Cold War
on Campus

Cold War
on Campus

A Study of the Politics of Organizational Control

Lionel S. Lewis

Transaction Books
New Brunswick (USA) and Oxford (UK)

Library of Congress Catalog Number: 87-16254
ISBN: 0-88738-178-2
Printed in the United States of America

Library of Congress Cataloging-in-Publication Data

Lewis, Lionel S. (Lionel Stanley)
  Cold war on campus.

  Includes index.
  1. Academic freedom—United States—History—20th
century—Case studies. 2. College teachers—United
States—Political activity—History—20th century—
Case studies. 3. Anti-communist movements—United
States—History—Case studies. I. Title.
LC72.2.L49   1987   378′.121   87-16254
ISBN 0-88738-178-2

For Peter and Andrew, with affection and high regard

Contents

Acknowledgments

Because this study was carried out over a long period of time, I have incurred many obligations. The book could not have been completed without the resourceful and incomparable assistance of Andrew P. Lewis. I would like to thank the many librarians, archivists, and administrative officers—especially Evelyn Miller of the American Association of University Professors—who helped in the search for relevant documents. I am also grateful to the following individuals for reading and commenting on various chapters of the manuscript: Professors Ben Agger, Philip G. Altbach, Jackson I. Cope, Richard E. Ellis, Irving L. Horowitz, Joel I. Nelson, and Dr. Jordan E. Kurland.

Introduction

Appearing before the House Committee on Un-American Activities in Washington, D.C., in April 1953, a 36-year-old physical chemist on the faculty of Rensselaer Polytechnic Institute refused to tell the congressmen whether he had once been engaged in communist activities. Although he admitted membership in the controversial American Labor Party, he declined to say whether, years before, he had been affiliated with a Communist Party student group in New Haven, Connecticut, and whether he had attempted to recruit anyone into the Communist Party. He invoked the First and Fifth amendments, pleading possible self-incrimination.

After having completed his graduate studies at Yale University, the chemist had joined the faculty of Rensselaer as an instructor in 1948. He was subsequently promoted to assistant professor, and won a Ford Foundation fellowship to study methods being used to teach physical chemistry to students in biology and medicine. Between the time he received his B.A. and Ph.D., he had served in the army, and at the end of World War II was discharged as a first lieutenant. He was a member of the American Veterans' Committee, an organization well to the left of the American Legion.

The day after he testified, Rensselaer proceeded to launch an investigation into his background and associations. Part of the rationale for this was that "though his indefinite testimony . . . throws doubt upon him, for the present we do not have sufficient information to take action that will change his faculty status."[1] It soon became apparent that as a result of what had happened in Washington his status at Rensselaer had become uncertain.

In late summer, in response to questions from off campus, the dean announced that no action in the matter had yet been taken by institutional authorities. Given the tenet common among academic administrators that "invocation of the Fifth Amendment places upon a professor a heavy burden of proof of his fitness to hold a teaching position and lays upon his university an obligation to re-examine his qualifications for membership in its society," the president decided that the matter should be "referred to the Trustees for consideration at a subsequent meeting."[2] The following month the president traveled to New York City, where the chemist was at the time

1

doing research, and dismissed him. In light of the questions raised by his public actions, the Board of Trustees found the chemist "unfit and to have forfeited his right to continue as an assistant professor upon the faculty."[3]

The episode was quickly over, receiving only local and passing attention. The statements from official sources, as well as the brief press accounts, indicate that it was viewed as a personal matter, an issue that had developed between an individual and an institution. What is significant, however, is that the case was by no means an isolated incident. Beginning about a half dozen years earlier, and continuing for another three years after 1953 (that is, during a decade from 1947 to 1956), it was commonplace to hear about campus investigations of alleged political radicals and of firings, near firings, or forced resignations. There were stories of some faculty defiantly refusing to discuss their political beliefs or activities; there were as many stories of others being forced to publicly recant their political beliefs or activities. These were expressions of the Cold War on campus, and the individuals caught in these incidents were some of the casualties.

This book is an examination of a significant number of the political controversies in American colleges and universities that had some bearing on the larger question of academic freedom during the first decade of the Cold War. More precisely, it is a study of the reactions, and the factors that prompted the reactions, of academic authorities to the "red scare" in America in the years following World War II. It is not a history of the Cold War; it is a review of events on some American campuses during the Cold War years. The following chapters take a close, careful look at how those responsible for the stewardship of institutions of higher learning responded to the public's or their own apprehension about faculty who might be communists, radicals, or somewhere on the left.

It hardly needs to be said that the Cold War created tensions throughout society, and colleges and universities were affected by these no less than other institutions. One manifestation of these tensions was pressure for conformity in all forms of political expression—in beliefs, in speech, in actions, in associations. A great deal has been written and said about how compliance took on a new urgency. It has been taken on faith by many that the Cold War made inevitable an inquisition, "a search for and punishment of nonbelievers or heretics," "any strict or arbitrary suppression or punishment of those believed to be dangerous to the ruling powers." Such a theme seems overly deterministic. The thesis developed here is that the secondary pressures and conflict generated by the political constraints on college and university faculties took on a life of their own, and in the last analysis these intramural pressures—largely the result of the definition of the situation by academic authorities—ulimately determined who would or who would not lose his job and who would or who would not be forced to recant his political beliefs or activities; intramural pressures weighed more heavily than did the beliefs, speech, actions, or associations of individuals or even public pressure produced by the disquiet about communism on campus.

The fact that the Cold War put some academics at risk becomes a doubly interesting sociological question when juxtaposed with the fact that an individual at the Rensselaer Polytechnic Institute identified as a political undesirable could lose his job while another individual at the Massachusetts Institute of Technology given the same label could keep his. Because there were no agreed-upon criteria to guard faculty against infringements of academic freedom and other academic principles, the face of the Cold War was not the same on all American campuses—and this matter needs analysis and explanation.

What may in the beginning have been insignificant differences in defining the amount of academic freedom or the political rights due faculty members, most particularly so-called radical faculty, became the source of other sorts of conflict, for example, that over defining the managerial prerogatives of academic administrators. Disagreement and debate on more general questions of political ideology that touched on freedom of speech, the interpretation of the Fifth Amendment, the meaning of loyalty, and the like hemorrhaged to intramural loci of friction between faculty and administrative authorities—for instance, to questions about the obligation of the individual to the institution and the obligation of the institution to the individual. These latter questions have nothing to do with political ideology.

The analysis that follows considers for the first time the relative importance of a number of sociological factors—for example, characteristics of individuals (faculty members and academic authorities), academic institutions, and the wider community—in shaping the outcome of controversies over academic freedom that were rooted in the troubled political climate of the Cold War.

There may appear to be a circularity in arguing and attempting to demonstrate that nonpolitical factors weighed heavily in what it turns out were political events only on the surface. Yet, the question of whether qualities of faculty members (e.g., their seniority or record as teachers or researchers), of academic authorities (e.g., how their decisions were affected by their definitions of their responsibilities to the faculty and of faculty responsibilities to them), or of institutions (e.g., their size or control or location) sometimes played more than an incidental role in the resolution of these controversies must be addressed in order to determine if at bottom they were political in a narrow sense.

Those who have looked into the incidents involving faculty who lost or nearly lost their positions during the Cold War years have not moved beyond the commonplace that political conflict was at the core of each case. Almost all publications, incidentally, have only been concerned with a single institution,[4] and all are marked by a predictable and tiresome onesidedness. The possibility that other factors beyond how far to the left someone was reported to have been may also have had just as great a bearing on the resolution of these incidents has been overlooked. In forming a realistic or valid characterization of how these controversies played themselves out, this omission is implausible, and sociologically naive; multiple causality is an undeniable fact of the social world.

Essentially all discussion of the pressures brought to bear on faculty as a result of the concern with communism on campus turns on the assumption that this tension was purely a product and reflection of the Cold War. It is commonly believed that matters were simply and solely shaped by events that were occurring in the larger society. The analysis that follows examines this premise in detail.

This is not an attempt to gloss over the fact that political events precipitated these cases of actual or barely avoided nonappointment, nonreappointment, or dismissal. What becomes obvious from the myriad cases discussed in chapters 2 through 9, however, is that political considerations, defined literally, were important only in determining who was picked out and labeled, whose career was threatened; political considerations hardly figured in how matters on campus evolved and were resolved. Political beliefs and associations were important in getting some faculty labeled as deviant or dangerous, and this put their careers in jeopardy. Yet, in the final analysis they were not the controlling factors in determining who was fired and who was not.

What moved academic administrators to respond as they did? (Certainly it was not political events on campus, as there were no incidents of subversive activity, few communists, and hardly any left-wing activity.) In the analysis that follows, the patterns that overspread academia to cope with the pressures that developed in the wake of the unusually large number of controversies over academic freedom are specified. The study begins with, but moves well beyond, considering how political concerns initially shaped these cases. To put events in perspective, all facets of these incidents—the background of faculty who were under a cloud, the characteristics of the institutions where they worked, and the turn of mind of those charged with their administration—require detailed examination. We are interested in more than political beliefs and behavior, and in more than the reactions to these; it is necessary, for example, to give some attention to the administrative arrangements in institutions of higher learning that make faculty vulnerable to the control of academic administrators.

Considering various aspects, characteristics, or qualities of a large number of the institutions in which political matters exacerbated tensions between some faculty and administrative authorities produces a great deal of suggestive information about how controversies developed and were resolved, and about the balance of power in, and normative structures of, American institutions of higher learning.

Since controversies invariably transcended simple and paramount concerns about communism and communists, understanding the political context is necessary but not sufficient for understanding how the Cold War played itself out in American colleges and universities. What happened on American campuses was not the inevitable result of the fact that the Cold War in the larger society was gathering force. Faculty whose jobs were lost or only threatened were victims for reasons other than their identification as radicals when radicalism was more out of fashion than usual in American society.

The Cold War may have set the stage, but for the most part the key players who determined the form it took on campus were those charged with the governance of institutions of higher learning. Academic authorities, particularly campus presidents, were responsible for the Cold War on campus; they brought the Cold War to campus. Their assumptions, their attitudes, and their actions were primarily responsible for what happened at Rensselaer Polytechnic Institute and, in the end, on scores of campuses across the country. Academic authorities were as much a threat to faculty and to their academic freedom as were the ominous political forces off campus. Academic administrators were at the core of the Cold War on campus, and for this reason they—along with faculty whose political beliefs or associations had made them principals in a campus controversy—are at the core of this study.

It is not unreasonable to expect that academic administrators would protect faculty, institutions of higher learning, and academic freedom from the frenzy generated by the Cold War. There are not enough instances when they met this responsibility, and too many instances when they did not. A surprising number showed little capacity to stand up to the pressures of the Cold War. Many seemed eager to carry out the programs of the radical right and to impose economic sanctions against vulnerable faculty. Few administrators addressed the question of whether it was more dangerous to the quality of the teaching and research programs and to the morale of their faculty to purge wantonly suspected communists, or, for that matter, radicals correctly identified as communists, or to permit members of this mostly benign and innocuous minority to pursue their careers unobtrusively. Rarely did an administrator explain to the public the risks inherent in any assault on academic freedom, and why it might be necessary to defend it without compromise.

The American campus today seems marked by a mindless tolerance of all ideas, of all ideologies. Some might conclude that this tolerance is part of the heritage of the Cold War in that the academic community has adopted a value system that would not again allow the systematic elimination of unpopular ideas or minorities. However, it seems that it is not tolerance that is the legacy of the Cold War but mindlessness. What happened on American campuses in the decade after World War II narrowed the range of ideas that were given serious attention. Moreover, it may have made some individuals with ideas to contribute to serious academic dialogue reluctant to pursue an academic career. To be sure, the number of individuals, particularly in the social sciences, involved in partisan expression and political activities clearly increased in the 1960s and 1970s, but this is not really academic work. Today, in part because of the Cold War, there may be fewer ideas to debate and fewer people interested in debating them. Hence the appearance of tolerance.

Since the Cold War, the distribution of authority in institutions of higher learning has remained mostly unchanged. The responsibility for the governance of colleges and universities still ultimately rests with academic administrators. It thus seems appropriate to wonder what we can expect of them in dealing with fluctuating enrollments, budgetary crises, and the myriad problems that now confront institutions of higher learning, and will continue to confront them in the foreseeable future. Will academic administrators be able to contend with the forces of social and economic change in society any better than they were able to contend with the winds of political change in the decade after World War II? The evidence in the chapters that follow would suggest that there is considerable risk in trusting them.

Notes

1. Livingston W. Houston, statement, 23 April 1953.
2. Livingston W. Houston, statement, 13 May 1953.
3. Livingston W. Houston, announcement, 28 September 1953.
4. The single exception is Ellen W. Schrecker's study of the denouement of a number of left-wing academics who were called before various congressional investigating committees and took the Fifth Amendment, *No Ivory Tower: McCarthyism and the Universities* (New York: Oxford University Press, 1986).

1

The Cold War in America and on Campus

There seems to be no end to the detailed analysis of the mounting Cold War tensions that swept across America in the decade following World War II. Nor should there be. There was barely a pause following the armed conflict before a frightening series of events began to unfold. International friction increased, and an iron curtain partitioned Western and Eastern Europe. Many nations became directly and indirectly embroiled in the civil wars that raged around the globe—in Greece, in China, in Korea. The Soviet Union exploded its first atomic bomb. The British Empire appeared in dissolution. Sensational spy trials involving Alger Hiss, Whittaker Chambers, Judith Coplon, Klaus Fuchs, and Julius and Ethel Rosenberg increased the public's sense of vulnerability. Americans feared communism and Soviet intentions; this fear was deeply ingrained, easily aroused, and acute. Not only had Soviet aggression made the world an unsafe place, but hardly anyone doubted that there were some Americans—communists— who were working to undermine American freedoms.

There was, of course, a strong undercurrent of anticommunism in America that went back to the Great Red Scare (which included the Palmer Raids) of 1919–20. Even during the years when the United States and Russia were becoming wartime allies, numerous surveys of opinion showed that the majority of Americans considered communists to be the single greatest menace to our way of life.[1]

The inquisitorial activities of politicians, most notably senators Joseph R. McCarthy of Wisconsin and William E. Jenner of Indiana, and Representative Harold H. Velde of Illinois, fed on and inflamed the frustration; the fear of the Soviet Union, of Red China, of internal subversion; and the all too common unfocused feeling of panic. Because many Americans were convinced, for example, that Russia did not by itself have the scientific capability to develop the atomic bomb as early as it had, it was widely assumed that the secret must have been stolen by communist spies. Among others, Congressman Velde nurtured this belief:

The Russians undoubtedly gained 3 to 5 years in producing the atomic bomb because our government from the White House down has been sympathetic toward the views of communists and fellow travelers, with the result that it has been infiltrated by a network of spies. . . .[2]

The well-publicized hearings in Hollywood in the late fall of 1947 and subsequent investigations around the country by the House Committee on Un-American Activities and other governmental bodies made headlines and projected the Cold War as the central fact of American politics. The Cold War became a dominant force in American life.

More and more events reported in the press could be characterized as what students of collective behavior call mass hysteria. Apace with the growing perception and consensus that communism posed an ominous threat to societal survival, irrational and sometimes compulsive beliefs and behavior spread among all segments of the public. It seemed that America had become dominated by a single impulse or purpose, the control of communism. This unanimity—and unanimity is one of the salient characteristics of all collective behavior—was merely one manifestation of the frenzy. Anything or anyone displeasing was labeled communistic; anything or anyone who could be even tangentially linked to communism became displeasing. Suspicion was everywhere, and, often, to be suspected was to be branded guilty. Much of the mass media contributed to this process. The public did not always have a clear picture of what the source of its apprehension was, and the critical judgment of those who sought to explain current events often failed. Scapegoats were found. It seemed easier to hunt for so-called crypto-communists or fellow travelers than to confront communism in the international arena.

Communism: The Growing Furor

One reaction was a predictable quest for national security. As a result there were encroachments on civil liberties. The Internal Security Act of 1950 (the Mundt-Nixon bill), which was passed over President Truman's veto, included, among others, the following provisions: (1) "Communist-action organizations" and "communist-front organizations" were required to register with the Attorney General and to report names of officers, sources of funds, and, in the case of the former, membership lists, to the government; (2) members in these registered organizations were barred from government employment and employment in private industries with defense contracts, and from applying for or using a passport; (3) registered organizations were denied tax-exempt status and contributions to them were not considered tax-exempt deductions; (4) registered organizations were required to label their publications and broadcasts as originating from a "communist organization;" (5) in the event of an invasion, war, or insurrection and a declaration of "an internal security emergency," the Attorney General was empowered to detain those who could reasonably be expected to "engage in, or . . . conspire with others to engage in, the acts of espionage or sabotage." Individuals would not be granted the right of a court trial or the opportunity to cross examine witnesses, but they would be entitled to administrative hearings, appeals, and judicial review; (6) aliens who had been members of or affiliated with communist or other totalitarian parties in other countries or who advocated totalitarian doctrines or who engaged in activities prejudicial or dangerous to the public interest were barred from entering the United States or could be deported without a hearing; and (7) individuals naturalized after 1951 could lose their citizenship if within five years they became members of registered organizations, and aliens who were members of communist-front organizations could not become naturalized unless they left these organizations within three months after they had become registered.

State and local governments followed the federal example, and sometimes, in fact, even went beyond it. Between 1947 and 1954, more than half of the states passed laws designed to prevent "subversives" from holding government employment. Four states made it a crime to belong to the Communist Party; a great many more barred members of the Communist Party or seditious organizations, or advocates of violent overthrow of the government, from the ballot.

Indiana passed legislation that declared it state policy to "exterminate communism and communists and any teachings of the same." Texas outlawed all parties that "entertained any thought or principle contrary to the Constitution."

In Maryland the Ober Act became law, restricting the rights of citizens to join organizations officially regarded as treasonous ("subversive"), banning "subversives" from running for or holding public office, and imposing fines of up to $20,000 and prison sentences to twenty years. This law was copied in part or whole by at least ten other states, including Mississippi, which, according to the Federal Bureau of Investigation (FBI), had a Communist Party of one individual. A Tennessee law provided the death penalty for those convicted of treason, in part defined as advocating the unlawful overthrow of the government. In order to vote in Alabama, an oath disavowing belief in or affiliation with any group advocating unlawful overthrow of the government was required. In Birmingham, Alabama, the city commission adopted an ordinance making it unlawful for members of the Communist Party to be "within the corporate limits" on penalty of a fine and/or 180 days in jail. A Jacksonville, Florida, law made possible the expulsion of any person who distributed "communist literature" or who communicated with a present or former communist.[3]

Observing this ferment, Robert M. Hutchins remarked that "it is now fashionable to call anybody with whom you disagree a communist or a fellow-traveler. . . . The danger to our institutions is . . . from those who would mistakenly repress the free spirit upon which those institutions are built. The miasma of thought control that is now spreading over the country is the greatest menace to the United States since Hitler."[4] Assessments such as this did little to moderate the misuse of legal procedures and the stifling of controversy or dissent through the banning and censorship of books and other media.

Morris has observed that "the years following World War I can be viewed as a time of repression and brittleness—as a time when America lacked that vital sustenance of flowing humanism that had seen her through earlier crises."[5] This characterization would apparently also apply to the years following World War II. This was indeed a time of great national perturbation. Most were caught up in the *Zeitgeist*, and Hutchins' concerns were those of a minority. The pressures were difficult to withstand. As Alan Barth noted in 1951, loyalty had become "a cult, an obsession."[6]

The concern of most Americans about national security cannot be exaggerated. John Dos Passos reflected the climate of opinion in his description of the existence of "a conspiracy of assassins bent on the destruction"[7] of the freedom Americans take for granted. It was a natural progression, as Barth observed, that un-Americanism would become "a hyphenated synonym for unorthodoxy." Barth went on to add that disloyalty "as it is commonly used today is nothing more or less than a circumlocution for treason."[8] Thus, it is not surprising that those suspected of what were said to be un-American beliefs, behavior, or associations were often swept up and aside in the maelstrom, their families, their careers, and their lives disrupted.

The struggle between East and West for political and economic domination resulted in the greater legitimacy of rightist pressure groups and ideology; indeed, a near consensus developed that the Communist Party was a fifth column. In the pursuit of subversion and subversives, no aspect of life or institution escaped scrutiny. In 1946, the FBI's J. Edgar Hoover claimed that communism had made deep inroads into our national life and called for a crusade against it in labor unions, in newspapers, magazines, and book publishing, in radio and movies, in schools and colleges, in government, and even in fraternal orders.[9] His figures showed that in 1947 one in every 1,814 Americans was a communist, a higher ratio than the one in every 2,277 Russians who were Bolsheviks in 1917.[10] "The disloyalty of American communists is no longer a matter of conjecture," he declared.

They were traitors. A few years later, Hoover estimated that the United States harbored 55,000 communists.[11] The government, the media, labor, the church, independent foundations, the schools, even the military were the objects of public agitation, of investigations for communist influence or sympathies, and of loyalty oath programs.

Communism on Campus: The Furor Intensifies

This is a study of one such focus of attention of the anticommunist zeal—institutions of higher learning. The concern is with how those responsible for the stewardship of colleges and universities—primarily academic administrators—reacted to the pressures generated by the public's apprehension about communist influence.

In large part due to the perception that they have a critical responsibility in molding the nation's youth—and consequently its future—educators seemed faced with unique problems. Even in normal times, schools are likely to be a matter of special interest to the public, and most people would agree that in the decade or so after 1947 the political climate was far from normal. In his assessment of the special problems of subversion in education, Iversen concludes that the public impression was that the schools were "the most sensitive sector and the most vulnerable to communist penetration."[12] After all, Iversen notes, "internal and external stress [on the schools] constituted an arena too inviting for a group bent upon controlling society to ignore. Such a group was the Communist Party."[13]

There was a great deal of hyperbole. According to a former staff director of a Senate investigating subcommittee, J. B. Matthews:

> For more than seventeen years, the Communist Party of the United States has put forth every effort to infiltrate the teaching profession of this country. In this endeavor to corrupt the teachers of youth, the agents of the Kremlin have been remarkably successful, especially among the professors in our colleges and universities.
>
> In these few years, the Communist Party has enlisted the support of at least thirty-five hundred professors—many of them as dues-paying members, many others as fellow travelers, some as out-and-out espionage agents, some as adherents of the Party line in varying degrees, and some as the unwitting dupes of subversion.
>
> Congressional committees, which are now investigating communists in the colleges, are on the track of a national scandal.[14]
>
> A conservative estimate places at close to 3,500 the number of professors in colleges and universities who have collaborated with the communist-front apparatus, since its inception about seventeen years ago. They represent every state in the union and the District of Columbia. They have been con-

nected with some 400 institutions of higher learning. More than 1,000 of
them have been active collaborators with the communist-front apparatus
since the beginning of Cold War I.[15]

Given that in 1952 there were almost 1,900 institutions of higher learning
with one-quarter million faculty in the United States (see Appendix B),
these figures would mean that between 20 and 25 percent of the colleges
and universities had at least one faculty member who was working for the
communist cause, and that overall about .5 percent were Party members
and between 1 and 2 percent of the faculty had collaborated.

Estimates like those of Matthews were repeated often enough—in the
example below by Senator McCarthy in response to the question: What
can I do to fight communism?—to become an accepted truth, and, along
with other lavish assertions, to contribute to the overcharged emotional
atmosphere.

> Approximately 28 percent of all the top collaborators with the deceitful com-
> munist-front movement in recent years have been college and university
> professors.
>
> Exhaustive research into the personnel of communist-front organizations
> reveals that some 3,000 professors from approximately 600 institutions of
> higher learning have been affiliated more than 26,000 times with these instru-
> ments of the Communist Party. This is not 'guilt by association' but guilt by
> collaboration.

McCarthy added:

> Every man and woman in America can appoint himself or herself to undo the
> damage which is being done by communist infiltration of our schools and
> colleges through communist-minded teachers and communist-line text-
> books.
>
> Countless times I have heard parents throughout the country complain that
> their sons and daughters were sent to college as good Americans and returned
> four years later as wild-eyed radicals. The educational system of this country
> cannot be cleansed of communist influence by legislation. It can only be
> scrubbed and flushed and swept clean if the mothers and fathers, and the sons
> and daughters, of this nation individually decide to do this job. This can be
> your greatest contribution to America. This is a job which you can do. This is
> a job which you must do if America and Western civilization are to live.[16]

Not only for McCarthy, but for many Americans, communism in education presented a risk greater than communism in any branch of the government; it was "a danger much greater than any threat"[17] from the Soviet
Union.

Following this line of thinking, the Subcommittee to Investigate the

Administration of the Internal Security Act and Other Internal Security
Laws of the Committee on the Judiciary of the Senate (the Senate Internal
Security Subcommittee) asserted "that the Soviet organization was continuously engaged in a plan to penetrate our educational institutions at every
possible point, thus posing a serious threat to our national security. The
communist agents who spun the very real web of conspiracy and intrigue
within the framework of the United States government departments, in
almost all cases, were cradled in our distinguished universities and colleges."[18] Governmental investigators were led to such exaggeration by testimony that "we had ... in the Boston area ... professors—and by
professors I mean those in the higher institutions of learning in the colleges
and universities—a number ranging between 20 to 30 pro group Communist Party members. This was the largest single element of individuals in
the pro section of Boston."[19] The Senate Internal Security Subcommittee
report continues:

> One witness testified that in the early 1940s there were 30 to 40 members in a
> faculty branch of the Communist Party at City College in New York. In
> addition he had attended several meetings of a New York City-wide unit of
> college professors and instructors that contained more than a hundred com-
> munist members from all colleges in New York City. Another testified to the
> size of the Brooklyn College unit of the Party. Two contemptuous witnesses
> acknowledged that they belonged to a unit at Columbia made up of almost a
> dozen faculty members and units at Pennsylvania and Yale made up of a
> dozen faculty members and students respectively. Bella Dodd gave a list of
> colleges [including: "All of the city colleges here in New York, I mean the four
> city colleges; Columbia University, Long Island University, New York Uni-
> versity, Vassar College, Wellesley, Smith, Harvard, M.I.T., University of
> Michigan, Chicago, Northwestern University, University of California, the
> University of Minnesota, Howard University"] that contained to her knowl-
> edge communist cells of one or more faculty members. And finally, there
> were the 82 educators from 16 universities and various other educational
> institutions and services selectively subpoenaed by the subcommittee to give
> a concrete sketch of successful communist penetration.[20]

Hearing such testimony, one could easily be left with the impression that
institutions of higher learning had become the hub and fount of all communist activities in the United States.

In light of such disclosures, the Senate subcommittee arrived at a series
of conclusions and recommendations. The most salient points were:

1. World communist leaders have made schools and colleges of the United
   States a target of infiltration and activity as part of their program to destroy the United States.
2. A communist educator, because of his submission to a totalitarian organi-

zation, cannot maintain the standards of academic freedom and objective scholarship and be loyal to the regulations of local authorities.

3. Communist teachers use their positions in the classroom and in extracurricular activities to subvert students and other teachers and the public to promote the objectives of communism.

4. Communist teachers exercise as part of an organized conspiracy an influence far more extensive than their numbers would indicate.

5. Communist penetration of the schools is becoming more covert, and communist teachers are being organized into a secret underground more difficult to detect. . . .

The subcommittee makes the following recommendations:

That educational authorities give consideration to the establishment of criteria and the initiation of procedures whereby schools, colleges and universities can eliminate teachers who have demonstrated their unsuitability to teach, because of their collaboration with the communist conspiracy.[21]

It is of some interest that a review of "communism and American education" in 1949 suggested that the problem was not widespread. *The School Review* stated: "It was also a fact that the number of *avowed* [emphasis added] communists teaching in American schools was extremely small. Estimates varied from ten to a hundred as the total, in all public schools, and in all colleges and universities."[22] This assessment and others that departed so much from the large number of higher estimates were hardly ever noticed in the formulation of policies and programs to halt the spread of communism in education.

Reactions

Advice thrust at the academic community, in general, and administrators, in particular, weighed heavily, and it was only a matter of time, of course, before it began to find its way into the rules and bylaws that governed academic appointments. One institution, for example, added to its regulations this statement: "Because of the well known aim of the Communist Party to infiltrate our educational institutions and, by calculated deceit, to pervert education for its own ends, the university . . . deems it necessary to state that it cannot harbor on its faculty any present member of the Communist Party." This posture, in fact, was quite similar to principles adopted not only by many other colleges and universities, but by the Association of American Universities, an organization representing the administrations of thirty-five of the nation's leading graduate centers. Their March 1953 published statement in part read: "Above all, a scholar must have integrity and independence. This renders impossible adherence to such a regime as that of Russia and its satellites. No person who accepts or advocates such principles and methods has any place in a university. Since present membership in the Communist Party requires the acceptance of these principles and methods, such membership extinguishes the right to a university position."[23]

The political rectitude of faculty became a matter of great concern on many campuses. The president of Temple University expressed keen interest in the suggestion "that a loyalty oath be printed on the back of each paycheck so that no person might receive a compensation without automatically signing an oath," but he had to settle for departmental committees to certify loyalty. Department chairmen at Temple were reminded that investigations should be more than perfunctory.

The criteria guiding academic appointment and retention had become quite similar to those mandated for the appointment and retention of government employees by President Truman's 1947 executive order (Executive Order 9835 which established a loyalty-security program). The federal program called for extensive background checks on all civilian workers in the executive branch of government. On the strength of the belief that the "presence within the government service of any disloyal or subversive person constitutes a threat to our democratic process," it became the practice to investigate all present or prospective employees to establish if they had been involved in (1) sabotage, espionage, and related activities; (2) treason or sedition; (3) advocacy of illegal overthrow of the government; (4) the disclosure of confidential information; (5) serving a foreign government in preference to the interests of the United States; and/ or (6) an organization, association, or movement designated by the Attorney General "as totalitarian, fascist, communist or subversive, or as having adopted a policy of advocating or approving the commission of acts of force or violence." Dismissal would be occasioned if there were "reasonable grounds . . . for the belief that the person . . . is disloyal to the government of the United States."[24] Asking and expecting academics to at least measure up to such minimal standards hardly seemed unfair.

The impetus against permitting communists, most particularly, Communist Party members, from holding academic appointments was the suppositions that they were committed to a dogma that precluded objectivity, and that members were obligated to use any and all means—including dishonesty—to achieve the ends of the Party. These ends essentially were the advancement of doctrines formulated in the Soviet Union to support its causes and that of world revolution, the final objective being totalitarian rule by the proletariat.

Many wondered how members of the Communist Party who were supposed to sign a statement that concluded "I pledge myself to spare no effort in uniting the workers in militant struggle against fascism and war. . . . I pledge myself to rally the masses to defend the Soviet Union, the land of victorious socialism. I pledge myself to remain at all times a vigilant and firm defender of the Leninist line of the Party, the only line that insures the triumph of Soviet power in the United States"[25] could be objective scholars and scientists. Sidney Hook quoted from the "directives from the official organ of the Communist Party" in the *New York Times*:

> "Party and Y.C.L. fractions [sic] set up within classes and departments must supplement and combat by means of discussions, brochures, etc., bourgeois omissions or distortions in the regular curriculum. *Marxist-Leninist analysis must be injected into every class* [emphasis added in Hook]. . . .

> "Communist teachers . . . must take advantage of their positions, without exposing themselves, to give their students to the best of their ability working-class education.

> "To enable the teachers in the Party to do the latter, the Party must take careful steps to see that all teacher comrades are given thorough education in the teachings of Marxism-Leninism. Only when teachers have really mastered Marxism-Leninism will they be able skillfully to inject it into their teaching at the least risk of exposure and at the same time to conduct struggles around the schools in a truly Bolshevik manner."[26]

To be sure, the pledge of the Communist Party of Massachusetts in 1937 seems more tempered: "I solemnly pledge to remain true to the principles of the Communist Party, to maintain its unity of purpose and action, and to work to the best of my ability to fulfill its program. With firm loyalty to the best interests of the working class and with full devotion to all progressive movements of the people, I pledge to work actively for the preservation and extension of democracy, for the defeat of fascism and all forms of national oppression, and for the establishment of world peace and socialism."[27] Yet, the analysis and social change suggested by the Communist Party's "Declaration of Principles and Constitution" were undoubtedly sweeping enough to threaten some:

> It is an unquestioned fact that a small group of men, bankers and industrialists, have gathered unto themselves the fruits of the labor of hundreds of thousands of workers, farmers and middle class people. A small number of families constituting a DISTINCT CLASS own and control the factories, mills, railroads, public utilities and banks. They run these for their PRIVATE PROFIT. They have accumulated great power and influence as the result of their wealth. They enjoy special privileges.

> Sixty families rule America, their profits soar to $5 billion. They strive feverishly to bind state and national legislatures to their will. Theirs is a program for self enrichment and for the impoverishment of the American people. They have usurped power and drunk with wealth, are recklessly pushing the

nation to an abyss of injustice, intolerance and poverty. They are giving ear to "alien and subversive" doctrines coming in from fascist countries, aiding in the weakening of democracy in all parts of the world. They are undermining and seeking to destroy democracy at home. They are destroying the "happiness, prosperity, and safety" of the American people. And the people have the right when such conditions exist "to reform, alter or totally change" this situation.

The Communist Party, while being the best fighter for the improvement of conditions thru immediate demands and objectives, educates and organizes the masses for socialism. Only socialism can solve the fundamental problems of the people and make secure progress, peace and prosperity. A WORKERS AND FARMERS GOVERNMENT, supported by the majority of the people, will usher in socialism. . . . Socialism will abolish forever the ownership by big bankers and industrialists of the vital means of production, the mines, mills, factories, public utilities, banks, big landed estates and all natural resources of America. It will abolish classes by the creation of a society that will end production for profit and the exploitation of man by man.[28]

Most Americans believed that communist principles put their way of life in grave danger. The evidence for this appeared overwhelming. For proof, it was argued, one need only be familiar with Party maxims to understand that it demanded from members something well beyond accepted political practice. Here is a not atypical description of the ethics of Party members:

Those consecrating themselves to communism must not only cast out truth, mercy, justice, and personal honor, but undergo a sickening discipline in lies, cruelty, crime, and self-abasement. They must endorse such "Leninist" maxims as these:

"We do not believe in external principles of morality. . . . Communist morality is identical with the fight to strengthen the dictatorship of the proletariat."

"We must be ready to employ trickery, deceit, lawbreaking, withholding and concealing truth."

"We can and must write . . . in a language which sows among the masses hate, revulsion, scorn and the like toward those of differing opinion."

This doctrine of immorality on principle, invented by Marx, brought into focus by Lenin, and carried into limitless action by Stalin, is playing a major role in the disintegration of our Graeco-Christian civilization.[29]

Communist Party members, of course, disclaimed this characterization out of hand. The fact that materials could be and were cited and presented to controvert it did not become part of the public's consciousness. It hardly mattered, for example, that the Constitution of the Communist Party of Massachusetts read in part:

Party members found to be strike-breakers, degenerates, habitual drunkards,

betrayers of Party confidence, provocateurs who advocate terrorism or violence as a method of Party procedure, or members whose actions are detrimental to the Party and the working class, shall be summarily dismissed from
positions of responsibility, expelled as traitors, and exposed before the general
public.[30]

In ascertaining the nature of communism, there was no attempt to sift the
evidence, to distinguish fact from fiction.

Hook illustrated to newspaper readers how following the ever-changing
Party line precluded any pretense of the dispassionate search for truth on
the part of beguiled faculty:

> In the social sciences, Communist Party teachers taught in 1934 that Roos-
> evelt was a Fascist; in 1936, during the Popular Front , a progressive; in 1940,
> during the Nazi-Stalin pact, a warmonger and imperialist; in 1941, after
> Hitler invaded the Soviet Union, a leader of the oppressed peoples of the
> world.[31]

For most this was proof enough that Communist Party members were
unqualified to hold academic appointments.

No quarter of society challenged these tenets; these were not questions
that divided the Left and the Right, academics and nonacademics, or faculty and administrators. Senator Wayne Morse of Oregon, a former law
school dean, fairly represented the liberal view that the employment of
communists by colleges and universities was inimical to academic freedom:

> True communists do not possess free minds but rather are indoctrinators of a
> philosophy which seeks to promote revolution and reduce our people to the
> dictates of a totalitarian form of government. . . . Such teachers do not pos-
> sess the devotion of the scientists to the findings of the facts but rather such
> communist teachers, in order to carry out their indoctrination objectives,
> must necessarily slant their teachings away from the facts.[32]

The most distinguished leaders and spokesmen for higher education
contributed to this negative climate of opinion, arguing that those committed to communism had surrendered their intellectual integrity and
were unfit to teach. President Edmund Ezra Day of Cornell University
expressed the view that:

> The faculty of any college or university should be made up of free, honest,
> competent, inquiring minds, seeking to find and disseminate the truth. The
> mind of a member of the Communist Party is enslaved to the Party line. It
> cannot possibly claim to be either free or honest. It is manifestly disqualified

for membership in a faculty of higher learning in a free and freedom-loving society such as ours.[33]

The Board of Trustees of Columbia University was briefer and clearer: "The trustees would not countenance the presence of an avowed communist on the teaching staff."[34]

Although the American Association of University Professors (AAUP) took the position that the test of competence must lie in actual teaching or scholarship, not in affiliations or associations, its 1947 statement on the matter was close enough to the temper of the time so as not to give others pause:

> If a teacher as an individual should advocate the forcible overthrow of the government or should incite others to do so; if he should use his classes as a forum for communism or otherwise abuse his relationship with his students for that purpose; if his thinking should show more than normal bias or be so uncritical as to evidence professional unfitness, these are the charges that should be brought against him.[35]

It was well implanted in the public mind that communism was less a body of doctrine than a sinister political program that readily employed dishonesty, propaganda, conspiracy, and violence; that because communism was less interested in freedom than in power and political expediency, its threat could not be taken lightly. It was the enemy of traditional American freedom. All communists, including college and university faculty, were forced to conform to the shifting Party line, which would preclude objective or even rational thinking. It was imperative that their efforts to interrupt and undermine legitimate academic pursuits be withstood by almost any means. Resisting the corruption of the Red menace had become a given, an accepted and seemingly unalterable article of the American belief system.

One clear result of such concern was that, among others, the Feinberg Law in New York, the Pennsylvania Loyalty Act (the Pechan Act), Michigan's Trucks Act, and provisions of the Government Code in California required loyalty oaths solely for teachers, and made dismissal without due process mandatory for those who failed to execute them. The Feinberg Law, for example, required both written reports on the loyalty of all teachers and the dismissal of individuals who were members of organizations designated subversive by the New York State Board of Regents. State education officials were required to compile a list of such organizations and to report annually on the loyalty of all school employees. Anyone belonging to a subversive organization was automatically disqualified "for appointment to or retention in any office or position in the public schools." The state commissioner of education described the law's comprehensiveness:

> The writing of articles, the distribution of pamphlets, the endorsement of speeches made or articles written or acts performed by others, all may constitute subversive activity.
>
> Nor need such activity be confined to the classroom. Treasonable or subversive acts or statements outside the school are as much a basis for dismissal as are similar activities in school or in the presence of school children.[36]

In 1951, Colorado discovered in its statute books a loyalty oath for teachers that had not been enforced since 1935. The state's attorney general ruled that it could be applied to the faculty of the state university, so that a punishment of up to a $100 fine or six months in jail, or both, could be imposed on administrators who permitted faculty to assume their duties before an oath was administered. The fact that the law had been permitted to lapse and was publicly characterized as "discriminatory" since it pertained to only one profession did not delay its immediate implementation after the attorney general's ruling. "Irked" by a voluble communist student, the Texas legislature passed a bill requiring all faculty and students in state colleges to sign affidavits swearing loyalty and disclaiming membership in subversive organizations.

Faculty and administrative authorities could do little but fully comply with state-mandated loyalty programs. The pressures and penalties for doing otherwise were too great. On the individual level the threat was the loss of employment; for institutions, budgets could be adversely affected. Section 13 of the Pennsylvania Loyalty Act read:

> State-aided Institutions of Learning. No appropriation of public funds made after the first day of May, one thousand nine hundred fifty-two, of any character shall be paid by the Commonwealth to any State-aided institution of learning not a part of the public school system unless there shall be filed annually, on or before the first day of September, with the Governor (with copies furnished to the president of the Senate and to the Speaker of the House of Representatives), on behalf of the institution, a written report setting forth what procedures the institution has adopted to determine whether it has reason to believe that any subversive persons are in its employ and what steps, if any, have been or are being taken to terminate such employment. The report also shall unequivocally set forth that the institution has no reason to believe that any subversive persons are in its employ. If the report shall be approved by the Governor, he shall notify the Auditor General and the State Treasurer that the provisions of this section have been complied with.

To some, such developments were not unexpected. Even before World

War II ended in the Pacific, the social analyst Bernard DeVoto had predicted that colleges and universities would be caught up in the overcharged political atmosphere of the day. There "is a powerful sentiment" that the country would be better off if we "get rid of the communist professors— who are all homosexuals and New Dealers anyway—and everything will be all right once more. We will be back in the days before there was a depression, before the New Deal conspiracy was hatched, before labor unions had to be dealt with, before the sacred rights of corporations were invaded, . . . before the foundations of our society were undermined by atheism and bolshevism."

> As the waves of reaction gather strength in the years immediately ahead of the United States, the same attack will be made repeatedly in many colleges. . . . That Texan has not only attacked the University of Texas, he has put Yale and Stanford in peril too—and there will be many others dressed in shirts of the same color to take up where he leaves off. The academic community is one, the world of inquiry and appraisal, of the search for truth and progress, is one. When Texas has lost its freedom, we have lost ours.[37]

DeVoto's suspicions that the patriotism fostered by World War II would persist with as strong an edge of hatred and intolerance against those identified as the enemy (or their sympathizers) proved true. Since it was commonly believed that colleges and universities were hotbeds of radicalism, there was near unanimity that the professoriate should be closely watched. The FBI's J. Edgar Hoover spoke for many with his observation that "some professors have aided the communist cause by tearing down respect for agencies of government, belittling tradition and moral custom and by creating doubts in the validity of the American way of life."[38] He advised the House Appropriations Committee: "Every communist uprooted from our educational system is one more assurance that it will not degenerate into a medium of propaganda for Marxism."[39]

Thus it is not surprising that in interviews with over 6,000 individuals in 1954 regarding "the communist conspiracy outside and inside the country," about one-fifth of the respondents felt that an individual teaching in a college or university should be fired if his loyalty was criticized or questioned even if he swore he was not a communist.[40] Approximately 90 percent expressed the belief that a known communist teaching in a college should be fired, whereas, by comparison, less than two out of three thought that such an action should be taken against an "admitted communist [who, for example] is a radio singer."[41]

There is no question that more than a small minority of the public was particularly determined to keep radical influences away from institutions of higher learning. This was made apparent by the fact that the respondents

nated in good faith and that the Party principles were in good faith repudiated. . . .

Most faculty acceded to such rules as fair and proper. Of course, some liberal faculty spoke out in opposition, but not many.

Only a handful of academic administrators offered any resistance to the anticommunist tide. Those like President Charles Seymour of Yale University who pledged to oppose any "hysterical witch hunt" on his campus—"we shall not impose an oath of loyalty on our faculty appointees"—could be counted on one's fingers.[51] Even rarer were affirmations of principles such as that by the Board of Trustees of the University of Chicago: "Academic freedom is important not because of its benefits to professors but because of its benefits to all of us. Today our tradition of freedom is under attack. There are those who are afraid of freedom. We do not share these fears." Chancellor Robert Hutchins of the University of Chicago was by far the most outspoken academic administrator. His testimony before the Subversive Activities Commission of the Illinois State Legislature was often blunt and sometimes quoted: "The policy of repression of ideas cannot work and never has worked."[52] His directness and combativeness were rarely emulated.

As the Cold War gained momentum, there were more and more stories, from one end of the country to the other, of politically controversial faculty members losing their positions. The Senate Internal Security Subcommittee boasted in 1953 that "in all but a few of the cases before the subcommittee, the university officials and local authorities suspended the teachers who invoked their privilege against incrimination when asked about Communist Party membership."[53] This assertion may be an exaggeration, but it points up the fact that the appointments of some, perhaps most, faculty identified as being too far to the Left were at greater risk during the Cold War than at other times.

Some academic administrators were in agreement with the prevailing Cold War sentiment that radicals and radical ideas did not belong on campus. To the degree that they acted on this belief, the Cold War on campus can be seen as but a reflection of the political climate in the country. When academic administrators responded for reasons other than concerns about communism, loyalty, patriotism, and national security, however, the Cold War on campus became different enough from the Cold War in America to warrant a careful scrutiny in order to delineate its special features. When this is done, the Cold War on campus appears to be something more than a simple reflection of the Cold War in America.

Academic folklore alleges instances of administrators using the uncertain political mood in the decade after World War II as a pretext for taking revenge on their enemies or those who had shown less than full support for institutional policies. This was generally found to be an undemonstrable charge. What the body of materials reviewed in this study makes clear, however, is that controversies between faculty and administrative authorities invariably did move beyond simple and paramount concerns about communism, loyalty, patriotism, and national security. For example, in building cases against faculty identified as being radical, academic administrators were more interested in public relations than in larger political or ideological considerations. The chapters that follow examine how the Cold War in America manifested itself on college and university campuses and what conditions beyond the Cold War in America helped shape the Cold War on campus.

Notes

1. Warren B. Walsh, "What the American People Think of Russia," *Public Opinion Quarterly* 8, no. 4 (1944): 515.
2. *Congressional Record* (83), 1949, p. 4372, in David M. Oshinsky, *A Conspiracy So Immense* (New York: Free Press, 1983), p. 102.
3. Such details are repeated in, among other places, Francis Biddle, *The Fear of Freedom* (Garden City, N.Y.: Doubleday, 1952), p. 94; Robert Justin Goldstein, *Political Repression in Modern America: From 1870 to the Present* (Cambridge, Mass.: Schenkman, 1978), pp. 348–60; David Caute, *The Great Fear: The Anti-Communist Purge under Truman and Eisenhower* (New York: Simon and Schuster, 1978), pp. 70–75.
4. Robert M. Hutchins, "Statement to the Subversive Activities Commission of the Illinois State Legislature," April 1949, in Howard Mumford Jones, ed., *Primer of Intellectual Freedom* (Cambridge: Harvard University Press, 1949), pp. 8–9.
5. Arval A. Morris, "The University of Washington Loyalty Oath Case," *AAUP Bulletin* 50, no. 3 (1964): 222.
6. Alan Barth, *The Loyalty of Free Men* (New York: Viking Press, 1951; New York: Archon Books, 1965), p. 7.
7. Quoted in E. Merrill Root, *Collectivism on Campus* (New York: Devin-Adair, 1956), p. 229.
8. Barth, p. 7.
9. William R. Tanner and Robert Griffith, "Legislative Politics and 'McCarthyism,'" in Robert Griffith and Athan Theoharis, ed., *The Specter: Original Essays on the Cold War and the Origins of McCarthysim* (New York: New Viewpoints, 1974), p. 178.
10. Hoover's testimony is quoted in *100 Things You Should Know about Communism in the U.S.A.*, prepared and released by the Committee on Un-American Activities, U.S. House of Representatives, Washington D.C., revised 1 December 1950, Question 31.
11. "J. Edgar Hoover Tells How Communists Operate," *U.S. News & World Report*, 11 August 1950, p. 32.
12. Robert W. Iversen, *The Communists and the Schools* (New York: Harcourt, Brace, 1959), p. 332.

13. Ibid., p. 8.
14. J. B. Matthews, "Communism and the Colleges," *American Mercury* 76, no. 352 (1953): 111.
15. Ibid., p. 116.
16. Joseph R. McCarthy, *McCarthyism: The Fight for America* (New York: Arno Press, 1977), p. 101.
17. Ibid.
18. "Subversive Influence in the Educational Process," report to the Committee on the Judiciary, U.S. Senate, Eighty-third Congress, 17 July 1953, p. 1.
19. Ibid., p. 10.
20. Ibid., p. 11.
21. Ibid., pp. 28–29.
22. "Educational News and Editorial Comment," *The School Review* 57, no. 9 (1949): 454–55.
23. "The Rights and Responsibilities of Universities and Their Faculties," policy statement of the Association of American Universities, 30 March 1953.
24. In Henry Steele Commager, ed., *Documents of American History*, 7th ed. (New York: Appleton-Century-Crofts, 1963), pp. 527–30.
25. This is just one of many quotations repeated by anticommunists that was said to typify communist goals. It was part of a pledge read by Earl Browder to party initiates in New York in 1935. It was reprinted in the *Daily Worker*, 2 April 1936, p. 7.
26. Sidney Hook, "Should Communists Be Permitted to Teach?" *New York Times Magazine*, 27 February 1949, sec. 6, p. 24. This quotation is found in Richard Frank, "The Schools and the People's Front," *Communist: Journal for the Theory & Practice of Marxism* (1937), pp. 445, 440.
27. *Declaration of Principles and Constitution of the Communist Party of Massachusetts*, adopted September 1937, Boston, art. 2, sec. 2, p. 16.
28. Ibid., pp. 6–8.
29. Max Eastman, in Foreword, to *The Whole of Their Lives* by Benjamin Gitlow (New York: Scribner's, 1948), p. ix.
30. *Declaration of Principles and Constitution, art. 8, sec. 6, p. 23.*
31. Hook, p. 26.
32. Wayne Morse, "Academic Freedom Versus Communistic Indoctrination," delivered to the graduating class of the Federal Bureau of Investigation, National Academy, Washington, D.C., 1 April 1949. (Reprinted in *Vital Speeches of the Day*.)
33. Quoted in Benjamin Fine, "Educators Insist on Ouster of Reds," *New York Times*, 30 May 1949, p. 14.
34. Quoted in "Columbia's Board Bars Communists," *New York Times*, 29 March 1952. (Statement "approved by the Board at its meeting on March 3.")
35. "Report of Committee A for 1947," *AAUP Bulletin* 34, no. 1 (1948): 126.
36. Quoted in Lawrence H. Chamberlain, *Loyalty and Legislative Action* (Ithaca, N.Y.: Cornell University Press, 1951), pp. 197–98.
37. Bernard DeVoto, "The Easy Chair," *Harper's Magazine*, August 1945, pp. 136–37.
38. Walter Goodman, *The Committee: The Extraordinary Career of the House Committee on Un-American Activities* (New York: Farrar, Straus, Giroux, 1964), p. 326.
39. Ibid., p. 332.

40. Samuel A. Stouffer, *Communism, Conformity, and Civil Liberties: A Cross-section of the Nation Speaks Its Mind* (New York: Doubleday, 1955; Gloucester, Mass.: Peter Smith, 1963), p. 38.
41. Ibid., p. 43.
42. Ibid., p. 59.
43. Paul F. Lazarsfeld and Wagner Thielens, Jr., *The Academic Mind* (Glencoe, Ill.: Free Press, 1958).
44. Albert Einstein, correspondence to William Frauenglass, *New York Times*, 12 June 1953.
45. Kalman Seigel, "College Freedoms Being Stifled by Students' Fear of Red Label" and "Colleges Fighting Repressive Forces," *New York Times*, 10 May 1951 (p. 1) and 11 May 1951 (p. 29), especially pp. 1, 28, May 10.
46. Lazarsfeld and Thielens, pp. 84–85.
47. Ibid., p. 192.
48. Ibid., p. 197.
49. Ibid., pp. 204ff.
50. Harold W. Stoke, "Freedom Is Not Academic," *Journal of Higher Education* 20, no. 7 (1949): 348.
51. Quoted in Murray Schumach, "Head of Yale Bars Oath for Faculty," *New York Times*, 22 June 1949, p. 34.
52. Hutchins, p. 9.
53. "Subversive Influence in the Educational Process," p. 14.

2

Studying the Cold War on Campus

Needlesss to say, even if communism, loyalty, patriotism, and national security were paramount concerns of those who governed and managed institutions of higher learning during the height of the Cold War, the fact that social phenomena have multiple, overlapping causes suggests that a great deal could still be learned by considering how other factors may have affected the Cold War on campus. One would have to ignore a great deal that was important to believe that only the Cold War in America had consequences for the Cold War on campus. Although nearly all academic administrators pursued the Cold War on campus, a number frankly stated that it had never occurred to them that the political beliefs or behavior of any faculty member might be dangerous. In fact, only a small minority saw the spread of world communism as being a direct or major threat to the integrity of academic programs on their campus. Moreover, it is likely that some of those academic administrators who were truly concerned about communism, loyalty, patriotism, and national security would have gone out of their way to avoid controversy with faculty over political issues, as had been their inclination in the previous decade. During the early Cold War years, there were many more academic administrators who pursued controversy with faculty than who shunned it. Did this controversy occur only because faculty and administrators found themselves on different sides of political questions, or was there more to it?

Critics on the Left have generally assumed that because of their rabid anticommunism, liberals could not bring themselves to protect radicals or radical ideas from the furor generated by the Cold War.[1] It was and is still widely believed, in fact, that liberals were instrumental in initiating and perpetuating the Cold War on campus. It has become an article of faith that liberal faculty contributed as much to the misfortunes of those colleagues who seemed to be somewhere to the left of them as did conservative or reactionary academic authorities. This is a variation on the theme that the Cold War on campus was rooted in ideological conflict and was essentially political in nature.

In order to establish that ideological conflict was not by itself at the heart of the Cold War on campus, as is commonly believed, it was necessary to show which other factors were involved. To do this, an array of instances from a number of colleges and universities in which the appointments of faculty were lost or threatened because of alleged political beliefs or behavior were examined with an eye on identifying other elements that were common to these cases, most particularly those elements which were clearly tangential to political beliefs or behavior. Were there factors other than those political in nature that had some bearing on who became embroiled in political controversy on campus during the early years of the Cold War and on how this controversy was eventually resolved? Put another way, what other characteristics of individuals besides their political beliefs or behavior had a substantial effect on whether, after they were identified as political undesirables by sources off campus, they became the focus of a campus investigation? Since not everyone who was the focus of a campus investigation lost his job, what distinquished those who were dismissed from those who were not?

To answer these questions, it is first necessary to examine the effects of various individual characteristics (e.g., discipline, rank, academic accomplishments) and institutional features (e.g., size, control, location)—beyond those bearing on political beliefs and behavior—on a significant number of cases involving academic freedom that were undeniably rooted in the Cold War.

The foci of this study are institutions of higher learning in which, between 1947 and 1956, the appointment of one or more faculty was threatened because of the concern of academic authorities about alleged radical (i.e., left-wing, Marxist, communist, socialist, progressive) political beliefs or behavior. Significant and pertinent events mark the beginning and end of this period. In 1947, President Truman's first loyalty program was begun, and in 1956, the American Association of University Professors published its lengthy "Academic Freedom and Tenure in the Quest for National Security."[2] This widely circulated publication brought added attention to, and may have helped to reduce, the impact of the Cold War on campus.

It should be noted that it is more likely that there would be a record of incidents in which someone actually did lose a job than of incidents that were quickly settled with no faculty punished or displaced. The former would be more widely known and there is thus a greater probability that they would come to the attention of a researcher. As a consequence, the institutions actually studied are often those in which there was a precipitous dismissal, and, more often than not, a subsequent accusation that there had been a violation of academic freedom. This latter aspect of the controversy would have been debated in public, and there is a greater likelihood it would have found its way into the materials used for this study. Some of these incidents attracted national attention, while, at the other extreme, a few passed largely unnoticed. Appendix A describes how the list of colleges and universities that became part of the study was developed.

Using primary and secondary sources (such as original correspondence, transcripts of hearings, minutes of meetings, government documents, institutional records), published and unpublished, up to fifty pieces of ancillary information were gathered about each case in which the appointment of a faculty member was lost or threatened because of alleged political beliefs or behavior.

The first category of information bears on the personal characteristics of those faculty whose positions were jeopardized. These include gender, highest earned degree, discipline, rank, years of experience, years of service to the institution, tenure status, teaching record, research record, personal reputation, professional reputation, institutional associations and relationships, professional associations and relationships, and political activities and involvement. Of all the facts accumulated, by far the most gaps are in the biographical data of the faculty who were at the center of these controversies. Information that may well have contributed to a full understanding of the denouement of many cases was missing.

The information coded for institutions includes their size, control (that is, private or public), location, range of programs, and the degree of faculty involvement in their governance.

The particulars of a case, from the precipitating incident (such as failure to execute a loyalty oath; reliance on the Fifth Amendment; activity in the Progressive Party presidential candidacy of Henry Wallace; or an accusation by a public figure, other persons in the community, the press, institutional authorities, or students) to its resolution, were also coded. Of particular importance here was the threat (i.e., what was at stake, whether it was dismissal, nonappointment, nonreappointment, nonpromotion); the charge (whether it was disloyalty, lack of patriotism, Communist Party membership, subversion); tangential issues that became a focus (e.g., noncooperation with institutional authorities); the defense; and how the outcome (dismissal, dismissal and reinstatement, nonrenewal, probation, no action) was explained or justified.

Finally, data on how an institution's administration handled the matter were assembled. Information coded includes career histories of administrators and governing board members who were actively involved in an incident as well as their degree of involvement and their sympathies and general attitudes, and whether an investigation committee was established, along with the process of selecting such a committee, the composition of the committee, the procedures and activities of the committee, the recommendations of the committee, and the force of the recommendations of the committee.

For 84 percent of the cases it was also possible to obtain the complete record of the part played by administrators and governing board members in the final resolution, and all pertinent data were coded. Any evidence of administrative support, indifference, or hostility to faculty; all indications of eagerness to pursue a dismissal; and any act of vindictiveness, dissimulation, cooperation, and/or accommodation was noted. If there were any other considerations that seemed to bear on the outcome of a case, they were noted, although on the surface they may appear extraneous. These include such things as concern with the reputation of the institution, concern with the reputation or survival of the administration, and the need on the part of academic administrators to assert authority, control, or discipline over faculty.

The Statistical Profile of the American Campus

As is evident from a great deal of statistical material (see Appendix B), campus life was marked by fairly steady growth during the decade after World War II. In spite of this fact, there is no reason to believe that this expansion or its consequences had a good deal to do with the evolution of the Cold War on campus. The rate of growth was not unusual, and was in line with what we have come to expect in American institutions of higher learning; increases were nonlinear and long term. Higher education was expanding, but not in a manner that seemed unmanageable. The bulge in enrollments was the result of the return of many veterans to campus. The actual increase in the number of students affected only public and not private institutions.

Compared to the period that would follow, the growth in higher education was in fact quite modest. The number of four-year institutions increased by a little over 5 percent. Expenditures and income increased faster than inflation, but the rate was not remarkable given the growth in enrollments. Faculty, particularly males, increased at a rate faster than students. The relative economic position of faculty did not improve; however, like some of the other statistical changes, the consequences of this on the dynamics of campus life are unclear.

The Fifty-eight Institutions

A variety of institutions are represented in the study, and they can be characterized in a number of ways. Using standard definitions, those offering a general four-year course leading to a bachelor's degree were designated as colleges; those with more than one undergraduate school along with programs of graduate and/or professional study, and with authorization to confer various degrees, such as the bachelor's, master's, and doctor's, were designated as universities.

The schools range in size from small colleges with faculties of fewer than 40 and student bodies of not more than 300 to large, multifaceted university centers. Nine are among the eighty-five oldest colleges and universities (all founded before 1826) in the United States. They vary in visibility and prestige. An incident at Columbia University is included in the analysis, as is one at Fairmont State College in West Virginia. This was not the first time some of the fifty-eight institutions were party to well-publicized dismissals in which it was claimed that the academic freedom of faculty had been curtailed. Prior to World War I, the University of Washington and the University of Colorado were involved in cases investigated by the American Association of University Professors. Years earlier, there had also been a much-discussed academic freedom case at Ohio State University.

The schools are found in all areas of the country, from Burlington, Vermont, to San Diego, California. No region is conspicuously underrepresented or overrepresented; more institutions are located in the northeast than elsewhere, reflecting the facts that in general this is where most colleges and universities are found and that congressional committees investigating subversive influences in education focused a major part of their attention there. Perhaps some faculty with less conventional political views avoided accepting positions in those parts of the country such as the southeastern states that would be most inhospitable to their social or political views. If this were so, there would simply be fewer faculty with ideas that were out of the ordinary to be found in certain areas. Finally, as far as sponsorship is concerned, approximately half of the schools are publicly controlled, with most of their revenue derived from government appropriations; the rest are private, some secular and some under the auspices of a religious organization. Of the former, most are funded by the state rather than locally; of the latter, the largest number are sponsored by Protestant denominations. Almost all institutions have at least a full, four-year liberal arts program.

Colleges and Universities: Some Differences

Faculty under a cloud of suspicion were treated differently in colleges than in universities. In the smaller institutions, mostly colleges, where all relationships are more personalized, there was a greater likelihood that those in authority would first appeal directly to faculty not to further embarrass their friends, their associates, or the community by their actions. Colleagues were also asked to remind those who were "bringing too much attention" to the college to be concerned with the welfare of the institution. At Evansville College, which had close ties to the Methodist Church and the local chamber of commerce (twenty-three of thirty-six trustees were residents of the local community, and only one lived outside the state), no one thought much of the fact that the president not only appealed to a close friend of an activist (George F. Parker) in the Wallace presidential campaign "to counsel with him," but even approached "various individuals," including student leaders, to do the same.

In the eyes of many college administrators, more so than university administrators, the hazards were such that anyone who could help should be enlisted to try "to point out the inevitable results of the course of action being followed":

> It has been my administrative policy to give maximum freedom to all members of the faculty in determining their activity, coveting for them the joy of creative work and activity. I fully assumed that Mr. Parker, as a member of the college staff that he had voluntarily joined, was as concerned for the welfare of Evansville College as I was and could be trusted to show the restraint necessary for the good of the college and the faculty.[3]

In such situations, in conjunction with the facade of paternalism there was commonly either a veiled or explicit threat:

> Upon my return from a vacation period on February 15th a clipping on my desk told of Mr. Parker's appointment as *temporary* chairman of the third party committee. It suggested the concern of the staff member who had placed it on my desk and I knew at once that serious trouble for Evansville College might well be involved.

> Within a week I called Mr. Parker in for a conference. I made it quite clear to him that further participation in such an official political capacity would prove embarrassing to me and would be certain to seriously harm Evansville College. I asked him if it were not possible for him to withdraw and not become the *permanent* chairman [of the county Citizens for Wallace Committee]. I made it quite clear that he had a right to vote, think, and talk as he desired—in fact could meet with the group if so desired—but urgently asked that he refrain from official activity for the sake of the college he had chosen to serve. Four times he asked if I had any specific proposal and each time I repeated that he must make the decision himself, clearly indicating what I knew was best for the college we both served. At the conclusion of the interview I further pointed out the danger that he, a liberal, by overstepping, might be responsible for forcing Evansville College into a much more conservative position.[4]

Although a college president might personally feel that someone "could be trusted to show the restraint necessary for the good of the college and the faculty," the interview, the conference, and the friendly meeting were used to remind a political "troublemaker" of his special obligations.

A larger proportion of colleges than universities were visibly tied to the local community. These relationships ranged from academic programs that were specifically developed to meet "the needs and desires of the community" to employing townspeople in key service positions. Under such circumstances, a number of college administrators were quick to acknowledge that they were especially sensitive to parochial interests and values. After a young teacher received some unwelcome attention for his political activities, the college president related that when he visited the Rotary Club he felt as if he had contracted smallpox.

In light of these local connections, there was a frequently expressed concern on the part of college administrators that controversial political activity associated with faculty would provoke a strong, adverse reaction. There was apprehension that conspicuous involvement in any politics left of center or expressions of unconventional ideology by faculty would be interpreted by the public as involving the college itself. Indeed, in the opinion of most it was in the best interest of the school if faculty did not call any unnecessary attention to themselves, for any reason. Faculty who exercised their rights as citizens did so at considerable risk: "His political activities, both on and off the campus, . . . in the opinion of the college, put an end to his usefulness to the institution." More than one college president argued that a teacher who disregarded the effect of his actions on the college was irresponsible, and "the college must protect itself"—by dismissing him as quickly and as publicly as possible.

In sum, it was assumed more often by college than university presidents that institutional welfare was dependent only on the approval of the immediate community. Placating the immediate community was so essential, it was felt, that other concerns, wider implications, could be ignored. The long view, involving questions of what impact some action might have on traditional ideals of higher learning and what the lasting negative consequences to the larger academic community might be, seems not to have been considered by half of the college presidents and more than a fifth of the university presidents. The possibility that faculty themselves might be competent to be the final judges of what should be the limit, if any, on political activity also was not an option given a great deal of attention, by either college presidents or other administrative officers.

Notwithstanding these findings, by and large it would appear that institutional characteristics did not have much of a bearing on the resolution of these cases. To be sure, there simply are not enough institutions in various categories to make adequate comparisons in order to settle the question with any certainty. Moreover, the sparseness of the data in places makes any interpretation or generalization hazardous, and at times it is possible to draw only the most tentative conclusions. The finding, for example, that three of the fifty-eight institutions are under the auspices of a single (the Methodist) church may be an intriguing fact, but a reliable inference could not possibly be drawn from it. It would also seem that administrators in private universities are less imperious than those in private colleges, public universities, or public colleges. Procedures in private universities appear to be more democratic than in other types of institutions. However, it cannot be concluded that during the Cold War years private universities were more tolerant of so-called radical faculty than other types of institutions. There are striking exceptions; there is no clear trend; and there are too few institutions to support this impression with believable statistics.

All in all, with the data on hand, it would appear that institutional characteristics had relatively little impact on how these cases got settled.

Only indirectly do institutional size and location affect outcomes, and this occurs in only a handful of cases. If an institution was located in a small, conservative community and if a local, prominent citizen—such as a newspaper publisher—was particularly concerned about or active in its affairs (as a member of the governing board, for instance), then the signs of external pressures on intramural decision making were easy to find. These situations almost invariably involved colleges rather than universities. In these few instances, institutional authorities were clearly responsive to external pressure, particularly if matters evolved slowly or were protracted. The intercession was quite straightforward. It was not denied, but instead was viewed as quite proper. The intervention was said to be the right and duty of an individual who simply had the interest of the institution at heart. It was not meddling or even a display of too much zeal, but only a patron taking charge, acting responsibly. Under these circumstances, academic administrators were more likely during the course of a controversy to adopt arguments originally heard off campus. These were never an endorsement of the faculty position, and commonly began with the premise that the good will and support of the public or local merchants or political figures would be dissipated if the institution harbored subversives. (Another standard contention was that it is always harmful to students to expose them to radical ideas.) This, of course, is not to suggest that academic administrators from larger institutions were not sensitive to the views of the public. A marginally smaller proportion were concerned, and this concern did not as obviously dominate the actions of nearly as many. More college than university presidents expressed the opinion that they could not expect community support if they retained faculty who were not considered "good citizens," and therefore they should not or would not attempt to do so.

Such considerations were introduced and held sway whether or not an institution was under secular or religious control. It is true that in the few institutions under the auspices of more traditional or conservative rather than liberal (e.g., Congregational) Protestant denominations and in which the presidents were clergymen, there was little support from any quarter on campus for ideas or faculty that strayed too far from what the public would find noncontroversial and acceptable. Yet there were too few documented instances in which orthodox, doctrinal tolerance was put to the test to conclude that this was completely lacking.

There is no evidence that religion, or religious beliefs, per se, intruded in matters in schools under church control. That is, one does not get the impression that on denominational campuses individuals were especially moved by a spiritual fervor to eradicate communism and communists. In fact, in the majority of institutions, denominational and secular, authorities were conventionally and abundantly pious. At a public institution, Rutgers University, to underline the sanctity of finding a sound method to keep "a member of the Communist Party, or . . . anyone who is under its discipline" off the faculty, the president opened a meeting of the governing board with a prayer. The deliberations ended a few hours later with a decision to dismiss two faculty who had invoked the Fifth Amendment before legislative committees. Those in public institutions were just as likely as those in institutions under religious control to display a crusader's zeal in their pursuit of heretics.

Members of governing boards were no less likely than so-called radical faculty to be irreverent. An associate professor of physiology and biochemistry at Jefferson Medical College related that when threatened during an interview with a board member, he responded with the following biblical story from the First Book of Samuel: After being accused of conspiracy by King Saul, David fled and came to the high priest Achimelech, begging for food and a sword. Achimelech gave these to him. Doeg the Edomite reported this to Saul who then accused Achimelech of conspiracy and ordered his guards to kill him. When they refused, Doeg the Edomite slew Achimelech and seventy priests. The principal described to an official of the American Association of University Professors how the meeting ended:

> This story infuriated [him]; he shouted, "Damn it, can't you keep the Lord out of this." Then he curtly told me that I was dismissed. I replied that he could not disturb my equanimity because the Lord was with me. Then he sneered and muttered, "See, if the Lord will get you out of this fix."[5]

The 126 Faculty (The Principals)

There are, of course, many more individuals than institutions represented. On half of the fifty-eight campuses the appointments of at least two
faculty were threatened. Usually, but not always, a single incident—a summons to give testimony to a legislative committee investigating the extent
of communist influence on education, the refusal to sign a loyalty oath, or
some involvement in the 1948 Wallace presidential campaign—precipitated a campus inquiry. Initially disputes over the demands by administrators, trustees, or governmental officials that faculty execute a loyalty
oath generally entangled several individuals.

In the coding, an effort was made to obtain twenty-four pieces of background data for each person in danger of losing his position. The 126
individuals for whom at least sixteen such pieces were found became the
principals of the study. (Four persons became involved more than once;
one had the dubious distinction of being terminated by four different
institutions, although information on only two of the incidents was
gathered for the study.) While not the primary foci of the study, an examination of these principals puts a number of issues in perspective, shedding
some light on both individual and institutional characteristics, the qualities
or conditions that might be expected to affect the outcome of academic
freedom controversies.

The academic backgrounds of the faculty involved in these controversies
seem unexceptional. The majority held a Ph.D. or the highest earned degree for their discipline. Some were just beginning their academic careers.
A larger number had twenty or more years of service. As many were full
professors as were instructors. More were associate professors than any
other single rank. Of those for whom information was available, about half
were on continuing appointments (i.e., they had tenure, presumably a
permanent position they could lose only because of gross negligence, incompetence, or moral turpitude), and about half had term appointments
(i.e., they were nontenured). As it turned out, having tenure was not a
protection against dismissal, although to revoke an individual's tenure is
obviously more punitive than simply deciding not to renew a contract.

Faculty were spread over almost the full range of academic disciplines,
coming in about equal numbers from the humanities (cinema, classics,
English, fine arts, history, languages, literature, music, philosophy) and the
sciences (anatomy, biochemistry, chemistry, mathematics, physics, physiology, zoology), and more infrequently from the social sciences (anthropology, economics, government, psychology), and the professional
schools (education and engineering). The large number from the biological
and physical sciences was due to the involvement of over a half dozen each

from mathematics and physics. Faculty from English, philosophy, and psychology were represented four or more times, while a number of professional fields (agriculture, architecture, dentistry, nursing) were completely free of incidents.

Aside perhaps from political beliefs or activities—86 percent saw themselves or, more importantly, were seen as political radicals, heretics or dissenters, and a somewhat smaller number were or had been involved in left-wing politics (some having been members of the Communist Party)—there was nothing about the personal lives of these individuals that made them stand out from their colleagues. All but five were white males. From an examination of surnames, admittedly a dubious scientific procedure, it would seem that Jews, who in the years after World War II made up less than 4 percent of the American population and a little more than twice that proportion of the faculty of colleges and universities, are overrepresented as principals.

Over the years only a few had had scrapes with colleagues, chairmen, or administrative officers. Most appear to have been quite unobtrusive. A handful had been known, open Marxists, a fact that in the past had attracted little attention. More resembled communists—they were members of organizations that had communist support, former members of such organizations, former communists, pacifists, socialists, antisegregationists—than had actual connections with the Communist Party.

Fewer than one-eighth were reported to have been constantly involved in political activities—from gathering signatures for petitions to participating in what one source felt "could have been a disorderly meeting" in the dean's office—that called unfavorable attention to themselves. It is possible that such activity prejudiced administrators against them prior to the particular incident under study. A few others had been involved in organizations working for faculty collective bargaining. Junior faculty were less conspicuous than those with eight or more years of service in these other intramural matters, but not necessarily in extramural activities. As a result of common political activities, some knew each other; a number of friendships had been made in graduate school.

Seldom did a story surface about idiosyncratic behavior that office mates, neighbors, or townspeople found offensive. Even when the ascot that someone sported or shorts and sandals were mentioned in testimony as sure proof of foreignness or "queerness" ("It's not the socialism, it's the beret," the secretary of the Board of Trustees of Olivet College reportedly complained), or sporadic church attendance was dredged up to show someone's dark side, it was mostly as an afterthought. Generally, old scores were not being settled; political opponents were not engaged in a contrived, systematic purge of dissidents or radicals. Departmental strife rarely fig-

ured in how a case developed or in its outcome. If there was jealousy or
interpersonal conflict it was pretty well masked.

Relations between principals and those who were to become their adversaries were no less cordial than ordinary faculty-administrative relations.
One individual had in the recent past lived for six weeks with the college
president "as a guest" before he and his family found adequate housing. A
number of others had been active in campus affairs, being tirelessly committed to administration and governance. Five were former or present
department chairmen. Five others had devoted considerable time to committees of the faculty senate. Altogether, almost one-quarter could be classified as being or having been very active or fairly active in campus administrative, governance, or service functions. Most of these held the rank of
associate or full professor.

Although most principals were not given unqualified support and a few
even encountered unyielding hostility, testimony about campus activities
that proved to be false was rarely given. In fact, when called upon, students,
former students, and colleagues were generally well-disposed and helpful.
On the other hand, in their assessments and testimony, deans and
chairmen were for the most part less charitable; more than a few were
sometimes clearly mean-spirited. Most of these seem to have been venting
irritation at the extra work, or the personal embarrassment, or the strain
on the institution that the affair had caused. Principals had been hired,
given salary increases, promoted, and given tenure and apparently had not
been special problems in the past.

Although not necessarily asked to, some deans and chairmen obviously
felt that they must account for this earlier support, preferment, or advancement:

> Mr. Margolis's classes seemed to have acquired considerable popularity
> among the students and he was well-known on the [University of Connecti-
> cut] campus in spite of his short service here. I would judge that he was
> competent in the subject matter taught. I was not fully satisfied with his
> maturity and judgment. He had a pleasing personality and got along well.
>
> A charge that he was a communist was brought during the 1952–53 academic
> year. This was not a matter of public knowledge. Mr. Margolis denied the
> truth of the charge to me. I have no way of deciding the truth of the charge. A
> faculty committee acting for the Board of Trustees held hearings in the mat-
> ter. Their conclusions were never brought to my attention.[6]

Apparently some deans and chairmen believed that by debasing a principal they might be absolved from their own past "errors." Yet only a
handful were drawn in to take an active role in the prosecution of a case. As
the example below of testimony given by a medical school administrator

and a department chairman to an advisory committee to the president of the University of Michigan illustrates, such witnesses could go far afield, and might not hesitate to offer unsubstantiated evidence and irrelevant testimony in painting an unfavorable picture of a principal. First the dean:

> *Committee Chairman Smith*: Do you care to express any opinion as to whether you think Doctor Nickerson has been honest and candid and forthright in his disclosures, in his statements as to his past affiliations with the Party, and as to his termination of these affiliations? . . .
>
> *Doctor Ferstenberg*: Well, I certainly am quite willing to express the conviction that he is not candid. I don't know how honest he may be, but certainly I have seen very little evidence of candor. He evades questions nicely, avoids others pretty well, and I think I express the judgment of the executive committee, when I say that he certainly has not been candid with us. He may very well be honest, I don't know.
>
> *Chairman Smith*: When you say he has not been candid, you mean in these conversations that you have had with him, relating to his communist affiliations?
>
> *Doctor Ferstenberg*: Yes. By candor, I mean there is no openness of mind. His mind is pretty much closed to his beliefs, and you have a great deal of difficulty in drawing out his beliefs, and when you do draw them out, he can support them by reasoning, reasoning of his own variety, and an evaluation of his reasoning of course is difficult for someone who does not know anything about communism.
>
> *Chairman Smith*: You do not mean by lack of candor, to imply, or do you, that he failed to state all the facts that you were asking him about?
>
> *Doctor Ferstenberg*: Well, it would be difficult to prove that he had failed to state all of the facts, but one must necessarily get that impression in visiting with him.
>
> Now the reason one gets that impression is because his replies are short and brief, and when you want to learn something definite about some of his answers, you have to draw him out. There is very little evidence of open-mindedness, and that is my definition of candor. He just is not open-minded enough to sit right down and discuss the situation with us, in all of its aspects. . . .
>
> *Chairman Smith*: Have you ever had a report from any student or any faculty member or any graduate student prior to these recent occurrences, which would suggest that Doctor Nickerson was a communist?
>
> *Doctor Ferstenberg*: No, no report of that kind. I had a deputation of students from the summer session of a year ago last summer, come to me because they felt they had been treated very badly during the summer session.
>
> One of the older members was in tears, stating that he was hostile, and his methods were roughshod, and that never in their experience in an educa-

tional institution, had they ever encountered a man of his manner and conduct in class. . . .[7]

The department chairman's observations were no kinder. More than once, he told the committee that there were questions about his colleague's integrity, but after raising this specter, he refused to elaborate. More than once, other faults of character were noted. The assessment was harsh; particulars were not mentioned:

> Nickerson has had, however, the reputation throughout the country . . . of being a troublemaker, an exceedingly difficult person to get along with, and one who has a type of personal arrogance and a lack of candor, and desire to get ahead, which means tromping on everybody else in the department and elsewhere.[8]

There is little question from these transcripts that any issue that could conceivably turn the committee against the principal, Nickerson, was introduced. The committee was reminded that if one department member could not get security clearance, than this would jeopardize the government funding of everyone. The chairman related how his department had become divided ("a sharp schism") over the matter of someone taking the Fifth Amendment. Nickerson's testimonials were depreciated because Nickerson, himself, had solicited them. The chairman went as far as to introduce the subject of lunch periods that had "become so unpleasantly political, that my staff, including myself, have pulled away from it, because it simply creates arguments, and has been of no value. My associate professor, L. A. Woods, did not feel that this was the type of a proper situation in which the general philosophy of anti-administration, anti-authority, anti-government, anti-everything, is held up and supported in defense of other types of philosophies."[9] In case someone missed the point, here he elaborated.

> *Chairman Smith*: You mean these are conversations of current political problems or issues?
>
> *Doctor Seevers*: Much more than that. I mean they are completely, well, I think I can put it in simple terms, it is basically following the communist line without saying so. I mean the word hasn't come up; it is a leftish type of conversation.
>
> I doubt very much if the term has ever been used, or that there was any inkling along that line.[10]

It should be noted that this case is not typical; it would have been better for Nickerson had this information not been volunteered. Although the majority of department chairmen had no opportunity to be heard, of those who were, more were advocates than were interested in having someone dismissed. On the whole, faculty—senior colleagues, junior colleagues, and, to a lesser extent, chairmen—even those who were inclined to overlook issues of justice, were interested in mercy. Doctor Seevers may not have been representative of department chairmen, but his thinking was representative of the specious reasoning of what had become a not insignificant number of individuals—off and on campus—when discussing the subject of communism.

After individuals were finally let go, this picture of widespread support changed somewhat. It was not uncommon for former associates to offer evaluations and opinions supportive of the decision to terminate. When asked by a professional organization looking into the nonrenewal of the contract of a chemist at Oregon State College whether he had "shown any evidence of a lack of scientific objectivity, intellectual integrity or other qualities which are essential to success in research or teaching," the department head wrote:

> Underscoring the words *in chemistry*, I can say that I have not detected any lack of scientific objectivity or intellectual integrity. I think, however, that there are other qualities which are highly essential, in which he has shown a definite lack. Among these is a serious lack of balance and a great desire to argue, merely for the sake of arguing.[11]

In response to a question about how "faithful" this individual had been "in the performance of his duties," the head continued:

> Staff members, townspeople and students began to harass me about his objectionable political tactics and so I became convinced that his accelerating political activity was the cause of the lack of attention to his duties which had been worrying me.[12]

The department head concluded his detailed assessment in a negative vein, failing to mention that according to the record the president made the decision to terminate without consulting the department. In fact, the department was formally notified after the principal had learned of the decision, and, in an effort to force the administration to back down, made it public. In turn, the department head took steps to give credence to the administration's actions.

> Summarizing in a sentence, however, this seems to us to present a situation in which a brilliant young man did not live up to his pre-appointment promise, and did not prove to be one whom we would wish to have as a permanent colleague.[13]

Almost instantly, the fact that political considerations were at the center of the dismissal was brushed aside.

Again at Oregon State College, a second department head just as readily justified and corroborated a decision by the president to terminate a second Wallace activist:

> The above incident [an anonymous complaint] together with the previous impressions made on my mind by second-hand reports placed me in a state of mind where I was willing to subscribe to the president's later declaration to me that he thought LaVallee's contract for the 1948–49 year should not be renewed. I promptly notified LaVallee the same day I had this consultation with the president that his contract would not be renewed.
>
> You will gather from the above that I did not take the initiative in proposing the termination of LaVallee's appointment, and that is correct, but I should add that I felt a distinct sense of relief that Dr. Strand had taken the bull by the horns if I may put it that way. Had I not exhibited indecision because I felt I lacked sufficiently concrete evidence and consequently did not come out with a recommendation for termination of appointment I am confident that a notice to terminate appointment would have gone out to LaVallee a year earlier. I early felt that Dr. Strand had a fuller knowledge about LaVallee's shortcomings both in and out of the classroom than I had from the standpoint of concrete evidence. . . .
>
> I will conclude by saying that hindsight reveals the mistake I made in not divulging to LaVallee the conviction growing in my mind that his objectivity of approach in the classroom was in question. As I see it now I was deterred by the feeling that I should not "open up to him" until I could face him with irrefutable, concrete evidence.[14]

It seems that the more egregious this sort of after-the-fact accommodation, the more likely the revisionist was a senior faculty member.

Notwithstanding such notable instances of rationalization or betrayal, in easily 70 percent of those cases where extensive materials were available, the character of individuals appears to have been above reproach. To be sure, over half of the positive portrayals were found in letters or statements of friends or partisans. Moreover, the evaluation of faculty performance and personality are generally quite laudatory. Nonetheless, in fewer than 10 percent of the cases was someone pictured as less than completely reputable. Even those making the case against an individual were over five times as likely to have positive rather than negative comments to make about trustworthiness, morality, or decency. The present ordeal was commonly seen as an isolated incident in an otherwise unblemished career, association, or life. Of course, when formal charges were enumerated, the behavior of a large minority was labeled as "misconduct," but there was essentially no evidence of misconduct in the record beyond the single issue that was putting the appointment in jeopardy. Those involved were often viewed as having been deceived, not deceivers—as having been misled rather than as misleading others.

Even in official reports, it is common to hear someone characterized as "a man of decency and honor" who is at the same time a "committed scientist" and who "undoubtedly is free from the taint of communism." Descriptions such as "a man of integrity" appear with regularity; denunciations such as "devious and disappointing" are rare—and, as in the case of "misconduct," mostly refer to behavior subsequent to the charge of political heresy. It was not personal character, but character of political affiliation that was at issue.

After a case was publicized in the local or national media, individuals were sketched in quite different terms. Flaws and heretofore unseen reprehensible traits suddenly became obvious. Arthur M. Schlesinger, Jr. felt that the evidence suggested that two Communist Party members and one suspected Party member who had been fired from the University of Washington were "contemptible individuals who have deliberately lived a political lie, pretending to be American liberals while secretly responding to the dictates of a foreign nation and of a totalitarian conspiracy."[15] Actually, words like "contemptible" were not commonly used. However, with hindsight, it was easy to find other defects, blemishes, or misdeeds—among others, evidence of insanity, immaturity, shallowness, discourtesy, and overzealousness.

As will become evident, almost 15 percent were, as some put it, unbending or, as others put it, highly principled. Yet even these individuals were no more "unbending" or "principled" than their detractors or others on campus. Neither trait seemed to attract any undue attention before their loyalty became a subject of general concern. Given that all 126 principals presumably held radical political and/or economic views, it is striking how many were not, or at least were not seen as, militant or strident; it is also striking how many clearly complied with all institutional requirements. In light of what they were said to be, on the whole they were a pretty conventional lot.

The principals did stand out from other faculty in one way: almost all were very much attuned to current events. Their answers to a flood of questions during administrative proceedings indicated that they may well have been more conscious of social issues than a random assortment of ten dozen of their colleagues. This is merely conjecture, but, if true, would hardly be surprising.

Administrators and Boards

The institutional records examined provided little background information about the administrators or members of the governing boards who played a part in these cases. Other materials such as catalogs, biographies, and directories such as *Who's Who* were used when practicable to supplement the few facts that were gleaned. In the end, however, what was learned is incomplete and its value is unclear. There were more clues about the experience and attitudes of administrative officers and members of the governing boards of universities than of colleges; for many college officials the only record was little more than a name. Moreover, although administrators were naturally more directly involved than members of governing boards in all facets of these incidents, it was actually possible to gather more facts about the latter from secondary sources.

Almost all senior academic administrators—presidents, executive vice presidents, and college deans—had at one time been faculty members. Many had not been in the classroom for a number of years, but at some point in their careers they had been in a position to gain familiarity and sympathy with the faculty point of view. On the other hand, only a few members of governing boards had had careers in education. The largest number were drawn from or engaged in business, finance, or law. There were also a substantial number of public officials and other professionals represented on boards. Members of the boards of public institutions were generally named by the governor or elected by the public. Members of the boards of private institutions were appointed by other board members to fill a vacancy. Notwithstanding this difference in the selection process, the compositions of boards were not too dissimilar. Boards were pretty homogeneous, consisting of white males affiliated with Protestant denominations.

There was some indication that a small minority of board members did not have very much information or knowledge about routine matters germane to higher education. At most institutions the boards appear to have been controlled by a minority of members; at least very few board members took an active or visible interest in campus affairs. Those who did were definitely the older members with the longest service. A few board members seem to have become very much involved in the administrative details and in monitoring day-to-day institutional affairs. These individuals were not only abreast of administrative matters on their own campuses, but were in touch with academic officials at other institutions. Board members saw themselves as guardians of the public interest, engaged in carrying out responsibilities that had been thrust upon them.

On the whole, academic administrators appeared to believe that faculty had a right to express their views on any subject, although at the same time some indicated specific reservations about faculty having complete academic freedom. By a margin of at least two to one, they felt that how faculty conducted themselves on or off campus was, because of their administrative authority, their business. It is unclear what the views of board members were on these issues. By a fairly larger margin, academic administrators agreed that it was reasonable to require a loyalty oath of faculty. Board members appeared to be almost unanimous in supporting this position. A number of board members, particularly at colleges, went as far as to express the opinion that no facts about communism should be taught in any educational institution.

It was rare that the political affiliation of board members could be determined; when it could, over twice as many indicated a preference for the Republican Party over the Democratic Party. How board members may have cast their ballots in a state or national election, however, did not appear to affect attitudes, public statements, or voting patterns to a significant degree during board meetings.

Notes

1. See, for example, Jesse Lemisch, *On Active Service in War and Peace: Politics and Ideology in the American Historical Profession* (Toronto: New Hogtown Press, 1975), pp. 46–52.
2. "Academic Freedom and Tenure in the Quest for National Security," report of a special committee of the American Association of University Professors, *AAUP Bulletin* 42, no. 1 (1956): 49–107.
3. Lincoln B. Hale, "Statement Relative to George F. Parker," p. 3.
4. Ibid., p. 2.
5. William H. Pearlman, correspondence to Ralph E. Himstead, 23 November 1953.
6. G. Lowell Field, correspondence to George E. McReynolds, 8 October 1953.
7. "Proceedings of the Special Advisory Committee to the President," 7 June 1954.
8. Ibid.
9. Ibid.
10. Ibid.
11. E.C. Gilbert, correspondence to George Pope Shannon, 23 June 1949.
12. Ibid.
13. Ibid.
14. Milton N. Nelson, correspondence to George Pope Shannon, 29 June 1949.
15. Arthur M. Schlesinger, Jr., "The Right to Loathsome Ideas," *Saturday Review of Literature*, 14 May 1949, p. 18.

3

Precipitating Events: "Catching the Spotlight"

Over 60 percent of the 126 cases were occasioned when individuals were called before some governmental body to give testimony about their knowledge of or contributions or connection to the communist influence on education. Most often these were formal hearings of the House of Representatives Committee on Un-American Activities or one of its sub-committees. A smaller number of individuals were called before investigators from the Subcommittee to Investigate the Administration of the Internal Security Act and Other Internal Security Laws of the Committee on the Judiciary of the Senate, other investigating committees of the Congress, state legislative committees or commissions on un-American activities, or state boards of education. As indicated, participation in the 1948 Wallace presidential campaign and the refusal to sign a loyalty oath were the two other prevailing reasons that drew individuals into one of these controversies. The remainder of the cases involved persons who, like a social scientist from Kansas State Teachers College who was one of 280 signers of a petition asking for amnesty for Communist Party members convicted under the Smith Act, brought unfavorable attention to themselves by some expression of their political views.

Masking the Truth

As a matter of course, administrative authorities ardently denied that acts of free expression, such as a contentious talk widely reported in the press, were controlling factors and put faculty at risk. Unless there was overwhelming evidence to the contrary—public statements, memoranda, and the like—these protestations were taken at face value in determining whether an incident was truly precipitated by the political expression or beliefs of a principal, and qualified for inclusion in the study.

Seven institutions that were said to have dismissed or in some other way punished faculty whose politics offended administrators were not included in the study as evidence supporting the charges was inconclusive. For example, it was believed by some and even reported in the press that because of his legal activities in defending individuals accused of being communists, Vern Countryman was denied a promotion to full professor—and in effect denied tenure—at Yale University after being unanimously recommended by the faculty of the School of Law. In defending the administration, the dean of the School of Law said that the promotion was not denied, but delayed. The dean wrote that:

> I was not convinced that the evidence of Countryman's objective scholarship warranted a full professorship at this time, but I believed him to have much promise and to be worthy of reappointment as associate professor for another term in which his qualifications for the full professorship could be established. The president, who had carefully studied the case, was of the same opinion. . . .
>
> I have emphatically denied from the beginning, and deny again, that the determination was based on these factors, . . . his political views and his activity in certain loyalty and court cases.[1]

No record could be found to refute the dean's statement.

About a year before the Yale University administration's decision to overrule the recommendation of the faculty of the School of Law, President A. Whitney Griswold received a lengthy letter from an influential alumnus, involved in a fund-raising campaign, in which critical remarks were made about the School of Law and some of its faculty, including Countryman:

> Probably the best introduction to my thinking will be made by a brief review of the progress of my committee in its attempt to raise an endowment fund for the account of the Forestry School. The present status of our efforts is that we have raised $480,000.00 and have it in the bank. In addition to this we have plans so well along towards the raising of the money for a building program in connection with the Forestry School setup that will total about $500,000.00 that I feel reasonably hopeful that we won't have too much difficulty in completing this next step. Beyond this, we have further contingent promises, favorable contacts and many other things that are in process, so that it would look as if we might get up to $1,500,000.00 as a minimum and $2,000,000.00 as a maximum in connection with our present mode of procedure. . . .
>
> Our opportunity seems obvious and unusually favorable in that the Watzek family (three brothers) are all graduates of the Forestry School and have a deep devotion to its welfare. They have made really large fortunes in the forest products field and have been very generous with the Forestry School over a period of many years as you no doubt are aware. . . . The problem of

our committee is that the Watzeks are deeply concerned over what they consider to be radical or socialistic trends in the Yale program. All of our committee, as well as Charlie O'Hearn, George Garratt, and a number of others have done a great deal of work with the Watzek people but they feel that they are well informed and up-to-date and we have not been successful in relieving their minds about their criticisms of the Yale program. When we once get this road block out of the way, I am hopeful that our undertaking in respect to setting up an endowment fund for the Forestry School will be quickly concluded. . . .

At any rate, it seems to me that the present criticisms that are directed at the School of Law are sound and are as a result of either weak leadership on the part of the present dean, or, as is believed by some, lack of sufficient authority in his office. The radicals and troublemakers are nearly always vocal and unusually active so that unless the more thoughtful majority and particularly the executive leadership of the program are alert and on the job, the result is that the vocal minority sometimes develop into great authority and assume leadership to which they are not entitled. . . .

The men I don't like are Harper, Emerson, and one or two more of their type but I have no great concern in their being kept there temporarily although I do feel that it would be desirable if they recognized that their paychecks come from Yale and they should tone down their activities away from the School of Law to an extent that will avoid the very serious damage to Yale that they have been resposible for during recent times. There is another type in the School of Law that I believe you do not know about because there is some unlikelihood that this sort of information would come to your attention. I refer to Vern Countryman. He went to Yale from the University of Washington so that I have been able to get rather complete information as to his life history and record before he went to New Haven. Top people here seem to feel that they are well enough informed to say positively that there are serious reasons why we should be very alert in respect to him.[2]

The following week, the same individual again wrote to the Yale administration, this time to the Secretary of the Yale Corporation.

Dear Ben:

I had intended to make a personal report to you when I was in New Haven on the subject of Vern Countryman. He is strictly "no good." I don't know this of my own knowledge, and, as a consequence, should not make such a flat statement as I have, but my information comes from people out here of the highest authority and in whose judgment I have complete confidence. Vern Countryman may not be a communist, but if not, it is simply because he thinks it is safer and more effective to work without taking on the risks and responsibility that are involved if he joins up with the Party. He goes with the wrong people and has always done so. He operates "in the woodwork," but is quite effective and is dangerous. It is impossible to determine whether he is a member of the Communist Party or not (my guess is that he is not), but he is just as dangerous if he is out of the Party, and possibly more so than if he was [*sic*] a Party member.

I realize that the above is not very conclusive but it seems to be about the end of the line where you end up with many of these people, and I thought I would send the story along to you as far as it is possible to obtain it at this time. . . .[3]

President Griswold assured those who wrote on Countryman's behalf that his decision not to recommend promotion was based solely on his evaluation of Countryman's scholarship.

To the former dean of the School of Law:

I can only say that I came to the decision after careful study and deliberation and with some knowledge of the field in which most of Countryman's published writings have appeared. . . .

I do suggest—and believe with my whole heart—that the principle followed by Yale College [making competition for the full professorship rigorous and nationwide in scope] is a good one.[4]

To Senator Estes Kefauver:

I should like to say that university policy looks to performance of the highest order, as well as to promise, in both teaching and scholarship, in all candidates for the full professorship. . . . It did not seem to me that Professor Countryman had, within this short time, produced sufficient evidence as teacher or scholar to justify a full professorship in what purports to be one of the country's leading law schools.[5]

To Justice William O. Douglas:

I assure you that this [that Mr. Countryman is not being promoted because of disagreement with his political views] is not the case. In the first place, I do not know enough about Mr. Countryman's views to know how much I might agree or disagree with them, though I doubt that the area of disagreement would be any greater than it would be with respect to many other members of the faculty. With his general concern for the rights of individuals under the Constitution, I am in complete sympathy. In the second place, I agree with you in thinking that a law school "should not be a 'conservative' school, a 'radical' school, a 'New Deal' school," etc. To attempt to recruit or maintain a faculty on any such basis would be ridiculous. . . . The reason why Mr. Countryman's promotion was delayed has been fully and accurately stated by Dean Shulman.[6]

In a reply to a committee of the Association of American Law Schools interested in the matter, Countryman stated:

Frankly, I don't believe that the reason assigned for denying my promotion— the inadequacy of my legal writing—is the real reason. [President] Griswold is not qualified to pass judgment on legal scholarship and [Dean] Shulman was not the sort of man who would pit his judgment on that issue against the unanimous decision of the Permanent Board. This, however, is merely my opinion based on my appraisal of the men who made the decision. There is no objective evidence to prove that my opinion is right.[7]

This case and six others in which there was a charge that an unfavorable outcome for an individual was mostly or partially due to his taking an unpopular political stand, but for which there was no substantiating evidence, were excluded from the analysis.

On the other hand, the University of Minnesota and Tulane University are two of six institutions included in the study in spite of denials on the part of academic authorities that political considerations may have been even tangentially involved in the dismissal of faculty. The claims by the administrations that relevant criteria—competence at the University of Minnesota and an inability to get along and work with colleagues at Tulane University—were at the heart of these dismissals were hardly supported by the evidence.

Competence as a Pretext

At the University of Minnesota, the administration terminated an instructor of philosophy, Forrest Wiggins, ignoring his department's unanimous recommendation that he be reappointed. The Department of Philosophy decided that Wiggins should be continued for another year, at which time his record would be reviewed and he would either be granted tenure or terminated. The dean wanted him fired. The department proceeded and recommended that he be continued; the dean overturned the recommendation and the president concurred.

In defending the administration's decision, the dean of the College of Sciences, Literature and Arts argued that "continuance is not justified on the basis of his scholarship record or his potential contribution to the Philosophy Department."[8] The president also stated that Wiggins had been terminated because he was a poor scholar and that political considerations did not figure in the decision.

Since his appointment to the faculty, Wiggins's left-wing politics had brought him a good deal of attention. He was active in Henry Wallace's Progressive Party, serving as a vice president for the State of Minnesota. There had also been some unfavorable comment about a leftward slant in his teaching. However, a surreptitious investigation by the administration did not support a charge of bias in the assigned readings he gave to undergraduates.

In one talk before a business club Wiggins argued that business was "destructive of the public good." The university president was forced to comment: "When we brought him to the Minnesota faculty three or four years ago . . . there was no hint of the views that he now seems occasionally in public addresses to espouse."[9]

In reaction to a highly ideological public address on social and political questions two years before Wiggins was terminated, the former dean had written to the chairman of the Department of Philosophy wondering "how analytical, systematic, rational, and objective his teaching really is. . . ."[10] Noting that Wiggins's speeches were generating criticism of the university, he added, "I think we will need the most careful documentation of his scholarship and philosophy and of his competence as a teacher when the question of permanent tenure arises." The assistant to the director of university relations, who had heard Wiggins's address reported to the administration that it was his impression that Wiggins was a Soviet apologist and a disciple of socialism. He accused Wiggins of using rhetorical tricks to condition his audience to "communist dogma."[11]

The present dean also found fault with the scholarship of the speech: "The Ideology of Interest." The dean accused Wiggins of misrepresentation of quoted sources, use of unscholarly sources, and careless documentation. It was apparent, however, that it was more than the presentation's scholarly qualities that caught the attention of the dean—and a number of members of the state legislature who publicly and privately urged the president to dismiss Wiggins. His assertion that America was more militaristic than other countries raised the most controversy:

> Conflict of interest is telescoped and brought into sharp focus by means of war. We ought to ask ourselves, "who are the people who want war at the present time?" The Koreans? Their towns and villages and cities and hospitals and schools and huts are reduced to rubble. More than three-fourths of Korea is destroyed. The population has suffered a loss of more than one hundred thousand casualties. The Koreans do not want war. The Chinese, in a period of some twenty years in which they have been struggling for independence, have lost more than ten million lives. They are only one year out of an internal civil war. The great job of the Chinese is that of reconstruction and industrialization. The Chinese do not want war. The German elections show that the German people will not shoulder arms in defense of the Western democracies. The Russians don't want war. Who is it, then, who wants war?
>
> The answer is that it is the capitalists and the militarists in the United States who want war.[12]

Although some of the inquiries into the dismissal by various faculty and student organizations concluded that some of Wiggins's public talks had indeed contributed to the unfavorable evaluation that led to his dismissal, members of the University of Minnesota chapter of the American Association of University Professors investigating the matter were bothered by his stridency:

> We cannot say that Dean McDiarmid's conclusion respecting this address was outside the area of permissible administrative discretion, particularly when we ourselves find it impossible to understand how an able and conscientious philosopher and teacher of logic—or indeed an able and conscientious scholar in any of the disciplines of the university—could deliberately and sincerely reach the above-quoted conclusion from the given premise.[13]

This faculty committee, in fact, was so disapproving that it accepted the administration's contention that the dismissal of Wiggins was a routine and unexceptional use of its discretion. Inasmuch as the tenure code allowed for the removal of untenured faculty without cause, the burden of proof was on Wiggins to show otherwise. He would have to prove that the refusal to reappoint was "predicated exclusively or even primarily on . . . political prejudice."[14] (Apparently, it would have been insufficient to establish that it was secondary, marginal, or peripheral.) This, of course, was an impossible task inasmuch as Wiggins was not given access to all of the records. Even if he had been, it would have been difficult to make his case, since it is unlikely that such evidence would be readily found. Throughout the controversy, the administration claimed that Wiggins was not being fired, but, because there were questions about his competency, only being denied reappointment.

Interpersonal Conflict as a Pretext

At Tulane University where Robert Hodes, a professor of neurophysiology and experimental neurology, was charged with "creating friction in the department," the authorities also went to great lengths in an attempt to hide the fact that his politics had anything to do with his being told to "look for another job." From the beginning to his final appeal to a committee of the Board of Administrators of the Tulane Educational Fund, Hodes' claim that the charges were "a subterfuge by means of which . . . dismissal could be effected without revealing the allegedly true cause thereof" was not given any credence. He was terminated because, the administration alleged, his "character and personality [were] of such a nature that conflict between him and others was almost inevitable."[15] The fact that he had gathered a group of faculty together to hear a request for aid from an individual from the China Welfare Appeal (declared by the United States Attorney General to be a subversive organization) in the form of medical and other supplies for the People's Republic of China was, the administration claimed, completely incidental. This was a matter, the university said, in which it had no interest.

The testimony of administrators and faculty in the preliminary proceedings and in the hearing itself makes it obvious that the dismissal had more to do with politics than with the lack of interpersonal skills. From statements not only by disinterested faculty but even by the department chairman, who pressed the case for the administration, there is little doubt that the Medical School dean and the president of the university were being disingenuous when they denied that they knew or cared about Hodes' political or social views. The observations of a number of faculty refute this contention.

Dr. Rucker:

> Q. You think, doctor, that Dr. Hodes was dismissed for political reasons or for his political views?
>
> A. I think that was a factor. I think it is an important factor.[16]

Dr. Ervin:

> It was my impression that the general conclusion, the only reasonable explanation, for this occurrence was in terms of Dr. Hodes' unpopular political and social views, and there was no other explanation that seems to suffice at the time to explain what happened, and the impression that we had [was that] he was in danger of dismissal at that time.[17]

Dr. Smith:

> The statement was made on this occasion that there would very soon be a dismissal from the faculty and that the person who was going to be dismissed was Dr. Hodes, and that he was going to be dismissed because he was a communist. And the statement was made [that] he was not only a communist but was a leader of the Communist Party in New Orleans, and that evidence for this was said to have been obtained from two medical students who were FBI agents. It was said that Dr. Hodes would be dismissed very shortly because it was not possible to keep communists on the faculty. It was a very startling piece of information. It was so startling that some of us had a serious discussion later about the matter.[18]

Dr. Heath, chairman of the Department of Psychiatry and Neurology:

> It was stated that at one occasion that I mentioned to him—and this is the first episode he mentioned—that he had held a political meeting at his home in the spring. It was my information that this meeting was held in the fall.

This was the information that had been given to me. He stated that I had more or less reprimanded him because funds were collected for "Red" China at that meeting and I called this treason and [it] was an act that violated the law of the nation. But these things are true. I did make this statement to him.
. . .

I always spoke to him about politics in the overall framework and context of causing friction, I never pointed out that politics was the sole reason for his dismissal as he apparently quoted from that book, and to the best of my knowledge it was not, that it was one of the factors leading to the friction.[19]

There was considerably more than what the Tulane administration called "dissension, disharmony, and difficulty" that made Hodes' "continuance in the department intolerable."[20]

Congressional and Other Committees

Those required to give testimony before a congressional committee almost always cited the Fifth Amendment ("no person . . . shall be compelled in any criminal case to be a witness against himself, nor be deprived of life, liberty, or property, without due process of law . . ." [see Appendix G, Part 1]) as their reason for not answering questions. Since the courts had ruled that it was an inadequate justification for not giving testimony, principals less often sought the protection of the First Amendment (that a hearing was an abridgment of someone's freedom of speech). Sometimes reference was made to both the First and Fifth amendments by those who "refused to testify fully" or who did not, as one principal put it, "respond to the grilling about personal political beliefs and associations."

Most of the time, witnesses who were required to come before a congressional committee would make a grudging effort to be helpful, although anything less than full cooperation was seldom viewed approvingly either by government or university officials. A small number of principals were difficult, recalcitrant and argumentative witnesses; a slightly larger number were fully accommodating. The complaint that it was not easy to remember particulars about conversations, meetings, rallies, or petitions a decade or so in the past was a common defense against the charge of antipathy to the "civic duty" of uncovering subversion.

Frequently, the procedures of governmental committees were viewed with suspicion and openly criticized. Many witnesses would not go beyond testifying that they were not "presently" Communist Party members. In what became a widely publicized appearance before the House Committee on Un-American Activities, an instructor of psychology at Vassar College who objected to the questions themselves, declined to answer them, citing numerous Supreme Court decisions to support his position:

1. I . . . hereby respectfully object to the power and jurisdiction of this committee to inquire into:
   (a) My political beliefs
   (b) My religious beliefs
   (c) Any other personal and private affairs
   (d) My associational activities.
2. I am a private citizen engaged in work in the fields of education and research and in writing and speaking in connection therewith. I hold no office of public honor or trust. I am not employed by any governmental department. I am not under salary or grant from any governmental department.[21]

There were numerous challenges by witnesses to the right of governmental investigators to ask political questions. Some principals maintained that, because they were completely ignorant of Communist Party affairs, tangential to the radical movement, or had not been involved in any political matters for a number of years, they were unable to provide substantial information. They were not balky witnesses, they claimed, only ignorant. Many were willing to talk freely about their own beliefs and participation in political activities, but were unwilling to implicate friends, colleagues, co-workers, or acquaintances from years past.

As in this brief example from the testimony of an anthropologist from Sarah Lawrence College, there was a particular reluctance on the part of most to name names:

Committee Counsel: Mr. Goldman will you tell us who was the head, who was the leader, of the communist unit at Columbia [University] while you were a member of that unit?
Witness: I am sorry, as I told you and the committee in executive session, I cannot as a matter of principle reveal those names. . . .
Committee Counsel: What is the principle that you mentioned then?
Witness: The principle, I think, is a simple one which is that I cannot inform on others to get others into trouble, particularly since I have no knowledge that any of these individuals had ever committed any offense against the security of the United States. So far as I know, they had violated no law. . . .
Committee Counsel: Mr. Goldman, will you tell us the name of the leader of the Brooklyn [College] unit while you were in Brooklyn, of the Communist Party?
Witness: I cannot tell you the name for the same reason I have just stated.
Senator: Will you repeat that reason again?
Witness: I rest primarily, and as far as I know perhaps that is the only reason I have got, [on] a moral principle. I simply could not live with my conscience if I informed on other people who, to the best of my knowledge, have done no harm.

Whether those who took the Fifth Amendment did so to avert the danger of prosecution for perjury in case their testimony was later contradicted or because they were protesting what they believed was a congressional violation of due process, the decision to refuse to answer these sorts of questions is precisely what led to their becoming principals.

Those represented by legal counsel followed counsel's advice. A number insisted that too many questions were not pertinent; some would not answer queries that to them were not germane to the task of the investigating committee, although they did not seek the protection of the Fifth Amendment. A few would not produce records; a half dozen were cited for contempt of Congress. Some may have lied, some may have forgotten, some may have been too high-minded, some may have been frightened, some may have had something to hide. Very few were eager to discuss events of ten, fifteen, or twenty years in the past. All caught the attention of academic authorities.

The general pattern of congressional investigations was quite similar. The committee usually relied on the testimony of a former member of the Communist Party—a Bella Dodd, Herbert Philbrick, Dorothy Fann, or Anne Kinney—who offered the names of past associates or membership lists of organizations with which they were affiliated or both. Then the persons named were called to testify in a closed hearing. If in these semiprivate meetings they answered questions to the committee's satisfaction, further action was seldom taken. If they were thought evasive, they were asked to give evidence publicly about groups of which they were members, campaigns and causes they had supported, meetings they had attended, articles by or about them in left-wing publications, friendships they had formed, and the like. About one-fifth of the questions and answers about communist associations from a single individual's one and a half hours of testimony before the House Committee on Un-American Activities in May 1953 is reproduced in Appendix C and is fairly representative of the sparring and uneasiness that characterized appearances of faculty before these investigative bodies.

The most common reaction of academic administrators to notification that someone on the faculty had been subpoenaed to give testimony was to urge full cooperation. The most common reaction after the individual testified was to suspend him and initiate an investigation, regardless of what was said or uncovered during the hearings. The long-run consequence was most often censure, probation, nonrenewal, or dismissal. How one behaved before a legislative committee may have had little bearing on whether the matter was pursued on campus, but it did have a significant impact on the eventual outcome of a case: the more unfriendly a witness, the more inclined academic authorities were to mete out some punishment, and the swifter and more severe this punishment was. No evidence was found that there was pressure on academic authorities from the congressional committees themselves to retaliate against unfriendly witnesses.

Uncooperative Witnesses

What resulted from merely being compelled to make an appearance before an investigating committee was inconsequential compared to the repercussions from being "a difficult witness." In the first place, as indicated previously, those who gave a committee the information it wanted were often absolved and excused without any or with little attendant publicity. When in February 1953, Robert Gorham Davis, a professor of English at Smith College, admitted that he had been a Communist Party member from 1937 to 1939, described his activities, and identified eleven associates in the Harvard University cell to the House Committee on Un-American Activities, he was thanked "effusively for his cooperation" (another description was "warmly praised") by the congressmen, and the college president and the chairman of the Board of Trustees promptly issued a statement that "his testimony before the House Committee on Un-American Activities seems to us to afford no basis for an investigation concerning his fitness to teach nor does it raise any questions concerning his loyalty."

> Professor Robert G. Davis is a valuable and highly respected member of the Smith College faculty. ... His break with the Communist Party took place four years before he joined the Smith faculty and he has long been known as a staunch and effective opponent of communism. As the members of the House Committee have said, Professor Davis deserves nothing except praise and gratitude for his testimony.[22]

On the other hand, the slight majority of faculty witnesses who invoked the Fifth Amendment or who were thought to be less than candid were given no quarter by college and university authorities. As the result of a decisiveness and alacrity not often found among administrators, over 25 percent of the principals found themselves suspended from their teaching duties within twenty-four hours after their recalcitrance was reported in the press. They were commonly informed of this decision by telegram or special delivery letter. It is evident that the primary concern of academic authorities was getting rid of a source of immense embarrassment immediately. A few principals who had made it known that they had no intention of giving testimony were relieved of their academic responsibilities prior to their legislative hearing.

At some point, all principals who were uncooperative experienced summary suspension, most with pay, most until after a campus inquiry and a final disposition of their case. It is worth noting that in the end, when all of the processes and procedures had completely played themselves out, fewer than 20 percent of these individuals still held their appointments. Almost all had resigned, or their contracts had been terminated or not renewed.

From their public statements, which appeared with timeliness in local newspapers, it seems that in the opinion of a majority of academic administrators, seeking protection under the Fifth Amendment was "a pretty good sign that there was something to hide." Given such an assumption, it is hardly surprising that administrative authorities felt the need to sever an institution's relationship with such individuals as quickly as possible.

It is unclear how many on campus shared the view that those who took the Fifth Amendment were guilty of something. If a small, unsystematic survey at the University of Michigan is at all indicative, there was little consensus on this question among faculty. Twenty-five faculty were asked: "What would your attitude be, in the event of a congressional investigation on our campus, toward a colleague who had invoked the Fifth Amendment in response to questions concerning his political affiliations?" It was reported that "there are almost as many views and shades of feeling as faculty members interviewed." Responses ranged from, on the one hand, "the refusal to answer is, of course, a privilege, but it has been well described as a 'dirty privilege,'" to, on the other hand, "to refuse to answer questions put by such an investigating committee is the best thing a man can do." More faculty, however, seemed closer to the former than to the latter position. As one individual put it: "I would not take the refusal to answer questions as an indication of guilt, but rather as an indication of lack of wisdom." Academic authorities were less tolerant.

Some administrators pressed for dismissal (successfully, as it turned out) simply on the grounds of "improper use" of the Fifth Amendment. The president of Fisk University argued that "invoking the Fifth Amendment when there is a clear opportunity to confirm or deny is for all practical purposes tantamount to admission of membership [in the Communist Party]. Under such circumstances Fisk University would have to take prompt steps to release the person from its faculty."

Ohio State: The Darling Case

A dismissal at Ohio State University is one of the most obvious examples of prejudgment, a case where the failure to testify fully in public was the only fact that mattered in the decision to dismiss a principal. In the words of the university president who outlined to Byron T. Darling, the offending faculty member, "the grounds upon which I may find it necessary to recommend your dismissal":

During the course of your public testimony you refused to answer many questions directed to you, citing the First and Fifth Amendments as reasons for your refusal. In particular you refused to answer questions as to your membership in the Communist Party or in related or affiliated organizations. . . . You also refused to answer other questions of similar import. . . .[23]

Darling, an associate professor of physics who was working on an Air Force project, had not only refused to tell the House Committee on Un-American Activities whether he had been involved with the Communist Party (even refusing to say whether he had ever performed services for the Party for which he received compensation), but he would not reveal whether he had access to or was in possession of classified information. As soon as the president, Howard L. Bevis, learned that Darling had taken the Fifth Amendment, he suspended him:

Until the university can make a complete study of the . . . appearance before the Velde Committee, Professor Byron T. Darling is relieved of all duties at the Ohio State University. . . .[24]

The university requested and received the complete transcript of the hearing. Its study and a detailed check of Darling's record at the university and in previous positions brought no evidence of communist activity to light. In Darling's mind, he had only done what was right:

The Velde Un-American Activities Committee had no legitimate cause for requiring me to appear before it and for badgering me in an open session yesterday. I have never done anything disloyal and against the interest of my country . . . and the Velde Un-American Activities Committee has not produced a single shred of evidence to the contrary. I deplore the activities of this committee in its performance of a typical witch hunt against the scientists and teachers of the United States. . . .

Darling's colleagues in the Department of Physics agreed that the question of loyalty was not an issue:

At no time during the entire period of his association with us have we had the slightest reason to doubt his loyalty to the university he serves and to his country. . . .[25]

Students also attested that Darling had never said or done anything that could be construed as disloyal.

The president's response was more popular off campus than with faculty or students. Immediately after he acted, a resolution was introduced in the Ohio House of Representatives praising his swift and firm action:

RESOLUTION

Commending Dr. Howard L. Bevis, president of Ohio State University, for his action in suspending those who do not subscribe to our form of free government by a free people.

WHEREAS, at a day and hour when the preservation of the tenets of a free people, and the passing on to posterity of the principles of the American way of life, unmarred and unblemished, is eminent in the hearts and minds of all liberty-loving people, the safeguarding of these rights challenges every member of the House of Representatives of the 100th General Assembly of Ohio; therefore be it RESOLVED, that the members of this House hereby take note of the alertness of Dr. Howard L. Bevis, president of Ohio State University, and commend him for his accustomed dispatch in suspending those who do not subscribe to our form of free government by a free people. . . .[26]

Darling stated that he was "not, and never [had] been, a member of the Communist Party or of any organization which, to my knowledge or belief, was affiliated or connected with the Communist Party. I have no knowledge of the existence of a Communist Party group in the university, nor do I know whether any faculty member or student is a member of the Communist Party. . . . I have never consciously violated any law, I am and always have been loyal to my country. . . . I have tried to be an ethical and honest scientist and teacher and an honorable citizen." He had three reasons for taking the First and Fifth amendments rather than answering the committee's questions: (1) he felt he had the legal and moral right to refuse; (2) though innocent, he felt he would be in a position of undeserved danger if he answered the questions; and (3) he felt the committee's inquiry into education was a violation of academic freedom and freedoms of speech and association guaranteed by the First Amendment. He described his quandary:

I could not, as apparently the committee wanted me to, testify that I am or was a communist, or disloyal, or had done anything wrong. Such testimony would have been completely false. But if I testified to the truth, then I ran the risk of being charged, and even convicted, of perjury on the basis of evidence in the committee's possession, which evidence was either false or capable of being falsely interpreted.

In ordinary times and circumstances, I probably would not have regarded this situation as presenting a serious dilemma. I would have, I think, denied the accusations, without any serious apprehension that I might, through a miscarriage of justice, be accused of committing perjury by telling the truth. But these were not ordinary times, nor was I in ordinary circumstances. . . .[27]

To President Bevis, however, reliance on the Fifth Amendment was an incontrovertible offense:

Your refusal to answer these questions raises serious doubt as to your fitness to hold the position you occupy. Doubt is raised as to your ability to answer these questions truthfully without self-incrimination. Doubt is raised as to your moral integrity. Doubt is cast upon the loyalty of your colleagues and the integrity of the university itself.[28]

In an attempt to keep his appointment, Darling first appealed to the president:

If you dismiss me, you do so not because I am a communist, for I am not, but because I have relied on the Constitution. This is indeed a blow at the rights of teachers.[29]

He then appealed directly to the faculty.

I wish to emphasize that these charges . . . arise exclusively from my refusal to answer the questions described on the basis of the Fifth Amendment, as well as the First. No charge or suggestion is made that I have been an incompetent teacher, that I have engaged in any misconduct other than . . . my refusals to answer certain questions of the committee. No question as to my loyalty is raised except insofar as it is suggested that disloyalty may be inferred from my refusals. The same thing is true as to my integrity, morality, compliance with university requirements, and, I suppose, as to whether I am or ever have been a member of the Communist Party or any other organization alleged to advocate the overthrow of the government by force and violence.[30]

In pleading not guilty to the charges, Darling based his defense on two points. First, he noted that a claim of the Fifth Amendment is not, and cannot be, a proper basis for finding immorality, gross insubordination, conduct clearly inimical to the best interests of the university, or, for that matter, any kind of misconduct or defect of character. He also pointed out that not only in the abstract, but in his own particular case, the assertion of the Fifth Amendment warrants no such finding.

The president, however, could not be moved. He announced his final decision to abrogate tenure:

In re-examining [his] qualifications it should be said at once that on our campus and indeed throughout the country, he is regarded as an outstanding research man in his field, and that he is a very good teacher.

Moreover he appears to have conducted himself while on our campus with scrupulous propriety. There is no evidence of any kind of political activity and there is common agreement that he gave no indication of bias or leaning toward communist ideology. He appeared consistently during all the time he was on our campus as a competent and devoted man of science. There appeared from his conduct no reason to question his loyalty.

A number of his colleagues have made a statement to this effect. Their statements are a part of the record of the hearing.

Forty-eight graduate students and six others who have recently completed their graduate work, all of whom had sat in [his] classes, presented to me a statement testifying to the complete objectivity of [his] teaching and the absence of anything approaching propaganda or indoctrination in his contacts with students. Their statement is included in the record of this hearing.

These facts are relevant and would carry weight were it not for [his] public refusal to answer pertinent questions.

The crux of the matter, indeed, is in his refusal to answer these pertinent questions.[31]

Darling's claim that in invoking the Fifth Amendment he was acting within his rights as a citizen was never taken seriously by university authorities. The president reasoned that since each faculty member had signed an oath denying membership in any organization or political party that advocated the overthrow of the government, this would imply that one has conducted and should "conduct himself so that he shall be able to testify on such matters without fear of self-incrimination." Moreover, subscribing to the loyalty oath also implied a duty to be candid and truthful. However, the refusal to answer the questions of a legislative committee constituted "gross insubordination of university policy" and a lack of "moral integrity." The president insisted that insubordination and immorality were such grave charges that the university should not even honor the obligation of a one-year notice of dismissal.

The chairman of the Board of Trustees also insisted that Darling had a legal obligation to answer, not a legal right to invoke the Fifth Amendment. He claimed that he and his colleagues would protect faculty whose rights as citizens were abused:

The Board of Trustees has thoroughly examined the record in the case of Byron Thorwell Darling, and after so doing approved the recommendation of the president that Darling be discharged from his position as associate professor and from the Ohio State University. . . .

Darling's statement that the reason he did not testify before the congressional committee was that "he ran the risk of being charged, and even convicted of perjury on the basis of evidence in the committee's possession, which was either false or capable of being falsely interpreted." This was a clear-cut evasion of his responsibility as a university professor and citizen. If the statement that he was not a communist were true, he had nothing to fear from anything, including an indictment for perjury. Unless previous testimony had been given under oath, the contention that an answer to a question may subject one to perjury is untenable. "It is neither sound in law, nor [in] morals." Cf. State v. Cox, 87 Ohio t., 313, 348.

The question of Darling's tenure is not a legal one, but rather one of what should be the attitude of an educator toward his university and government, when summoned to give information as President Bevis so well pointed out in his recommendation.

No true American can find fault with the announced purpose of investigations by congressional committees. There may be criticism by some that at times the investigators have not complied with all the procedures and standards set forth by our courts. This was not, however, apparent in reference to Professor Darling's appearance before the committee.

The duty is imposed upon all called to testify that they must testify truthfully and honestly, except those who would incriminate themselves by so doing. Their refusal is not mitigated by opposition to the interrogators or their methods, unless Congress or the courts otherwise determine.

If a legislative committee should abuse its prerogatives by unfair or improper questions to wrongfully harass any member of the university faculty or staff, which was not done in the case of Professor Darling, the Board of Trustees, as well as the public at large, would immediately rise to the defense of that person. . . .[32]

In the minds of the university authorities there clearly was nothing that would justify Darling's failure to cooperate with the congressional investigators.

Some schools, in fact, adopted "a fixed policy" that in essence called for the automatic dismissal of faculty who were difficult witnesses. In all cases these were public institutions. At the other extreme, a handful of private institutions had "no blanket rule." Where more flexibility was permitted regarding those who took the Fifth Amendment, there was naturally a greater probability that the punishment would be something less than dismissal. A comparison of a case from Rutgers University with one from Harvard University illustrates how in the first instance, at an institution with a fixed policy, someone who to all appearances was completely blameless was forced out of his job, while in the second instance, at an institution with no blanket rule, someone who was found to be dishonest at the minimum escaped with a reprimand and probation.

Rutgers: The Glasser Case

In December 1952, the Board of Trustees of Rutgers University passed a resolution making it "cause for the immediate dismissal"[33] of faculty who refused on the grounds of the Fifth Amendment to answer questions of any duly constituted investigatory body as to past or present membership in the Communist Party. The following March, Abraham Glasser, an associate professor of law on indefinite tenure, was called before a congressional committee and pleaded the Fifth Amendment. Glasser was suspended and brought before a committee of faculty from the Law School to answer the charge that "he did not bear his responsibilities as a citizen, a member of a learned profession, and a representative of the university in mind and seek to conduct himself appropriately." The committee noted:

> that there is not before us in any sense a question as to the fitness of Mr. Glasser in his professional capacity as a teacher or as a member of the legal profession. . . .
>
> We are satisfied that there is involved in the present proceeding in no sense any concept of limitation on freedom of thought or freedom of speech, either within or outside the classroom, nor any challenge to the right of Mr. Glasser to hold and to express opinions popular or unpopular, and to dissent from accepted political or ideological views. . . . The committee is of the opinion . . . that the matter is excluded from our consideration by the specific questions referred to us.
>
> Third, we take the position that the merits or demerits of the policy expressed in the resolution of the Trustees of December 12 concerning the invocation of the Fifth Amendment are outside the scope of our deliberations. The letter of referral characterizes it as "a fixed policy"; the committee has functioned on the assumption that the resolution represents the basic law governing our activity.[34]

In 1941, Glasser had been charged with having passed on to an unauthorized individual official information of the Justice Department relating to the Spanish Civil War. He was absolved of the charges of communism and espionage, but it was determined that he had been negligent. He was permitted to resign without prejudice and to accept a position with another government agency. After he began work with the other agency, he was informed that the same charges had been sent to his new superiors.

In 1946, he was assigned to argue a case before the United States Supreme Court, and in his application for admission to the bar of the Supreme Court he was obliged to disclose the facts pertaining to the 1941 proceedings. Nonetheless, his application was granted by the court. The same year, following his application for permanent civil service status, he received inquiries from the Civil Service Commission regarding the 1941 charges. He answered these fully and under oath. Even after he resigned from government service, questions about the charges were raised frequently in connection with attempts to obtain other employment.

In 1949, he received a subpoena from the House Committee on Un-American Activities, but this was later withdrawn.

In 1950, a newspaper published a story that a secret intelligence report had been given to the White House describing the activities of Alger Hiss and mentioning "an attorney fired by the Department of Justice for leaking secrets," who "immediately obtained a good job with the OPA." A second article titled "Department of Justice Lawyer Aided Soviet Spy," unmistakably referring to Glasser, stated that the case of the former Justice Department and OPA lawyer would prove "similar in size and seriousness to the Hiss-Chambers operations." The following year the House Committee on Un-American Activities published a booklet titled "The Shameful Years—Thirty Years of Soviet Espionage in the United States." Again there was a reference to Glasser, without mentioning his name, comparing him with Alger Hiss and Judith Coplon.

After Glasser received his subpoena in 1953, he learned that the House Committee on Un-American Activities considered him to be "a serious malefactor," and that memoranda from two federal judges would be introduced against him.

Glasser expressed "a feeling of being hunted and hounded,"[35] and he decided "that I would answer all questions of the Velde Committee on any subject on which I had not previously answered under oath before government bodies. . . ." He stated that he would not have made this decision if the only charge against him had been membership in the Communist Party. He was concerned that if he testified fully he might have to face a perjury indictment. Although he was innocent of the 1941 charges, he would, "in the mystique of the Hiss case," have no chance to be believed if it were his word "against two or three or I don't know how many government witnesses." He was convinced that "such a trial would be the further feeding of hysteria, the further hoopla, the further barbaric war dance of the Velde tribe on the prostrate corpse of the New Deal." He was also convinced that "the federal government at highest levels engages in the frame-up technique in times of social tension . . . ." Under the circumstances, he could not accept the advice of university authorities to cooperate with the Velde committee:

> Now, that's the personal inner story of how I made up my mind. . . . I realize that there are these further avenues of evaluation. I hope that whatever advantage may accrue to my cause from these other avenues of evaluation would commend themselves to the minds of this committee and that I would have the benefit of them. But I cannot in conscience maintain before you that the reason why I resisted the Velde committee was double jeopardy, equitable estoppel. . . . But in all simple candor and conscience, . . . I cannot state to you other than that my deciding considerations were these which I have described, these considerations of a purely inner moral nature.[36]

Regardless of such circumstances, the faculty committee took the position that Glasser's actions were "incompatible with the Trustees' mandate of cooperation with congressional committees in answering their inquiries about Communist Party membership."

> In evaluating the balance of the factors, we have concluded that the determination of the violation of the fixed policy establishes as strong a *prima facie* case that it would require a substantial preponderance to overcome it, and that such preponderance does not appear.
>
> Therefore, we feel that we cannot recommend that he be absolved from the consequences of his violation of the policy.[37]

After a hearing, the committee concluded that Glasser had violated the trustees' standards, which made the use of the Fifth Amendment incompatible with the special obligations and responsibilities of "candor to be expected of one devoted to the pursuit of truth." It did not find that there were "extraordinary facts" to "counteract the adverse public impression" created by Glasser's refusal to testify. He "was fully aware that his conduct was injurious to the university, but that that fact was subordinate in his thinking to the position he felt he must assume as a matter of principle." Indeed, his reasons for not cooperating were "of a purely inner moral nature"; he regarded "Veldeism as an evil."[38]

> The conduct resulting from Mr. Glasser's intensity of feeling with respect to the House Committee far surpasses the limits of reasoned criticism of its procedures.

The faculty committee felt that in light of the overriding principles of the trustees, the best that it could recommend was that Glasser be permitted to resign without prejudice, which he did.[39]

In essence, a policy making the refusal to testify before a congressional committee a punishable act transferred the decision to terminate to the committee, in that it was able to force a principal from his job if it insisted in a public hearing on asking questions that it knew he would not answer.

Harvard: The Furry Case

The case at Harvard University began in 1953 when Wendell H. Furry, an associate professor of physics, was identified by at least three witnesses before the House Committee on Un-American Activities as having been a member of the Communist Party before and during World War II. When he was called before the committee, Furry declined to respond to questions about past or present Communist Party membership and related matters on the grounds of possible self-incrimination. He refused to answer the direct question: "Are you a member of a cell at Harvard or anywhere else?" He would only say that he had never engaged in any activity that was against the best interest of the United States.

At the conclusion of the hearing, Furry issued a statement assuring "my friends and colleagues that I am not a member of the Communist Party, that I have no personal knowledge as to whether or not there is any Communist Party activity at Harvard or anywhere else." Unlike many others across the country who relied on the Fifth Amendment, Furry was not suspended. Harvard's provost simply announced: "Professor Wendell H. Furry's reported refusal to answer certain questions put to him by the House Committee on Un-American Activities will be given full and deliberate consideration."[40]

During a second appearance before the congressional committee two months later, Furry testified that he had not been a member of the Communist Party since at least 1 March 1951 and that he knew of no organized communist activities at Harvard since that date. He continued to invoke the Fifth Amendment on all other questions about his connection with the Communist Party prior to 1951.

Furry admitted to university authorities that he had been a member of the Communist Party from 1938 to 1947. He also told of having participated in activities that were in varying degrees secret or deceptive. He admitted that he had been involved with others in attempting to dominate the local teachers' union and that on several occasions he had furnished incomplete or false information to government investigators. For example, he told one such investigator that he had no reason to believe that an applicant for classified government work had been a member of the Communist Party, although he knew this to be false. This revelation that he had lied could readily have been used as a reason for dismissal. There were few other cases where the evidence against a principal was so damning.

The uneasiness about the Cold War was as evident at Harvard as on other campuses, and the inquiry into Furry's political activities was no more or less comprehensive. Harvard's president had stated that he believed that communists should not be permitted to be on the faculty. Those appointed to look into the Furry case stated that they "would regard membership in the Communist Party by a member of our faculty as grave misconduct, justifying removal."[41] They noted, however, that Furry was not a member of the Communist Party:

> The facts available to us indicate that Dr. Furry is not now under the domination of the Communist Party. He has not been active in the Communist Party since 1947. He has stated under oath to the Velde Committee that he is not now, and has not recently been, a member of the Communist Party. He has at no time permitted his connection with the Party to affect his teaching, nor

has he attempted otherwise to influence the political thinking of his students.[42]

In the affirmative they added: "Dr. Furry's teaching is of high quality." As far as the use of the Fifth Amendment was concerned, this too, they reasoned, fell short of grounds for dismissal: "The use of the Fifth Amendment by a member of our teaching staff within the critical field of his possible domination by the Communist Party . . . we regard . . . as misconduct, though not necessarily grave misconduct."[43]

The governing body with the authority to dismiss Furry, the Harvard Corporation, expressed concern over the fact that Furry had not told the truth, that his conduct "fell so far below the standard of moral conduct to be expected of a member of our faculty as to constitute grave misconduct." He had not shown the "candor to be expected of one devoted to the pursuit of truth." Yet, rather than dismissing Furry, it felt that by punishing him with probation for three years, "the interest of the university will be best served. . . . Some other action than the removal of Dr. Furry at this time" would suffice.

A finding of grave misconduct left the university the option of dismissing Furry at some later time if the situation warranted. If "either because of Dr. Furry's future conduct or because of contrary evidence as to his past conduct, we should deem it to be for the best interests of the university to remove him, we will do so."[44] Furry's probation was for three years.

The matter was still far from over for Furry or Harvard. In November, Furry made another appearance before a congressional committee; this time the hearing was conducted by Senator Joseph McCarthy. Furry reaffirmed the general fact that he had never engaged in subversive activities, and specifically he assured the committee that he had not taken any secret or confidential material out of the laboratory while working on secret research for the government.

Senator McCarthy: Did you know of anyone who was removing classified material from the laboratory and giving that material either to espionage agents or any other personnel who were not authorized to receive it?

Furry: I did not, sir, and I would like to add a factual statement to that. That I have never had any connection with espionage or plans for espionage myself and I have never known of any other person having any connection with such things. . . .

Senator McCarthy: Did you ever remove classified material from the M.I.T. laboratories?

Furry: I can remember only one instance, sir. The instance in question was when I left the employ of the laboratory in August 1945. There was a document classified restricted, which, as you know, is the lowest brand of classification, and I would, of course, be entitled to remove that at any time for my own study. I think the material, this document, was of general science interest, and copies of it have been made available to lots of people since. I took a copy of it home. I was told the next day by my group leader that had been improper; that I should wait until the time it was made available, as it was later.

Senator McCarthy: With the exception of this one document marked restricted, did you ever take home any document marked confidential or secret?

Furry: Certainly not to my memory.

Senator McCarthy: And to your knowledge you never had any confidential or secret material in your home? Is that correct?

Furry: No, sir, not in my home, only in my office.[45]

Furry also denied that he discussed classified material with anyone except authorized laboratory personnel. He again invoked the Fifth Amendment about communist activities prior to March 1951.

Senator McCarthy: You said you were not a communist since March 1, 1951. Have you ever attended any Communist Party meetings since that time?

Furry: No, sir.

Senator McCarthy: Did you since that time ever attempt to indoctrinate your students with the communist philosophy?

Furry: No, sir.

Senator McCarthy: Do you believe in the communist system?

Furry: No, sir.

Senator McCarthy: Did you in February of 1951 believe in it?

Furry: [No answer]

Senator McCarthy: What is your answer to that question?

Furry: I will claim the privilege on that, sir.[46]

Although Senator McCarthy threatened to initiate contempt of Congress proceedings against Furry for refusing to answer a question as to whom he had discussed secret radar data with, as far as the Harvard administration was concerned, no new evidence that could change its earlier conclusions had come to light in the exchange.

In a telegram, Senator McCarthy demanded that President Nathan M. Pusey tell him "what, if any, actions the university intends to take in Furry's case and what your attitude generally is toward retaining teachers at Harvard who refused to state whether they are communists on the ground that the truth would incriminate them." Pusey's reply was as direct as the question:

Since there are conflicting reports concerning what Dr. Furry said before your committee at the private session and since you have not made the complete testimony public, I am quite unable to comment on the significance of his latest refusal to answer questions, nor can I say whether any further action will be taken by us concerning Dr. Furry.[47]

Pusey also rejected McCarthy's assumption that it was necessary to do anything about Furry:

> My information is that Dr. Furry has not been connected with the Communist Party in recent years . . . also that Dr. Furry has never given secret material to unauthorized persons or sought to indoctrinate his students.[48]

Pusey told Senator McCarthy that he agreed that a member of the Communist Party should not be on the Harvard faculty because he would not have the necessary independence of thought and judgment. He added, however, that as far as he knew, there were no communists on the Harvard faculty.

McCarthy denigrated Harvard and pressed the president to dismiss Furry. More than once he made reference to the "smelly mess" at Harvard where students were open to indoctrination by communist professors. McCarthy noted that he was referring not only to Furry, but to a number of Harvard professors "whom Pusey is keeping on at Harvard":

> You've got a sizable number with long records of apparent assistance to the Party and . . . of serving the communist cause. . . .

> These are the professors who have refused to say whether or not they are communists. This means they are communists and under the discipline of the Party, they must indoctrinate their students.

In the face of the steady torrent Harvard remained steadfast. The mood on campus was anything but grim; in many quarters, in fact, there was obvious pride in Harvard's response to the challenge in such remarks by McCarthy as:

> Even the most soft-headed and fuzzy-minded cannot help but realize that a witness' refusal to answer whether or not he is a communist on the ground that his answer would tend to incriminate him, is the most positive proof obtainable that the witness is a communist. You and the Harvard Corporation can of course continue to keep Fifth Amendment communists teaching the sons and daughters of America.

Many at Harvard seemed hardly perturbed by the attacks. President Pusey's response was cool. In a press conference Pusey chastized McCarthy for even making Furry's testimony a public issue: "It is against all the principles of our country to make statements about secret testimony without releasing it." Pusey reiterated that he was unable to discuss or make a judgment about the matter: "I don't know what Furry said because I haven't got the testimony."

After the first of the year, Senator McCarthy came to Boston as a one-man committee and Furry was again summoned to give testimony. The hearing was widely publicized.

Waiving the Fifth Amendment, Furry admitted his own Party affiliations and activities. He had come to feel that continued reliance on the Fifth Amendment "would bring undue harm to me and the great institution with which I am connected." He said that he was now willing to discuss his own Party activities, but that he still would not disclose the names of others who had been in the Party with him. He acknowledged that there were "about a half dozen" communists who had worked with him in the radar laboratory, but would discuss their identities only in the most general way. He was ordered to name them and was threatened with jail for contempt when he refused to do so. He said that he would disclose names only if he were convinced the person involved was guilty of a substantive crime—espionage, treason, or sabotage—but not in "political cases":

> I am not seeking to protect the guilty from prosecution. I wish merely to secure the innocent from prosecution.

Furry testified that no present member of the permanent Harvard faculty was known to him to be a member of the Communist Party. When asked if he knew of other present or former communists "connected" with Harvard, he refused to answer. McCarthy urged him to reconsider his position: "We have no pleasure in seeing people go to jail, but it would give me a great deal of satisfaction if Professor Furry decided to do something for himself and for his country."

Given the continued refusal to disclose the names of his "co-conspirators," Senator McCarthy questioned whether Furry had truly left the Party. He blamed Furry and other communists for "the deaths of thousands of American boys," and said that he did not deserve the protection of the country. He expressed hope that President Eisenhower's new proposal to strip those involved in conspiracy to overthrow the government by force and violence of their citizenship would become law so that Furry would lose his citizenship.

McCarthy again heaped scorn and ridicule on Harvard and its president. He thought it "inconceivable that a university that has had the reputation of a great university should keep this kind of creature teaching young Americans." He accused President Pusey of "maintaining a privileged sanctuary for Fifth Amendment communists," of "sheltering and harboring" them. McCarthy expressed the opinion that pressing for a contempt citation "will be another way, perhaps, of getting rid of some of Mr. Pusey's Fifth Amendment communists."

Furry was indicted by a federal grand jury on ten counts of contempt, primarily for refusing to name names and to tell Senator McCarthy about the activities of the Communist Party when he was a member. Harvard still did not suspend him as other institutions had done to faculty in similar situations. In fact, President Pusey immediately announced that until the court ruled on the case there would be no change in the university's policy toward Furry. The president's formal statement was sympathetic to Furry; he noted that none of the counts made any reference to Furry's own relationship with or activities in the Communist Party, that his testimony indicated that he had been out of the Party for a number of years, and that he was not hiding behind the Fifth Amendment:

> Indictment has been found against Dr. Furry charging him with the misdemeanor of refusing to answer questions of a senatorial committee concerning other people. He has not been indicted for refusing to answer questions about his own connection with the Communist Party; he testified under oath that he dropped out of the Communist Party a number of years ago. He also abandoned reliance on the Fifth Amendment, the use of which we had deplored. We continue to favor full disclosure in these matters, but the legal consequences of his refusal will presumably be determined by the courts. So long as the case is pending, we do not think it appropriate to make any further statement on the subject.[49]

During the entire period, Furry's appointment was left undisturbed although the government did not drop the charges against him until 1956.

Thus, by no means did everyone who sought the protection of the Fifth Amendment or in other ways failed to cooperate with civil authorities automatically suffer negative consequences. Yet even faculty at colleges (such as Sarah Lawrence) and universities (such as Cornell) who were not summarily discharged for "hiding behind it" (the Fifth Amendment) were "expected" (essentially required, as will become more evident in later chapters) to explain or justify its use.

Almost 35 percent of the principals who were uncooperative witnesses were jettisoned or written off by their college or university within two weeks after institutional authorities learned about their appearance or scheduled appearance. A number of presidents did not wait to review the testimony, but made their decision on the basis of press reports. A few made preparations to terminate faculty before they were scheduled to testify, and those plans were often set in motion before the reluctant witness returned home. A larger number of senior administrators seemed initially to have the intention of supporting faculty, but abandoned such plans in the face of real or imagined pressure or unfavorable publicity. The institutions that made a determined effort to stand by faculty were not numerous.

Sometimes at the same institution one principal who invoked the Fifth Amendment was given every consideration while another who did the same was driven out with little regard. Differences in response on the part of institutional authorities were seldom due to differences in how principals conducted themselves before congressional committees. Sometimes they were the consequence of how much support a principal received from his colleagues or from his dean. Backing from these sources, however, was less critical than vacillation on the part of the highest administrative authorities. All in all, there were no consistent patterns. An exception to any rule could always be found. Generally, institutions more readily discovered reasons or excuses or provocations to fire those who took the Fifth Amendment than those who became principals due to other circumstances. Congressional investigations made the headlines, and witnesses who were less than fully cooperative could generate a great deal of unfavorable publicity for a college or university.

It was rare for institutional authorities to turn a hand for those whose conduct made termination seem plausible or justifiable. There were fewer problems from sometime civil libertarians when someone whose public behavior was controversial, perhaps even repellent, was eased out. Only friends, partisans, or the American Civil Liberties Union would be interested in defending the indefensible. In only three instances did an institution stand firm behind someone who could easily have been sacrificed without extensive repercussions.

Notes

1. Harry Shulman, correspondence to Melvin Gittleman, 10 January 1955.
2. Charles F. Clise, correspondence to A. Whitney Griswold, 27 November 1953.
3. Charles F. Clise, correspondence to Reuben A. Holden, 1 December 1953.
4. A. Whitney Griswold, correspondence to Wesley A. Sturges, 17 January 1955.
5. A. Whitney Griswold, correspondence to Estes Kefauver, 20 January 1955.
6. A. Whitney Griswold, correspondence to William O. Douglas, 31 January 1955.
7. Vern Countryman, correspondence to the Committee on Academic Freedom and Tenure, Association of American Law Schools.
8. "A Chronology of the Controversy regarding Dr. Wiggins's Dismissal," *On the Dismissal of Dr. Forrest O. Wiggins*, December 1951, p. 3.
9. James L. Morrill, correspondence to Howard Ottinger, 17 April 1950.
10. T. R. McConnell, correspondence to George P. Conger, 28 November 1949.
11. William T. Harris, correspondence to Malcolm Willey, 24 January 1951.
12. Forrest O. Wiggins, reported in "Report of Committee on Academic Freedom and Tenure," p. 14.
13. "Report of Committee of Academic Freedom and Tenure," p. 14.
14. Ibid., p. 2.

15. "In the Matter of the Hearing concerning the Termination of Employment of Dr. Robert Hodes at Tulane University," p. 3.
16. Testimony before a Committee of the Board of Administrators of Tulane University, February–April 1953 in "In the Matter of: Dr. Robert Hodes and Tulane University," Vol. 2, pp. 66–68.
17. Ibid., Vol. 2, p. 230.
18. Ibid., Vol. 3, p. 28.
19. Ibid., Vol. 3, pp. 226ff.
20. "In the Matter of the Hearing," p. 1.
21. Lloyd Barenblatt, "Objection to Jurisdiction of the Committee on Un-American Activities and to Questions Propounded by It," 1954, p. 1.
22. Benjamin F. Wright and Amanda Bryan Kane, 27 February 1953.
23. Howard L. Bevis, correspondence to Byron T. Darling, 24 March 1953.
24. Howard L. Bevis, statement to press, 13 March 1953.
25. Dudley Williams, "Hearing of the Case of Byron Thorwell Darling," 4 April 1953, p. 36.
26. Resolution of the 100th General Assembly of the State of Ohio.
27. "Hearing," p. 29.
28. Bevis, correspondence to Darling.
29. "Hearing," p. 33.
30. Ibid., p. 21.
31. "Recommendation of President Howard L. Bevis to the Board of Trustees in the Case of Dr. Byron T. Darling," released 7 April 1953, pp. 5–6.
32. "Statement of Robert N. Gorman, Chairman of the Board of Trustees of Ohio State University."
33. "Resolution of the Board of Trustees of Rutgers University," 12 December 1952.
34. "Report of the Faculty Committee of Review of the Law School of Rutgers, The State University of New Jersey, on the Matter of Abraham Glasser, Associate Professor of Law," 26 August 1953.
35. "Transcript," Faculty Committee of Review, p. 6.
36. Ibid., pp. 233–34.
37. "Report of the Faculty Committee."
38. "Transcript," p. 235.
39. Abraham Glasser, correspondence to Lewis Webster Jones, 7 September 1953.
40. Paul H. Buck, "Memorandum of Announcement of Provost Buck at Faculty Meeting," 3 March 1953.
41. "Statement by the Harvard Corporation in regard to Associate Professor Wendell H. Furry," 20 May 1953.
42. Ibid.
43. Ibid.
44. Ibid.
45. Testimony, 4 November 1953.
46. Ibid.
47. Nathan M. Pusey, correspondence to Joseph R. McCarthy, 9 November 1953.
48. Ibid.
49. Nathan M. Pusey, statement, 16 December 1954.

4

Pressure and Reaction

For the most part, the executive officers of institutions, not members of governing boards and not deans or department chairmen, initiated the actions against faculty. In those instances when a dean framed a charge, it was at the urging of the higher administration. At fewer than one-fifth of the institutions was there an indication that the impetus for a loyalty investigation came from any source, on or off campus, other than the central administration. The majority of these latter cases were set in motion by one or two unrestrained members of the governing board, a highly visible public figure, or a steady drumbeat from the press.

Governing Boards

It was usually difficult to determine not only if members of a governing board actually did press for an investigation or dismissal, but precisely when this occurred and the degree of involvement. Trustees and regents were most visible as members of hearing committees or as spokesmen for these committees. It is very likely, of course, that some board members expressed opinions during the initial phases of these cases more often than is indicated by the written record. However, unless there was actual evidence of some action (for example, a letter or minutes from a meeting) by someone on the governing board or an admission that one of its members had prompted administrative officials to launch an inquiry, it was assumed that none had. Charges by principals or their supporters that administrators had been forced by certain members of the board to act against them had to be discounted as partisan speculation, even though it is inconceivable that academic administrators were unaware or unconcerned with the wishes of those to whom they were responsible.

There were instances when members of a governing board went out of their way to tender cooperation and resources to government investigating committees, to announce publicly that faculty were expected to cooperate or possibly face dismissal, and to make statements that indicated hostility toward left-of-center political beliefs and activities. It was reported in two different newspapers that three members of the board of regents of one state university were eager to purge the faculty of not only those "engaged in subversive activities," but anyone who could not dispel all doubt about his loyalty. Other such incidents and the suspicion that governing boards may, indeed, have exerted more influence than is shown by available documents does not diminish the controlling role played by administrators—from beginning to end—in these cases.

Whether or not they were active participants, governing boards as a rule readily supported the decision of administrators to press for an inquiry—or dismissal. By the same token, in those rare instances when an administration passed up an opportunity to conduct an internal investigation—or dismiss someone—governing boards also supported that decision. Whether or not they were openly working together, boards and institutional administrative officers were of one mind, a fact that made any appeal to a board for an independent judgment—particularly to overturn an unfavorable administrative decision—a useless exercise. Governing boards were never more forgiving than administrators; in fact, sometimes the punishment they meted out to faculty was more severe than that recommended by a college or university president.

The Press, Politicians, and Others

As in the case of governing boards, it is difficult to assess the impact, if any, of advice from newspapers and government officials to academic authorities on how best to rid a campus of suspected subversives. The extent of the agitation by newspapers and politicians was considerable. It seemed that the newspapers never missed an opportunity to repeat a charge by an elected official against a faculty member or highlight a campus investigation. Incidents in which faculty at other institutions were dismissed were sometimes publicized in the local press, making it clear that there were precedents for resolve and for punitive action against those who were suspected of being disloyal. Newspaper accounts of hearings and terminations at other campuses were found in the official papers of the administration or governing board of over a dozen of the fifty-eight institutions in the study.

Not surprisingly, administrators maintained that they ignored all lobbying or any form of pressure. In fact, numerous presidents went out of their way to claim their independence. However, themes first found in newspapers or given credence in a public forum were often precisely the arguments repeated by academic administrators to justify an action, and in more than one instance a theme became part of official rhetoric within hours after being seen in print. Although it was not possible to measure the media's impact with precision, it is clear that academic administrators were very aware of what was in the press. A case involving David Hawkins, a professor of philosophy at the University of Colorado, clearly illustrates this point.

Taking Heed: The Hawkins Case

After the House Committee on Un-American Activities released testimony that disclosed that Hawkins had at one time been a member of the Communist Party, the *Denver Post*[1] called on the administration to move decisively and "clean house." It was said that this strong stand by the newspaper was a good-faith attempt to safeguard the institution from detractors and discredit. Whether this was truly the case, the concern was expressed that here was yet another academic who would talk about himself but declined to provide congressional investigators with information about former associates. Hawkins testified that he had been a member of the Communist Party between 1938 and 1943 (prior to and while working at Los Alamos) and declined to confirm or deny Communist Party membership of other persons. The newspaper took the position that this cast doubt on his loyalty to "American standards of life" and to his fitness to hold his appointment.

The university, the newspaper argued, could not overlook the fact that Hawkins had not informed it about his past political affiliations, and that, moreover, he had been a member of the Communist Party for a period of five years.

> President Stearns has been a good university president, by and large, but if he is not willing to take strong action, the Regents should get a new president who is willing to preserve the American way of education and academic resposibility as well as academic freedom.

The newspaper further editorialized that the university should begin with an investigation of the faculty: "The doubt has been cast. The university must clear the air, or a legislative investigation may manage to dirty it up even more."

Acting swiftly, the Board of Regents instructed President Robert Stearns to file charges against Hawkins, to appoint investigators to make a study of communist activity on campus, and to require faculty to sign an oath of allegiance. (Not only did the Board of Regents accept without question the ruling by the Colorado attorney general that a loyalty oath that had not been used since 1935 could be applied to faculty, but by making it more elaborate and restrictive the Board changed its nature from a simple affirmation to part of an anticommunist campaign.) Declaring that the university would not knowingly hire a communist, the president drew up charges against Hawkins, and hired two former FBI agents to conduct a confidential probe of the faculty. In an effort to protect itself and maintain favorable community relations, the university was forced to conduct a trial.

Hawkins was examined by a six-member faculty committee that serially considered seven allegations (See Appendix D). Two of the allegations—that he had been a member of the Communist Party from 1938 to 1943 and that he did not disclose this fact to his superiors when he was appointed to the position of historian to the Los Alamos project in 1943—were about events prior to his appointment to the faculty of the University of Colorado in 1947. Three—that he refused to answer certain questions put to him by the House Committee on Un-American Activities, that other responses were evasive, and that his separation from the Communist Party was nominal rather than real—were about actions of only tangential interest to university authorities. Only two of the allegations, that when he was hired by the university he did not tell the administration that he had once been a member of the Communist Party and that he permitted a Marxist study group of which he was a sponsor to become a political action committee, were immediately germane to his appointment at the University of Colorado.

Over a two month period, the committee questioned Hawkins, heard numerous witnesses, and deliberated in executive session. In spite of taking the strictly conventional position that past membership in the Communist Party "raises a presumption that a teacher may be unfit if the break with the Party was not genuine, if the old Party practices and methods continue, if the teaching is slanted to fit the changes in the Party line," the committee still concluded that the charges against Hawkins were contrary to fact or insufficient to warrant dismissal. It thus unanimously held that Hawkins was not subversive or disloyal, had not slanted his teaching, and that he was otherwise fully qualified to hold an appointment at the university.[2]

The Regents voted to uphold the committee's report; Hawkins was cleared and returned to his normal academic duties. In Appendix D are excerpts from three meetings of the Board of Regents of the University of Colorado at which this matter was discussed and the decision was made not to terminate or otherwise punish Hawkins. It should be noted that these deliberations are more representative of the form that such inquiries took at universities than at colleges. At over half of the colleges in the study, in fact, very few documents were uncovered that shed light on the practices or procedures of governing boards.

Influencing Public Opinion

Most newspaper stories describing the Cold War on campus were not sympathetic to faculty said to be advocates or defenders of left-wing causes. The press paid greater attention to charges against principals than to evidence that what was being said was exaggerated, out of context, or simply false. Stories about the misadventures of principals struggling to hold on to their reputations and jobs were front-page stories. The many elected officials who used the newspapers to warn the public about the great harm that would result if so-called radical college and university faculty were not dealt with firmly represented both major political parties. Few newspapers or politicians urged academic administrators to proceed deliberately or cautiously.

A major newspaper in New Jersey insisted that, since it operated with public funds, Rutgers University must require faculty to provide a congressional committee the information it sought.[3] The governor concurred: "In my judgment, the professors should have answered the questions—or get out. That is my personal feeling. If someone asks me whether I am a Republican or Democrat, I would be glad to answer." This idea of the special obligation of public employees was a central theme in the case Rutgers eventually built (see chapter 6) to remove two faculty members who would not provide congressional investigators with the information they wanted.

New Jersey was not the only state where a politician postured or attempted to intimidate academic authorities. The governor of Massachusetts asked the president of Harvard University to dismiss faculty who used the Fifth Amendment. A few years later, another governor of Massachusetts told the press that he would insist on firing two faculty members at a public institution who took the First and Fifth amendments before the House Committee on Un-American Activities.

The state auditor of Ohio, James A. Rhodes, publicly maintained that, regardless of the decision taken by Ohio State University authorities, he would not pay the salary of physicist Byron Darling after Darling had been suspended—but before he was terminated—for refusing "to answer a great many questions" put to him by the House Committee on Un-American Activities. In the glare of publicity, Rhodes sent a letter to the Board of Trustees and President Bevis and asked the university to justify its meeting minimal contractual obligations.

Gentlemen:

On Monday, March 16, after inquiries from the public press, we made our

position known concerning payment of salary in the Darling case. This letter
is being sent to inform you of our position.

We learned through the local newspapers that the president of Ohio State
University had suspended Professor B.T. Darling as of noon, March 13, 1953.
The payroll of Ohio State University as submitted to this office for the month
of March, 1953, contained the name of Professor Darling for the entire
month. We feel that he is not entitled to remain on the payroll after March 13,
noon, until he has been fully reinstated by the Board of Trustees of Ohio State
University. We are, therefore, asking that the proper officials send to this
office a supplementary payroll for the 13 ½ days that he performed his official
duties as associate professor at Ohio State University.

Insofar as the case of Barbara Ann Darling, clerk-stenographer II, is concerned, this office would appreciate the submission of information as to
whether or not she accompanied her husband, Professor B.T. Darling, to
Washington with the permission of university officials and whether such
permission was in conformance with the civil service rules and regulations
covering vacation time or compensatory time. We would appreciate clarification of her status in this matter. Until such information is received her check,
too, will be held.

We want to cooperate to the fullest degree with the officials of Ohio State
University but due to the conditions and circumstances involved in the Darling case it would not be within the law to pay Professor Darling and his wife
for services not rendered until such clearance is received.

This is only to verify their status and does not change our position from the
original information we gave the payroll officials of Ohio State University on
Monday, March 16.[4]

There were other rumors and newspaper accounts of how political figures persuaded members of governing boards who in turn persuaded administrators to file charges against willful faculty. Although almost always
unconfirmed, these reports at least suggest that the actions of administrators were often closely scrutinized, sometimes by public officials,
sometimes by the press, and sometimes by both.

With the materials at hand there is really no way of determining how
intrusive public figures were and how much harm, if any, they caused once
a case became the subject of discussion off campus. It is part of the my-
thology of academia that, basically, politicians are full of mischief. The
general impression of a number of observers was that they did harry administrators at some public institutions, or at least administrators at some
public institutions felt harried by them. (This matter will be dealt with in
some detail in later chapters.) There is, however, only anecdotal material,
and no systematic data to support such claims. Moreover, even when research turned up what were presumed to be details of meddling and vindictiveness, it was often not possible to substantiate such accusations. In
short, this entire issue is quite hazy. Appendix E, which again is drawn

from the files of the University of Colorado, documents one of the handful of cases when a public figure openly went out of his way, and on record, to prompt academic authorities to fire someone. In this case the accused faculty member, David Hawkins, had been exonerated by a faculty committee. The state repesentative was offering testimony just prior to the Board of Regents' vote on whether to follow the committee's recommendation. It is of interest that in this instance the majority of the Board of Regents was not swayed by this legislator, and it promptly voted to adopt and approve the recommendation that the case against Hawkins be dropped.

How much the public, lawmakers, or pressure groups influenced administrators is unclear. It is quite obvious that academic authorities could not always be induced to follow a particular course. Prodding or advocacy that was not prompted by some formal group or organization or that was uncoordinated or not recurrent could be, and for the most part was, ignored. The occasional last-ditch efforts on behalf of a principal whose case seemed to be going badly—whether the advocacy was by departmental colleagues, sympathetic alumni, students, or the American Civil Liberties Union—almost always came to naught. A flood of letters from eminent mathematicians from major universities—for example, the University of California at Berkeley, the University of Chicago, Columbia University, the Massachusetts Institute of Technology, the University of Michigan, New York University, Stanford University—to the president of Fisk University expressing high regard for a department chairman, Lee Lorch, who had been cited for contempt of Congress for refusing to answer questions about his membership in the Communist Party had no effect on the decision to terminate him. In fact, the minutes of the executive committee of the Fisk Board of Trustees simply noted that the president had "indicated . . . that the letter campaign was continuing."[5]

Administrators were obviously mindful of the possible loss of financial support—allocations from the legislature for public institutions and gifts and bequests, perhaps for a new student union, for private institutions. Public relations were of particular concern for administrators, not only of those private institutions located in small communities, but of all public institutions. A counsel to a large state university publicly argued that in light of the "present state of public opinion" not even a former communist could be allowed on the faculty. A brief prepared for a case at another state university was as explicit: "Membership in the Party by a university teacher casts a false stigma on the university and fellow teachers in the public mind. In a state institution it makes it more difficult to obtain the public support essential to discovering and teaching the truth in all fields of education."

Pressure and an Inquiry: Indiana University

Although, more often than not, how a pressure group may have kindled an inquiry into the politics of a faculty was not apparent from the available evidence, some organizations did act conspicuously and their involvement became quite public. In an initial and notable salvo of the Cold War on campus, the American Legion in Indiana openly brought pressure to bear on the governor to force the Board of Trustees to conduct an investigation of communism at the state university. Many members of the Legion had become concerned about political activities at Indiana University after it was learned that faculty from "a tax supported institution" had signed a petition asking that the Communist Party be put on the ballot in a state-wide election. The incident only marginally qualifies for inclusion in the study, as the question of faculty actually losing their jobs seems to have been taken more seriously by the press and some segments of the public than by campus authorities. Nonetheless, it perfectly exemplifies that not only were campuses not seen as enclaves where it was best for combatants to back away from virulent ideological conflict, they were seen as one of the main battlegrounds.

The incident began with the 1946 Indiana senatorial election when the election commissioners ruled that the Communist Party's symbol and candidate's name would not be allowed on the ballot. Eleven individuals signed a widely publicized petition addressed to the governor arguing that the effect of the decision would be undemocratic and illegal:

> On July 29th, the nominees of the Communist Party filed a petition signed by 11,000 electors requesting that the said nominees be placed upon the ballot. The Communist Party in Indiana is a tiny minority and none of the undersigned are either members or political sympathizers with the Communist Party. However, its members and those other citizens who wish to support that Party cannot in justice be deprived of that opportunity.
>
> Accordingly, we call upon the State and Marion County Boards of Election Commissioners to cause the names of these candidates to be printed on the ballot, as provided in Section 106 of the Official Election Code of Indiana, and the Governor to certify the names of said candidates to the various clerks of courts, as provided in Section III of the Election Code. . . .[6]

A great deal of public attention quickly began to focus on three of the signers who were on the faculty of the Law School of Indiana University. This in turn prompted the American Legion to pass a resolution urging the governor to investigate state college and university faculty and to fire those with "communistic tendencies":

BE IT RESOLVED, that Case County Post #60, American Legion Department of Indiana, respectfully asks the Governor of the State of Indiana to cause to be investigated any act of any person engaged as an instructor in any state institution of learning which might be classed as pro-communistic or un-American, and if such investigation finds such act to be pro-communistic or un-American, it shall be cause for dismissal from such service as an instructor.[7]

The governor referred the matter to the Board of Trustees. He felt that faculty in tax-supported institutions were properly the subject of scrutiny of the Trustees and that "subversive activities" had no place on campus. He thus requested that the Board investigate the faculty and report their findings to him:

Recently I received a petition requesting that the State Board of Election Commissioners place the Communist Party on the ballot this fall. This petition was signed by three members of the faculty of the Law School of Indiana University. They signed this petition in their official capacity with the university.

I do not question the right of any individual to assert his own personal views at any time, but I do feel that as members of the faculty of a tax-supported institution such as Indiana University, their acts in this instance are certainly subject to scrutiny by the Board of Trustees of Indiana University.

The American Legion, at its state convention, adopted a resolution requesting an investigation as to communistic activities in our state universities. I have received numerous letters objecting to the action of members of the university faculty in petitioning, as such, in behalf of the Communist Party.

I personally feel that subversive activities of any nature have no place in our state universities and colleges. I am requesting, therefore, that your Board of Trustees make a thorough investigation of this matter, to the end that all such influences be eliminated from the teaching staff of the university. I request that you report to me the result of your investigation and such action as you may take in this matter.[8]

A full inquiry was set in motion and students and faculty witnesses were told that because "the hearing was informal . . . technical rules would be ignored with hearsay or rumor evidence being welcomed." The Board set itself the task of learning:

1. Whether teachers at Indiana University have used their position of advantage to promote any communistic, un-American, unpatriotic or subversive philosophy.
2. Whether any such philosophies which are communistic, un-American, unpatriotic or subversive have existed or exist among faculty or students.
3. The specific charge relating to the signing by three law professors of the

petition to include the Communist Party on the state ballot at the last election.[9]

The American Legion representatives who gave testimony asked the Board to look into any act of any instructor that could be classed as "pro-communist" or "un-American."[10] The commander of the Indiana Legion cautioned that "those given the great trust of directing the destiny of this splendid school be alert to infiltration of communists and fascists alike."[11]

The Board of Trustees asked individuals having knowledge of communist activities on campus to come forward. Among others, the eleven campus deans were called as witnesses. Everyone who appeared denied knowledge of any communist or un-American activities on campus. No subversion was turned up in the two days of testimony, and this was underscored in the 400-page report. The Board highlighted this fact in its report to the governor, and took pains to vindicate the three faculty who had signed the petition:

> Each [is a] veteran of one of our world wars, appeared at his own request, [and all] testified that they were not members of the Communist Party and detested its philosophy. Two of them testified that they were regular members of one of the two major political parties. The other said that he had voted independently for candidates of one or the other of such parties. Each earnestly asserted his profound admiration for the Constitution and the American way of life. During World War II, each of them was in the service of the government of the United States and, as a condition of . . . employment, underwent the customary investigation by the Federal Bureau of Investigation.[12]

The Board also expressed its appreciation to the American Legion, taking care to note the "cordial and friendly attitude of cooperation" of those who "honored" the Board by their attendance. "There could not have been and was not any clash of interests, but rather a sincere cooperative effort to get to the bottom of a troublesome subject." The Board of Trustees' official report concluded on this key:

> Because of the importance and sincerity of purpose of the American Legion and your own continuously friendly activity in favor of education generally, including Indiana University, this Board has taken extra time to conclude this investigation as it completes what is probably the most ambitious program for the housing and education of returning veterans in the nation, as well as concurrent care for their wives and children. The Board expresses its deep appreciation to you and the Legion for extending to it this opportunity to serve the state by clarifying the matter under consideration.[13]

The president's attitude toward the Legion was no less obsequious: "We again wish to thank you and, through you, the great organization of which you are a part for your courtesy in coming to Bloomington and for the helpful testimony which you presented."[14]

Although administrators (particularly from private colleges) fretted that even the smallest loss of prestige would hurt enrollments, oddly enough it was not a concern that left-wing faculty would drive students away that resulted in a concerted effort to exclude Communist Party members from the faculty. It was the conviction that they would be safeguarding their institution's budget, reputation, integrity, or autonomy (i.e., classroom freedom) that moved most administrators to action. The belief that public relations and compromise were essential for an institution's well being was seldom questioned.

Pressure and No Inquiry: Sarah Lawrence College

One exception to the common administrative position that it was imperative for institutions to heed what was represented as public opinion was Sarah Lawrence College's response to a barrage of criticism, mostly from the leadership of the American Legion (their Americanism Committee and magazine) but also from the Hearst press and the publication *Counterattack*. The pressure on Sarah Lawrence was so intense that it was even asked by community leaders to justify its real estate tax exemption. The commander of the local Legion post wrote the school and demanded, under threat of the "fullest publicity," that the president give an "official" answer to questions about Communist Party members or sympathizers on the faculty. President Harold Taylor and the chairman of the Board of Trustees responded in a public statement:

> Teachers who meet the test of candor, honesty and scholarly integrity may not be deprived of any rights they hold as citizens of this country, including the right to belong to any legal political organization of their own choosing. . . .
>
> The Board of Trustees and the president have confidence in the integrity and scholarship of the members of the Sarah Lawrence faculty, and will continue to stand on these principles of free inquiry and intellectual independence. They do so for serious and considered reasons.[15]

Less than three months later the American Legion renewed its offensive, this time accusing the college of ignoring the warning that one of its faculty was a communist, or at least "an academic security risk." Actually, the individual denied the charge before the Senate Subcommittee on Internal Security. The Legion passed two resolutions, one asking for a congressional investigation of the college and the other requesting that the legislature either make the college forfeit its tax exemption or rid itself of subversive faculty.

Against the charge that by entrusting an individual said to have communist leanings to teach a course on "Contemporary Issues" the college was guilty of "academic betrayal," the president characterized the young faculty member as "a valuable addition to our faculty" and refused to accept his offer to resign. The administration held to the principle that in order to dismiss an individual, it had to be proven that he was incompetent. President Taylor would not budge from his position that faculty must be individually evaluated on the basis of personal qualifications.

The following year after the college gained additional notoriety as a result of congressional hearings, the Board of Trustees was again solidly supportive of the faculty:

> During recent weeks, two members of the faculty of Sarah Lawrence College testified before the Senate Subcommittee on Internal Security.
>
> One of them, who came to Sarah Lawrence in 1947, answered all questions which concerned himself. He testified that he had been a member of the Communist Party prior to 1942, had left it in that year, and had had no other association with it since. When asked for the names of others in the Communist Party at that time, he declined to answer, saying "I simply could not live with my conscience if I informed on other people who to the best of my knowledge have done no harm. . . . I have no knowledge that any of these individuals had ever committed any offense against the security of the United States."
>
> The other faculty member denied present membership in the Communist Party but, on advice of counsel and in reliance upon the Fifth Amendment, declined to answer as to past membership on the ground that he might incriminate himself. He similarly declined to answer a number of other questions on advice of counsel that his answers might constitute a waiver of the privilege.
>
> A subcommittee of the Board of Trustees interviewed these teachers. The Board asked for and received reports from the appropriate faculty committees, President Taylor and Dean Raushenbush as to the qualifications of the two faculty members in question.
>
> On the basis of these reports and the transcript of the testimony, the Board of Trustees concluded that the teacher who refused to name former associates in the Communist Party did so on the basis of his personal standard of fair dealing and not for the purpose of defying the committee. This called for no action by the Board of Trustees. The reports as to his character and teaching showed that he was qualified to continue as a member of the faculty of Sarah Lawrence College.
>
> In considering the facts of the second case, the Board affirmed the postition

that exercise of the privilege of the Fifth Amendment is not a ground for suspension or dismissal but that this action calls for a careful reexamination of the qualifications of the teacher. In this instance, the faculty member resigned before any conclusion had been reached by the Board and at a time when no unfavorable action had been contemplated.[16]

Many academic administrators across the country expressed the belief that Sarah Lawrence was able to respond as it did because it was a private institution. Administrators at public institutions were convinced that such an independent stance was a "luxury" not afforded them. When asked by a faculty member during a formal inquiry whether, if he were in a favorable position, that is, in a private institution, he would hire an avowed communist, the president of the University of Washington responded in the affirmative, but added that in a public institution this was an "illusory hope . . . a pious hope."[17] He also stated that he agreed with President Conant of Harvard that if someone had professed membership in the Communist Party at some prior time and "were qualified in their respective fields of teaching and scholarship, I think . . . I would defend their profession, because I feel that it was an honest profession. But I hasten to say that I do not think that I would have a prayer of a chance of getting away with it in a public institution now. At one time I think that it might have been accomplished."[18]

Such statements left the general impression, still found today, that administrators in tax-supported institutions were more sensitive and diffident than those in private institutions to questions or criticisms from the public. It would not be fair to draw this conclusion from these data. To be sure, the institutions that did not punish faculty for invoking the Fifth Amendment were, with rare exceptions, private universities. However, enough private universities did punish or pressure faculty to suggest that their administrators and governing boards also often felt the same need to assuage what they saw as public sentiment.

Pressure on Smith College

In point of fact, colleges and universities could hardly ignore a widely circulated charge no matter how mean-spirited or vague or unfounded. For example, over the signature of an alumna from a wealthy and prominent politically reactionary family, the following letter, using the letterhead "Committee for Discrimination in Giving," went out to "several thousand" Smith College graduates:

Dear Fellow Alumna:

All of us, of course, realize that a contribution to a cause or an institution implies, on the part of the contributor, not merely a gesture of loyalty, but an active assumption of moral responsibility for that cause or institution.

How many, then, of those who bear a real affection for Smith, wish to sponsor the employment of men and women who, through their teaching positions, may be influencing young minds in a direction contrary to the philosophical principles in which most of us believe?

Newton Arvin, professor of English; Harold Underwood Faulkner, professor of history; Vera Micheles Dean, visiting professor of government; Oliver Larkin, professor of art; Mervin Jules, associate professor of art, and other members of the Smith College faculty have been or are presently associated with many organizations cited as communist or communist-front by the Attorney General of the United States and the Committee on Un-American Activities.

Even with full knowledge of the political associations of the above-mentioned professors, some of us will choose to contribute to Smith College the money which helps make their employment possible. We suggest, however, that any alumna who cannot conscientiously, and with complete awareness of its implications, follow this course, withhold her donation until the Smith administration explains its educational policy to her personal satisfaction.[19]

Within the month, the Smith authorities, with reluctance, found it necessary to respond to the attack. The president, Benjamin F. Wright, and the acting dean met with the faculty named in the letter. A statement was then issued by the president and chairman of the Board of Trustees:

For your guidance and information, this letter was not presented for investigation to the administration or to the Trustees of Smith College, who learned of it only after letters were received by some alumnae. The charges were not made known to the persons named nor were they given any opportunity to comment on them.

We are informed by the persons named, all of whom have taken the Massachusetts State Teachers' Oath pledging support of the Constitution of the United States and of the Commonwealth of Massachusetts, that they are not communists, that they are engaged in no disloyal or subversive activity and that they do not attempt to influence their students in the direction of any political doctrine. They particularly resent the insinuation that they might be guilty of abuse of academic freedom.[20]

In great detail, the president explained the administration's position and action to the faculty:

As soon as the text of the letter had been taken down by telephonic dictation, we tried to get in touch with the five members of the faculty named in the letter. . . .

Thursday evening Mr. Larkin and Mr. Arvin met at my house with Miss Kirkpatrick, Mr. Hill and myself. We discussed at some length the best way of dealing with the unhappy situation. All agreed that it would be most unfortunate if this letter with its vague charges, its insinuations and innuendoes were to get to the newspapers, but that we should be prepared with a statement if the newspapers did hear of it and ask us for comment. We also agreed that a letter should go to all member of the Board of Trustees, to all members of the Board of Counselors, and to all presidents of Smith alumnae clubs, and that such a letter should be sent out as quickly as possible in order that those persons might be in a position to answer inquiries being made by alumnae throughout the country.

The letter sent to Trustees, Counselors, and presidents of Smith clubs was drafted after several discussions and went through several revisions. All of the persons named in the original letter were either present or were kept informed of the nature of the statement. All of them gave their consent to the phrasing of the final draft.

You may well ask why this matter was not referred to the committees of the Board of Trustees and the faculty which were set up last year in the event that any case involving a faculty member should arise. We did not do so for two reasons: first, because of the impossibility of getting the members of the Trustee committee together immediately; second, because in the opinion of everyone concerned, this was not a case warranting investigation or discussion of the kind contemplated in the action taken by the Trustees and the faculty at their regular meetings last February.

You will be interested to know that though several of us have received many letters from alumnae as a result of the letter sent to them by the "Committee for Discrimination in Giving," not one, so far as I know, has indicated sympathy with the point of view of Mrs. Heath. One letter raised questions about the need for an investigation, but a telephone conversation between Mrs. Kane and that alumna immediately resulted in a statement that the alumna understood and sympathized with the policy pursued by the Trustees and the administration of Smith College. All of the other letters contain either statements of great indignation at the nature of the letter, or statements of complete confidence in the administration and the faculty of the college. It seems clear that the effect of the letter will be to strengthen the loyalty of the Smith alumnae to their college. But I deeply regret the pain and anxiety caused these members of the faculty and their families by this letter. I hope you will agree with me that, though the college might not suffer, the individuals involved should be protected against newspaper publicity, which would only mean further unhappiness for them. As we all know, denials and refutations rarely catch up with charges, expecially when they are broad and unsubstantiated, concerning loyalty or affiliation with allegedly subversive organizations.

I should also like to add that if there seems to be any need to do so I shall immediately call a meeting of the Trustee and faculty committees for further discussions of the question involved.[21]

An eight-member joint committee of trustees and faculty asked the administration to make an inquiry into the question of whether there had been "indoctrination in subversive, communistic, [or] communist-front doctrines." This largely involved interviews with the faculty named in the letter from the Committee for Discrimination in Giving. Individuals were asked about their political affiliations:

> Have You ever been a member of the Communist Party?
>
> If so, when did you leave the Party?
>
> Did you take the Massachusetts State Teachers' Oath in good faith?
>
> Have you supported any organization knowing that it was listed by the Attorney General of the United States as being a communist front?[22]

A subcommittee of the Commission on Communism in Massachusetts was also brought into the investigation.

The joint committee concluded "that there is absolutely no evidence" to support any charges of "teaching subversive doctrines": "There is a complete absence of any evidence that any member of the faculty had engaged in any such teaching or indoctrinal efforts. . . . None of the five members of the faculty named in the letter to alumnae are members of the Communist Party."[23]

The Board of Trustees of Smith College unanimously approved the report of the joint committee and a statement to this effect was widely circulated.

Sometimes administrators overestimated the risks they were taking in standing behind faculty members labeled as subversive. One told of his college being put on notice that financial support would be withdrawn if no steps were taken to curtail the political activities of an individual who was prominent in the Progressive Party. When this report was looked into, it was found that there had been one or, at the most, two telephone calls that involved vague warnings.

Whether or not it is possible to determine who or what moved academic administrators to act, it is clear that in at least one sense they were not acting independently but were reacting to political breezes as they gathered force. Perhaps by their complaisance they even stirred the winds, turning a breeze into a storm.

Instead of taking a firm stand in the face of exaggerated charges that colleges and universities condoned and fostered disloyalty, administrators often went well beyond simple cooperation. Before the fact, they generally extolled the fairness and integrity of any review, by all public figures; after the fact, they endorsed all methods and findings. Few stood their ground. "We welcome any investigation," a university president declared. "We will make our facilities available, and we delight at this opportunity." A college dean told a newspaper editor that anyone has a right to investigate a school.

The work and responsibilities of the university were for the most part left unexplained. Principles of academic freedom were rarely defined or defended. Administrators at public institutions seemed particularly eager to praise the wisdom, zeal, and patriotism of crusading politicians. It seems that there was as much concern with anticommunist politicians and newspapers—some inquisitorial, some vociferous—as with communism itself.

Routinely and with uncommon dispatch institutions launched their own investigations. As is evident from an internal memorandum of the American Association of University Professors, it was often not readily apparent to others why academic administrators pursued a particular course:

> For some reason or other, the Administration and Board of Trustees of Jefferson Medical College decided this summer to investigate certain members of the faculty regarding their loyalty. Without previous warning, Professors . . . (together with five or six other faculty members) were summoned, on June 17, to appear at the Board of Trustees' Room. No reason was given for their summons. . . . Each teacher was interrogated with respect to his loyalty. The following questions were asked: Is there a Soviet peril? Are you now, or have you ever been, a communist? Do you know of any communists on the Faculty? The proceedings were recorded on a disc.
>
> . . . stated that the faculty has not been informed about what is going on. . . .[24]

What was clearly understood was that invariably the work of legislative investigating committees would lead to the filing of charges against faculty and campus investigations. More often than not, these activities led to the dismissal of faculty.

Notes

1. *Denver Post*, 29 January 1951; and 1 February 1951.
2. Senate Committee on Privilege and Tenure, "Report and Recommendations in the Matter of David Hawkins."
3. *Newark Star-Ledger*, 26 September 1952, pp. 1 and 14.
4. James A. Rhodes, correspondence to Howard L. Bevis, 18 March 1953.
5. "Minutes of the Meeting of the Executive Committee of the Board of Trustees of Fisk University," 19 November 1954, p. 1.
6. "Petition to Governor Ralph F. Gates and the Indiana State and Marion County Boards of Election."
7. "Statement made by W. I. Brunton, Department Commander of the American Legion, to the Board of Trustees of Indiana University," p. 2.
8. Ralph F. Gates, correspondence to Ora L. Wildermuth, 5 September 1946.
9. Board of Trustees of Indiana University, report to Governor Ralph F. Gates, 15 December 1946, p. 2.
10. "Statement made by W. I. Brunton," p. 3.
11. Ibid, p. 6.
12. Board of Trustees, report to Governor, p. 5.
13. Ibid.

14. Herman B. Wells, correspondence to W. I. Brunton.
15. Harold Taylor and Harrison Tweed, statement, 22 January 1952.
16. Statement of Board of Trustees of Sarah Lawrence College, 21 April 1953.
17. Tenure hearings, University of Washington, pp. 733–34.
18. Ibid., pp. 707–8.
19. Aloise B. Heath, Committee for Discrimination in Giving, correspondence to Alumnae, February 1954.
20. Statement of Benjamin F. Wright and Amanda Bryan Kane, 26 February 1954.
21. Benjamin F. Wright, correspondence to members of the Smith College faculty, 1 March 1954.
22. "Meeting of Joint Committee of Trustees and Faculty," 16 March 1954.
23. Joint Committee of Trustees and Faculty, correspondence to the Board of Trustees of Smith College, 23 April 1954.
24. Warren C. Middleton, correspondence to Ralph E. Himstead, 21 July 1953.

5

Concerns and Charges

Politics as a Matter of Interest

All of the 126 cases involve individuals whose appointments were threatened because of alleged political beliefs or activities. Yet it is surprising how seldom, relatively speaking, political beliefs or activities were referred to when formal charges were specified and became the focus of proceedings. Looking at the charges alone, one often would hardly know that the cases were about politics. It would, of course, create unnecessary problems for administrators to acknowledge publicly that they were attempting to monitor the thinking of faculty or that they might be abridging someone's civil rights. Nonetheless, even when it was most evident that there was nothing else that had put an appointment in jeopardy, the complaint frequently specified matters other than political expression.

In the first place, most deliberations about those involved in the 1948 Wallace presidential campaign would perhaps have never mentioned this fact if those faculty defending themselves had not made reference to it, attempting to gain faculty and community support for their claim that their privilege and duty as citizens to engage in political activity was being curtailed. When involvement in the Wallace presidential campaign figured in a case, there were marked differences—significantly larger than in other cases—in how it was characterized on the one hand by institutional authorities and on the other hand by a principal.

For the most part, when political activities or affiliations were explicitly mentioned and became the indispensable focus of an action—albeit not necessarily as part of the formal charges—it was with reference to questions about past or present membership in the Communist Party or in other communist-dominated organizations that the principal had refused to answer before legislative committees. It was nearly universally accepted that a faculty member had a responsibility to provide these answers to

institutional authorities as a minimum condition of employment, even if
he had refused to cooperate with civil authorities. Those who would not
answer questions about their politics were obviously, as far as most academic administrators were concerned, violating the conditions of employment. Indeed, the starting point for those with the responsibility of
determining if someone was fit to hold an academic appointment was to
establish the extent of his connection to the Communist Party, his sympathy with the communist movement, and his affinity to communist ideology. A faculty committee appointed to advise the president at the
University of Michigan on what to do about faculty who did not cooperate
with the House Committee on Un-American Activities was reminded in a
memorandum from him that it must get "answers, freely and candidly
given, to the following questions":

> Were you ever a member of the Communist Party?
>
> Are you now?
>
> When did you sever the relationship? Why?
>
> How did you sever this relationship?
>
> What contacts, if any, have you had with members or their activities since
> that time?[1]

The committee, for its part, in outlining its "lines of inquiry," agreed on
a more detailed series of questions that would enable it to pursue this tack.

> 1. Do you believe in or advocate the overthrow of our present system of
>   government by force or violence?
> 2. Are you now a member of the Communist Party or associated with the
>   communist movement in any way? If so—
>   (a) When did you join the Party or become associated with the commu-
>   nist movement? Explain the circumstances of your joining or association,
>   and the activities in which you have been engaged in such capacity.
>   (b) Do you consider your Party membership or your association with the
>   communist movement fully compatible with your responsibilities as a
>   member of the university faculty? If so, on what basis?
>   (c) Have you, while employed by the university, sought to promote or
>   advance the interests or objectives of the Communist Party or the com-
>   munist movement in any way? If so, explain. If not, have you ever done
>   so? Explain. If you were once active, but are not now active, why?
> 3. If the answer to (2) is "no," have you at any time in the past been a
>   member of the Communist Party or associated with the communist move-
>   ment? If so—
>   (a) Why did you join the party or become associated with the movement?
>   (b) Indicate the period or periods of such membership or association.
>   (c) Why did you cease such membership or association?

(d) Are you able to prove that you terminated membership or association? How?[2]

Once such questions were addressed and principals had denied that they were active in Communist Party affairs, attention quickly turned to matters other than politics.

Perhaps if individuals had been enmeshed in illegal, revolutionary, or ultraistic activities, more references would have been made to radical politics. No one, however, seems to have been entangled in espionage, sabotage, or advocating the use of force or violence to overthrow the government or legally constituted institutions. There was no evidence of anyone being involved in a conspiracy or other criminal conduct. No subversive action was ever cited. However, the fact that someone was supporting an organization that may have engaged in political activities outside the mainstream was often noted. There was a general mistrust of those who had given money, time, or their name to any group designated as subversive by the Attorney General of the United States. There were accusations, but there was no real proof of disloyalty. Evidence that someone was involved in political organizing beyond working in the 1948 Wallace presidential campaign almost invariably proved to be hearsay. No one had been convicted of a felony. One individual had been named by the FBI as a member of "a spy ring" that had passed on information "to an espionage courier," but he fled the country, and the institution at which he held an appointment never got to the bottom of the matter. These were academic intramural—not civic, legal, or judicial—matters. Some individuals, approximately a dozen, had been cited for contempt of Congress, for refusing to answer questions or for "making misrepresentations" or false statements. From the data on hand, it would appear that only about half of them were ever tried and convicted.

At every possible opportunity—at a hearing, in meetings with colleagues, in open letters to the public, in statements to the press—a number of principals went to great lengths to attest that they did not subscribe to any unlawful organization or treasonous dogma. Nothing was uncovered to refute these claims. With five or, perhaps, six exceptions, the question of character or ethics was never even raised in a context other than a situation that touched on politics. To be sure, misgivings were often expressed about the morality of principals who had not indicated that they had lost interest in social change. This was to be expected given the widespread presumption that socialists, communists, fellow travelers, radicals, party-liners, sympathizers, and the like were reprobate. Yet, the doubts were general; they were not put in concrete terms. Reference was not made to plans or actions.

When the question of dishonesty was raised it was not about something obvious but came after a detailed review of someone's record. Horace B. Davis who had failed to "disclose . . . pertinent information"[3]—that he had once worked for a so-called communist-front organization—in an application for employment and in subsequent interviews with institutional authorities was brought before a committee of the Board of Trustees of the University of Kansas City. The committee piously claimed that it was not concerned with his having taken the Fifth Amendment or his generally noncooperative attitude. What mattered was the omission, and it was judged not inadvertent or unintentional but "a fraudulent concealment of material facts" by someone who was "less than frank."

As a result of testimony, not always reliable, of peripatetic anticommunist informers, many of the older principals, those at least 45 years of age, were asked to give an account of their participation in radical politics in the decade before World War II, a period when Marxism was somewhat fashionable on campus. Not much beyond what government investigators had made public was learned from this line of questioning, and it seldom generated new charges.

When institutional authorities produced concrete information about someone's involvement in radical politics, it was generally concerning events or actions that had occurred prior to the individual's present appointment. Regardless of the number of specific facts produced, these matters almost never became central to a case. Apparently someone's politics when he was a graduate student, for instance, or what he may have signed or joined during the Spanish Civil War, were seen as irrelevant to the present situation. There was no instance in which this issue was used seriously or with determination to prejudice a case. Some may well have been Stalinists or Trotskyites in the 1930s; others admitted past and present sympathies with collectivist ends. Yet, on only a few campuses was the argument ever made that someone was zealous and involved to the point of being even a remote danger to the political order. Moreover, only one-third of the principals could be objectively or appropriately characterized as being somewhere between mildly to very radical. As noted in chapter 2, many more resembled communists than actually were communists.

Thus, in spite of all of this probing, in institutions where there were formal hearings, the content of past activities rarely influenced the outcome of a case. What proved important during the course of the proceedings was whether someone chose to respond to questions about his past, not what the answers revealed. There is no way of knowing how relevant such considerations were in instances where decisions were made or actions were taken by more ad hoc procedures.

Although the accusation of being a communist or, more frequently, a communist sympathizer, was made against many more individuals than the few who admitted present Communist Party membership, it was made less often than expected. It was never assumed that those who refused to subscribe to a loyalty oath were involved in the Communist Party or communist activities of any sort. It was not suggested, for example, that any of the three dozen individuals forced to resign or finally dismissed from the University of California by the Board of Regents for not signing the disclaimer affidavit had in the past been communists or involved in communist affairs. On the other hand, those singled out because of their work on behalf of the 1948 Wallace presidential candidacy were frequently labeled by someone—not always officially—as communists or communist dupes.

The charge that someone was a communist invariably entailed additional charges. Given the belief that communists were disloyal, followed authoritarian rather than democratic principles, and were dogmatic (having closed minds inconsistent with an honest and impartial search for and use of facts), it was assumed that they were capable of "misrepresenting the truth," using the classroom to "indoctrinate students," and advocating the overthrow of the government "by force." Most of the time such an accusation was not explicitly made; it was assumed, made after the fact, hinted at, or "understood."

When such charges were made, they were not based on anything that principals had said or done but on what individuals with communist or radical political opinions or affiliations ostensibly "stand for," profess, or do. Needless to say, there was no way of defending oneself against such imputations. An attorney in one such case expressed the frustration of many when he observed:

> We are trained, and many of us in this law school have been trained in the theory that a person must stand for the act that he has committed and he is not responsible for the act of others. And now, we are faced for the first time in my experience as a lawyer, and the rest of us, with a new theory, where we are charged with guilt, as alleged, and responsible for the acts of someone else over whom we have no control.[4]

When the charge was at bottom guilt by association, even the most tenuous connection to those sympathetic with the ends of communism could put someone at risk. Denunciations were most general. Because, for example, it was never stated or written that someone had actually slanted his teaching, it was not easy for those so accused to convince others that they did not advocate or practice objectives attributed to communists.

Teaching as a Matter of Interest

A central tenet of the argument of those opposed to allowing communists or communist sympathizers to teach was that their presence on campus would invariably be harmful to students. It was reasoned that if communists were permitted to "infiltrate" educational institutions and with slanted teaching "deceitfully pervert [subvert] the educational process for Party ends," truth would not be served and students would not learn. To indoctrinate students with communistic ideas and principles, the argument continued, would be an abuse of authority and a gross violation of the trust given to teachers. Anyone who would engage in such subterfuge (and, of course, a communist could be expected to do so) was, quite simply, unfit to teach.

In the years after World War II, the corollary of this position, namely, that Communist Party membership, ipso facto, disqualified one from holding a faculty position, steadily gained currency. Seldom was it viewed as a personal attack or an attack on the liberty of a political minority, or on those who held unpopular beliefs or who were members of an unpopular political movement. No one questioned the premise that since the Communist Party was totalitarian in that it required obedience from its members on all issues, they were not intellectually free and should not be allowed to teach in free colleges and universities. Repeated almost as often was the argument that the Communist Party U.S.A. represented the interests of the Soviet Union, and therefore its members did not have the same rights as those in a domestic political party. They certainly did not have the right to indoctrinate college students. The counterargument articulated by the American Association of University Professors was seldom heard:

> There is, then, nothing in the nature of the teaching profession which requires the automatic exclusion of communists, and the attempt to exclude them would threaten our educational system. ... There is nothing now apparent in reference to the Communist Party in the United States, or to international conditions, that calls for a departure from the principles of freedom and tenure. ... This association regards any attempts to subject college teachers to civic limitations not imposed upon other citizens as a threat against the academic profession, and against the society that profession serves.[5]

A number of variations on these general themes can be found in these data. The president of one university defined incompetence as "any action, condition, or attitude which interferes with the proper performance of ... duties." He then reasoned that since one cannot be a sincere communist and a "sincere seeker after truth, which is the first obligation of the teacher," by definition being a communist makes one "incompetent." Of the ten academic administrators whose views on this matter most closely resembled this view, eight were from universities and two were from colleges.

Most often, when the question of teaching was raised, it was maintained that it was not necessary to examine someone's teaching to take the measure of it. The assessment of someone's ability in the classroom was not the only consideration in determining if, as it was put at the University of Kansas City, he is or "is not of the caliber for teaching in this university."

> We are not questioning [Davis's] competence. We are saying that he is bound by commitments which would prevent his continuing in a position of educational trust with this institution. That has nothing to do with competence of the teacher in some other institution.[6]

Efforts on the part of principals to make what they did or did not do in the classroom central to their cases were mostly unsuccessful. Here is an exchange between Horace Davis and a member of the Board of Trustees of the University of Kansas City:

Dr. Davis: I gave my teaching record when I came to this institution. I was not asked to give any political undertakings or disclaimers. I was employed here for six and a half years, I was put on tenure, and this whole field of questioning was never brought up, it was never considered necessary. Now, if it is brought up at this time it seems to me that the Board must be under some misapprehension. You must think that this line of questioning has something to do with my competence as a teacher, with my ability to conduct classes.

Mr. Howard: Of course the question of your competence as a teacher has never been raised by the Board.

Dr. Davis: All I have to say before the Board, Mr. Chairman, is that I hope that I will be judged on legitimate grounds, that is, on grounds of my competence as a teacher and my integrity as a person, and in this period that I have been on the campus there should have been ample time to check up on both.[7]

Davis was not judged on the basis of his teaching, and was fired. The introduction of other criteria, in this case a political test to establish how someone might perform in the classroom, if nothing else, clouded and complicated professional assessment and quite clearly aggravated the tensions between some faculty and administrators.

In light of the contention that the communist point of view would unbalance a sound educational program, it is of some interest that in fully one-third of the cases, there is absolutely no reference to teaching practices or performance, not only in the charges, but anywhere in the entire proceedings. It is clear that for the most part academic administrators neither knew nor cared much about the quality of the teaching of those they suspended from their teaching responsibilities, and whose careers were still in the balance, ostensibly in order to avoid putting students at risk.

The president of Rutgers University was apparently reflecting the opinion of many when he acknowledged that

> professional competence was not in question; nor did the Trustees attempt to inquire into this matter, which is clearly the province of the faculty and administrative officers. No suggestions of lack of professional competence, or of improper conduct, had been made. The inquiry into the teaching records of the two professors was irrelevant to the issue.[8]

The president of the University of Washington perhaps provided one explanation for this view while detailing to a historian the complexities in prosecuting a number of cases: "There was no time to study the record of an individual and his effect on students." In the course of testifying against an individual, an administrator was asked if he had any particular criticisms of the defendant's teaching. He responded, "I wouldn't know anything about that." The testimony and speeches of presidents of public universities, such as Ohio State University, the University of Michigan, and the University of Vermont, were most likely to reflect this attitude.

At the outset of one hearing, the committee chairman, speaking for his colleagues, made it clear that there was "no interest" in "classroom presentation"; they would be addressing other issues. A report from another committee twice emphasized that it had not inquired "into the substance" of any teaching.

Offers from principals to have materials about their teaching introduced into the record (e.g., "I am perfectly willing, if it seems desirable, to enter into the evidence here all the available views . . .") were generally declined. It was said that such evidence was irrelevant or unnecesary. If a letter or other testimony was admitted, seldom was further reference made to it.

When there was some mention of classroom behavior, it was, in all but three instances, favorable. Principals were not charged with propagandizing in class, indoctrinating students, or recruiting students for Party causes. Only once was it suggested that someone might be using the classroom to teach "false doctrine." It was not implied that this was being done under orders. There was but a hint from Oregon State College that students might not be hearing the whole truth, nothing more:

> Reports came to me in second-hand fashion which led me to think that [LaVallee] might be spending an undue amount of classroom time discussing political matters not pertinent to scheduled assignments of subject matter.
> . . .
>
> Reports of strong resentment coming to me for the most part second-hand . . . [townspeople, faculty in other schools] have led me to the definite con-

clusion that [he] failed to manifest a reasonable degree of scientific objectivity in the classroom.[9]

LaVallee, an economist, was said to have brought too many of his personal views into his course material; he was not accused of sowing partisan propaganda in place of content.

Another case was built around improperly influencing students, and that concerned the principal's participating in and being "responsible for" an improper and potentially disorderly demonstration directed at a dean. It was concluded that the teaching of a faculty member at New York University might be one-sided since "officers in radical student organizations were enrolled in [his] undergraduate courses."

There was never any indication that students were being recruited, even for the most innocuous activities. Although many were asked about the matter, there was no instance in which individuals were charged with misusing other relationships with students.

When the subject was raised, principals were most often praised for their teaching. Some examples:

He is by general repute a stimulating teacher.

[His teaching is] more than satisfactory.

[He is] one of the few teachers . . . about whom there has been no complaints.

Faculty are commonly rated as capable teachers, and the principals are not unusual in this regard.

At times, and with no particular explanation, even academic administrators went out of their way to make it clear that faculty were under a cloud for reasons other than their teaching or their work with students. The following are typical comments; this sort of assessment came from administrators at colleges, such as Evansville and Dickinson, as well as universities, such as Fisk, Temple, and Harvard:

[His culpability is] . . . not from an improper performance of teaching duties.

[This teacher] has never given a communist slant to . . . teaching, nor has . . . sought otherwise to influence the political views of . . . students. . . . teaching and research are of a high order.

[There is] no evidence that he had acted unprofessionally as a teacher. . . . [There is] nothing to show that he had attempted to indoctrinate any of his students.

[There is] no evidence that [he] . . . misused his position as a teacher to propagandize students. Evidence produced . . . show[s] the absence of any such conduct.

> Misuse of his classroom or of his relationship with students, in the interest of his political ideas, was [not] attributed to him.

When faculty or students were queried or volunteered information about the teaching of one of the principals, their assessments were overwhelmingly favorable. There was testimony about objectivity; there was no mention of bias. Competence was never called into question. At worst, classroom procedures were described as "conventional":

> [He apppeared to be involved] in a careful examination of all the relevant facts and theories and hypotheses.

> [He had a] high reputation as a very fine teacher and most competent, not only as a teacher of philosophy and a student of philosophy, but as a philosopher. [The chairman also stated that] he was probably the best teacher [in the department].

> [He] has not discussed in the classroom matters not germane to ... [the] course.

A review committee of faculty may have hit upon the point that lay behind this near consensus:

> It is impossible to conceive how the mere fact of membership in the Communist Party could, in any way, affect the competency of respondent Butterworth as a teacher of Old English literature.[10]

Quite simply, given their academic specialties, most principals would have found it difficult to introduce slanted or communist-tainted materials into their teaching.

Scholarship as a Matter of Interest

The performance of other academic duties, for example, research, or professional effectiveness in general also seldom seemed to be a concern of academic authorities. As it turned out, these considerations were even less important as a matter of interest than was teaching. This fact was due to a number of reasons, the most obvious being the peremptory contention on the part of many academic administrators that under a variety of circumstances "professional competence was irrelevant." Since quality of work was assumed, it was not a subject given much attention. There were situations, it was reasoned, when other factors simply took precedence over how well someone may have done his work. For example, a president of a large state institution, arguing that the university was a public trust, held that "academic freedom entails the obligation to render an explanation as clearly and rationally as possible, whenever such an explanation is called for by duly constituted governmental bodies acting within the limits of their authority." It follows, he continued, that regardless of what service someone might have given or the quality of that service or however firmly one might be convinced that silence was justifiable, faculty did not have the right to invoke the Fifth Amendment:

> It is no invasion of privacy but a necessary measure of protection of the freedom of all of us to seek to determine whether teachers and others in public positions of trust are committed to the discipline and program of the Communist Party.

Other administrators were persuaded that the fact of holding an academic appointment was in itself proof of qualification and ability. From this perspective, the particulars of what someone had actually done in carrying out his academic functions—what had been written or what committee service had been rendered—were unimportant. Some of the time this view was put forth with elaborate logic; other times it was stated matter-of-factly:

> ... we will indulge in the conclusive presumption that every person here charged is sufficiently learned in his field and sufficiently skillful in his teaching. . . .[11]

In the eyes of still other academic administrators—perhaps not fully appreciating the implications of this position—focusing on the academic dimension was specious. This premise was introduced more often and expressed more plainly at universities than at colleges. Before setting forth any accusations, the administration at a large university made it clear that the proceedings against faculty were not an inquiry "into technical competency" but into their relation to or involvement in the "communist conspiratorial movement."

Administrative officials were mostly interested in professional competence only insofar as it could be inferred from political affiliations or activities. There was no interest in the converse. If the contents of an individual's published work had reflected poorly on him, these may well have been given more attention. As it was, it is reasonable to conclude that because the professional writing of the principals—with three exceptions— received absolutely no attention in the deliberations, there was little or nothing in it of a political nature.

Even those administrators who made it evident that they did not approve of the alleged political views of the principals or who appeared to be the strongest advocates of anticipatory dismissal generally conceded—

often only when pressed—that the research of "these dissident faculty" with which they were familiar was "highly competent," of "excellent quality," "quite good," or the like. Two individuals at different ends of the country were described as being "without academic fault." The colleagues of another principal unanimously agreed that he had "conscientiously and ably performed" his duties, "cooperated fully," and showed "complete devotion to his work in teaching and research." The academic fitness of only two individuals was ever openly and seriously questioned. The scholarship of the rest was not challenged or discredited. In letters and testimony there was seldom a suggestion that someone was not meeting all of his professional obligations. Here is how a president described someone about to be fired: "He appeared consistently during all the time he was on campus as a competent and devoted man of science. There appeared from his conduct no reason to question his loyalty."

At bottom, as far as the majority of academic administrators were concerned, the criterion of competence was not actual performance as a teacher or researcher but political orientation, behavior with respect to a political matter, membership in some organization, or a cooperative attitude.

Time and again, with little success, those who were, in effect, pleading for their jobs attempted to keep the focus of the inquiry on the quality of their academic work. At the University of Washington, the defense, holding that competence was at the heart of any valid case for dismissal, appealed that the review committee

> . . . should stand on the well established principle that a man on the faculty of the University of Washington so long as he is competent in the usual sense of that term, as it was certainly meant, so long as he is honest and moral in the usual sense of that term, without any stretching of meanings, so long as he has been responsive to his duties as a teacher, has taught his classes, has taught them well, he may hold any political opinion he sincerely believes in and he may belong to any political party that he chooses, so long as he deports himself in his academic life in a proper way.[12]

A majority of eight faculty members on the committee reviewing the case agreed, holding that the question of competence, indeed, revolves around how well one carries out his academic work. The president disagreed. In overturning the committee's recommendation, he simply redefined the term:

> Because reasonable doubt is cast upon the objectivity, integrity and intellectual honesty of these men by the secrecy of both their affiliations and of the nature of the organizations to which they presumably belong, they are in my opinion, incompetent to hold their positions.[13]

The contention that "a teacher may be rendered incompetent ... by any action, condition, or attitude which, interferes with the proper and adequate performance of his duties" was substituted for the usual, narrower meaning of competency as something that could only be judged within a field of scholarship or teaching. Under the broad construction, at Fisk University the mathematician, Lee Lorch, who in five years had received one contract renewal, two increases in salary, and a promotion to full professor was judged incompetent—and was in the end terminated. For the most part, however, the question of competence in teaching or research was either unmentioned or conceded.

Charges

In eighteen cases on eleven different campuses, academic authorities disregarded evidence that clearly indicated excellence in teaching or research. It is evident from the context in which this was done that they were reluctant to acknowledge any fact that would be inconsistent with the charges they had framed.

Both legally and morally the charges were seen to be at the center of a case. In light of the great significance given to them, it was surprising that so much of the time there was considerable guesswork involved in determining what in fact the true charges were against a principal. A variety of approaches to the categorization of the data did nothing to eliminate any of the ambiguity. Since from campus to campus the same action might be labeled differently, efforts to set up a reliable classification system were not successful. The examples below bring into comparison similar behavior that at one institution was called or characterized as *incompetence* and that at another was called or characterized as *insubordination*.

Incompetence

1. Refusal to disclose information to the college
2. Refusal to identify a signature; refusal to verify questions under oath
3. Querulous and insolent to investigators
4. Holding unpopular ideas; making statements such as the "Communist Party is not a danger to the United States"
5. Secretive

Insubordination

1. Refusal to answer questions about past associations
2. Refusal to sign a statement
3. Losing temper; discourtesy

4. Refusal to acknowledge that the Communist Party was dangerous and threatened the country
5. Evasive attitude

   Along with incompetence and insubordination, the most omnibus charge was "being disloyal." At one college, the president's description of an individual's disloyalty both to the United States and the college included, among others, the charges of "illegally" claiming the protection of the Fifth Amendment, refusing to assure college authorities that he had never been a communist, being identified as "a member of a communist cell," obtaining a letter of recommendation from a "known" communist, having "evaded" identifying "the Communist Party as a conspiracy," publicly complaining that evidence had been fabricated, and being generally uncooperative. For his part, it was the faculty member's contention in this instance that he had never been a member of the Communist Party or even a "fellow traveler," that the president was being "another McCarthy," and that he was acting on the advice of counsel. Here and with most of the materials we reviewed, where there were inconsistent or contradictory accounts, it was not really possible to determine where the actual truth lay. As a consequence, how any complaint or case was categorized is somewhat arbitrary. (Of course, it is not unlikely that some entangled in these controversies would question any interpretation of events that was necessarily arrived at almost entirely from available records.)

   Delineating with appreciable confidence the grounds in each case was obviously difficult when these were not precisely specified. Even when, initially, the principal charges were concrete and clearly spelled out, these often proved to be only incidental as a case developed, as an institution attempted to strengthen its case through the addition of irrelevant or marginal charges. For instance, by the time hearings began at the University of Washington, the president through formal hearings initiated by the dean (see Appendix F) had augmented the simple and straightforward accusation that a principal "is and for many years has been a member of the Communist Party" (Appendix F, Charge I) with the compounded and vague "his behavior has been bad; he has neglected his duty; he has been dishonest and incompetent" (Appendix F, Conclusion and Prayer). This was an obvious example of an administration attempting to frame a case so that dismissal would be consistent with the institution's faculty code or bylaws.

   In the eyes of the president, this elaboration clarified matters, and did not make the case any less "clear-cut." For him, the new charges simply spelled out the implications of Communist Party membership, specifically, "following the Party line," spending too much time on political activities, and having allegiances and commitments that precluded being open or cooperative with civic or academic authorities. Moreover, individuals who were members of the Communist Party "brought contumely and disrespect" upon themselves and their colleagues. It was the University of Washington administration's view that any one of these charges, and certainly any combination, would demonstrate "professional unfitness."

It was the university president's position that nothing could offset such inadequacies, even if an examination of actions or behavior in the classroom or testimony indicated that none of his suspicions were true. The elaboration of charges, the institution's attorney ironically insisted, served to narrow the grounds so that a more "clear-cut" case could be presented.

The continued introduction of additional considerations by academic authorities, on top of the failure to give full particulars contributed to the impression that many proceedings had little focus or coherence. The somewhat novel practice of adding to the charges after a decision to dismiss had been made also suggests that all of this may only have been dust thrown in the eyes. The charges as enunciated by administrators and the true reasons for dismissal may well have been only tenuously related.

To be sure, the hearings were not legal proceedings. And because they often were not bound by judicial formalities, they could go in unpredictable directions—marked by what frequently seemed to be the haphazard introduction of new issues. For still unfathomable reasons, some questions were unexpectedly raised, desperately pursued, and just as unexpectedly dropped. Public statements and the tack taken during a formal inquiry might only be tangentially related. It was not uncommon for a principal to be charged with one thing and be relentlessly questioned about completely unrelated matters.

As one might guess in light of the foregoing example from the University of Washington, it was not uncommon for there to be a number of allegations, one or another being emphasized as events unfolded. Many cases shifted ground—some suddenly, others almost imperceptibly; some once, others more often. It was not unusual for a case to be reshaped in accordance with changing circumstances, for instance, reports of military action in Korea, that were in no way related to it. Principals were often left bewildered at being charged with one action and being convicted of another.

Fairmont State College

Like those at the University of Washington, events at Fairmont State College illustrate perfectly how a case might unpredictably move from issue to issue. In this instance, the chairman of the Department of Art,

Luella R. Mundel, (one of two females who were principals in a case) with a three-year contract subject to an annual review brought unfavorable attention to herself at an antisubversive seminar sponsored by the American Legion. She asked a speaker what his evidence was that Owen Lattimore was a communist, questioned another about how he or the ordinary citizen could tell a communist when he saw one, and expressed annoyance at statements linking liberals and communists and at the suggestion that radicals were overrepresented on college and university faculties. She suggested that the measures the journalist Victor Lasky, one of the participants, had recommended to deal with subversion were a threat to civil liberties and were similar to those used in fascist countries.

Two months later a recommendation was made that she be terminated because "she's a poor security risk." When at that time the president declared that he did not believe anyone on the faculty was a communist, the board member who had suggested that she might be one was asked to elaborate. The response to this challenge was that it really meant "a poor teacher." Making his own inquiries, the college president went to the local office of the FBI, but no evidence was turned up to contradict the faculty member's statement to him that "she had never been, was not then, and never wanted to be a communist."

To evaluate the second charge relating to her teaching, eighteen students were interviewed, and she was evaluated favorably by essentially all of the art majors and the majority of the nonmajors. On this matter, the president's report concluded:

> In summarizing the notes on my personal conferences it was discovered that eight (8) of the nine (9) majors liked Dr. Mundel as a person and the ninth felt that he was not qualified to say. Five (5) of the nine (9) non-majors liked Dr. Mundel, while four (4) of them disliked her.[14]

Ten faculty and administrators were asked "Do you believe the criticism you have heard against Dr. Mundel as a teacher and as a person would justify her immediate release?" Eight answered in the negative.

Nonetheless, at the board meeting at which this report was presented, she was dismissed "for the good of the school." Just prior to the vote, the claim that she was "an atheist" was heard for the first time. The president had reported that he had heard a rumor "that she has said she was an atheist. I had heard her say in a faculty meeting that she was a socialist and I heard her use such language indiscreetly." When later asked by the president whether this was true, she replied, "no, I am not." The president reported that

> at that time the Board did not consider it [the question of atheism] serious enough to give it as a reason for dismissal or cause for an investigation.

The Board never did ask for an investigation of the atheism rumor, but it did use it as justification for Dr. Mundel's dismissal following a later meeting in September at which the Board denied Dr. Mundel's request for a hearing.[15]

(Her nemesis on the Board was later reported to have said, "I am a theist . . . and would expect to stand judgment if I condoned its opposite.") Finally, it was alleged that she was part of a clique that had become dangerous because of "certain opinions" held by its members.

The Board's minutes of the vote begin: "After conducting a thorough investigation . . . ." The president, however, wrote:

> I have no knowledge of such an investigation other than a faint memory that I had heard it mentioned that several board members in this area had been designated to check into the problem. No evidence has come to my attention that such a committee made a "thorough" investigation or reported its findings.[16]

The Board's minutes report:

> Upon motion duly made, seconded, and unanimously carried, the Board denied the request of Dr. Luella R. Mundel for a hearing before the Board concerning its former action declining to reemploy her as a member of the faculty of Fairmont State College. . . .
>
> In deciding not to reemploy Dr. Mundel for a third probationary year various factors were considered. These included the allegation reported to the Board by President George H. Hand, that Dr. Mundel had on occasion declared herself an atheist.
>
> President Hand nevertheless recommended Dr. Mundel's reemployment for a third probationary year although he expressed to the Board serious reservations as to her satisfactory adaptability to the various demands of the position and the soundness of her judgment in her public expressions.[17]

The grounds for dismissal had widened considerably. Even the president seemed embarrassed by how they had grown in scope.

> I object to this interpretation because it does not make clear that I merely reported an uninvestigated rumor to the Board that Dr. Mundel has said she was an atheist; and because it used its own interpretation and not mine when it said my reservations on Dr. Mundel were serious (obviously I did not think they were serious or I would have recommended her dismissal).[18]

Hoping to clear her name and to bring to light what in fact the issues were, Mundel filed a $100,000 slander suit against the board member who had led the attack against her, claiming defamation of character. She charged that being branded with terms such as poor security risk, atheist, and incompetent, as well as bad personal traits, did her irreparable harm professionally. In a special plea the defense attorney argued that it was a board member's duty "to ascertain the qualifications of all instructors, present and prospective, including their ability, education, character, loyalty to the United States and its form of government, and their freedom from atheistic, communistic, or any other anti-religious or un-American 'taints or infirmities.'" During the trial, the defense attorney argued for the Board of Education's right "to purge its schools of teachers it believes incompetent, atheists, communists, horse thieves, murderers, or just too ignorant to teach children." He described Mundel as someone who would "tear down the the man of Galilee from the Cross"—a woman who "boasted of painting pictures which arouse sexual desires in men." This new assault resulted only in Mundel's collapse in the courtroom, but not in a clarification of the particulars of the charges and case against her.

Wayne University

On the other hand, administrative authorities could become fixated on a single issue, letting it determine the outcome of a case. At Wayne University in Detroit, the governing board, the administration, and a substantial number of senior faculty felt themselves bound by Michigan's Public Act 117 (or Trucks Act), which was designed to create legal difficulties for those who sought recourse in the Fifth Amendment. The law in part read that:

> No persons may hold any non-elective position, job or office for the State of Michigan, or any political subdivision thereof, . . . where reasonable grounds exist, on all of the evidence, from which, after a hearing, the employer or superior of such person can say with reasonable certainty that such person is a communist or a knowing member of a communist-front organization.

and further that:

> . . . the refusal of any person who holds a non-elective position, job or office . . . who, upon being called before a duly authorized tribunal or in an investigation, under authority of law, to testify concerning his being a communist or a member of a communist-front organization, on the grounds that his answers might tend to incriminate him, shall be, in the hearing provided for in this section, *prima facie* evidence that such person is a communist or a knowing member of a communist-front organization.[19]

In effect, the law made claiming the privilege against self-incrimination itself incriminating. It not only set aside the principle of innocence until guilt is proven, but it did not specify how an individual under suspicion could establish his innocence.

When two Wayne University faculty, Gerald Harrison, who had a tenure appointment in the Department of Mathematics, and Irving Stein, who had a term contract in the Department of Physics, took the Fifth Amendment before the Clardy Subcommittee of the House Committee on Un-American Activities, the university president immediately suspended them in light of provisions of the Trucks Act that had been formally incorporated into Board policy and administrative procedure. Policy and procedure also made it necessary for Harrison and Stein to stand trial: Since an "employee has a *prima facie* case against him[,] he will be expected to clear himself of the charge of being a communist or knowingly a member of a front organization."[20] The university presumed guilt, and the burden of proof was on Harrison and Stein to show otherwise, to prove that they were not communists.

The congressional committee had made no charges against Harrison, although one witness had testified that Stein was a member of a communist-front organization. The university committee appointed to investigate the matter asked the congressmen for any derogatory information they might have on either man, but received no response.

During the hearing, Harrison and Stein were questioned by the committee about a wide number of matters, many of a personal nature. The committee felt that answers to general and personal questions were necessary to confute the case established by the use of the Fifth Amendment. Among other things, they were asked about areas of agreement and disagreement with Communist Party dogma, membership in organizations, personal associations, attendance at meetings, why the Fifth Amendment was invoked, and what they read. Although neither taught biology, they were asked about Lysenkoism, and it was thought significant that they were even aware of such ideas.[21]

Harrison answered all questions and the committee prepared and signed a report clearing him. He was recalled and asked to sign an affidavit. After conferring with his attorney and being reminded that the document could be used in a perjury trial, he balked. Two pages were added to the report, and the final recommendation of the committee was that he not be reinstated.

After Stein refuted the one direct charge against him, he took the position that his activities and beliefs were his own affair and he appeared to be less cooperative or forthcoming. Nonreinstatement was also recommended in his case.

Although both had support and testimonials from colleagues and students, the committee justified the dismissals on the grounds that "both men by refusing to testify before a congressional investigating committee had under the law 'incriminated' themselves."

In answer to questions from our colleagues we can only reply that in the judgment of the committee Dr. Harrison and Mr. Stein did not rebut the *prima facie* evidence. One specific question is likely to be, "was there any substantial evidence against them?" Our answer is "No." It probably won't help much at this point to explain that the clear-cut intent of the Michigan Communist Control Act is to bring about the dismissal of teachers who are unable or unwilling to rebut presumptive evidence even though there is no substantial evidence against them.[22]

The committee felt that it was bound to follow the law and that it was necessary for Harrison and Stein to rebut beyond all reasonable doubt the presumption of guilt: "A committee is obligated to take seriously the presumption that the accused is a communist."

The committee also made it clear that it believed Harrison and Stein invoked the Fifth Amendment in bad faith, that they were not motivated by conscientious scruples and were not standing on principle. Since there was no evidence against them, and at least one answered every question the committee asked, the opportunity for exculpation seems to have become a means of inculpation. Whatever the committee members found Harrison and Stein guilty of, they apparently furnished themselves.

A second committee also held that under the law and institutional policies a mere affirmation of innocence would not be sufficient to clear anyone, and sustained the recommendation that Harrison and Stein not be reinstated.

At a substantial minority of institutions, no charge was ever specified or detailed, administrators or the governing board apparently believing that they had no obligation to state their reasons publicly.

At Jefferson Medical College in Philadelphia, when three individuals who had been abruptly dismissed after interviews with some administrative officers and members of the governing board asked for an explanation, the dean responded that he had "been instructed to tell . . . nothing more." He also refused to make known the findings of the College Loyalty Committee. Requests for copies of the findings of the inquiry by an ad hoc committee were also denied. Institutional authorities would not furnish any explanation for the dismissals. The official reason for the dismissals given to the press was that the retention of the three was not "in the best interest of the institution."[23] This was a fairly standard rationale, more frequently offered by college than university administrators. It was said that the institution's action was precipitated by a five-month long investigation. On the basis of rumors, it was concluded that the three had "communist associations." Some time later, the institution sent each a letter that stated that there had been no finding that any had been involved in acts to undermine the government:

I can assure you that the decision of the Board of Trustees to terminate your service as a member of [the] faculty was not based upon a finding that you were a subversive person as that term is defined in the Pennsylvania Loyalty Act.[24]

At three other institutions, as curious as it might seem, the principals were never told what they were being charged with, even after formal hearings.

Most frequently, charges were vague. For about 40 percent of the institutions it was impossible to identify with any degree of certainty what the administration saw as the central issue or issues. The more years the principal had served at an institution, the less likely that the charges would be clear and unequivocal. Searching out and examining more information seldom helped shed additional light on this question. In fact, the more closely some cases were studied, the more difficult it became to determine what offense a principal purportedly committed. One thing that became readily apparent was that some academic administrators were reluctant to make statements that could be contradicted, disproven, or, most importantly, used in a legal action against them.

Because charges were often quite different from the issues that emerged in the prosecution of a case, it was not unusual for faculty to have difficulty defending themselves.

Oregon State College

The common problem of figuring out what exactly the allegations were is clearly shown through an examination of several documents from a case at Oregon State College. In this dispute, not only had a young associate professor of chemistry and his wife attracted undue attention because of their activities in Progressive Party politics, but a letter that he had published in the *Chemical and Engineering News*, in response to an editorial about science in the Soviet Union, greatly angered the president. The chemist, Ralph Spitzer, had written:

The editorial of Dec. 27, discussing H. J. Muller's charge that science is being destroyed in the Soviet Union, advises us that "this indictment should be read by every scientist." In the interests of scientific objectivity, the editor might better have advised us to read the 536-page stenographic transcript of the last session of the V.I. Lenin All-Union Academy of Sciences . . . at which the state of biological science was discussed by 57 agricultural and biological scientists representing both the classical and the Michurin schools of genetics and development.

The major paper of this meeting, by T. D. Lysenko, is now available in the

United States (International Publishers, 1948) and should be read by scientists in preference to the numerous polemics and "indictments" which are current. Contrary to Dr. Muller's assertion that, "despite the pretenses of communist officials and their followers, this matter is not a controversy between scientists or a dispute over the relative merits of two scientific theories. It is a brutal attack on human knowledge," a perusal of Lysenko's report shows that the issue is largely over matters of biological and technological fact and theory. Are vegetative hybrids possible? Mr. Lysenko has samples. Can the heredity of organisms be changed by changing the environment at an appropriate time and in an appropriate way? The Michurinists have changed 28 chromosome spring wheats to 42 chromosome winter wheats by suitable temperature treatment during several generations. Finally, it is asserted that the Lysenko theory and techniques are far more productive of economic results than the classical theory, which is also assailed as being "idealist," a term which in the Soviet Union has roughly the connotations of supernaturalist or unscientific. . . .

It is important—literally vitally so in the present international situation—for us to try to understand the problems of the Soviet Union and the methods used to solve them. In the Soviet Union, no less than in other countries, decisions must be made to support one field of research or another, or to establish or abolish university chairs. . . . Judged in the light of the Soviet social structure, this method of allotting funds and responsibilities does not seem less democratic than our method of allowing boards of directors, Congress, or the military to decide (often on a smaller scale) which branches of science and which projects to encourage. . . .

This rejection of any possible use of biological law for ideological or propaganda purposes makes it difficult to see just what the Communist Party could hope to gain by replacing a functioning science by a "medieval superstition" as Muller charges. Remembering the tremendous need for reconstruction of Soviet agriculture after the wartime destruction, it is more reasonable to conclude that this controversy revealed facts which made the majority of those involved decide that the Michurin-Lysenko trend is probably more fruitful than classical genetics. It can be presumed from past behavior that the controversy on this subject, as well as on all other subjects of importance, will be reopened periodically as new facts and methods emerge. . . .[25]

To the university president, A. L. Strand, the letter was clear proof of support for "the charlatan Lysenko in preference to what he must know to be the truth. . . . He went far out of his way to combat the influence of [other geneticists]. . . . Why should a chemist bother to stir up controversy in the field of genetics? I can tell you. It is because he goes right down the Party line without any noticeable deviation and is an active protagonist for it."[26]

The president's argument was less qualified, complex, or subtle than Spitzer's. It was the latter's contention that his letter in no way "support[s] or accept[s] Lysenko's theories."

Without taking a position with regard to the validity of the scientific hypotheses involved, I referred to some of Lysenko's arguments and urged American scientists to investigate these controversies from first-hand sources.

The fact that I did not make a judgment on the subject does not mean that I did not have a right to do so. Most American scientists would agree that the individual scientist has not only the right, but the obligation, to make up his mind on the basis of the facts, as he sees them. In so doing, he cannot be influenced by the approval or disapproval of college presidents, Nobel prize winner or the other spokesmen for the dominant scientific theories of the day.[27]

The president's initial broadside essentially focused on a single issue: Spitzer's "letter, above all else, shows but one thing, namely, his devotion to the Communist Party line." As far as the president was concerned, his own action was justified by the fact that Spitzer was not "free from the compulsions of a political party" that had denounced ideas of western civilization—including freedom—as bourgeois, was the enemy of freedom, had no freedom itself, and had established itself and its institutions as the final arbitrators of truth:

He accepts Lysenko's pamphlet in preference to evidence from American and British scientists. . . . He is very much in accord with the Soviet policy as enunciated by the Moscow press.[28]

When publicity and controversy began to surround the case, the grounds began to widen. Vaguely and lamely, President Strand took the offensive: "It [the letter] was far from being the sole reason for indeed our conclusion in regard to him had been reached before the letter was available to us."[29] Although Spitzer was never accused of being a member of the Communist Party, there was the appendant claim that he had been very active in communist work on campus, "carried out through the Young Progressives." The president also indicated that because those outside of mainstream politics were a threat to society and a threat to a smoothly functioning college, they were quite naturally not welcome as faculty members. Alongside his insistence that free political expression had nothing to do with his decision to fire Spitzer, was the admission that "their [the chemist and an economist, another member of the Progressive Party,] very activity indicates we would not make permanent members of the staff out of them. Anybody's politics is all right down here, but . . . I don't think I'd better say anything further."[30]

The pretext that Spitzer's political affiliation had affected his ability to think objectively followed. Party dogma was said to have clouded his judgment in all matters, academic and otherwise. His devotion to Communist

Party policy regardless of the evident truth was apparently obvious, unassailable, and unacceptable:

> Any scientist who has such poor power of discrimination so as to choose to support Lysenko's Michurin genetics against all the weight of evidence against it is not much of a scientist, or, a priori, has lost the freedom that an instructor and investigator should possess.[31]

Pursuing this theme, it was suggested by the president that in a more general way intense involvement in political activities could have a deleterious effect on academic functions:

> It [the letter] follows true to form his proselyting activities on this campus for at least two years, activities which have taken on the nature of a campaign and which have become so absorbing for him that they have begun to interfere with his regular work, although no claim in that regard has been made in connection with the decision not to renew his contract.[32]

When asked directly if Spitzer had been negligent in his duties, the president responded, "not at all." Yet, a newspaperman for the *Oregon Journal* wrote, "[President Strand] told this reporter that he had received student complaints regarding both men [the chemist and the instructor of economics]. . . . [The] dean of the School of Science said no students had griped to him . . ., but he understood several had gone to the president's office."[33]

As far as the president was concerned, Spitzer's true "loyalties and beliefs" were quite easy to discern. His ideas were contaminated; he was contaminated; and he should no longer be permitted to contaminate students. That Spitzer was not silent about his nonrenewal was taken as further evidence of his true politics, for it was typical of persons "in that category [Party liners] to set up their case as a *cause célèbre*."[34] The very fact that Spitzer relied on Soviet sources was also said to afford inviolable proof of his guilt.

Administrators at other institutions were as wide-ranging and inventive in raking up gossip and introducing a canard, and were no more able to provide evidence or specifics to substantiate their accusations.

Balky Witnesses

As indicated in chapter 3, the largest number of cases and of charges were the direct result of individuals simply having been called before a legislative committee or some governmental agency—such as the state police—and of having failed to respond fully to questions about past or, less frequently, present political affiliations. Those who invoked the Fifth or First amendment were said to have acted in a way that "was inimical to the best interests" of the college or university. (The official using this phrase was arguing that any behavior that incurs the displeasure of some portion of the community is to some degree "inimical to the best interests" of an institution.)

For the most part, campus officials believed that any and all questions put to faculty should be answered. With few exceptions, there was the feeling that even questions about events that presumably occurred a dozen or more years prior to a subpoena, and that were not unlawful or improper, were not inappropriate and could not be ignored. It was taken for granted not only by administrators, but by most faculty that at the very minimum institutions were "require[d] . . . to reassess the fitness of a faculty member who invokes it [the Fifth Amendment privilege]." (It was the published view of the Association of American Universities [see chapter 1, note 23] that invoking the Fifth Amendment "places upon a professor a heavy burden of proof of his fitness to hold a teaching position and lays upon his university an obligation to re-examine his qualifications for membership in its society." Remembering the Introduction, this was the standard the chemist from Rensselaer Polytechnic Institute did not measure up to, according to the president and the Board of Trustees.)

Many principals who had been recalcitrant witnesses before civil authorities acknowledged that it was legitimate for academic authorities to ask the same sorts of questions. Consequently, they were more forthcoming during proceedings on campus. This more open attitude may have prevented a few—by no means very many—from being fired.

Those who failed to cooperate with a legislative investigation were assaulted from all sides. Some were called to account for evading their civic responsibilities. A philosopher at Temple University whose tenure was eventually revoked was reminded that he had failed in his duty to "maintain the highest example of good citizenship." His "false use of a constitutional privilege in manifest contempt of a proper governmental body" was, he was told, nothing other than a violation of a "cardinal duty."[35] Someone else who also refused to cooperate with a legislative committee and lost his tenure was many times over criticized for failing to show the "candor that would be reasonably expected of faculty," "not conducting himself with the dignity expected of educated men and women," as well as "ignoring what he must know were his duties and responsibilities." The president of Rutgers University summarized the case against two other faculty:

> The sole question concerned their special obligations as members of a learned profession and as representatives of the university in making public statements.[36]

In addition to the accusation of neglecting "these singular duties incumbent on academics," there were a number of cognate charges made against those who used the Fifth Amendment. Depending on how an academic administrator may have interpreted institutional regulations or bylaws, faculty who would not give evidence were deemed culpable for having failed to act in the best interest of the institution, for putting their own interest before the interest of the institution, for unnecessarily embarrassing the institution, for injuring the good name of the institution, for placing the institution in a vulnerable position, or for insubordination. Terms such as "improper conduct" and "moral delinquency" were never defined but were indiscriminately thrown about. When the president of Ohio State University was asked to explain what he meant by "insubordination," he responded:

> I don't think any precise definition has ever been formulated and probably none could be except as a result of a series of cases. I suspect this is the first case that has arisen in which that word has been called into question.[37]

There was also near consensus among academic administrators that a refusal to testify was a misuse of the Fifth Amendment that "abused the high constitutional privilege ... invoked." Regardless of an individual's record of service or motives, "seeking refuge in the Fifth Amendment" was considered contrary to institutional policy—and at a number of institutions it was made clear that such an act would not or could not be tolerated. Most who failed "to display the qualities of responsibility, integrity, and frankness" brought so much criticism and discredit to the institution that they were summarily suspended. Although they were not an immediate threat to the welfare of students or colleagues, that is, they were not unfit to continue their work, it was believed essential that the institution distance itself from them as quickly and completely as possible.

The contention of a handful of faculty that they had no obligation to testify about personal matters was disregarded out of hand as self-serving. Many administrative officers wanted to know what there was to hide. The idea that someone might be moved by a desire to uphold a higher truth or by other principles was given absolutely no credence or consideration. As far as most academic administrators were concerned, there was no difference between those who might be motivated by ideals and those who remained silent so as not to reveal Party membership or conspiratorial activities and thus subject themselves to criminal prosecution. Indeed, to defy and frustrate an inquiry when one's background was "entirely unexceptionable," was seen by some academic administrators as more unacceptable than if one had some reason for caution:

It is obvious that truthful answers to questions of the committee could not possibly have tended in the slightest respect to incriminate him. . . . It is plain that he deliberately undertook to misuse the constitutional privilege against self-incrimination as a means of evading the duty of giving his testimony.[38]

It was "intellectual arrogance," authorities at Temple University asserted, to believe that one could choose, for whatever reason, not to cooperate.

In about 80 percent of these cases where individuals were balky witnesses, an administrator denied faculty the right to use the Fifth Amendment. In these instances, academic authorities were clearly denying faculty a constitutional right. The often-heard argument that the use of the Fifth Amendment was inimical to the rules of a college or university was in effect saying that the Constitution—which argues the right to believe whatever one wants—itself was inimical to the rules of a college or university.

Evidence

Regardless of how concrete or precisely spelled out charges may have been, administrative authorities generally had little evidence to support them. It would, of course, be difficult to establish such charges as "he was exploiting his connection with the university" or, in another case, "he was not a free agent." These allegations are quite vague. At the same time, however, it would be expected that an academic administrator would be able to point to some specific shortcoming in someone's academic work given the charge that his "day-to-day, extra-curricular activities were infringing on the time necessary for the performance of professional duties." In this particular case this did not happen. Nor did it occur in similar circumstances: regardless of how specific charges were, seldom was evidence produced that had some bearing on them.

The allegations themselves seemed to serve as evidence. Often, academic administrators thought it unnecessary to back up their charges. In a surprisingly large minority of institutions they were not asked or expected to; it was enough that a faculty member stood accused. If someone was said to be acting in a way that led someone else to conclude that he was less than fully competent, this was never openly examined or substantiated by testimony or documents.

Even in the most completely developed and extensive cases, the evidence produced by institutional authorities to support their charges was generally quite thin. The only exception to this was when individuals were in difficulty simply for invoking the Fifth Amendment (in addition to the few instances when there was an admission of Communist Party membership). These, incidentally, were the very situations the American Association of

University Professors throughout the period insisted were by themselves not enough to justify dismissal. Besides, in many of these cases there was no need to prove the charges. Those who took the Fifth Amendment did so publicly and never denied doing so.

Universities were more careful than colleges to collect and provide details, particularly if the principal had a tenure appointment. As the following example illustrates, however, the accumulation of a great deal of factual and circumstantial material did not always add up to a convincing indictment.

New York University

In testifying before the Senate Subcommittee of the Committee on the Judiciary, Edwin Berry Burgum, an associate professor of English at New York University, refused to answer fifteen questions including, "Have you ever been a member of the Communist Party?" Under the circumstances, the charges filed by the dean were not surprising:

> 1. . . . By refusing to tell the truth frankly in response to legitimate questions related to an issue of major concern to the American people which were asked by a duly constituted agency of the United States Senate, he has exercised his legal right to avoid being a witness against himself in a criminal case, but he has violated an obligation of a member of the teaching profession who has the privileges of academic freedom.
> 2. He refused to tell the truth frankly in this connection not, in my considered judgment, because of his stated desire to uphold freedom of speech, but rather because of his fear of testifying to acts which would reveal the truth concerning the relation of himself and others to the Communist Party and subject him to criminal prosecution. Previous evidence which leads to this inference is:
> a. He was reported to be affiliated with from thirty-one to forty communist-front organizations by the Committee on Un-American Activites of the United States House of Representatives.
> b. He has been identified as a member of the Communist Party in testimony given under oath.[39]

Not only did the university have two witnesses testify as to Burgum's membership in the Communist Party, but sixty-two exhibits were introduced to bolster the charges, and to establish that over the past twenty years his "conduct coincided with the path of the Communist Party." One of the witnesses testified that among the material that was required reading for members of the Communist Party was *Science and Society*:

> I would buy my copy and copies for the pro group meetings, as one of my official tasks, at the Marxist bookstore and carry them in my portfolio as one

of the top communist publications. One of the original editors of *Science and Society* was Professor Edwin Berry Burgum. He is still an editor of the magazine.[40]

One piece of evidence was a 1942 State of New York document which in part read:

> Actual organization of the college section was deferred until November 1930 by which time the split in the union had occurred and the rank and file group was in control. Professor Edwin Berry Burgum of New York University was elected chairman of the section.[41]

The report added that other evidence identified Burgum as a member of the Communist Party. There was a photograph of him marching with the communist teachers' union instead of with Norman Thomas's socialists in the 1938 May Day Parade, the year there was a split among the parade's sponsors. There was a photostat of a page from the *Daily Worker* that carried a news article listing him as a member of the May Day Parade Committee.

The list of Burgum's radical activities was expansive:

> He wrote at least 42 articles, book reviews, and other contributions for the *New Masses* between 1934 and 1936.

> He was mentioned at least 51 times, with his picture appearing at least twice, in the *Daily Worker* from 1933 to 1952.

> He urged the support of the Communist Party platform and candidates in the 1933 mayoralty election in New York City.

> He expressed his support for the Soviet Union in 1936 by attending a meeting which greeted the Soviet constitution with enthusiasm.

> He contributed in 1937 and 1938 to *Soviet Russia Today*.

> He defended the Moscow Purge Trials and signed a statement in 1938 saying the defendants were guilty by "sheer weight of evidence."

> He signed a statement in 1939 calling for closer cooperation with the Soviet Union and saying that the Soviet Union works unceasingly for the goal of a peaceful international order.

> He appealed in 1942 for the release of Earl Browder.

> He lectured in the 1940s at the Jefferson School for Social Science.

> He signed an open letter in 1942 in defense of Harry Bridges.

> He opposed in mid-1943 "the current anti-Soviet campaign as a grave disservice to our own country in her hour of peril" and opposed "any delay in the opening of the second front in Europe."

He asked in 1949 for the suspension of the trials of the twelve top indicted communists.

He solicited funds for the Civil Rights Congress which put up $50,000 bail for Gerhardt Eisler and financed the defense of the now convicted twelve top communist leaders.

He asked in 1951 for money to finance cargoes of supplies to send to Communist China.

He spoke at meetings in the fall of 1952 to raise funds to save the Rosenbergs, whose conviction the Supreme Court of the United States has twice refused to reverse and for whom the President of the United States has declined to intervene.

He solicited funds in 1952 for the defense of Elizabeth Gurley Flynn and other now convicted "second-string" communists.[42]

This was largely the evidence used to remove Burgum from New York University. In most other instances evidence was not as detailed.

For the most part, claims of neglect of duty, moral turpitude, incompetence, or other commonly accepted justifications used by institutional authorities to proceed against faculty could be documented in only the most tenuous and unconvincing way. No time and place were cited in an action against the individual referred to earlier who allegedly was instrumental in creating a "campus disturbance" that was "detrimental to instruction." No specifics were given about someone said to have engaged in "conduct unbecoming a teacher [academic turpitude] in his chosen community activities outside the university."

When nothing could be produced to establish that an individual who was said to be a member of the Communist Party was in fact one, it was countered that this was only because he had failed or refused to disclose his membership. Quite simply, he was successfully "hiding the truth." Moreover, this "shifty" behavior was "evidence in itself," and "proved" what administrative authorities knew all along: he was "not a free and honest man." After all, communists "always lied."

The University of Vermont

Evidence introduced to sustain charges, was often only tangential to them. Arguments that were made against Alex Novikoff, a professor of experimental pathology and associate professor of biochemistry at the University of Vermont (see Appendix G, the summary and presentation of evidence in Parts II and III) who had claimed the privilege of the Fifth Amendment before a subcommittee of the Senate Judiciary Committee, illustrate this point well.

To protect himself against what to him seemed to be the committee's inquisitorial methods, Novikoff had refused to answer any questions about his activities prior to his appointment to the university. As a consequence, he was brought before a university board of review—twenty of the twenty-four members were trustees—on the grounds of (1) claiming "privilege under the Fifth Amendment" before a legislative committee, (2) "improperly invok[ing] the Fifth Amendment for the protection of others and not for his own protection," and (3) being guilty of "conduct which justifies his discharge in that he has refused to disclose fully his connection with the Communist Party prior to 1948, if any."[43] After the public hearing,[44] a recommendation was made that Novikoff should be terminated, and the full Board of Trustees concurred.

It was the contention of the Board that "he has failed to display to a sufficient degree in his actions and statements during the past five months, both before the committee of Congress and before the university bodies, the qualities of responsibility, integrity, and frankness that are the fundamental requirements of a faculty member. The actions referred to include, but are not limited to, his invoking of the Fifth Amendment."[45]

These reasons had little bearing on the initial charges. This is made most evident by the fact that in announcing its decision the Board reaffirmed its policy "that the invoking of privilege under the Fifth Amendment is not, in and of itself, cause for dismissal."[46] Apparently, then, the first charge could not have determined the Board's action. The Board next stated that the second charge was not a factor in its decision. No reference is made to the third charge.

The only evidence of lack of responsibility, integrity, or frankness that could be found was in Novikoff's decision on advice of counsel not to testify during an open hearing on campus about events prior to his appointment to the faculty. Against this, however, he did agree to answer all questions in a closed session (off the record). This offer was refused.

In regard to the question of his character, it is worth noting that an earlier trustee-faculty committee (see Part I of Appendix G) had been unanimous in finding Novikoff "a sincere and tireless" research scientist, having a "sense of scientific honesty." It was noted that "his candid attitude, his willingness to testify in all honesty, and to cooperate with the committee, were of the highest level." This original investigating committee uncovered no communist connections or advocacy of communist ideas during his tenure at the University of Vermont. It found instead that he was widely respected, both personally and professionally. Indeed, by a margin of five to one it voted that he be retained on the faculty. Finally, it was concluded in a report published by the American Association of University Professors (written by academics not connected with the University of Vermont who reviewed the dismissal) that "virtually no evidence of any sort bearing on [his] personal fitness was presented at this hearing, and nothing at all concerning any 'unfitness to teach because of incompetence, lack of scholarly objectivity or integrity, serious misuse of the classroom or of academic prestige, gross personal misconduct, or conscious participation in conspiracy against the government,'" (criteria developed by the Association).[47]

The situation at the University of Vermont was in no sense atypical.

Notes

1. Harlan H. Hatcher, "Memorandum to Advisory Committee," read at meeting of the Special Advisory Committee to the President, 7 June 1954.
2. Proceedings of the Special Advisory Committee to the President, 7 June 1954, pp. 12–14.
3. Roy J. Rinehart, correspondence to Horace B. Davis, 10 August 1953. The full charge against Davis and a more detailed discussion of the case can be found in chapter 7.
4. Tenure hearings, University of Washington, pp. 1360–61.
5. "Academic Freedom and Tenure: Report of Committee A for 1947," *AAUP Bulletin* 34, no. 1, (Spring, 1948): 127–28.
6. Hearing before the Executive Committee of the Board of Trustees and the President's Advisory Council, 1 December 1953.
7. Proceedings of the meeting of the Board of Trustees of the University of Kansas City, 4 August 1953, p. 29.
8. "Statement of President Lewis Webster Jones of Rutgers University on the Heimlich-Finley Cases," 4 January 1953.
9. Milton N. Nelson, correspondence to George Pope Shannon, 1 June 1949.
10. "The Cases of Lauer vs. Butterworth and Lauer vs. Phillips: Statement of Professors Densmore, Gose, Hatch, Rowntree, and Thompson."
11. Tenure hearings, University of Washington, p. 1822.
12. Ibid., p. 3496.
13. Raymond B. Allen, memorandum, 20 August 1948.
14. George H. Hand, "Report to the West Virginia Board of Education on Dr. Luella Raab Mundel," 9–10 July 1951.
15. George H. Hand, "A Report on the Fairmont State College Case," p. 10.
16. West Virginia Board of Education, minutes, 9–10 July 1951.
17. West Virginia Board of Education, minutes, 5 September 1951.
18. Hand, "A Report on the Fairmont State College Case," p. 40.
19. Michigan Statutes Annotated, 28.243 (18).
20. Wayne University, "University Procedure under the Trucks Act," 26 January 1954.
21. George Pope Shannon, correspondence to Chester H. Cable, 1 September 1954.
22. University Committee on Rights and Responsibilities, report to President Clarence B. Hilberry, 14 December 1954.
23. Jefferson Medical College, press announcement, 1 December 1953.

24. J. Warren Brock (solicitor for Jefferson Medical College), correspondence to dismissed faculty.
25. Ralph Spitzer, letter, *Chemical and Engineering News*, 31 January 1949.
26. A. L. Strand, address to the academic staff, 23 February 1949, pp. 4–5.
27. Ralph Spitzer, statement on President Strand's charges, 24 February 1949.
28. Strand, address, p. 5.
29. A. L. Strand, open letter, n.d., p. 1.
30. A. L. Strand, statement, in *Oregonian*, 15 February 1949.
31. Strand, address, p. 6.
32. Strand, open letter, p. 2.
33. F. A. Gilfillan, statement, in *Oregon Journal*, 27 March 1949.
34. Russell Sackett, "'Red Scare' Case at Oregon State College Refuses to Lie Dormant," *Oregon Journal*, 27 March 1949.
35. "The Case of Dr. Barrows Dunham," AAUP, 23 September 1953.
36. Lewis Webster Jones, correspondence to Ralph S. Brown, 5 January 1953.
37. Howard L. Bevis, "Hearing of the Case of Byron Thorwell Darling," 4 April 1953, p. 67.
38. "The Case of Dr. Barrows Dunham."
39. Thomas Clark Pollock, correspondence to Henry T. Heald, 24 November 1952.
40. Hearings before the Faculty Committee of New York University, 18 February–6 March 1953.
41. Rapp-Coudert Report, Legislative Document Number 49 (1942).
42. "New York University Statement on the Suspension, Hearing, and Dismissal of Edwin Berry Burgum," 30 April 1953, pp. 7–8.
43. T. M. Adams (Secretary, Board of Review of the University of Vermont and State Agricultural College), correspondence to Alex B. Novikoff, 14 August 1953.
44. "In Re: Dr. Alex Novikoff before Board of Review," University of Vermont and State Agricultural College, 29 August 1953.
45. Carl W. Borgmann, correspondence to Alex B. Novikoff, 5 September 1953.
46. Ibid.
47. "The University of Vermont," *AAUP Bulletin* 44, no. 1, (March 1958): 15–16.

6

Committees

Administrators and the Administration of Committees

As a rule, those whose politics became the object of attention of academic authorities did not suddenly find themselves without jobs. Dismissal, when it occurred, generally followed a protracted course of investigations, hearings, meetings, inquiries, and the like. The fact of the prevalence of these procedures cannot in any way be taken to mean that colleges and universities across the country adopted a collective policy or response with regard to faculty who had become a liability during the Cold War years. Committees are as much the lifeblood of colleges and universities as is freedom of inquiry.

Although the American Association of University Professors and the academic profession had had some success in making due process—which involves having charges "stated in writing in specific terms" and "a fair trial on those charges before a special or permanent judicial committee chosen by the faculty"—standard practice, procedures were invariably set in motion by administrators. In effect, the procedures were a political test, as they compelled principals to discuss their political beliefs. By no means were these procedures initiated by the individuals whose appointments were threatened. In a sense, then, faculty were being put on trial. This chapter could fairly accurately be titled "Administrative Proceedings." (Some materials were gathered on a handful of individuals who chose to resign rather than further defend or embarrass or pain themselves before a committee. This information was so spotty that in the end none was included in the study.)

At close to two-thirds of the institutions, at least one committee was appointed or elected and given the responsibility of looking into the concerns of administrative authorities. The committees were quasi-judicial in nature. Their task did not usually go beyond clarifying questions about political affiliations, activities, ideology, or commitments. They were in most cases advisory bodies; they were empowered only to hear evidence and make recommendations and/or report their findings to institutional authorities for final action.

Some committees had names—the Faculty Committee on Tenure and Academic Freedom, the President's Advisory Council, the Committee on Personnel of the Board of Trustees, the Joint Faculty/Trustee Committee on Review, the Bylaws Committee, the Executive Committee, the Executive Committee of Trustees, the Faculty Advisory Committee—that in a general way described their responsibilities, and were standing committees within the institution. Others—the Special Senate Committee, the Special Trial Committee, the Loyalty Committee, the Advisory Committee on Loyalty, the Faculty-Administration Loyalty Council, the College Loyalty Board, the Board of Review, the Faculty Committee of Review, the Faculty-Trustee Committee—were newly created (appointed by a president, by a dean, by a faculty senate, or by a governing board) to deal with events as they unfolded. Fewer than 10 percent of the committees comprised individuals who were all elected by their constituencies, and in almost all of these instances administrative authorities had the final authority in making committee appointments.

Sometimes a special committee—typically a standing committee—was charged merely with determining if there were grounds for a full, formal investigation. If it recommended that the college or university administration should or could proceed, a larger and more diverse body would convene to hear the case.

All in all, a great many committees with responsibilities ranging from affirming decisions already taken or denouncing principals to intellectualizing about the permanence of the Cold War and its effect on rightist politics busied themselves with these matters. Eighty-six committees from the fifty-eight institutions left some record of their work. The proliferation of committees may have been unprecedented and remarkable even by college and university standards. Sarah Lawrence College's announcement that "no new committee was elected or appointed to deal with issues raised by recent congressional investigations" was quite unusual.

More typical was Wayne University, where, to establish a "policy in respect to loyalty issues," a Special Committee on Rights and Responsibilities proposed and the University Council unanimously adopted "a definite structure, an operational machinery" of two committees—the University Committee on Rights and Responsibilities and the Advisory Committee on Loyalty. The former, consisting of five faculty and two administrators, was appointed by the university president from a panel chosen by the steering committee of the University Council. One of its functions was to provide for a hearing when there were "charges of disloyalty or subversion." The Advisory Committee on Loyalty was to provide "tangible evidence of university intention to cooperate fully with governmental investigative bodies to develop a program of internal self-discipline and just action" in "dealing with issues of loyalty and subversion."[1] The president originally suggested the establishment of this four-member committee of the provost, dean of administration, and two faculty members to "handle certain highly confidential requests and communications . . . from the FBI, some from the police, some from other sources including letters by citizens."[2] It was agreed that the faculty committee members "must be fully acceptable to the president" who would also "participate in their election" since "he holds, as a matter of course, final veto power in [their] selection."

Not only did the Advisory Committee on Loyalty have a charge to "call in" faculty "if discussion is necessary," but it could invite

> any member of the university community to take initiative, to come in for consultation, if in the individual's judgment the need exists. For example, a person may feel that his past associations, utterances or writings may be brought into question, that it will be to his best interests to take the committee into his confidence. If he elects to do this, he will then assist the group in finding relevant facts. Once the committee is assured of the person's innocence, it will be in a position to defend him against irresponsible charges. If, on the contrary, the evidence available permits no such assurance, the case would be referred to the president.[3]

It was thought that "the effect of such a committee on campus morale could be considerable," although the direction of this effect was not predicted or examined.

It was widely believed that all committees served to safeguard the integrity of the academic community and uphold the law of the land. More committee members than not expressed the view that, in itself, Communist Party membership was grounds for dismissal, irrespective of behavior in the classroom, relationships with students or colleagues, or conduct as a citizen. The task of all Americans was to combat communism.

Committees varied in size and composition. The two smallest were made up of a college president and one of his associates, and of two members of a governing board, and the largest had thirty-nine members. Some committees consisted of only faculty or only administrators or only members of the governing board. Most had representatives from at least two of these constituencies. When there was a mix, faculty were often not well represented, or in a distinct minority. At one college where three ostensibly independent committees were charged serially with ferreting out possible communist associations within the faculty, the first consisted of five members of the Board of Trustees, the second was simply the full thirteen-member Board, and the third was the Board and seven members of the Faculty Council. At a handful of institutions, faculty were completely excluded not only from selecting but from serving on committees. All in all, the principles of faculty self-government and shared responsibility were not controlling in the empanelment of committees.

The president or chairman of the governing board presided over nearly one-fourth of the tribunals. Only a minority of committees seemed suited to secure independent faculty judgments—for example, where the structure was such that faculty were free from the constraints of being in a minority to deans, members of governing boards, vice-presidents, and the like.

Only occasionally did a committee complete its business in a single session. When this occurred, the committee was almost always one whose membership was limited to trustees or regents who were taking final action on a dismissal. Sometimes, hearings seemed without end. In thirty-three sessions, one committee called seventy-three witnesses and produced over three thousand pages of testimony. Most transcripts were more spare, the majority running between one and two hundred pages. The median number of hours committees met to consider a case was forty.

Approximately half of the time, the campus president had the sole responsibility of choosing committee members. The selection was often done in consultation with some individuals from the governing board, and less often in consultation with any faculty. Even when it appeared that faculty were adequately represented on a committee, the campus president often conspicuously dominated the proceedings. Not only did he many times select all of the faculty who sat on a committee, but he could also determine the rules under which it operated. His questions and general attitude could set the tone or climate of an inquiry. On both college and university campuses, he, more than all others combined, defined the situation. At the University of Washington, the president helped to draw up the charges, was an unfriendly witness, cross-examined defense witnesses, and made procedural rulings.

The unedited transcript of the first session in what the president characterized as "a fair hearing" at Ohio State University in Appendix H perfectly exemplifies these points. Since the three faculty (a professor of business organization, a professor of animal science, and an emeritus dean) among the seven observers who were present for this session were completely silent, there is no way of determining what their opinions were on either specific or general questions. Throughout this entire administrative hearing only one member of the committee other than the president asked any questions of the individual facing dismissal or of his counsel or of any witness who appeared before it. The determination by the president in the initial skirmish that the principal be given no more than a forty-eight-hour continuance, in spite of the fact that he still had not found an attorney to represent him and that there was no obvious urgency to proceed since he had already been suspended, testifies to administrative control over the shape of the Cold War on campus. The principal, Byron T. Darling, had been slow in writing to the university president asking for additional time to prepare his case:

Dear Dr. Bevis:

This is a request for a postponement of the hearing which you have tendered me and which is scheduled for tomorrow. For this request I submit the following reasons:

At meetings held yesterday by both the Conference Committee and the Association of American University Professors [sic] I was urged by resolution of those bodies to obtain someone to represent me at the hearing. This recommendation was apparently occasioned by the belief that it is a requisite of a proper hearing that I have assistance in preparing a statement of my position. It was further occasioned by its opinion that it is a matter of great importance to the faculty that the hearing be in every way as useful as possible. This resolution also tendered the services of its Conference Committee in providing me with representation. I enclose a copy of this resolution for your information.

I had not previously intended to ask anyone to represent me, but I now feel it desirable to follow the recommendation of these faculty groups. It is apparent, however, that any person who is willing to act for me in this way will need more than these few hours to familiarize himself with my situation and to organize his materials.

Moreover, I am sure you will appreciate that the strain of these past three weeks has been very great. It has made my own preparation far more difficult than I could have realized. I can therefore assure you that with a further week in which to procure a representative, to inform him, to enable him to formulate his position, and to gain for myself some greater composure, I shall be able to make a more complete and more helpful contribution to your understanding of my position and to the usefulness of the hearing.[4]

The president chose not only not to take seriously the needs of Darling but the advice of a faculty organization that supported his request for administrative flexibility.

Whether a case resulted in dismissal was obviously less closely related to the number of committees or subcommittes involved in reviewing materials or making recommendations, or even, ultimately, to their composition, than to administrative attitudes and procedures before and during the course of a hearing. Committee transcripts make it apparent that when a college or university administration selected the members of a committee without any faculty counsel, it was not always careful in naming enough individuals who truly understood the faculty point of view or who seemed willing to exercise much independence during the proceedings.

Sometimes there was not even the semblance or claim that the proceedings would be thoughtful, thorough, or fair. At more than one hearing no concrete suspicions were openly voiced, no testimony was given, no accusations were made, no misdeeds were described, and no evidence was put forth. At one institution, an assistant attorney general for the state conducted the hearing before the Board of Trustees while acting as counsel to the administration. The charges were never specified, key witnesses were not required to testify, there was no judgment on the evidence, there were no findings, representatives from the American Association of University Professors were excluded as observers while a lieutenant of the state police was permitted to attend, and in the end no reasons were given for the inevitable dismissal. It was clear from this situation, and others, that it was easier to predict a case's outcome from how vigorously it was prosecuted than from how thoroughly it was investigated. To be sure, only a handful of proceedings were Kafkaesque. In nearly one-sixth of the hearings the defense was intransigent in its refusal to cooperate. Often, there was no way of determining on which side, if any, the responsibility for an impasse could be placed.

The fact that individuals were granted hearings did not guarantee that they would be equitably treated. Even the existence of adequate procedures to assure due process did not mean that rights were automatically protected. It was not unusual for the president of an institution to sit with a committee, even when he was not officially a member. In many instances when a senior administrator, usually a president, took an active part in the proceedings, it would not be unfair to characterize his role as that of prosecutor, jury, and, in the end, judge. Sometimes a college or university administration was served by a counsel who vigorously played the role of a determined prosecuting attorney, conducting the proceedings as if they were a criminal trial. The sense of informality of some hearings may have falsely convinced principals that they were not actual defendants, that the purpose of a session was merely didactic, but in a number of instances this impression must have been short-lived given the unforseen and staggering speed with which many lost their jobs.

At approximately one-third of the institutions, more than one committee had the responsibility of hearing a case. The second (or even third) committee was generally set up to review the work and findings of the original tribunal and to make its own recommendations to the full governing board. It often consisted totally or mostly of members of the governing board, and seldom went over ground not considered by the initial investigating committee. As will become evident later in the chapter, even with no new information it was not unusual for its members to reach conclusions completely at variance with those of its predecessors, particularly if the first contained mostly faculty and the second did not.

Almost one-third of the time when a faculty committee found no basis for dismissal, the administration or governing board rejected this conclusion. The data show that this was more likely to happen at large public universities, for example, the University of California, the University of Michigan, Rutgers University, the University of Vermont, the University of Washington, than at smaller colleges. As material presented later in this chapter makes obvious, faculty committees often could do little to shield their colleagues against an administrator or governing board determined that dismissal was the only possible outcome. If there was a minority report, administrators or governing board members who publicly defended overriding a faculty committee's recommendation would find some point in it to justify the action. Belonging to the Communist Party, a minority of a faculty committee at the University of Washington concluded, is "reckless, uncritical, and intemperate," and "sufficient grounds for dismissal."[5] The large majority of the governing board concurred.

In a sense, the committee was the backdrop for all but a few of the 126 cases. Most of what could be understood about them was gotten from committee records. A case generally took its form before a committee, although, of course, neither this form nor whatever evidence came to light was necessarily a very important determinant of its resolution. It was before a committee that much of what became known about a principal's beliefs and activities was learned. It was to committees that administrators looked for advice or affirmation. There was a convergence of people and facts before committees.

Obviously, no two committees—not even two on a single campus—functioned in the exact same way. Given the diversity in the structure and procedures of committees, any generalizations about them must be somewhat inaccurate. Nonetheless, a number of the features in the following example are fairly typical of how a case developed and was formed, how it moved through a committee, and how in this setting the Cold War on campus took shape. This case usefully puts in concrete terms some of the abstractions discussed in the above paragraphs and in the remainder of the chapter. The one outstanding difference between this incident and most others was that it did not end in a dismissal, loss of tenure, or some other punishment.

Illinois Institute of Technology: The Matchett Case

Gerald J. Matchett, a professor of economics at Illinois Institute of Technology (I.I.T.), was one of forty-five former government employees named as Communist Party members by Herbert Fuchs in testimony before the House Committee on Un-American Activities. Matchett was said to be associated with six other Party members while working in the regional office of the War Labor Board in Denver during World War II.

When Matchett was called to appear before the congressional committee, he would only say that he was not presently a member of the Communist Party; he failed to respond to a series of questions "on the grounds that any answer may tend to incriminate me." When asked "were you [a communist] yesterday?" Matchett replied, "I refuse to answer, relying on the Fifth Amendment." The question, "were you this morning?" brought the same response.[6] Matchett only gave the committee his name, present occupation, educational history, and facts about his military service. He would not tell the congressmen whether he had worked for the government, whether he had resided in Denver, whether he recognized his signature on a government form, or what subjects he taught, and his recalcitrance brought the threat of a contempt citation.

The following day, the president of I.I.T., John T. Rettaliata, suspended Matchett "because of your refusal to answer questions . . . regarding your association with the Communist Party . . . pending review by appropriate institute bodies."[7] At the time, President Rettaliata said that the school "does not assume Matchett is a communist, and I do not believe he is," but "the institute does not condone refusal of its professors to answer questions by claiming protection of the Fifth Amendment." It is important to note that an assumption of innocence on the part of academic authorities always loomed large, as it lent support to a balanced and sober inquiry in which equal weight was given to information that could clear as well as condemn a principal.

President Rettaliata described the situation to members of the Executive Committee of I.I.T. as "important and serious":

> Not only has the institution been embarrassed already, but we can probably expect more unfavorable publicity regardless of the ultimate disposition of the case. More and more people are getting into the act. . . .[8]

As formally specified, the charge against Matchett was that his behavior

> before the House Un-American Activities Committee is in conflict with the following pertinent paragraph of a statement on "The Rights and Respon-

sibilities of Universities and Their Faculties" adopted by the Association of American Universities in March, 1953:

> As in all acts of association, the professor accepts conventions which become morally binding. Above all, he owes his colleagues in the university complete candor and perfect integrity, precluding any kind of clandestine or conspiratorial activities. He owes equal candor to the public. If he is called upon to answer for his convictions it is his duty as a citizen to speak out. It is even more definitely his duty as a professor. Refusal to do so, on whatever legal grounds, cannot fail to reflect upon a profession that claims itself the fullest freedom to speak and the maximum protection of that freedom available in our society. In this respect, invocation of the Fifth Amendment places upon a professor a heavy burden of proof of his fitness to hold a teaching position and lays upon his university an obligation to reexamine his qualifications for membership in its society.[9]

(As noted in the last chapter, this was the criterion applied at Rensselaer Polytechnic Institute.)

Prior to a hearing, I.I.T. attempted to unearth Matchett's true political colors. Within three weeks the administration had the results of a confidential security check it had requested on him. The investigators apparently did not see a need to look beyond Fuchs' charge, which they affirmed. As a consequence, no new information was uncovered.

> Type of Report: Special
> Date of Report: 1-5-56
> Security Files: See Below
> Police Records: Not Checked

> The name of this subject first appeared in our security files in December of 1955 as a result of his being named under oath as a member of the Communist Party during hearings held in Chicago by the House Un-American Activities Committee. . . .

> We find that Gerald J. Matchett and his wife Margaret Ellen Matchett apparently came to the Chicago area in 1947 coming from Denver. We find them listed as residing at 1551 E. 65th Street with the telephone number of Midway 3-1593 in 1947 and through 1951. In 1952 through the present date, we find them listed as residing at 5536 S. Kimbark with the same telephone number of Midway 3-1593.

> As you will note from the attached photostats, Gerald J. Matchett was named under oath as a member of the Communist Party in hearings held by the House Committee on Un-American Activities in Chicago on December 14, 1955. On the following day or on December 15, 1955, Gerald J. Matchett and his wife Margaret Ellen Matchett appeared as witnesses before the committee. Both refused to deny membership in the Communist Party.

> SUMMARY AND CONCLUSIONS: It is assumed that these people either are or have been members of the Communist Party.

This concludes our report as of this date.[10]

Authorities from other institutions were contacted for advice, but this effort also did not provide much to give I.I.T.'s inquiry direction. President Jones from Rutgers could not give "any pointers":

Dear President Rettaliata:

Thank you for your letter of January 23. As far as I know, there is no one who has any wisdom about these Fifth Amendment investigations. They are extremely difficult questions, as you well know. I have nothing to add to my statement of January 24, 1953.

I wish you well.
Sincerely,[11]

Others made more of an effort to be helpful, but in the end I.I.T. was left to develop its own guidelines.

Seven faculty members, all full professors, were selected to review the Matchett case. Five were designated by the Faculty Council and two were named by the campus chapter of the American Association of University Professors. The president had the ultimate authority over the appointments of committee members.

Dear Professor:

The chairman of the Faculty Council has informed me that you have been designated by the Council as a regular member of a seven-man Committee of Inquiry to consider the situation which has developed regarding Professor Matchett.

It is my understanding that you are willing to serve in such a capacity. I, therefore, appoint you a regular member of the committee.

For your guidance, I enclose a statement of the procedure applying to this consideration, including the hearing of Professor Matchett.[12]

The committee's charge was layed out by the president. It was given the responsibility of hearing testimony from Matchett and others "in his behalf or by the institute administration, and such other persons as the committee deems desirable." It was to evaluate the "facts, testimony, and evidence" and prepare a report and recommendation for final action by the Board of Trustees. Matchett was free to attend all sessions where evidence was being taken, was given the right to counsel, and was to have access to the complete verbatim transcript. The president set the opening day for the trial to begin, and the committee was given fifteen days after all of the testimony was received to file its recommendation.[13]

In setting down explicit procedures and guidelines, the committee decided that it would work within standards promulgated by the American Association of University Professors rather than those of the Association of American Universities, which represents the views of academic administrators.

After consideration of several positions, the following was adopted by the committee:

> A scholar dedicated to the pursuit of truth owes his colleagues and the public a level of conduct involving complete integrity, precluding clandestine or conspiratorial activities having any objective that could be allegedly harmful to his colleagues, his fellow countrymen or his country by other than democratic methods provided in the Constitution. He therefore has an obligation to cooperate with governmental authorities seeking relevant information on subjects within the scope of their power of inquiry. A professor's refusal to testify fully before a legislative committee is likely to cause an adverse reaction among his colleagues and particularly with the public, and this is a source of possible embarrassment to himself and the institution with which he is associated. A professor called upon to testify before a legislative committee should make every effort to show that his conduct justifies the position of responsibility that he enjoys, and he should therefore weigh carefully the likely implications and consequences of a refusal to testify.

> Refusal to answer proper questions of legislative committees and invocation of the Fifth Amendment justify an inquiry by a properly constituted college or university authority to determine the fitness of the professor to continue in a position of moral trust. The inquiry is justified not because claim of the Fifth Amendment or other constitutional privilege is itself immoral or automatically warrants the inference that he has committed an immoral or disqualifying act, but because the use of this privilege raises an unresolved question. Such claims and refusals to testify have been and can be used to conceal misconduct of a nature that disqualifies the witness for the position he holds. The college or university, in seeking to confirm its own integrity must seek an answer to the unresolved question regarding the qualification of a faculty member.

> This hearing is an opportunity for Professor Matchett to explain his conduct. To allow him maximum freedom in developing his position, Mr. Matchett will have the opportunity, with the help of such counsel as he may desire, to:

> a. Make a statement related to the situation, at the beginning of the hearing, and at any time he may have the floor,
> b. Answer all questions as he fully desires,
> c. Challenge any question as inadmissible because it violates his rights or is irrelevant to the situation.

> The hearing will be conducted with the following procedure as a guide. Additions and amendments may be necessary during the course of the hearing.

> 1. (a) Mr. Matchett will present the statement of his position.
>   (b) Mr. Larkin [the dean] will present his statement of the administra-

tion's position.

(c) Questions will be asked of Mr. Matchett by committee members and alternates in rotation.

(d) Questions will be asked of Mr. Matchett by Mr. Larkin.

(e) Other witnesses may be introduced at the request of Mr. Matchett, Mr. Larkin, or the committee, and questioned in a similar manner.

(f) Committee members will have a final opportunity to question Mr. Matchett and Mr. Larkin.

2. In admitting a witness who is not a principal in this inquiry, the chairman will first ask his name, occupation, employer and place of employment, and his position. Such a witness presented by any one of the three interests at the hearing (faculty committee, administration representative, Mr. Matchett) may be questioned by the other two directly following his statement. He will then be asked to retire from the room, although he should if possible be available for recall before the end of the hearing.

3. A recess may be requested at any time by any member of the committee, including the chairman. The member requesting the recess must state its purpose.[14]

Matchett's statement to the committee was candid, personal (starting from his childhood), and lengthy (covering twenty typewritten pages). He was emphatic in denying the charge made against him to the House Committee on Un-American Activities, and took pains to explain why he invoked the Fifth Amendment:

My appearance before the House Committee, and the position I took before it, stems from my activities and associations in Denver, Colorado during a 15-month period in the years 1943 and 1944. I wish to present fully to you the facts as I recall them of my Denver experience, and to explain why I invoked the Fifth Amendment in spite of the fact that neither my wife nor I have ever been members of the Communist Party. . . .

Mr. Fuchs is mistaken. Neither of us [my wife or I] is now or ever has been a member of the Communist Party. . . .

Confronted with Mr. Fuchs's bare and unsupported assertion I can answer only with a counter-assertion: I have never been a communist. . . .

Under the law I had two choices: to answer fully whatever questions were asked by the committee, or to invoke the Fifth Amendment as to certain questions. Several considerations influenced my final decision.

First, despite the fact that I was never a member of the Communist Party I believed that under the circumstances I was in danger of prosecution for violation of the Smith Act. Let me explain why. Mr. Fuchs had testified under oath that I was a member of a communist cell in Denver, and presumably he would be ready so to testify in court proceedings. As I have indicated, I was acquainted with some of the persons Mr. Fuchs had named as communists. If I had testified as to my acquaintance with these people my own testimony, together with that of Mr. Fuchs, might be regarded by a court or jury as sufficient evidence to convict me of violation of the Smith Act even though I was entirely innocent of membership in the Communist Party or, indeed, of any illegal activity.

I believed, moreover, that in the face of Mr. Fuchs's testimony my own statement that I had never been a communist might not be accepted by the House Committee. Having expressed confidence in Mr. Fuchs's story, the committee might well bring charges of perjury against anyone who contradicted some element of it. I do not know how I could find any positive evidence to refute the charge that I had been a communist, any more that I know what evidence would support it.

The prospect of being indicted either for violation of the Smith Act or for perjury was an unhappy one at best. Certain personal considerations reinforced my unwillingness to face such hazards. I have two small children, a son barely six and a baby daughter. They need above all, now and in the years immediately ahead, the care and attention of their parents. My wife, as well as I, was involved in the whole matter, and if I became more deeply involved in legal proceedings so might she be. The weeks before we appeared before the House committee were a time of great strain and tension, difficult for our children as well as ourselves. I was deeply conscious that any decision I made was a decision for my family as well as myself. . . .

In summary, testifying fully before the House committee would have subjected me to the hazards of a charge of violation of the Smith Act or of perjury. In spite of my innocence, neither risk was remote or unreal. Testifying fully, moreover, unquestionably would have required me to injure others, and the circumstances made this act appear to me to be unprincipled.

I was far from being unmindful of the adverse effects of an invocation of the Fifth Amendment, both as to myself and as to Illinois Tech. But I saw no clear way of achieving a favorable outcome for anyone concerned. Whatever I did, however I handled the situation, adverse publicity would probably result, damaging alike to myself, to my family, and to Illinois Tech. This was a crisis that was forced upon me. If I was the prey to conflicting emotions and considerations, it was because they were inherent in the circumstances.

I reviewed my situation in detail with my attorneys, Richard J. Stevens and Irving Askow, and invoked the Fifth Amendment on their advice. Mr. Stevens and Mr. Askow are members of the Chicago bar in excellent standing. Their services were secured for my wife and myself through my wife's father, a prominent attorney in Indianapolis. . . .[15]

After intensive and complete questioning, the committee found no grounds that "would warrant any punitive action" and recommended Matchett's immediate reinstatement.[16] After examining his written work and teaching as well as his record as an administrator to determine the character of his economic beliefs, it was convinced that he was not concealing any misconduct and that he was not shielding others. His actions did not appear to be dominated by communist ideology. There was no evidence that he had ever engaged in "clandestine, conspiratorial, or other questionable activities." The committee judged him to be fully fit to keep his position. In fact, it found his economic philosophy to be conservative: "It is not in any way tainted with Marxist or communist ideas." The committee also remarked that he had been completely cooperative and had answered "all of our questions."[17]

In light of what it observed, the committee unanimously concluded that there was "no case."[18] Matchett was not guilty of any misconduct.

A number of documents make it clear that members of the Board of Trustees of I.I.T. were no less politically conservative and were not any less likely to see faculty simply as their employees than individuals on other boards, and were just as likely to express their views on political and social issues. One wrote to President Rettaliata in early March:

> Dear Jack:
>
> Over the weekend, I went over the material which you sent me regarding the Fifth Amendment case that happened at Harvard. I am rather surprised at the statement made by President Conant on page 360, which reads as follows:
>
> "Outside of his classroom a professor speaks and acts as a private citizen. What his views may be or how wisely or foolishly he speaks is no concern of the university administration, provided he is not acting illegally. . . ."
>
> In industry, we feel that the conduct of an employee detrimental to the welfare of a company, even when it occurs outside of business hours, is very much our concern and I would think the same ought to be the position of any employer, even that of Harvard University.
>
> On the whole, Harvard certainly went out of its way to find reasons why they should not discipline those of their staff who resorted to the protection of the Fifth Amendment.
>
> Thanks for sending me the material.
> Most sincerely,[19]

Nonetheless, in early April the Board upheld the Committee of Inquiry's decision and reinstated Matchett without prejudice. In the announcement and in the president's letter to Matchett there was an expression of "displeasure" at the invocation of the Fifth Amendment: "The Board considers inappropriate the use of the Fifth Amendment by a member of a profession devoted to the pursuit of truth. Such action casts suspicion on the individual, his institution and his profession."[20] With this gesture to the public, the matter was closed.

The Special Problems of Junior Faculty

Committees were generally more supportive of senior faculty than of junior faculty. At one university a committee of faculty and administrators, none of whom knew much about a new faculty member who had taken the Fifth Amendment before the House Committee on Un-American Activities, recommended that he be relieved of all academic duties, even before he had taught his first class. The committee simply concluded that it did "not possess sufficient confidence in . . . as a colleague and teacher to justify its continued recommendation of him for appointment."

Sometimes committees (or a faculty senate) chose not to take action on or review an appeal from an untenured faculty member. As is clear from Appendix I, the problems of junior faculty were sometimes given short shrift by senior colleagues. In the face of a lack of support by other faculty members, a principal's situation was essentially hopeless.

The University of Southern California

At the University of Southern California, Andries Deinum, an instructor of cinema who had been immediately suspended after being called before a subcommittee of the House Committee on Un-American Activities, wrote to the faculty senate requesting a hearing. Deinum had openly shared his views with the congressmen and had answered all questions except those asking him to name and implicate others. The week following his appearance, he had fully explained his refusal to name names in a letter to the university president.

> I would like it to be understood that while my refusal to name names in front of the committee had, out of necessity, to be couched in legal terms, the basic reason was a *moral* and *ethical* one. It was a question of conscience. I could not bring upon people who were to my knowledge innocent of any subversive intent the mental suffering that has befallen me.
>
> I was willing and I am still willing to answer questions freely about anything except names, and I would like to make clear now why I must draw the line there. I told the committee under oath, and I will tell you now, that in the four years that I was a member of the Communist Party I never observed anyone engaged in any criminal, subversive, or illegal act. I belonged to a cultural study group. We discussed books and articles, largely in the fields of aesthetics and the social history of literature, art, and film. There was little talk of politics. We were innocent of any wrongdoing.[21]

A month later Deinum was informed by the chairman of the university senate that he would not be given a hearing. When he made the fact of this denial public in a letter to the student newspaper, the full senate reversed its executive committee, and a special committee was appointed to review the matter. Its report, two months later, concluded that the policy "requiring all persons to testify fully before duly constituted governmental bodies

under penalty of suspension from the university" was known by inference
to the petitioner and that by his suspension and nonreappointment Deinum "was not deprived of his teaching position without cause. The question of tenure was not involved."[22] It was clear that he had to "answer all
questions." This was in accordance with the university president's view that
the use of the Fifth Amendment was an indication "that he was not, in the
fullest sense, a good American citizen."

> Indeed, there is considerable evidence, corroborated by Mr. Deinum to indi-
> cate that Mr. Raubenheimer [the vice president for educational affairs] coun-
> seled with Mr. Deinum on several occasions as though Mr. Deinum were his
> son, treated him warmly, spoke Dutch with him, and virtually pleaded with
> him to make a clean breast of things for the good of the university and for his
> own good so that he might be continued on the faculty. The committee finds
> many indications of the administration's interest in "saving" Mr. Deinum
> because of his recognized competence as a teacher.[23]

Acknowledging that "from the vantage point of hindsight," it would have
been best if "a frank, explicit, written statement of the specific university
policy" had been sent, and that "it would have been better procedure for
the administration to have called Mr. Deinum in for a final hearing before
sanctions were imposed,"[24] the board was satisfied that he had been
granted full due process. After all, when "he left the stand in his appearance
. . . he went to the telephone and called his department chairman . . . and
said 'I have just finished testifying. What happens next? Have you heard
anything?' Apparently Mr. Deinum was acutely aware of the probability of
some impending disciplinary action by the university as a result of his
refusal to testify fully."

> Finally, the special committee finds that, even assuming, without the com-
> mittee's admitting, that Mr. Deinum could not and did not infer the exact or
> approximate nature of the administration's policy with respect to his possible
> suspension in the event that he refused to answer all questions of the House
> committee, he knowingly *assumed the risk* of whatever policy the admin-
> istration did have.[25]

In light of what it took as the essential facts, the special committee recommended "that no further action be taken by the university senate."[26]

The University of Colorado

At the University of Colorado, statements were made by administrators
that the contract of an instructor of philosophy, Morris Judd, would not be
renewed because of incompetence, failure to make satisfactory progress

toward his doctorate, a lack of intellectual honesty, and noncooperation. The chairman of the Department of Philosophy was told by the administration that some students had complained that Judd's teaching was dull, and that his refusal to answer questions regarding past political affiliations raised questions about his character. The Board of Regents had made the decision to terminate Judd after the time when other reappointments had been made.

Judd had refused to respond to questions of two former FBI agents conducting an investigation of communist activities on campus on the grounds that this was a political test, a violation of academic principles, and an invasion of constitutional rights. In conversations with the university president and vice president he was asked political questions to which he objected, claiming a commitment to certain moral convictions that prevented him from submitting to pressures that he as a faculty member considered oppressive and degrading. He had assured President Stearns, however, that he was not presently a member of the Communist Party. He declined to answer further inquiries about his past affiliations with political organizations.

Less than a year earlier, Judd had been recommended for retention by his colleagues, although the department had been forced to cut its staff due to declining enrollments. When his departmental colleagues learned that he had been given a terminal appointment they protested to President Stearns. The fact that the president had taken the action without consultation was what galled them most.

Judd appealed the administration's decision to the Senate Committee on Privilege and Tenure. He contended that his rights as a faculty member had been violated, and the department added that its autonomy had been abridged. The committee agreed to review the situation.

Not surprisingly the Department of Philosophy determinedly supported Judd's complaint. His colleagues believed that the "case is, in fact, a case involving academic freedom."[27] The administration at first declined to appear before the committee since, it contended, Judd had not been dismissed. His contract had simply not been renewed. Moreover, it noted, the question of tenure was not involved. The administration, under the signature of the president and vice president, appealed to the full senate:

> If the Committee of Privilege and Tenure proposes to assume jurisdiction and hear cases where a short-term appointment is not renewed, it is in effect proposing to make difficult the legitimate and necessary changes of staff during the probationary period.[28]

The full senate decided that the committee should hear the case.

The president refused to tell the committee what the reasons were for the nonreappointment:

President: In answer to that question, Mr. Judd—in the first place, I don't recall it; and in the second place, that might be regarded as attempting to compel me to make statements, specific reasons which I have sedulously tried not to do.
Judd: Do you have any evidence that I was non-cooperative with the administrative authority, Mr. Stearns?
President: I'm afraid I'm going to have to decline to answer that, because to do so would be to specify particular grounds.
Judd: In other words, Mr. Stearns, any questions which I might ask you concerning anything specific about the implication, would be considered by you to be irrelevant?
President: I would conceive that it is not the obligation of the administrative officers specifically to give reasons for the actions which they find it necessary to take, and I don't feel that it is incumbent upon them to be placed in a position where they are required to give specific reasons under these circumstances.[29]

....

Professor Garnsey: No, my question was, what were the reasons for the decision not to reappoint?
President: Again, I'm going to have to decline.
Professor Garnsey: Was the decision not to reappoint related to information submitted to you by the investigators?
President: Again, I'll have to decline.
Professor Garnsey: Was the decision related to your conversation with Mr. Judd and his refusal to answer questions concerning political affiliations?
President: Again, I'll have to decline.
Professor Garnsey: Were the reasons by which you arrived at your decision in any way different from the reasons included in the statement of Mr. Machle and Dean Van Ek?
President: Again I'm going to decline, Mr. Garnsey, because you are attempting to make me specify particular charges which I said at the outset I would prefer not to do.[30]

Since this was not a congressional inquiry, it was not necessary for the president, when questioned here, to invoke the Fifth Amendment, and the majority of the committee held that the administration was not obligated to reveal any more than it chose to. The committee then concluded that without formal charges the unofficial explanations first bruited about were merely hearsay.

Not only did the committee decline to consider circumstantial evidence, but the view was expressed that there was nothing to show that Judd's nonreappointment was not properly motivated and carried out. Just because there were "anonymous accusers" and the instructor had been subjected to questioning on political matters by the president did not mean, the committee reasoned, these had anything to do with his being terminated. It was concluded by a vote of four to two that "Judd's privilege of academic freedom was not violated." Nothing in the five-point conclusion was conceded to Judd:

> The majority of the committee is of the opinion that before the consideration of any evidence upon the question at issue, the administration is aided by the presumption that in the making of decisions on matters of reappointment and in the performance of its administrative duties and functions, the administration acts, and acted in this instance, legally, fairly, and honestly, and with due regard to the individual's right of academic freedom, a right recognized by the administration and understood by it; and that such presumption is a strong one which can and ought to be dispelled only by evidence to the contrary of a clear and convincing character. In the case of anyone disputing the legality, fairness, or honesty of an administrative action on a matter in which the administration has jurisdiction to act, the burden is clearly upon the proponent of such assertion to establish the same by satisfactory evidence of sufficient weight to reasonably convince the minds of the triers of fact— and without such weight the claim must fail.[31]

The minority of the committee who dissented believed that the weight of the evidence—some of which the majority had rejected for technical reasons—in fact provided ample "proof of a violation of academic freedom":

1. Mr. Judd was singled out for questioning about political affiliations, and there is a causal nexus between this interrogation and the non-renewal of his contract;
2. When the Board of Regents discussed, in quite unusual fashion, the non-renewal of an instructor's contract, Regent Austin made it clear that Mr. Judd had been the object of accusations concerned with matters outside his professional record as a teacher;
3. The decision not to renew Mr. Judd's contract was made by the president's office without concurrence of the department concerned;
4. The reasons which the president offered for his decision have frequently changed; no explanation has been given for such a change in motivation.[32]

When the matter finally came before the university senate, it agreed that Judd had been given a "full and fair opportunity" to present his case; by a decisive majority[33] it voted to adopt the committee's decision.

The Work of Committees

For the most part, members of faculty-dominated committees rarely even raised the possibility of outright dismissal. A smaller proportion of faculty than administrators shared or were willing to act on the widely held assumption that communists—actual or suspected—fell outside the pale of legitimate politics; that because they were a direct and immediate threat to American democracy, their political rights could be abridged.

Although faculty who sat on committees were generally sympathetic to colleagues whose careers were in jeopardy, they could be openly hostile to a defendant if they were convinced that they were being intentionally deceived. In the New York University case touched upon in the last chapter, and which will be examined in greater detail in the following one, a majority on a faculty committee, believing that the defendant, Edwin Berry Burgum, had been disingenuous, sustained the administration's charge that he had refused "to tell the truth frankly" to a congressional committee because his testimony "would reveal the truth concerning the relation of himself and others to the Communist Party and subject him to criminal prosecution."[34] In a few other instances, the support of some faculty on committees for principals who were defending themselves against both civil and institutional authorities, for example, those who stood under the threat of contempt of Congress and who as a consequence were in the glare of much unfavorable publicity, seemed to waver.

Without exception, the greater the proportion of faculty on a committee, the more likely it was to recommend against dismissal. In fact, with three exceptions, the only time faculty-dominated committees did not show considerable solicitude for principals was when the latter did not recognize their authority, did not appear to be forthright, and/or refused to cooperate. Principals who were defiant before a committee greatly increased the probability that they would be dismissed. (This question is examined in detail in chapter 7.)

In light of the general pattern of sympathy for principals by faculty-dominated committees, it is fair to conclude that faculty were not in the vanguard of any movement to rid campuses of colleagues labeled as communists, procommunists, former communists, communist sympathizers, and the like. This said, it is important to recognize that faculty on the committees accepted without question the assumptions that investigations into the politics of colleagues were necessary and that principals had an obligation to account to institutional authorities for their political beliefs and activities. Few questioned the premise that principals could and should be asked about their political views and associations. There was near consensus that the political climate in America made it imperative that faculty provide administrative authorities with sufficient information "to allow them to safeguard the welfare of the institutions in their charge." A committee inquiry was a setting where the question of a principal's loyalty could be put to rest: Was he under the sway of communist ideology? Could he be depended on to behave with professional integrity?

Although many questions were personal and perhaps beyond the proper scope of inquiry, almost everyone on campus believed that all questions should be answered. As a consequence, principals were quizzed about family, friendships, and leisure activities. They were expected to explain and justify their values, beliefs, and attitudes. Their work history was probed. They were cross-examined about their political—foreign and domestic—and religious views. They were not asked very much about teaching and research. Any question—no matter how hypothetical—that might shed some light on the depth of someone's commitment to communism or loyalty to the Communist Party was considered appropriate. Committees seemed equally concerned with matters of morality and ideological purity. In fact, as this sampling of items from hearings at the University of Buffalo makes plain, there was no limit to what committees were interested in learning:

> Do you know of an example in this country where the "ruling class" has done this [resorted to the use of violence to thwart the will of the majority]?

> Do you think the word democracy is used in the same sense [when the Party pledge requires a member to work "actively for the preservation and extension of democracy and peace"] in which it is used in connection with the principles of our form of government?

> Do you still think that socialism on a world scale is necessary to avoid war? By "on a world scale" do you mean some sort of world-wide socialist government?

> Did members-at-large of the Party have to pay dues? If so, how were they expected to pay them?

> Is it part of the Communist Party pledge or discipline to refuse to divulge the names of other members of the Party?

> You stated that on one occasion you went into a book shop in Buffalo which sold Communist Party literature, and somebody spoke to you about joining or rejoining the Party. Is such literature still being sold? Do you think there is considerable demand for it locally? Did you buy or receive communist literature on the visit you mentioned? Have you bought communist literature there on other occasions? How recently?[35]

Appendix J, which consists of the first fifty pages of the transcript from a single session of fairly extensive hearings by the committee at the University of Buffalo, perfectly shows the range of issues scoured. The fact that the principal in this case, William Parry, only lost his tenure but not his job suggests that the intent of intensive cross-questioning, despite appearances to the contrary, was not necessarily to harm.

There were only a few instances when principals were grievously badgered and menaced by a committee, and no faculty sat on the offending tribunals. Faculty presence greatly reduced the possibility of harassment of principals or witnesses. During a session at one institution, a member of the Board of Trustees and the dean first asked to be told the names of "persons with whom you were associated in the Communist Party." This was followed by a request for additional information. The dean believed there was also an obligation to "tell us who were in with you" from the college: "You must aid and assist in uncovering those who have not left." He added, "We would like to have evidence that you have broken, other than to say that you have, and the best evidence you can possibly give is to become an informant." The trustee was quick to point out that "your refusal to tell us will undoubtedly have an effect upon your career [here]." This warning was repeated at the end of the hearing by the chairman of the Board of Trustees: "You realize that by your action [in not revealing the names of the others] you might be jeopardizing your whole future?" At the next meeting, a great deal of time was spent trying to find out with whom the principal had discussed the possibility of the investigation during the past six months, and with whom he had discussed the first hearing during the preceding five days.

At first glance, it would seem that the quasi-judicial course of an investigation offered principals a modicum of protection from unfair condemnation and punishment. There is the appearance that principals were being given an opportunity to explain, to clarify. Most of the time they were permitted the benefit of counsel. The idea of being judged by peers seemed fair. Being given the opportunity to exculpate oneself seemed fair. There was often a full stenographic record so that disinterested parties and history could judge how balanced the proceedings had been. The reality that principals faced, however, was somewhat different.

Over half of the time, faculty were not a majority on committees so that principals were not necessarily being judged by peers. Moreover, most individuals who were obliged to go through the ordeal of campus hearings—that is, who were given a chance to vindicate themselves—were assumed to be guilty of something. Unlike the American legal process, committee proceedings did not require that a case be made against them. They had to establish their innocence or loyalty or whatever. Some committees, bound by state laws or rules and procedures that presumed guilt and precluded finding some middle ground, "had to vote for dismissal." One committee wrote:

> Particularly we believe that, if respondent was not and is not a Party member, he could readily and voluntarily have advanced much better supporting proof.

As noted in chapter 5, a committee at Wayne University would (or could) not accept a mere affidavit of innocence of communist involvement from two individuals who had taken the Fifth Amendment before a legislative committee. The respondents, it was declared, would have to do more to clear themselves of "*prima facie* guilt."

More often than not, all committee members—not only those who were faculty—appeared to be objective and reasonably well-disposed toward principals. The hearings were also for the most part technically fair; however, in light of the fact that at about one-half of the institutions where a faculty-dominated committee produced findings exonerating a principal, this judgment was ignored by administrators and governing boards in their decision to dismiss, it is not unreasonable to infer from the material that follows that the collecting and sifting of evidence and the use of experts was many times largely a sham to lend an air of respectability to outcomes determined well before any faculty committee sat for the first time. This point needs to be emphasized because it has been written elsewhere that

> the freedom of the profession as a whole, its control over the terms of its own employment, remained pretty much intact. Professors everywhere not only endorsed the exclusion of communists and Fifth Amendment witnesses from the academy but also participated in the process of excluding them. In only a few, a very few, cases did a university's administrators and trustees impinge upon the prerogatives of the faculty and fire someone a faculty committee had wanted to retain.[36]

The materials considered here would not support this conclusion.

Aside from being asked to serve on one committee or another, whose recommendations in the end might be ignored, faculty other than principals were basically spectators to these events. The following examination of how two different faculty committees, administrative authorities, and the university senate at the University of Michigan acted preceding and subsequent to the dismissal of two individuals exemplifies this point, and a number of others being made in this chapter. This example is followed by two others—from Rutgers University and the University of Washington—where the process and outcome were remarkably similar.

The Disregard of a Faculty Committee

Example I: The University of Michigan

Three faculty at the University of Michigan were first suspended by President Harlan Hatcher for refusing to answer questions put to them by the House Committee on Un-American Activities. The president arranged with the university senate to have the three brought before a faculty committee so that it might advise whether to initiate dismissal proceedings or reinstate them. After holding hearings, the committee recommended that two should be censured and reinstated and that the third, who refused to cooperate, should be terminated. The president reinstated one and initiated dismissal proceedings against the other two.

The second set of hearings again produced no evidence that either principal had engaged in unlawful, improper, or immoral conduct, and this committee unanimously recommended that the one who had fully responded to its questions be reinstated and that the other who still refused to discuss Communist Party membership and other political matters be dismissed. President Hatcher recommended to the Board of Regents that neither should be continued. Both were dismissed by the Regents at their next meeting.

The president argued in the first case that the principal's (Mark Nickerson's) own testimony before the initial committee convinced him that he had not really turned his back on the Communist Party:

> Your answers to . . . questions leave grave doubts as to your fitness to hold your present position of responsibility and trust, and have raised in my mind and in the minds of the university committee serious concern about your integrity as a member of the teaching profession. . . .
>
> You have refused to answer pertinent questions put to you by a duly constituted legal body concerning your activities and affiliations with the Communist Party on the grounds that the answers might tend to incriminate you. Although you deny that you would overthrow the government of this country by force, you have vigorously asserted before the committees of your colleagues that you want it clearly understood that you hold the same views and beliefs now which you held while you were an active member and an officer in the Communist Party; and that, although you are not now an active communist, you drifted away from your activities only because you did not have enough time to devote to them, and not because you were in disagreement with the aims, policies, and methods of the communists. Under these circumstances it becomes difficult to accept your disavowal of the illegal and destructive aims of the Communist Party.
>
> These serious disqualifications which bring your case before me under the provision of Bylaw 5.101 become even more weighty when joined with the formal recommendation made to me by the dean and the executive committee of the Medical School that you be dismissed because your continued membership in the medical faculty would be harmful to the school and may injure the reputation of the university as a whole.[37]

For its part, the second faculty committee saw the matter quite differently, and expressed this to the president:

> . . . We have earnestly sought . . . to determine, as precisely as possible, the nature of the charges brought against Dr. Nickerson. . . .

It appears to us, after considering your letter to Dr. Nickerson, your memorandum . . ., the testimony as a whole, and the conclusions of the . . . [ad hoc committee], including the minority report, that the charges brought against Dr. Nickerson may be stated as follows:

1. Dr. Nickerson was in the past a member of the Communist Party.
2. Dr. Nickerson is at the present time a member of the Communist Party.
3. Dr. Nickerson remains a communist in spirit, and repudiates no part of the communist program or objectives.
4. Dr. Nickerson has given conflicting testimony concerning the time of his withdrawal from the Communist Party, and has been vague concerning the method and extent of his withdrawal.
5. Dr. Nickerson invoked the Fifth Amendment when asked by a duly constituted legislative committee to testify concerning his Communist Party activities, despite the advice of officials of the university that he should testify openly.
6. Dr. Nickerson, at the time he accepted employment in the university, signed the employment oath, and failed to disclose his past Communist Party activities.
7. Dr. Nickerson failed to disclose his past Communist Party affiliations to his department head, even though classified projects were under way in that department.
8. That even though the four foregoing items do not in themselves constitute grounds for dismissal, taken in the aggregate they indicate a lack of integrity.
9. That the retention of Dr. Nickerson on the Medical School faculty would not be in the best interests of the Medical School or of the university.

We believe that no charge has been made that Dr. Nickerson has failed to be candid in his testimony before his colleagues on the Special Advisory Committee to the president, and we believe there is no justification for any charge of such a nature. This was the unanimous opinion of the Special Advisory Committee to the president, including those who filed a minority report.[38]

In its vindication of Nickerson, this second committee was of one mind:

Dr. Nickerson has been, but is no longer, a member of the Communist Party, and is not under the domination of the Communist Party. His Marxist views on economic and political matters may coincide in some respects with those of the Communist Party, but this does not establish Party membership. He has disavowed both illegal political aims and the use of illegal methods to achieve what may be legal objectives. There is no evidence of illegal activity on the part of Dr. Nickerson in the past or at present and he has denied this under oath before the Clardy Committee. We have found him candid and open, and willing to discuss any matter we deemed relevant. He impressed [us] that he was honest in his answers, and we found him in no sense evasive.[39]

In justifying having ignored this faculty committee, President Hatcher contended that he had "read hopefully through the testimony taken by the

... [second committee], seeking to find some new evidence that might controvert that already presented. Not only was it not there to be found, but instead there appeared repeated reinforcements of previous evidence upon which the original recommendation had been framed."

The university senate's opposition to the president's decision to overrule both faculty committees may not have changed the outcome, but its public stand made it clear that the administration had acted unilaterally, that in this case the view of the faculty hardly mattered:

> WHEREAS, this university senate recognizes both the legal responsibility and the moral obligation of the president and the Regents of the University of Michigan to make final decisions in matters of faculty tenure, the senate believes that the long term interests of both the university and its supporting society are best served when such decisions reflect the considered opinion of the university senate.
>
> WHEREAS, the senate believes that the president and Regents are entitled to know the opinion of the senate on the broad issues involved in faculty tenure, therefore
>
> *Be it resolved*:
>
> 1. that this senate express its full approval of the general principles of intellectual freedom delineated in the report of the Senate Committee on Intellectual Freedom and Integrity in the case of Dr. Nickerson, especially
>   (a) We believe that we speak for faculty and administration alike when we assert that so long as ideas do not extend beyond the pale of legality, or accepted concepts of morality, the great tradition of academic freedom requires their protection.
>   (b) Dismissal from the university faculty, particularly in the case of a faculty member with tenure, is consistent with the ideals of intellectual freedom only when there is substantial evidence of grave misconduct on the part of the individual concerned.
>   (c) This case involves matters of university-wide policy with reference to a subject which transcends departmental and college lines. It involves questions of the freedom to hold unpopular ideas. It involves questions concerning the relations between the faculty and legislative bodies. It involves the meaning of tenure and the obligations of candor to the university. These are matters in which no department, no school, no college, as such, has any particular competence. These, it seems to us, are matters which must properly be considered at the university level.
> 2. that this senate express its satisfaction with the decision of the governing body of the university in the case of Professor Markert, and its regret that the decision in the case of Professor Nickerson was not in accord with the unanimous opinion of the special senate committee charged with reviewing this and similar cases.[40]

The president did not contravene the recommendations of the faculty committees when he acted to have the other defendant, H. Chandler Davis,

fired. This is what both committees had advised. Davis's refusal to cooperate with either committee was seen as an immature (he was only 28 years
old) act of defiance, as "evasiveness and deviousness." As chapter 7 will
make clear, when a principal challenged the legitimacy of an inquiry, the
reaction was invariably antagonistic, the outcome invariably dismissal.

Example II: Rutgers University

The fate of the final recommendation of a faculty committee at Rutgers
University was similar to that at the University of Michigan in that it too
was ignored by the president and Board of Trustees. After two individuals
refused to answer questions put to them by the Senate Internal Security
Subcommittee, President Jones appointed a committee of three trustees,
three faculty and one alumnus to review the situation and advise him on a
possible course of action. The committee was not interested in what political activities these individuals had been engaged in, as it was not charged
"to probe the lives and record of these men"; it was to determine if their
behavior before the congressional committee had raised "grave doubt"
about their fitness to teach. The committee was to determine if they had
violated their "special obligations" to Rutgers University. Initially President Jones did not consider the invocation of the Fifth Amendment sufficient grounds for suspension or dismissal.

At the urging of the president, one individual, Simon Heimlich, an
associate professor of physics and mathematics in the College of Pharmacy,
publicly explained why he had done what he had, and that he was not
concealing radical connections:

> At the base of all my behavior and thinking there has always been the princi-
> ple that my views on social, political and religious matters, as well as my
> affiliations, political or otherwise, are my private concern. I have always
> considered any intrusion into this area to be exceedingly offensive. This is the
> first reason for my refusal to answer questions relating to such matters when
> propounded by the [Senate] subcommittee. The second reason is the need for
> protecting myself against possible false testimony. In my opinion, the stand I
> took is fully in accord with all that is contained in our American heritage of
> freedom and democracy.
>
> Although I am not a member of the Communist Party and have never been
> one, I consistently refused to answer the [Senate] subcommittee's questions
> relative to any political affiliations. . . .
>
> Again, I affirm that I am not a member of the Communist Party and never
> have been one, nor have I ever used an alias. I am definitely not under any
> outside discipline or influence which would prejudice me in the unfettered
> search for truth in research or teaching. Finally, I have never done any re-
> cruiting for the American Youth for Democracy.[41]

When asked why he had been open with President Jones but not with the Senate subcommittee, Heimlich replied: "Here is a matter of principle: in one case I am faced with an organized group prying into my 'private conscience'; in the other case, President Jones, I was not asked to answer any questions, I volunteered to do so." Heimlich added that he would still decline to answer if he went back to the Senate subcommittee: "I believe it is no one's concern what my private ideas happen to be. I believe it is not the concern of the Trustees, nor has anyone any right to compel me to express them."[42]

The other individual, Moses I. Finley, an assistant professor of history, testified that he had declined to answer whether he had been a communist before the Senate subcommittee and could do no differently before his colleagues, since "it does me no good to be inconsistent." He would, however, say that he had not been a communist while teaching at Rutgers. When asked to explain his actions, he responded:

> Around 1938 or 1939 I was the executive secretary of the American Committee for Democracy and Intellectual Freedom, of which many prominent college people, including college presidents and top administrative personnel were members. The committee was attacked by the Dies Committee and it was involved in the Rugg textbook controversy and other things. The result is that it was called a communist front. Moreover, during the Rapp-Coudert investigations in 1940 or 1941, I was accused of being a communist by one William Canning. He and Mr. Wittfogel said I had been conducting communist study groups, which I denied. Then Bella Dodd testified similarly. I am now convinced that public denials accomplish nothing. A possible charge of perjury and conviction would lead to a jail sentence, and although I may be a coward, I am not enthusiastic about the prospect. There is nothing about my activity which I would be unwilling to discuss publicly. I have done nothing illegal in the broad sense of the term, nor have any of my acquaintances to the best of my knowledge, but I will not involve other people in possible trouble when I know nothing about their possible involvement.[43]

In its report, the seven-man committee noted that the use of the Fifth Amendment is "a right under the Constitution," and "as such it is not unlawful." The committee felt that the failure to respond to questions about one's relationship to the Communist Party was harmful to the university as it "raises in the mind of the average man a reasonable question concerning the witnesses' loyalty to the United States." Doubts about the loyalty of faculty "tend to affect the confidence which the public is entitled to feel in a university. . . . In the case of a state university, such a situation also may tend to impair the confidence of state officials and the legislature in the integrity and value of the university." Thus, it concluded, the

refusals of Professor Heimlich to answer questions of the Senate committee relative to his connection with the Communist Party, and of Professor Finley as to his previous connection with it, on the ground that to answer might tend to incriminate them, do raise a real question as to their fitness to continue as teachers on the university faculty. We believe that this question should be resolved, and recommend that you institute appropriate proceedings to this end.

It urged the appointment of a Special Faculty Committee of Review to study the matter further and to make recommendations.[44]

The second committee met sixteen times and invited individuals from the faculty, the legal profession, the alumni, the student body, the administration, and the executive offices of the American Association of University Professors to discuss the matter with it. Unlike the situation at the University of Michigan, both principals made an effort to be cooperative. The committee took the posture of a grand jury and saw the sole question before it as being whether the refusal to testify before a legislative committee made one unfit to continue to teach. It did share one fundamental premise with administrative authorities:

> The members of the Special Faculty Committee of Review stand unanimously behind the policy of the president that a member of the Communist Party should not be permitted to teach at Rutgers University.[45]

This committee also noted that legally the Fifth Amendment could be used, and that it was not necessarily improper to do so. Indeed, the committee understood Finley's refusal to answer the questions of the congressional committee on the "plausible and legally acceptable grounds" that he might otherwise "place himself in a position of being indicted for perjury" if the government decided to use the testimony of other witnesses as the basis of prosecuting him. The committee recognized that the failure to testify in full raised a question "as to the border line between such special obligations and responsibilities and the right and privilege of the teacher as a citizen in a free society." It was aware that although many might argue that the special position of the teacher involves waiving his constitutional rights,

> the committee believes that this would be discriminatory and in violation of the spirit and letter of the Constitution itself. It would tend to reduce the teacher to a status more appropriate to a totalitarian society than to a free America. The committee believes that it would be unfortunate if the privileges of the Constitution, which make the United States a symbol of freedom throughout the world, were denied to the very group which is responsible for the education of Americans. While it is a matter of regret to many that a teacher may find it necessary to invoke his constitutional privilege, it should be recognized that the unique position of the teacher which imposes upon

him special obligations and responsibilities, renders him likewise particularly vulnerable to criticism, and to public pressure. The committee believes that the teacher, given this special vulnerability, far from being denied his constitutional privileges, should, on the contrary, be given their full protection.[46]

It, therefore, unanimously agreed that refusal to testify before a legislative committee did not constitute unfitness to teach:

It is the view of this committee that neither Mr. Finley nor Mr. Heimlich in dealing with the university in the matter of his appearance before a legislative committee and in invoking his constitutional privileges in declining to answer certain questions, has acted in contravention of the university statute cited above or the standards of behavior prescribed by the AAUP in its pronouncement on academic freedom.[47]

The committee took note that both individuals were considered excellent, objective teachers. There was nothing to indicate either ever misused his position as a teacher to propagandize students. Indeed, the evidence showed "the absence of any such conduct." It was also emphasized that "no charge of irresponsible behavior has ever been brought against either. In fact, no suggestion has come to this committee other than that the academic record of each man has been exemplary."

It concluded its report:

After prolonged consideration of all the aspects of the case the Faculty Committee [of Review] has unanimously reached the conclusion that on the basis of the evidence available to the committee no charges should be preferred against Mr. Heimlich or Mr. Finley. It therefore recommends to the president that no further action be taken.[48]

In direct contrast to the Special Faculty Committee of Review's recommendation, the Board of Trustees was unanimous in agreeing that professors could not use their constitutional privilege to invoke the Fifth Amendment and remain on the faculty. It set a date by which Heimlich and Finley should either cooperate with the congressional committee or be dismissed.[49] In essence, it ignored the faculty report since the conclusions were not in keeping with its own and did not serve its purposes. In the words of President Jones:

The main criticism was this: that the faculty committee's report established at some length the legal right of the two professors to invoke the Fifth Amendment in refusing to testify, a right which was not in dispute, though the legal wisdom of its exercise is questioned; but it did not deal adequately, in the opinion of the Board, with the central issue: namely, the obligation of a member of the teaching profession, and a representative of the university, entitled by his position to freedom of teaching, research, thought, and expression, to state his position with respect to the Communist Party in the spirit of truth and courage upon the basis of which intellectual freedom is justified and valued. The faculty committee in effect endorsed the stand of the two professors, a stand which the Trustees felt to be wrong, and undermining to the integrity of this and other universities.

It is a matter of sincere regret that, on this central issue, the Trustees found themselves in unanimous disagreement with the Special Faculty Committee of Review.[50]

The president's criticism of the faculty committee was more restrained than that of one trustee who complained that it had treated "this whole thing as an abstract situation in which the niceties of the law and the regulations pertaining to the conduct of the teachers of the university are given preeminence. It seems to me that we lost sight of the fact that we are at war with communism."

The Board of Trustees made no allegation that either man was or had been a communist or was under the discipline of the Communist Party. There was no charge of disloyalty. The reversal of the faculty committee's recommendation was based on the allegation that refusal to answer the questions of the Senate subcommittee "impairs confidence in Heimlich's and Finley's fitness to teach." No factual evidence of that impairment was mentioned. Of course, impairment of confidence in fitness to teach is quite different from fitness to teach.

The Board of Trustees was asked to, but would not, reexamine its position.

No new considerations relevant to the fundamental issue of policy have been introduced at this time. The communications did not deal with the broad issues which have been discussed in the foregoing statement; they dealt narrowly with technical questions of professional self-regulation which were not at issue.[51]

One of its members explained its position: "The faculty committee was an advisory board and the Board of Trustees had sole responsibility for the final decision. The United States faces a menace to its very existence and freedom. Loyal citizens everywhere must guide their actions accordingly—professionals must be entirely above suspicion." He likened the action of the Board of Trustees to the decision of an appeals court, and said that the fact that it did not agree with the lower court, that is, the faculty committee, was not in any way an indication of "disrespect."[52]

As already noted, it was President Jones's contention that the only issue was whether faculty had an obligation to answer questions regarding membership in the Communist Party. He noted that academic freedom is not the same as freedom to be silent. "The freedom to be silent is a civil right guaranteed under special circumstances by the Constitution. But academic freedom entails the obligation to render an explanation, as clearly and rationally as possible, whenever such an explanation is called for by duly constituted governmental bodies acting within the limits of their authority."[53] In the eyes of the Board of Trustees and the president, the faculty committee's points were hardly relevant and could be readily ignored.

Example III: The University of Washington

At the University of Washington, the faculty Committee on Tenure and Academic Freedom heard the cases of six faculty whom the administration wanted discharged. All had been identified as being Communist Party members. Three had admitted to a legislative committee examining alleged communist activities at the university that they had once been members, and three had refused to provide information about their political activities.

After painstakingly examining a considerable amount of evidence over a seven-week period, the faculty committee determined that only one of the six should be terminated, and that the remaining five should be retained. President Allen recommended to the Board of Regents that the three who had been uncooperative be dismissed. The Board of Regents dismissed the three, and placed the others on probation for a two-year period, subject to their signing and filing noncommunist affidavits.

In the case of the latter three, the action of the Board of Regents came as a surprise to some, as the faculty committee had written:

> We are unanimous in the view that the tenure and employment of each of these three respondents should not be disturbed by reason of the charges filed and facts proved in the cases against them.[54]

The two that the committee agreed should be retained, but whom President Allen had dismissed, openly declared that they were and had been members of the Communist Party for thirteen years. The president was of the opinion that although the Communist Party was not illegal, belonging to an organization that was secret, advocated the overthrow of the American system, encouraged its members to engage in clandestine activities, and was involved in a "propagandistic mission" was sufficient grounds for dismissal. Party membership, in itself, was evidence of unfitness since one was subject to Party discipline and was dishonest and immoral. The Communist Party allowed no criticism of its principles and programs. Party members could not possibly be faithful to the higher academic responsibilities of impartiality and objectivity. Moreover, the president continued, membership in the Communist Party, which was directly controlled by the Soviet Union and therefore brought discredit and disrepute upon the institution, was a dereliction of duty. Finally, concealment of Communist Party membership made the original offense doubly heinous. Thus, not only was membership in the Communist Party by itself grounds for dismissal, but the subterfuge that Party membership entailed was evidence of unfitness to hold an academic appointment.

Five of eleven committee members believed that these arguments were irrelevant; Communist Party membership did not constitute grounds for dismissal since there was nothing prohibiting faculty from joining an organization that was not unlawful and that was not outlawed by the university. They felt that clarification or revision of the university administrative code that governed faculty appointments was in order, but that it was not the committee's charge to establish a policy that would ban faculty from joining the Communist Party. Three other committee members concurred in the recommendation against dismissal but made it clear that they disagreed that membership in the Communist Party could ever be a legitimate cause for dismissal, even if institutional bylaws were changed. At most, membership in the Communist Party was regrettable. As was noted earlier in this chapter, only a minority argued that membership in the Party was so "reckless, uncritical, and intemperate" that it was sufficient grounds for dismissal. In any case, in spite of, as it was put, a "division of opinion" in arriving at its conclusion, "a majority of the committee has agreed that there is no basis for recommending removal of respondents Butterworth and Phillips under the administrative code of the university."[55]

Given operating regulations and definitions, the president's and Board's decision to dismiss was based on a political test, and directly contravened the recommendation of eight of eleven members of the Committee on Tenure and Academic Freedom.

It was President Allen's contention that since five committee members who had voted for retention expressed disapproval of the Communist Party, a majority could be counted in favor of dismissal if these five were added to the three who all along held that Party membership made one ineligible to hold a faculty appointment. He was convinced, apparently, that a majority favored, and would have voted for, dismissal if the committee had taken a broad interpretation of the administrative code.

The main thrust of the university's case was that under the administrative code membership in the Communist Party precluded one from being a reliable faculty member. The majority of the committee did not accept this argument: "It must be kept in mind that nothing concerning the conduct of these respondents other than the simple fact of their Party membership, plus the necessary implications, is before us." In light of his failure to persuade the committee, President Allen suggested that the Board of Regents should simply ignore university policy in making its decision:

> I respectfully invite your attention to the fact that the Board of Regents never at any time specifically approved or ordered into effect the existing provisions of the administrative code. Rather, it authorized the president, if he saw fit, to approve an administrative code which the faculty itself had written and recommended as regulations for the management of the internal affairs of the university. This the president did. However, the Board of Regents is by law the governing body of the University of Washington, and, as such, retains clearly within its power the right to determine the conditions of employment of the faculty and staff generally.[56]

President Allen repeatedly argued that given their ideology, members of the Communist Party were disqualified from being faculty members regardless of how well they handled their teaching or research or the propriety of their conduct. Central to his argument was the tenet that any action, condition, or attitude that interferes with the proper and adequate performance of duties renders an individual incompetent. Embracing communist dogma precluded sincerely seeking truth—"the first obligation and duty of the teacher." It was his position that since no member of the Communist Party could ever be truthful, no member of the Communist Party should be allowed to teach, "because he is not a free man ... he is intellectually dishonest." Allen was not interested in an individual's character or behavior but what that character or behavior was assumed to be from the character of one's political affiliations.

Not only had the Communist Party not been outlawed, but it could hardly be expected that, given the administration's position with regard to it, faculty who were members would make this fact a topic of public discussion. Moreover, the administration apparently believed it had the authority to require faculty to reveal their political party membership and to dismiss those who failed to do so.

There was no evidence that either Butterworth or Phillips had engaged in illegal or improper activities. They were not charged with any overt act of force or violence, or even with conduct unbecoming a faculty member. Moreover, their competence as scholars and teachers was never in question, and there was no evidence that they had in any way abused their positions in the classroom or had neglected their academic duties. The committee said of Phillips:

> Although he does have occasion to discuss Marxian philosophy in his teach-

ing, it appears that his practice is to warn his students of his bias and to request that they evaluate his lectures in light of that fact.[57]

Both Butterworth and Phillips also attempted to make the point that the Party was not foreign dominated, did not advocate illegal means to achieve the goal of establishing socialism, did not discipline members or insist on unquestioning adherence to the Party line, and in general was lawful. They described their Party activities as mostly paying dues and attending discussions.

President Allen was more convinced of his premise that membership in the Communist Party was a priori evidence of incompetence than by the facts. Holding to his theory was what enabled him to conclude without examining particulars that any member of the Communist Party would be disqualified from holding an academic appointment.

Not intending any irony, the president wrote:

> First, it should be repeated that action was taken in these cases only after a full and scrupulously fair hearing, conducted in accordance with traditional safeguards against summary and capricious action by either the university president or the Board of Regents. While no attempt will be made here to review these procedures, it should be understood that "due process," as outlined by the faculty-written administrative code of the University of Washington, was observed to the letter. Respondents were represented by counsel of their own choice, there was no restriction upon their rights of producing or questioning evidence; and other traditions of Anglo-Saxon law were fully observed. Full hearings were provided by all individuals and agencies participating in the decision.[58]

Of course, the more said about the adequacy of the procedures, the more indefensible the president's and the Board of Regents' decision to overturn the recommendation of the faculty Committee on Tenure and Academic Freedom.

Notes

1. "Statement of Policy and Procedures relating to the Rights and Responsibilities of Employees of Wayne University," 4 June 1953, p. 11.
2. Ibid., p. 12.
3. Ibid., p. 13.
4. Byron T. Darling, correspondence to Howard L. Bevis, 1 April 1953.
5. "The Cases of Lauer vs. Butterworth and Lauer vs. Phillips: Separate and Dissenting Statement of Professors Benson and Goodspeed."
6. *Milwaukee Journal*, 15 December 1955; *Milwaukee Sentinel*, 15 December 1955.
7. John T. Rettaliata, correspondence to Gerald J. Matchett, 15 December 1955.
8. John T. Rettaliata, correspondence to Alex D. Bailey, 30 December 1955.

9. Exhibit E, materials sent to all members of the Executive Committee.
10. Special Report: Council for Industrial Security, 5 January 1956.
11. Lewis Webster Jones, correspondence to John T. Rettaliata, 9 February 1956.
12. John T. Rettaliata, correspondence to members of the Committee of Inquiry, 23 January 1956.
13. John T. Rettaliata, correspondence to the Illinois Institute of Technology Faculty Council, 20 January 1956.
14. "Objectives and Procedures, Matchett Hearing."
15. Gerald J. Matchett's statement to the Committee of Inquiry, 27 pp.
16. "Report and Recommendations of the Committee of Inquiry," 9 March 1956, p. 1.
17. Ibid., p. 5.
18. Ibid., p. 8.
19. R. J. Koch, correspondence to John T. Rettaliata, 5 March 1956.
20. John T. Rettaliata, correspondence to Gerald J. Matchett, 9 April 1956.
21. Andries Deinum, correspondence to Fred D. Fagg, Jr., 5 July 1955.
22. "Report of the Special Committee of the Andries Deinum Case," 14 December 1955, pp. 7–8.
23. Ibid., p. 5.
24. Ibid., p. 7.
25. Ibid., p. 6.
26. Ibid., p. 8; also see "Final Report," Senate Special Committee, March 1956.
27. Edward J. Machle, correspondence to Senate Committee on Privilege and Tenure, 8 January 1952.
28. Robert L. Stearns and W. F. Dyde, correspondence to the members of the University Senate, 24 March 1952.
29. Transcript of hearing concerning Morris Judd, p. 4.
30. Ibid., p. 16.
31. Committee on Privilege and Tenure, "Majority Statement," 19 May 1952, p. 2.
32. Committee on Privilege and Tenure, "Minority Statement," 19 May 1952, pp. 14–15.
33. "University of Colorado Situation; Judd Case," p. 2.
34. See note 39 in chapter 5.
35. Questions formulated 27 May 1953, questions 13, 15, 22, 26, 33, and 36.
36. Ellen W. Schrecker, "Academic Freedom: The Historical View," in Craig Kaplan and Ellen W. Schrecker, eds., Regulating the Intellectuals: Perspectives on Academic Freedom in the 1980s (New York: Praeger, 1983), p. 40.
37. Harlan H. Hatcher, correspondence to Mark Nickerson, 27 July 1954.
38. Bylaws Committee, "Analysis of Charges," Report to President Harlan H. Hatcher, 11 August 1954, pp. 3–4.
39. Bylaws Committee, Report to President Harlan H. Hatcher, 11 August 1954, p. 29.
40. University Senate, Resolution, 5 October 1954.
41. Simon W. Heimlich, correspondence to Lewis Webster Jones, 26 September 1952.
42. President's Special Advisory Committee, Minutes, 3 October 1952.
43. Ibid.
44. "Report of the Special Committee to Advise the President Concerning Simon W. Heimlich and Moses I. Finley."
45. "Report of the Special Faculty Committee of Review," 3 December 1952.

46. Ibid.
47. Ibid.
48. Ibid.
49. "Resolution of the Rutgers University Board of Trustees," 12 December 1952.
50. Lewis Webster Jones, "Statement on the Heimlich-Finley Cases," 24 January 1953.
51. Ibid.
52. George H. Holsten, notes on Assembly meeting, 18 December 1952.
53. Jones, "Statement."
54. "The Cases of Lauer vs. Eby, Lauer vs. Ethel, and Lauer vs. Jacobs: Statement of the Full Committee."
55. "The Cases of Lauer vs. Butterworth and Lauer vs. Phillips: Statement of Professors Densmore, Gose, Hatch, Rowntree, and Thompson."
56. "The President's Analysis: Concerning the Administrative Code."
57. "The Cases of Lauer vs. Butterworth and Lauer vs. Phillips: Statement of Professor Densmore et al."
58. Raymond B. Allen, "Statements by the President and the Dismissed Professors," *American Scholar* 18, no. 3, (1949), p. 326.

7

Rights and Obligations

At almost every college and university, secondary tensions developed between principals and academic authorities revolving around the question of the rights and obligations of the individual as opposed to the rights and obligations of the institution. Because there was no precedent, agreement, or formula regarding what each owed the other—the responsibilities of the individual to the institution and the responsibilities of the institution to the individual—five out of six controversies became inordinately complicated. Some conflict could be easily traced to diverse views on the subject of reciprocity and fairness.

At one extreme was the contention that institutions have no right to inquire about or punish faculty for conduct in any realm beyond the classroom. Quite simply, faculty have no duty to divulge more than they choose. One centrist position was that an institution should involve itself in non-academic matters only in instances where there is substantial evidence that there has been a violation of the academic process. Related to this was the view that faculty should be questioned only to address uncertainty, only to clear the air. The stand most distant from the first, and the one most common among academic administrators, was that since faculty generally owe their colleagues candor and integrity, they have a responsibility, when asked, to share information pertaining to political activities, beliefs, and associations with all members of the academic community, from members of the governing board to students. A detailed inquiry into the political lives of faculty going well beyond asking about membership in the Communist Party and including minute probing of an individual's mind to determine loyalty was not believed to be at all intrusive.

The matter of rights and obligations had apparently been given little thought on some campuses until these politically triggered controversies surfaced. Not surprisingly, at that point it often became a topic of considerable discussion, and more. The entanglements that grew out of the fact that there was no common understanding greatly decreased the probability that all sides would ever agree that a particular settlement, especially one that ended in a dismissal, had been reasonable or fair. Simple and standard solutions were quite rare; stalemates were quite common.

An impasse over rights and obligations could come about in a number of ways. First, the members of a governing board and academic officials generally believed that an obligation to the institution was the same as an obligation to its present administration. In their minds, their interests and institutional interests were identical. They equated loyalty to themselves with loyalty to the institution. Contrarily, numerous principals drew a sharp distinction between the institution and those who happened to be managing it.

There was, second, the perennial and more general question of whether faculty were autonomous professionals or merely employees. To this day, it has not been resolved whether faculty are holders of a public trust or are, like staff in any organization, required to follow orders given by those in higher positions or with formal authority. Although from the 1920s to the 1940s there appeared to be a trend in the direction of greater latitude and self-determination for faculty, these incidents suggest that a new definition on which all were agreed had not become firmly rooted.

More than one academic administrator alluded to his prerogative to assess faculty performance, to determine what was best for the institution, to have the final word. Members of governing boards, even more than academic administrators, were likely to take the position that faculty worked for them and were not really owed an explanation if called upon to do something. In the eyes of some of the more authoritarian board members, the mere failure to answer any question was sufficient grounds for dismissal. As far as numerous trustees and regents were concerned, whether a question was proper or pertinent or whether there might be reasons for not answering it was completely irrelevant. As a small but noteworthy paradox, faculty who were seen simply as employees, as individuals with narrowly delineated functions rather than as holders of an office or members of a profession, were more likely to be thought accountable by academic authorities for all of their actions—those that occurred on or off campus. Academic employment demanded relinquishing some privacy.

There was, finally, the practical question of the political climate in the country. It was widely believed, and probably true, that the heightened public concern about political matters increased the likelihood that budgets and enrollments of those institutions of higher learning seen as havens for individuals tainted by communism would be adversely affected. Under these circumstances, some argued, faculty had a special obligation to surrender some ground. It was unclear, of course, how much should be given up, how far faculty should go.

At Rutgers University, the president wrote that the principle of academic freedom made it inescapable that faculty who wished to keep their jobs forgo their right to use the Fifth Amendment:

> Under all the circumstances of our relations to world communism, a mini-
> mum responsibility would seem to be that members of the university state
> frankly where they stand on matters of such deep public concern, and of such
> relevance to academic integrity, as membership in the Communist Party;
> even when by a straightforward statement they believe they might incur
> certain personal risks.

> In the cases of Professors Heimlich and Finley, the legal risks suggested as
> possible were those of a charge of perjury or contempt. These risks must be
> balanced against the risk of damage to the entire university, and to the profes-
> sion to which the two men belong, incurred by refusal to testify on the
> grounds of possible self-incrimination. . . .

> I therefore agree with the policy stated by the Board of Trustees . . . requiring
> all members of the university faculty to answer questions concerning
> Communist Party membership put to them by any duly constituted public
> body. . . .[1]

As articulated here, the obligations of faculty to the institution were clearly seen as extending well beyond the campus. Given public opinion and the pressure—real or imagined—on colleges and universities, administrators held that it was not too much to expect faculty to give up some of their rights—which in any case were not always conceded or absolute—even if this in effect increased the rights of the institution. As will become apparent, a number of principals felt that this, indeed, was too much to ask.

Obstinacy

The probability that those thought not sufficiently accommodating to institutional needs as defined by administrative authorities would be terminated was exceedingly high. It was imperative that principals accede to all reasonable requests for information. Since some administrative authorities believed that all requests—particularly those to facilitate inquiries off and on campus or to sign loyalty oaths—were "reasonable," the options for most principals were quite limited. In addition, since there was no absolute or fixed point at which one became "sufficiently accommodating," this too could become as much a part of a label as a reflection of actual behavior.

This is not to suggest that all of those said to be uncooperative were arbitrarily misnamed as such. In the course of administrative efforts to determine what their politics were, seven individuals were dogmatic in maintaining that since such a question was of a personal nature, they were free not to abet any inquiry. They could only legitimately be asked about behavior in the classroom or behavior outside the classroom that had a bearing on moral turpitude. A larger category, about three times this number, put some limits on what they would share with others—this in the face of near unanimity in academia that one had a duty to disclose to colleagues or academic authorities information of a political nature if it would put their minds at rest. Although many times an individual might make an effort to convey the impression that there was nothing to hide, it was hard to find anyone other than a friend or close associate who did not feel that a response of silence or partial silence was simply posturing, that it was self-serving. As a result of seeming to hold back too much or to reveal too little, a number of principals put their appointments at risk.

The very worst tack any principal could take, in fact, was to withhold information or behave in any way that gave the appearance of being unwilling to cooperate. Those who were active in the Wallace presidential campaign were expected to curtail this activity if academic authorities were convinced that this reflected unfavorably on the institution. Being a good citizen on campus took precedence over general civic duties. Those who would not give a full account of their political beliefs were thought to be "defiant," "insubordinate," "out of whack," or perhaps, and more importantly, even guilty of something. The most detailed explanation of why a decision was made to remain silent on the most insignificant question was met with a great deal of skepticism; the most impassioned justification fell on deaf ears. Those who did not cooperate were thought to have no sense of their moral or social obligation. In a way, they were being labeled psychopaths.

The claim that the refusal to answer questions was a principled stand was almost always rejected out of hand. Even if the reasoning seemed particularly detailed or thoughtful, to most it was merely an elaborate ruse. Here is how Chandler Davis of the University of Michigan explained to a committee why he chose not to respond to questions that bore on political matters:

... What was my response to the questions of the [first] committee?

I was willing to answer questions pertinent to my integrity.

When questioned concerning certain specific charges of political chicanery that had been made against me by the Clardy (congressional) Committee, I answered. Though these things had been none of Clardy's business, my honesty *is* my colleagues' business. I denied the charges; if desired, I can prove my denial. Do I lack intellectual objectivity? Do I improperly influence students? Do I favor force and violence? I offered to answer all questions of this sort, in as much detail as required. I think I made good on the offer; the president does not claim otherwise. And the Special Advisory Committee had said it required *only* answers relating to my integrity.

I did refuse to answer questions as to my political preferences.

What is so bad about that? Now I know very well there is a doctrine currently in this country that one must say on demand, I am thus and thus far to the left (or better yet, far *from* the left). "The doctrine of compulsory self-labeling," it might be called.

The doctrine is pernicious. Many of its adherents admit its purpose is to facilitate punishment of anybody left of a certain line; some of its adherents admit that the line is movable. It certainly works that way in practice. Public intimidation has made many people terrified not merely of communism, but of anything they have been told might be construed as socialistic; many people have been so confused that they could not think of the subject, if they dared. My countrymen have been some of the world's finest, most critical-minded, most contentious citizens; when I see them being cowed it alarms me. I rebel. The doctrine of compulsory self-labeling has been one major instrument of this sad change, so I reject the doctrine. I will not talk politics under duress.

Do my colleagues on the Special Advisory Committee really insist on the doctrine? Presumably they would not want to punish me for my political position, whatever it might be. Do they nevertheless insist that I reveal my political position? Then they are unknowingly their enemies' accomplices. They should be as eager to see their error corrected as I am.

Some of you have objected, "but the Communist Party is *different*." The objection seems to be this (I will over-simplify it, but without distorting, I hope): "Members of the Communist Party are monsters, and your colleagues have a right to know if you are a monster, therefore your colleagues have a right to know if you are a member of the Communist Party." My answer is, in effect, "I deny that I am a monster. I promise to refute any alleged evidence that I am. If then I am not a monster you must believe one of two things, or both: (1) I am not a communist; or (2) some communists are not monsters, in which case your syllogism collapses."

This answer is not evasive or gratuitously complicated. It is implied by my criterion, which is simple. For the Communist Party, monstrous or not, is political; if a question concerning it amounts to both the question of morality and a question of politics, my criterion implies that I must split the question, answering the first part and not the second.

The reason I am especially careful to give no ground on the "$64 question" is that it has been made the central one by the congressional inquisitors whom I oppose.

I think my stand is the best one; if you were in my place I hope you would take it too. But surely, even if you prefer not to, you must realize it is not a dishonorable stand!

> The president says that in taking it I disdain the university's policies and ignore its responsibilities. How have I disdained or ignored them? I feel that on the contrary I have cooperated fully and patiently with the officers of the university concerned with my case. I have exhaustively explained the principles governing my conduct, and I have assisted every inquiry into my integrity.
>
> The basic policy and responsibility of the university is to advance learning by the fearless exercise of objective thought and observation. I think it is evident that I am far from disdaining or ignoring freedom of thought. In fact, I persist in what I consider the best defense of freedom of thought even when it is not expedient.[2]

The position of Davis that the questions were improper and therefore should not be answered was thought by committee members to be disingenuous and to lack merit. That his stand could be based on an adherence to principle was simply not believed. Thus, the committee's report to the president placed emphasis on his "dishonesty," and this question was a concern in subsequent proceedings.[3] In recommending that Davis be dismissed, the committee noted that he had violated his duty of "complete candor" to the university. Moreover, some were unsure whether he had relinquished his membership in the Communist Party, something that had never been established in the first place.

Whatever the case, the reasons Davis offered for his actions were not accepted as legitimate; his university colleagues (those on the committee, not the administration) argued that this cast a shadow on his character. A number of his departmental colleagues, incidentally, did not try to interpret what he said, believed him, and were supportive. From his silence the committee readily deduced that he was not truthful. The comments of a number of members suggest that the committee wanted to believe that he was not being "candid and sincere." There was a discernible reluctance, a resistance, to accepting his argument at face value.

Unhappily, Davis's problem was aggravated by the fact that he was seen as argumentative and impatient, an impression he almost seemed eager to cultivate. This abrasiveness was taken as simply more "convincing evidence of bad faith" and "lack of forthrightness." In response to the assertion that he had participated in a public forum in Ann Arbor with Howard Fast and Paul Robeson, both considered political undesirables, he responded:

> So far as I am aware, Paul Robeson has been in Ann Arbor only once during the time I was here, and Howard Fast wasn't in town at the same time, so neither I nor anyone else in Ann Arbor was part of the program with Howard Fast and Paul Robeson, so that can be easily proved.

When it was suggested that the event might have taken place outside Ann Arbor, he replied:

> In any event, it is not true. I don't mean to imply I would have been ashamed to appear on a program with Howard Fast and Paul Robeson, and as to being willing to appear on a platform with two such excellent Americans, I would be proud.

It is not surprising then that some on the committee were in the frame of mind to find his responses "unconvincing." More about Chandler Davis shortly.

A Case from the University of Kansas City

Curiously enough, the father of Chandler Davis, Horace B. Davis, an associate professor of economics at the University of Kansas City, had also resisted academic authorities in their investigation of his political activities. He too was fired.

In June 1953, Davis was called to appear before the Senate Internal Security Subcommitteee, and invoked the Fifth Amendment in refusing to answer questions concerning the following associations and activities:

> Communist Party; Columbia University; Cornell University; School for Democracy; Stockholm Peace Petition; Abraham Lincoln Brigade; American Investor's Union; Schappes Defense Committee; *New Masses* (contributor); International Labor Defense; Abraham Lincoln School; Maryland *CIO News* (editor); Federated Press Petition to Free Earl Browder; Workers' Alliance of the United States (executive board); Conference of Pan-American Democracy (sponsor); American League against War and Fascism (sponsor); American Friends of the Chinese People (advisory board); Appeal to Release Luis Carlos Prestes
>
> Authorship of *Labor and Steel* and *Shoes: The Workers and the Industry*, both published by International Publishers
>
> Date when he was in Brazil
>
> Whether he used *Labor and Steel* or *Shoes* in his teaching at the University of Kansas City

A month later, the advisory council to the university president recommended an investigation of Davis. Inviting him "to discuss with them his fitness to continue as a member of the faculty," members of the Board of Trustees were interested in the same questions as the congressional committee. The chairman of the Board asked him four questions, but since Davis believed that neither the Board of Trustees nor any institutional authority had a right to ask these questions, he did not feel obliged to respond:

Mr. Howard: First . . . are [you] or [have you] ever been a member of the Communist Party?

Dr. Davis: Well, Mr. Chairman, the general issue, of course, the general principle, is the same, whether it is a question put by the Senate Internal Security Subcommittee or this board, or any other place, that is, that—well, let let me put it this way. You wouldn't say that you had the right, let me put it that way, to ask me how I voted in the last election. People's views, people's political views, affiliations, are their own. They have a duty as Americans to maintain certain standards. [Davis's attorney also mentioned technical reasons, namely the principle of waiver. In addition, he raised the question of good faith with the congressional committee if Davis should answer to the Trustees what he refused to answer to it.]

Mr. Howard: I have a second question. We should like to ask you whether you now are or whether you ever have been active in the work of the Communist Party or employed by or associated with any of its organizations.

Dr. Davis: That seems to be the same question in another form. I am afraid the answer is the same. I don't quite know what you mean by its organizations, in any case. . . .

Mr. Howard: The third question, which might be similar in form, which we should also like to ask you, whether you now are supporting or whether you ever have supported communist activities?

Dr. Davis: Well, this is as vague as they come. What are communist activities?

Mr. Howard: Well, as I said before, I think what this Board would think of as communist activities are those activities commonly understood to be carried on by the Communist Party.

Dr. Davis: Now, when you ask the question that way, Mr. Howard, it puts me in a very difficult position, because there are so many things that the Communist Party stands for and has stood for at different times, which you or I or any member of this Board would consider to be worthy aims, and to say that I have never stood for any aims that the Communist Party was standing for, or even for several such, would be just to say that I haven't ever had any political ideas at all. . . .

Mr. Howard: As a matter of record, could you tell us whether in the period during 1941 to 1946 you were a member of any faculty of any school or college during those years?

Dr. Davis: Mr. Chairman, I see that I was under a misapprehension about the nature of this meeting. You are asking the same questions the Jenner Committee asked. You say this isn't an inquisition. I thought the Jenner Committee was an inquisition and I treated it so. I have no desire to defy the Board or refuse to cooperate with it in any legitimate way, but actually you are not any more entitled to ask these questions than the Jenner Committee.[4]

The following week, the chief executive administrator of the University of Kansas City responded by filing two charges against Davis:

The charges on which I am suggesting the termination of your services are that you failed to disclose in your application for employment to the University of Kansas City pertinent information in regard to your prior teaching experience, and that you refused to answer questions put to you by the Trustees of the University, or to cooperate with them in the performance of their duty to determine whether you are bound by commitments which render you unfit to continue in a position of educational trust.[5]

In attempting to establish the second charge in the hearing before the Executive Committee of the Board of Trustees and the President's Advisory Council, the counsel for the university pressed the point that Davis had commitments that would disqualify him from his position. On questioning by Davis's attorney, the counsel summed up what he saw as at the heart of the charge—"that he is a communist, that he has been a communist since 1929." He pointed to Davis's communist or possible communist connections, naming some additional organizations—the Council for American Democracy, the Friends of the Soviet Union, the National Committee to Aid Victims of German Fascism, the American Fund for Public Service, the Prisoners Release Fund, and the American Committee for the Protection of the Foreign Born. He noted Davis's book reviews not only in *New Masses*, but in *Science and Society*; the fact that his books were published by International Publishers; his role in bringing Herbert Phillips from the University of Washington to the campus; his connection with "peace fronts"; an article in the *Monthly Review* on the Rosenberg case; and the circulation on the campus of a pro-Rosenberg article by D. N. Pritt. Then he shifted ground and said that the issue was not whether Davis had commitments, but whether he had failed to cooperate with the Board of Trustees in their efforts to find out whether he had commitments.[6]

There seemed to be little reason for Davis's dismissal on the grounds of his having been engaged in ominously radical political behavior. The only substantial point in defending the revocation of tenure was that Davis had omitted biographical details on his job application. Yet, even this was never really the issue. The chairman of the Board of Trustees had earlier summarized what he saw as critical:

Mr. Howard: We are not a congressional committee and as I said to begin with, this is in no sense a trial. We are asking questions that we think as trustees of the university we have a right to ask. Whether the Congress of the United States or Justice Black or anybody asks or does not ask them, we feel we have a right to ask them.[7]

And five faculty on the President's Advisory Council concurred.

We did consider important, however, the fact that Dr. Davis had failed to include a considerable part of his past employment on his original application blank and, when asked to supply the missing part, refused to do so. . . .

It seems to us that a professor does not have a moral right to maintain a double standard in which on the one hand he claims protection under academic freedom but on the other hand refuses to communicate freely with his colleagues in the open market place on so important an issue as his possible allegiance to a system which would eventually destroy academic freedom. In other words, a university is not bound to tolerate intolerance or grant freedom to those who will not say whether or not they give adherence to a system which would destroy freedom. . . .

To refuse to answer an outside congressional committee which might be open to some legal and ethical question is one thing, but to refuse to reply to questions about employment and to refuse to communicate freely with colleagues is another thing. It may be that a university should tolerate heresy, but it should not tolerate a refusal to allow heresy or any other ideas to be examined, openly discussed, and subjected to the competition of the open market place.[8]

Davis was said not to have been sufficiently frank during the proceedings, but it is clear from the record that members of the hearing tribunal were most annoyed by his defiance of the Board of Trustees. The tribunal felt that the Board was in a difficult position, that it was uneasy, and that its desire for answers was quite reasonable. Davis would not bend, and a unanimous vote for dismissal was announced.[9] For the committee, the case was quite straightforward:

Those who at one moment claim the privilege of trading in the free market place of ideas may not, in the next, seek refuge in secrecy or a closed system of thought. In matters of basic social importance all members of an academic community must stand up and be counted. . . .

But the real issue is this: Shall a member of the academic community have the right to refuse to tell his associates whether he is a member of an organization, such as the Communist Party, which disqualifies him for academic life? Our answer is that he does not have this right. The present situation does not require us to enter the involved legal controversy concerning the educator's right to use the protection of the Fifth Amendment in refusing to answer questions put by congressional investigating committees. We need not go that far. This body has the responsiblity to decide only whether a member of this faculty, when questioned by other members of this academic community, can refuse to state that he is not a member of the Communist Party and continue to enjoy the privileges of a teacher in this institution. During the course of the hearings Dr. Davis did not avail himself of the opportunity to deny that he is a communist, or subject to communist influences.

No member of this institution may refuse to state his position on a matter of such fundamental importance not only to this academic body but to all of

American society. Dr. Davis has, therefore, disqualified himself for further membership in the faculty of the University of Kansas City.

The risks of taking the Fifth Amendment were particularly great. Once the question of someone's loyalty was raised, administrative authorities wanted verbal assurances that he was free of communist influences. Claims of conscience, letters of testimony from others, reading lists and course outlines, favorable professional evaluations, were all deemed immaterial; they were not enough to restore confidence. Convincing others that one was acting in good faith was unlikely if one was not fully pliant. Complete disclosure might not be enough to hold one's job, but anything short of it would certainly fail. In the eyes of some administrators, not to cooperate was yet another radical act. It seemed to suggest that an individual still adhered to the moral and political values that led him to have communist sympathies in the first place. It was believed that those who were not open were unrealistic, and were stigmatizing both themselves and the institution. It might be true that they were even disloyal. A dismissal at Dickinson College illustrates how such ideas developed and how events typically unfolded.

A Case from Dickinson College

L. R. LaVallee, an assistant professor of economics whose political activities on behalf of Henry Wallace had incensed authorities at Oregon State College in the late 1940s, had been identified as a clandestine member of an underground communist cell while employed ten years earlier by the National War Labor Board, and was called before the House Committee on Un-American Activities. In a conversation with the college president prior to being asked to give testimony, he stated that he had never been either a member of the Communist Party or a fellow traveler. He was warned by the president that if he took the Fifth Amendment this could affect his reappointment, but that he could expect reappointment if he explicitly stated that he had never been a communist or that he had once been a communist but was no longer one. In his appearance before the congressional committee he nonetheless pleaded the Fifth Amendment to fifty-one questions. This set in motion a campus inquiry.

During these proceedings, among other things, LaVallee refused to answer questions concerning past associations, refused to sign a written statement that he was "not a communist and had never been one," and refused to identify his own signature. (When asked whether he would under oath give a statement identifying particular exhibits containing his signature, he replied "since this might lead to a discussion of my political beliefs, I would not do so."[10]) He evaded answering questions about whether he believed the Communist Party was a conspiracy against the survival of the United States. When asked by the college president to state his opinion as to the purposes of the Communist Party, he replied that it was "a political party as are the Republican, Democrat, or Socialist Party." He would not say how he would answer a student who asked whether the Communist Party advocates the overthrow of the government. He would not tell campus authorities whether, while at the college, he had been in contact with any person or persons believed by him to be subversive. He then immediately denied that he had ever attempted to enlist any student or teacher into the Communist Party or any other subversive organization, and disclaimed any knowledge of anyone who wished to overthrow the government.

Campus authorities were determined to learn more about his politics, and he did not believe that this line of inquiry was proper. When asked whether he had ever been a member of the Communist Party, he replied, "under circumstances such as this, my political views or actions should not be answered by me." He was asked whether or not he knew a Gerald Matchett and stated, "I think you have the right to ask that question" but "this intrudes upon my associates which I do not think, out of conscience, I can answer."[11] When pressed on this issue, he refused to answer questions as to whether he knew Matchett was or had been a member of the Communist Party at the time he gave Matchett's name as a possible reference. He responded, "I do not care to discuss this or my associates."[12]

LaVallee correctly believed that these matters were being used to establish his competence or incompetence. This, he argued, intruded on his academic freedom, on a teacher's personal prerogatives.[13] Thus, to a trustee's question, "I would like to ask Dr. LaVallee if he thinks a communist should be permitted to teach on the faculty of an American college," he replied, "I don't think I should answer that question; it is too controversial." To another trustee's question, "do you know whether the Communist Party advocates the overthrow of our government?" he responded, "there is a lot of conflicting official information about this and I think it is too controversial for me to answer."[14]

In addition to claiming the right to personal privacy, he called a request of the president that he explain his position on the purposes of the Communist Party an "inquisition," and went on to accuse him of behaving like Senator McCarthy. The president testified that LaVallee's failure to answer such questions raised grave doubts in his mind whether an individual with so unrealistic an understanding of present-day history and world affairs should be teaching on any college faculty.

A faculty committee with no real jurisdiction in the case characterized LaVallee's intransigence as "imprudent and uncooperative," and recommended that he be given only a one-year instead of the customary three-year appointment.[15] The executive committee of the Board of Trustees was convinced that a more severe penalty was in order, that LaVallee should be dismissed on the charge of incompetence.

There was a widespread perception on campus "that it was *highly probable* (1) that the testimony against him was true, (2) that he feared perjury charges if he identified his signature, (3) that he had not been truthful when he said he had never been a communist, and (4) that he was a secret supporter of communism. Indeed, his lack of integrity was so highly probable as to be beyond any reasonable doubt. . . ."[16]

In the end, the Board took the position that not only did it have a right to information that it believed necessary to judge a faculty member's fitness, but that the mere failure to answer questions whether or not they were relevant in determining fitness, was sufficient grounds for dismissal:

> Dr. LaVallee's failure to disclose information to the college both in his interviews with Dr. Edel and with other members of the college administration, especially concerning his past associations, and his evasive attitude throughout the hearing before the executive committee on April 20, 1956, clearly disqualify him from being a member of the faculty of the College.[17]

The Partially Obstinate

Besides those who were determined to resist any inquiry into their activities, there were those who, as much as they might have tried, always revealed less than their interrogators wanted to know. They might, for example, be willing to talk about themselves, but not about others. To be sure, these principals did not provoke quite as negative a reponse as those who would not cooperate at all—those who in essence were telling institutional authorities to mind their own business. There were instances, in fact, when administrators showed a great deal of sympathy for someone willing to acknowledge that he had helped create a problem for the institution. Still, since administrative officers had no way of ascertaining if any claim of conscience was authentic, they expected faculty to meet institutional standards of full disclosure. Those who fell short were disadvantaged in efforts to hold their jobs.

In the end, any individual seen as a liability was dismissed. The less accommodating a principal was judged to be, the more likely he would be seen as a liability, and (1) the more promptly the dismissal would occur, and (2) the clearer it was that this would be the outcome.

At Jefferson Medical College, the administration insisted that three individuals give it the names of others with whom they had once been associated in Communist Party activities. They refused, pleading that giving this information would betray others, and they would find this intolerable. Two were willing to explain in detail why they had joined and why they had left the Communist Party. The administration insisted, however, that it was their duty as loyal citizens and employees to comply fully with the request. They must do so, they were told, so it could be certified that they were not subversive. As a trustee put it, it is

> incumbent on us to inquire whether any members of our faculty have been at any time members of the Communist Party or any subversive organization, and if any answer in the affirmative, then on what date they separated themselves, therefrom ... and then satisfy us that their separation is in fact a truthful separation.[18]

When asked to name names, one of the three insisted that he did not know of anyone at Jefferson with former Party affiliations who was not currently under investigation by the college. When he was next asked for the identities of individuals not connected with the institution, he was no more cooperative. He responded that he was willing to speak frankly about his political past, but would not answer questions that had bearing on the activities of others. He was called belligerent, evasive, and arrogant by administrative authorities.

None of the three was willing to provide the "evidence that you have broken, other than to say that you have." Since they all stood firm against the request to become an "informant," they were warned, "your refusal to tell us will undoubtedly have an effect upon your career at Jefferson."

During more formal hearings two months later,[19] they were told that the administration was not convinced and would not state that they were not subversive. Again, two described their experiences in the Communist Party but, when pressed, would not give the committee members any names. The school's authorities were not pleased. The lawyer for the college put it simply: "A status [of Party membership] once having been established, the burden of proof then shifts to the person who claims a change in that status to prove it, and the only proof which has been offered has been from Dr. Rutman's oath." Moreover, the three were reminded that at the request of the administration a faculty member has an "obligation" to identify others on the faculty who were and might still be communists.

The next time they were ordered to name others, they were threatened with an investigation by an outside "government" committee and with "public exposure and shame." A few weeks after they were summoned to the dean's office and introduced to a staff member of the House Committee on Un-American Activities, they were called in again and dismissed.

The college would not say why it took this step. Since two of the three answered all other questions,[20] were not found to be subversive, and were assured that past membership in the Communist Party would not jeopardize their appointments, a major, perhaps the major, reason for the college's action was their not revealing the identities of others, information that was not really needed for any purpose by the institution. It was apparent that administrative authorities saw the act of full cooperation as a test of character: those who did what they were asked were obviously loyal and trustworthy. The act of cooperating was more important than any information that might be imparted.

It is difficult to imagine why administrative authorities asked particular questions, and what sort of answers they hoped to get. To deal with the uncertainty, many principals took pains to leave the impression that they were fully sharing all of the information to which administrators felt they were entitled. Seeming to divulge all or nearly all was definitely a necessary, but not usually a sufficient, condition for holding on to an appointment.

Cooperating with Colleagues

Cooperation and Noncooperation at the University of Michigan

Not only did principals who were seen as open and cooperative fare better with administrators than principals who were thought to be holding back information, but they were also regarded more favorably by faculty charged with reviewing their cases. This is seen quite clearly in the following excerpts from the deliberations of a three-hour meeting between the executive committee of a college and the Special Advisory Committee to the president of the University of Michigan on the suspension of two young faculty who, because of their political affiliations, were in jeopardy of losing their jobs. A zoologist, Clement Markert, admitted past Communist Party membership and activity, including military service in the Spanish Civil War with the Abraham Lincoln Brigade for the Popular Front. He described to the committee how he slowly drifted away from the Party. Consistent with his public statements, Chandler Davis, the individual with whom Markert was compared, refused to answer any question that he felt the committee had no right to ask, and this included all questions touching on the subject of politics.

About Markert:

Dr. Haber: He took the position with us, and it may have a bearing on the question, that while he refused to comply with the questions of the Clardy Committee, that he had no hesitation whatsoever in discussing fully his entire history with a university group, formal or informal, or with anyone who asked him; that everything about him is known to the government; that they know every address he has lived, every time he goes out, every meeting or everything he reads. They have a complete record of everything, and he has no hesitation in discussing it. He just did not want to be in a position in replying to the questions of the committee, to involve other people. But as far as his colleagues were concerned, you asked the questions, and "I will answer them to the best of my ability."

Well, I should say that I for one was impressed that there was no deceit in his reference to us, that there was complete frankness.

Chairman Smith: He did not attempt to evade or avoid any questions?

Dr. Haber: No, we asked him for example, Russell, questions on his attitude about Korea, and Indo-China, we asked him questions of current policy on the current political scene. He expressed his views very frankly, and we asked him questions, I was interested as a student of these problems, about receiving orders from other people about intellectual freedom. He gave us his views.

I may not agree with his answers, but I certainly did not get any impression that he was evasive. That is the point I want to make.

Dr. Odegaard: I think for one thing, that perhaps this is a question which should go around the room, because it gets pretty close to the nub of the matter. Inevitably when you sit in a situation like this, you have whatever radar system you possess at work trying to form conclusions and reach generalizations about the character of the person to whom you are talking. This is not a scientific process, but it is one that we all have to live with, and use to the best of our ability, and I think that this statement with reference to Markert reveals our impression that he was not withholding anything.

As a matter of fact, a very enlarged portion of his story came out right at the beginning. He was aware of the problem which confronted the university, indicated he was sorry it happened that way, but that he had to do what he thought he had to do, and that he had not gone around asking for advice, I remember, on this point, from academic colleagues, because he felt that this was something where he had to make up his own mind. I do not mean on the legal matter, because he went to his lawyer and had counsel on that, but he said he did not see that it would have accomplished any good for him to have gone to administrative officers of the university, for example, with his problem, prior to the hearing, because that would come out in any case and he would have to do what in conscience he felt he had to do, and the way the thing shaped up he didn't see what there was that a university officer could say to him in the area; that he had to deal with that problem himself.

Now having taken that position, when he came before us, he recognized certainly that the university at least has to make an explanation of whatever happens in these cases, and I would like to say that he did his best to cooperate by being frank, with no trace of evasion in the answers which he gave to us.

So that in general our impression of the man was, however much one individually might disagree with some of his judgments about affairs, that there was what you could call integrity and honesty there.

Each one I think could go beyond that and make a judgment as to how he happens to end up in a particular philosophical position which he takes. His life history has some bearing on the explanation for that, but certainly that whole story came out with no trace of evasion in response to the questions which we put to him.

Now that is a general statement about the character of the man, as we tried to measure it in terms of the experience which we had had with him. I think it is a question that perhaps might go around the room, to be sure that I have stated the case as accurately as could be stated for itself, by each member of the committee.

Chairman Smith: I am wondering if any others would care to add to that?

Dr. Frankena: I would like to state I was impressed by the fact he stated his philosophical opinions as surely as he did, and he knew they were unpopular. He was not covering up on that point at all, he was quite frank by saying that.

Chairman Smith: You mean by that, he still thinks there is something to the communist economic theory?

Dr. Frankena: Yes, and he didn't want us to understand that he didn't.

Dr. Haber: . . . He convinced me insofar as one's intuitive impressions of an hour's conversation makes possible conviction, that he was in no part whatsoever active in the communist activities, the Communist Party, communist association, communist movement; that his philosophy was hardly what you might call a free enterprise philosophy; and as Bill Frankena said, he was rather startled at the complete frankness with which he outlined those points.

You would have thought that he might be somewhat less frank, in order not to complicate the problem which existed for him, and it is for that reason that when Charles Odegaard uses the word integrity, it needs to be outlined, there is no question.

I certainly differ with his conclusions, but there was no question that there was admiration for his bluntness and frankness. . . .

Chairman Smith: Has he been, as one might put it, fully cooperative with the suspension notice, in the sense that he has not protested as to any of the implications of it?

Dr. Odegaard: I recall in our meeting no reference whatsoever to the suspension. He simply took it as a matter of fact that it had occurred, and that this was a serious problem before the university. There was no disposition to deny that the university had a problem on its hands. I would say there was no disposition to try to complicate the problem, by virtue of the action he took before the Clardy Committee.

About Davis:

Dr. Odegaard: . . . In my own personal judgment, I am speaking now, I think this is a question which perhaps ought to go around the room, I could not help but feel that there was a certain evasiveness. . . . In terms of his presentation, there was a position I think which showed that he simply felt as far as the university was concerned, if it had a problem, it was its problem. . . .

Dr. Odegaard: Well, we all believe he reached the wrong conclusion, but as to the sincerity, we can only say that he could be sincere. We are not far enough into the story of the facts of the case, insofar as we have been able to determine them, to say that he is or he is not. . . .

Dr. Haber: . . . I have no question but what he is an entirely naive individual, and perhaps a fool.

Chairman Smith: I don't get your point. Are you saying this is an improper question?

Dr. Haber: No, I think if he were quite intelligent about it, there would be a more frank discussion. I think he is quite unintelligent, but an unintelligent person could be quite sincere.

President Hatcher: Well, members of the Communist Party are credited with sincerity, aren't they, Bill? . . .[21]

At this point in the investigation, committee members did not show any antipathy toward Davis, but his lack of cooperation obviously had raised questions in the minds of some about his integrity. The college committee, in fact, recommended that both Markert's and Davis's suspensions be lifted, although it's decision was less qualified for the former than for the latter: for Markert, "We therefore conclude that he should be reinstated as soon as possible"; for Davis, "We hope that a firmer basis of judgment may be forthcoming, but we believe that he should be reinstated unless conclusive evidence is found of his unfitness to be a member of our faculty."

Given his forthrightness, everything about Markert became a virtue; committee members were conspicuously tolerant, accepting, and not judgmental about his past. In contrast, before Davis's inquiry was completed, many senior faculty and all administrative officers were completely frustrated—and their patience was completely exhausted. Davis, who declined to answer questions about communist associations and certain political activities in a hearing before the Special Advisory Committee to the President, would only go as far as to state explicitly that he did not advocate the violent overthrow of the government or the use of deceit in the political arena.

The committee concluded that his failure to respond to detailed questions "forecloses to the university any assistance from him in evaluating these denials." It rejected his contention that it was no concern to the university whether he was or had been a member of the Communist Party as long as there was no evidence that he had done something illegal (or immoral). It was adamant in its position that the university was entitled to ask questions concerning past or present communist associations, and that a refusal on the part of a faculty member to answer was a "serious breach of obligation," and that, although it would not consider the matter solely on that basis, this fact created "a strong, if not absolutely convincing, case for disciplinary action or dismissal."

We cannot escape the conclusion, however, that Mr. Davis's attitude on the issues under consideration shows either that he is guilty of a gross imbalance of judgment or else that he has used a carefully contrived tactic to avoid a full and candid disclosure on his part of communist associations and activities. He does not necessarily disqualify himself to remain a member of the faculty

as a teacher of mathematics if the only charge against him is that his judgment on issues related to communism and the university's concern therewith
is very bad. On the other hand, if it appears highly probable that he is using
his professed principles as a means of avoiding full and candid disclosure of
communist affiliation, he has disqualified himself to be a member of the
faculty, in our opinion, not only and simply because of the fact alone that he
has refused to fulfill an obligation of candor, but also because of the probability that he has artfully contrived to preclude inquiry of him and thus
patently lacks the integrity which he claims to possess. In order to resolve the
doubt concerning his real motivation, we have had to make some use of
assertions made by government investigators concerning Dr. Davis's past and
present Communist Party affiliations, and have had to make an evaluation of
his good faith from his demeanor and responses to questions asked him at
our hearing.

The committee continued that Davis's failure to deny the allegations
against him on the grounds of principle was not made in good faith; he was
showing a lack of candor and was being dishonest. It found him guilty of
"deviousness, artfulness, or indirection hardly to be expected of a university colleague," and unanimously recommended dismissal.[22]

Appealing before yet another committee, Davis again refused to answer
questions about his political activities. In its report, this committee took
the same general position as the previous committee. Again the recommendation for dismissal was unanimous.

Although his departmental colleagues characterized him as "a man of
integrity," and there was no information that he misused the classroom to
promote political views or engaged in any other academic misconduct, and
there was also no supportable evidence that he engaged in illegal conduct
or advocated immoral ideas, it was generally believed that he was a member of the Communist Party and therefore accepted illegal and immoral
principles and methods of action—all because he would not cooperate.

Of course, in the end, he was fired, while Markert kept his job. The
resolution of these two cases shows that at bottom the impression—of
openness and contriteness or of silence and defiance—left with those in the
academic community could be as important as political ideology or activity in determining whether an appointment was ultimately lost. As the
following unhappy example illustrates, this principle held in colleges as
well as universities.

Reed College

The case of this unmistakably foredoomed principal played itself out at
Reed College, an institution with a reputation of tolerance for assorted
ideologies and behaviors. Here, Stanley Moore, a professor of philosophy

with a continuing appointment, was terminated after refusing to discuss questions concerning possible communist associations or Communist Party membership with campus authorities. He, too, insisted that others, particularly the president and the Board of Trustees, had no business concerning themselves with his political interests, activities, and affiliations:

> *Attorney*: You said it [whether someone was a communist] was none of their [members of the Board of Trustees] business.
> *Dr. Moore*: Excuse me. I said that was my own feeling, that if I had been asked the question, I would have given the same response.
> *Attorney*: You would have told them it was none of their business?
> *Dr. Moore*: That is right. . . .[23]

Even before the Board expressed its desire to talk to him, Moore expressed his ideas about the consequences of faculty being called before a congressional investigating committee and failing to cooperate:

> Though its victims cannot be punished legally, they can be persecuted economically. As citizens they go free: as employees they get fired.
>
> There is a quick treatment and a slow. In the quick treatment the teacher is dismissed out of hand, on the ground that failure to cooperate with the committee is misconduct or that pleading the constitutional privilege is an admission of guilt. I have stated already my reasons for disputing the adequacy of these grounds.
>
> In the slow treatment the charges are investigated, that is, the trustees or the administrators conduct a hearing at which, like congressmen, they question the teacher about his beliefs, associations, and political activities—not to mention those of his friends. I believe that academic officials have no more authority to ask these questions [about beliefs, associations, and political activities] than do congressmen. It is an abuse of power for an employer to question the employee about his politics. It is a travesty of justice to do so in an atmosphere created by pressure from influential demagogues. . . .
>
> Political beliefs and activites are not properly a matter for the college's official concern.[24]

Confident, then, that he had no burden to respond, Moore remained silent in the face of a number of appeals that he make some accommodation.

Obviously, the college authorities saw the issue quite differently; in their eyes the obligations of faculty were quite clear:

> You are charged with failure to cooperate with the Board of Trustees of Reed College in the particulars hereinafter stated. . . .
>
> The committee of the Board of Trustees of Reed College requested your cooperation in attending an informal meeting of the committee on August 3,

1954, for the purpose of discussing the above situation [of alleged communist associations].

You attended the meeting of said committee, but even though the committee agreed that any information given by you with respect to your past or present connection with the Communist Party would be held in confidence you refused to disclose any information with respect thereto.

Henry F. Cabell
Chairman, Board of Trustees[25]

There was such strong feeling on the part of the Board, in fact, that as its position hardened, the college's long and widely recognized tradition of faculty autonomy was largely disregarded.

The Board of Trustees took the stand that on the basis of Moore's conduct before the subcommittee of the House Committee on Un-American Activities and the testimony of other witnesses who named him as a communist, it had a right to ask him about political matters. Invoking both the First and Fifth amendments, he had refused to tell the subcommittee whether he had attended Communist Party meetings, whether he knew certain places and persons, and whether he had been or was presently a Party member. Since membership in the Communist Party "is not consistent with membership in a college faculty," an inquiry, the Board argued, was necessary and proper. Indeed, it had a duty to investigate, and he had a professional "duty to respond with full candor."

Many on campus, not only administrators and Board members, felt that against the background of the barrage of unfavorable publicity of which the college had been the object in recent months, faculty had a special obligation to redouble their effort to reduce some of the pressure, even if this resulted in some restraints on their taken-for-granted freedoms. Moore believed that to give in here would be too great a sacrifice:

Have I put Reed College in a difficult position? I admit that the college is in a difficult position, and I sympathize with it. I am in a difficult position myself. I do not think, however, that I as an individual or the college as an institution could have avoided this crisis. It is part of the national pattern. But though the causes which produced this attack were outside our control, the decision whether to submit or to resist is within our control, I have made mine. I await yours.

For institutions, as for men, to live is to compromise; but the character of both is revealed in the specific compromises they make. It is wisdom to compromise little things for great, foolishness to compromise great things for little. For myself, I know few greater things than self respect, intellectual independence, and the chance at least to argue what one has spent one's life to learn.[26]

Moore rejected the Board of Trustees's offer to talk informally and confidentially:

First, as to the completely informal opportunity for me to talk with the various investigators, I believe that the forms of procedure were established for my protection and that their strict observance is to my interests. For this reason and for the personal consideration of time and money I decline to avail myself of the informal opportunity you offer. I have nothing to add to my 3,000 word analysis of public charges and statement of relevant facts, but if any of the investigators wish to send me written questions, I shall be happy to reply on the understanding that eventually both questions and replies will be included in the public record.[27]

He accepted a second request ("I interpreted that as an order") to meet with a special committee of the Board. Even in this setting—in which he was told that what he said would "be released only as he desired it to be released"—he was not interested in making disclosures, and responded by challenging the Board to provide an open hearing so that all allegations against him could be laid out; he held that he should be judged only on the basis of his teaching ability and professional competence. It was the responsibility of the Board of Trustees, he insisted, to show evidence of misconduct, of moral turpitude, of incompetence, and the like.

The Board was not at all interested in the subtleties of Moore's argument. In its view the case was not complicated. Faculty have a duty to cooperate. Moore's reluctance to give information was a violation of this responsibility and, accordingly, "justifiable grounds for dismissal." In a word, "Professor Moore's refusal to cooperate has been misconduct." Everything else—including his contentions that the proceedings were unfair and departed from those recommended by the American Association of University Professors, and that they reflected a change in college policy of precluding political criteria for appointments or granting tenure—fell on deaf ears. As is apparent from Appendix K, faculty members were not as likely as administrators to be unnerved by noncooperation. This is not surprising.

The heart of Moore's argument was that cooperation or noncooperation was not an absolute, but had to be seen in context:

I want to say in connection with this to tie this up with the particular charges, it isn't a question of cooperation, of refusing to answer any questions. Noncooperation depends upon a refusal to answer proper questions, and the question of what are proper questions for the Trustees to ask can be affected by their past conduct, by the evidence as to what their policy was, and by an expectation and belief which arises on the part of their employees as to what they will and will not be held responsible for.[28]

This contention was ignored, and the charge of failing to cooperate with the Board of Trustees was sustained.

It is significant and worth noting that the Board did not dismiss two other members of the faculty who admitted past membership and denied present membership in the Communist Party, and who fully cooperated with inquiries. In its unanimous recommendation, the Special Trustee Committee was quite clear in specifying why Moore's case was different from the other two:

1. That, with reference to Messrs. Reynolds and Marsak, the committee recommends that no disciplinary action be taken in either case, but that Mr. Marsak be permitted to continue until the expiration of his contract (June, 1955), at which time further inquiry be made as to his attitudes, behavior and abilities to carry on as a teacher; and that Mr. Reynolds be continued in the employment of the college; but
2. That, in the case of Stanley Moore, with the aid of the Trustee's counsel appropriate charges be prepared in connection with his failure and refusal to cooperate with the members of the special committee, the college and other investigating bodies. . . .[29]

In describing his experience, the newspaper editor James Wechsler has written, "I had resolved much earlier that silence was suicidal in dealing with McCarthy. . . . To put it simply, I did not believe that my answers would tend to incriminate or degrade me but I was quite certain that silence would."[30] This principle was true not only with reference to congressional investigations.

Given the general feeling throughout society that the more that was known about the inner workings of the Communist Party, the less of a danger it would be, and given the resulting pressures on anyone who might have anything to reveal about it, it is surprising that any academics chose to remain silent. Those who did must have known that they were definitely expected to respond, even to volunteer information. They must have understood that they would be punished for not assisting in an inquiry. Unless one believes that these academics had more to hide than other suspected communists on or off campus, or that the counsel they received, legal or otherwise, was below standard, then it is not unreasonable to conclude that morality, principle, or conscience was at least one source of their defiance.

Noncooperation with Colleagues: Two Cases

Committees of faculty may not have demanded the same degree of cooperation as administrators, but there is little doubt that they expected cooperation. The counteraction against Edwin Berry Burgum at New York University for his position that he was not required to answer any of the charges against him illustrates this fact well. So does the fate of Ralph

Gundlach, who had been an undergraduate and a graduate student at the University of Washington, and had spent his entire professional career at the university before he ran afoul of institutional authorities and colleagues and, as a result, lost the job he had held for two decades. What set Gundlach apart from other suspected radicals at the University of Washington was the fact that he did not "communicate information" and "equivocated or failed to disclose" what others on campus believed they had a right to know. These two cases show that a point was quickly reached when the issue of cooperation took precedence over the issue of communism, even when faculty were sitting in judgment.

After he had invoked the Fifth Amendment in a congressional inquiry, Burgum was brought before a twelve-man faculty committee charged with conduct unbecoming a professor and with using the Fifth Amendment to avoid disclosing his and other people's relationship to the Communist Party.

Burgum held that not only was it a violation of his rights to be questioned about political matters, but that the hearings were a farce. He insisted that the charge was so drawn as to be unsusceptible to defense, that the evidence was mostly irrelevant, that many witnesses were professional informers who could not be believed, and that the questions were outside the scope of the inquiry. He was asked: "As far as the Communist Party is concerned, you have not recruited at the university, or as a result of university contacts, any person for the Communist Party?" And he replied: "I think you are now getting into an area that is beyond the ken of the university, and I should feel that it is inadvisable to answer that question one way or the other." He was asked: "You hail the Soviet Constitution as making a step forward in human development. Would you, and do you, approve all the provisions in the Soviet Constitution?" And he replied: "This matter would be very intriguing. In answering your question, I would have to go into a lot of detail and it would involve virtually a great deal of scholarly research. Therefore, it seems to me much better if I rest upon my claim that this is an area that is beyond the province of the committee."[31]

He had, however, at one point made an affirmative statement:

> I deny that I have ever used the classroom to indoctrinate communism. I deny that I have ever committed espionage. I deny that I have ever been under the control of a foreign power or that I have surrendered my free will to any domestic organization. I have never advocated violent overthrow of the government, in the classroom or elsewhere. I have never followed dictation from any source either in my writing or in my teaching.[32]

Most of the members of the faculty committee did not agree with Burgum's contention that the proceedings were improper and that no inferences were permissible from his responses. Moreover, his stand was seen as little more than defiance, as an attempt to block the committee's efforts to ascertain what to it were important facts. Many concluded that he was violating his ethical duty, to the government and to the university, by not cooperating. The committee felt that Burgum was entitled to the legal protection of the Fifth Amendment. However, it believed that his behavior had not met "the tests of responsible exercises of his rights of academic freedom." It concluded that dismissal "for his abuse of his university position under the cover of academic freedom would not be inconsistent" with institutional policy. The committee chairman added:

> He conducted himself with something less than the honest effort at coopera-
> tion I would expect from a colleague who had nothing to conceal. He had
> requested a hearing; the senate committee, representative of the faculties of
> New York University, sought for the whole truth. We were not bound by
> formal legal rules nor by trial practices; it was a hearing by colleagues with
> the widest latitude, both oral and documentary, being given the parties to the
> case. Any such hearing could be expected to open up wide vistas of a man's
> activities and motives; efforts to block this consequence of interrogation by
> the petitioner's colleagues through legal barriers could but confirm the im-
> plication of something to conceal. . . .
>
> The second—and in effect key—charge was attacked persistently and skill-
> fully from every angle with perfect teamwork between petitioner and his
> counsel. This was done with good reason under the direction of an astute
> lawyer because the charge opened up the case on the clearly understood
> though broad grounds of academic turpitude—conduct unbecoming a
> teacher in his chosen community activities outside the university, yet deliber-
> ately identified with the university for its prestige values. . . .
>
> Thus we come to values other than legal. Every right, be it legal, political or
> social, carries with it a duty. Academic freedom, however liberty-loving the
> scholar, is not anarchy; the responsibilities of scholarship are as profoundly
> social as intellectual. The petitioner, under the law of the land, has the right to
> stand on his judicial silence. Therefore he may continue his extra-curricular
> activities *legally* immune, within the protection of this carefully contrived
> vicious circle of alleged possible self-incrimination. But *morally* he cannot
> presume to force us to condone or to accept what appears to me by every
> academic yardstick to measure an anti-social civic attitude. The university
> community is not only free, it has the duty to disassociate itself from those
> who flagrantly abuse the freedom it confers upon its members. . . .[33]

Inferences were clearly drawn from Burgum's silence: he was not trustworthy; there was an unmistakable "impression of subterfuge, semantic sparring, and evasion, if not downright lying."

The chancellor of New York University found a great deal in the committee's judgment and its chairman's assertions with which he could agree:

It follows that a university may, in the interests of maintaining academic freedom, inquire into the beliefs and associations of any faculty member who it has reason to believe is conducting himself in such a way as to violate his obligations as a scholar and teacher.

Refusal of a member of a faculty to answer questions put to him by his university in an effort to determine whether he is bound by commitments which violate his own academic freedom renders him unfit to continue in a position of educational trust.

In the case of Mr. Burgum, an elected faculty committee of his peers, in the face of such evidence and in the face of Mr. Burgum's continued refusal to clarify his position with respect to such commitments, found that he was unworthy of continuing as a member of the academic community.

By its action, the faculty committee reaffirmed the traditional obligation of faculty members to themselves and to the community to avow openly and honestly their beliefs and not to conceal relationships which could be inimical to the welfare of their profession, the university, and the public.[34]

Twenty-eight years of service did not forestall Burgum's dismissal.

There are a number of parallels between Burgum's and Gundlach's cases. When directly asked by the president of the University of Washington whether he had been or presently was a member of the Communist Party, Gundlach, who was an associate professor of psychology, answered by saying that government officials could not prove that he was and that he, himself, could not prove that he was not. This reply was considered unacceptable; he was not being sufficiently "responsive." For being evasive here and in other meetings with university authorities, Gundlach was brought before a faculty committee and charged with, among other things, neglect of duty. As far as the university president was concerned, it made perfect sense to recommend the dismissal of someone involved in communist-front organizations since he was accepted as a Party member even though he may not actually have been one.

Seven of the eleven faculty on the committee recommended that Gundlach be dismissed, noting that his relations with the university administration were uncooperative and unsatisfactory. Four wrote: "We believe that the failure to respond directly to [the president's] question was a neglect of duty on [his] part within the meaning of that phrase in the university's administrative code. The duty of a member of the faculty does not begin and end with his teaching duties. It necessarily also includes, as a minimum, a reasonable measure of cooperation with the administrative officers of the university in matters affecting the welfare and reputation of the institution."[35] That his "lack of desire" to cooperate, as seen in his "failure to answer frankly questions relating to his Communist Party membership" (an assumption, in part "established" by the university counsel who produced evidence that Gundlach followed the Communist Party line on issues such as the advocacy of legislation dealing with lynching, price controls, and fair employment practices), brought such a severe sanction is not as noteworthy as the fact that of the ten individuals whom the administration had investigated, he, in the end, was the only one a majority of the committee agreed should be dismissed. The others had shown, which he had not, that they had the "general welfare of the institution and the problems of the administration in mind as well as [their] own problems." They were not "indifferent" or "hostile" to the university's concerns and reputation. In a curious twist of logic, it was concluded that if Gundlach

> was not and is not a Party member, he could readily and voluntarily have adduced much better supporting proof.[36]

It was thus perfectly clear that an individual's attitude toward an investigation was a dominant factor in how a case turned out—that it served one very badly, for example, to tell a president "I am opposed in principle to the setting up of political tests for teachers." Some faculty, in fact, were even assured by administrative authorities that they could be continued if they "made a clean breast of things," or would "communicate freely," or would "renounce" Henry Wallace in the press to show "complete withdrawal" from his presidential campaign.

From the first, it was unmistakable that all faculty had to be open with both administrative authorities and colleagues. During the 1949–50 loyalty oath controversy at the University of California (which will be discussed more fully presently), a committee charged with evaluating the petitions of the thirty-one individuals who had refused to sign the oath would not make favorable recommendations for one full professor, two associate professors, and two assistant professors. Each of the five had "refused to discuss with the committee either the question as to whether or not he had any connection with the Communist Party or his views with respect to this organization." Although the committee noted that there was no evidence of disloyalty, it felt that it could not recommend continuation of employment on the grounds that the five had "not complied with the conditions of employment established by the Regents." For the chairman of the committee, the matter revolved around a single issue—cooperation:

> [They] did not cooperate as we thought they should have, and we advised the Regents, through the president, that we could see no reason why their employment should be continued. We did not make the positive assertion that they were communists, however. That is a difficult thing to say. We said that we did not think we could advise the continuation of their employment

because they had not met the terms of the resolution of April 21 [which demanded cooperation].[37]

Although institutional committees were not performing the same function as congressional committees, there was little doubt in the minds of their members that they were entitled to full disclosure. No one but a few principals ever asked whether committees needed all of the information they requested. If their function was to determine whether subversive ideas were being propagated on campus, one might wonder why they did not spend more time inquiring into what, in fact, was taught or said to students. However, if their true function was to determine loyalty to the institution, then answers to questions were necessary, as the act of responding suggested that a principal recognized his institutional obligations. Silence indicated that the right of the individual took precedence over the right of the institution. In any case, even if those principals who would not assist these inquiries were active communists, it was arguable whether they were in any way a threat to the institutional or social order.

Full Cooperation

Convincing others that one was not holding back names and other information was not the only thing a principal could do to help himself. A number of principals were made to go beyond simply responding to direct questions. When that occurred, few discovered that the more obsequiously one acted, the better one's chances of holding an appointment. Those who explained the political activism of their student days as a consequence of having grown up during the economic depression of the 1930s, or of an impoverished childhood, or of the folly of youth, or of naive idealism were accorded more sympathy than those who did not appear to recant. By no means did as many principals as would have pleased academic authorities formally shift ground. Nor did many move as far as academic authorities would have liked. If such had been their nature, they would perhaps have been better able to avoid the predicament in which they found themselves.

Beyond repudiating the past, five individuals from three different universities were able to keep their jobs by signing and filing affidavits affirming that they were not members of the Communist Party or engaged in communist work. A much publicized affidavit that William Parry from the University of Buffalo was forced to sign read in part:

> I am not in any sense a member of the Communist Party or in any sense affiliated with such Party and have not been in any sense a member of the Communist Party or in any sense affiliated with such Party since December 1946.

I do not believe in, and I am not a member of nor do I support any organization that believes in or teaches, the overthrow of the United States government by force or by illegal or unconstitutional methods and since December 1946 I have not believed in and I have not been a member of nor have I supported any organization that believed in or taught the overthrow of the United States government by force or by any illegal or unconstitutional methods; and I have at no time taught or advocated the forcible overthrow of the United States government.[38]

Not only were these five principals made to affirm their loyalty publicly, but their tenure was revoked. Being placed on annual appointments, in effect, on probation, of course extended their trial. Authorities could continue to check to make sure that they had truly repudiated their past political beliefs.

Not surprisingly, one discernible reaction to degrading inquisitorial practices and public humiliation seemed to be a diminished interest in political matters. An attorney in one case assured the regents that his clients had "no desire to engage in any political affray from now on." Echoed on campuses across the country, this attitude undoubtedly helped lay the foundation of the "placid decade" that was to follow.

Exercising Control: The University of California

It is unclear whether academic authorities who forced faculty to abjure under oath any sympathy or connection with the communist movement did so to alleviate their concerns or those of the public. It is clear that other considerations were as important in influencing their judgments and actions as apprehension about communism or disloyalty. They were without question interested in maintaining institutional stability—so much so, in fact, that instead of its being a means to an end, it became an end in itself.

Academic authorities were also interested in maintaining the distribution of power within institutions of higher learning. Their problem was to hold their positions, vis-à-vis faculty and over time. Principals who cooperated were publicly acknowledging that they recognized who ultimately controlled the college or university. They also were in effect saying that they did not wish to embarrass or weaken the authority of academic administrators. The much discussed loyalty oath controversy at the University of California exemplifies this in detail, perhaps more transparently than any other case in the study.

At the suggestion of the administration, the Board of Regents of the University of California amended a disclaimer affidavit to what for a number of years had been a noncontroversial oath of allegiance expected of faculty. The new requirement called for faculty to attest to nonmembership and nonbelief in any organization that advocated the overthrow of the government. With this policy, the administration presumably would be assured that there were no members of the Communist Party on the faculty.

The action by the Board of Regents precipitated considerable debate among faculty over whether to sign such a document. For one or more of the following reasons a number of individuals refused to sign: it was an assault on their honor; there was no loyalty problem on campus; the whole business only added to the hysteria on the subject of communism; it was a political test; it intruded on their prerogatives; the academic profession was being picked on; tenure might be violated; the policy would not work; the entire plan was suddenly being forced upon the faculty by the administration. In short, many felt that faculty rights were being threatened.

As the weeks wore on, the pressure to sign increased, and the number of faculty who continued to resist decreased. At the same time, the unrest among faculty increased, while the issues slowly narrowed and changed.

Initially, the administration was primarily interested in reaffirming the university's opposition to communism and in barring communists from university service. And even as the matter played itself out, some members of the Board of Regents remained troubled by the issue of communism. One was sure that "if the original loyalty oath were rescinded the flag would fly in the Kremlin."[39] Yet another acknowledged that it was "not worth the paper it was printed on."

At the early stages of the controversy there was bickering about who was right and who should back down. Many members of the Board felt that since the faculty played some part in formulating the new policy, they would be committing a breach of good faith if they backed away from it. A regent said that

> Dr. Grant has stated it very well. I think we are in a situation here where this Board adopted a policy nine years ago, which it has reaffirmed. I think the Board has properly had the right to assume that, not once, but twice, the faculty through its representatives has agreed to a restatement of that policy. I do not believe this Board out of decent respect for public respect in California can abandon its position. I think you are utterly unrealistic, and I think you are theorizing despite the fact. . . .[40]

At this time, there was also a widespread belief among the Regents that much of the discontent on the part of the faculty was being stoked by a small minority of dissidents. One regent spoke of an "irreconcilable minority of the faculty [who] had ruthlessly maneuvered the situation." He warned his fellow regents: "We are up against here a situation in which there is a great reluctance to recognize the fact that there can never be unity on this thing, except by abject submission on the part of the Regents, the president, and the senate to a minority of that faculty."[41] He summed up what were at that point many of the concerns of the Board of Regents:

> Now then, having made that statement to the public and the statement of September 30, and then to come out now and tell the public some nebulous thing like this, it would be a disaster and I would not share the responsibility. You have to realize this Board had a right to stand on what it understood was complete agreement with representatives of the faculty. If you go behind these agreements constantly you create a situation of irresponsibility. It means that an aggressive minority of that faculty, stressing unity—an aggressive minority constantly can exercise a veto power embroiling this faculty and the Regents in constant turmoil. I beg of you to look at this thing in a realistic light. You cannot make agreements and abandon them as if they were a nullity. I know the Regents will be shocked that there is no agreement.[42]

Under the circumstances, the president was confident that the best thing that the authorities could do was to hold their course. "We are in midstream and have a substantial majority of the faculty going along with us and to back down now would put us in a most difficult position."

The faculty saw matters differently. One told the Board of Regents:

> I simply cannot come to the conclusion that there has been repudiation on the part of the faculty. You time and again have stated that the faculty has repudiated an obligation. That is completely false to any understanding I have as a faculty member. The president already has indicated that, assuming you were as far apart as north and south in agreement with the advisory committee, the committee could not bind the senate. It has to go back always to the senate. That is important to the honor of the senate.[43]

The controversy smoldered and began to change focus. The faculty's opposition no longer centered on the oath itself and on a threat to academic freedom that a political test might pose. Each side moved away from its most conciliatory position. Behind all of the finger pointing and lecturing, what now emerged as the fundamental issue was who should govern the university. The faculty spoke of their rights of self-government and shared responsibility; the Regents held that in the final analysis it was their prerogative to appoint or dismiss faculty.

The Regents finally issued an ultimatum demanding that faculty sign the disavowal. To avoid a showdown, a plan was devised to have committees (one in northern California and one in southern California) evaluate the loyalty of those who refused to do so.

Almost all (73 of 79) who came before the committee were found to be objective teachers and scholars. Those about whom there was no suspicion were recommended for retention. The president concurred. However, the

Board of Regents decided by a two-vote majority to fire thirty-one who had cleared themselves before a committee but had refused to sign the disavowal. In effect, they were being dismissed for insubordination; flouting the Regent's authority was an act of disobedience. The Board of Regents was not prepared to accept this resistance to its straightforward demand, even if this meant that the principle of tenure would be violated. The controversy at the University of California was now only about control, with the majority of the Board holding a managerial view of university governance: the relationship between it and the faculty was similar to that between management and labor.

Thus, the Board of Regents made it plain that it was less interested in saving the university from harm by politically subversive faculty or a concerned public than it was in defeating the challenge to its authority. The concern with barring communists from university service had faded into the background. In the words of one regent, "the real issue has nothing to do with communism, the loyalty oath or anything else." It is, he added, a question of "whether this faculty is to be permitted to select its own members and govern itself without encroachment or interference by the Trustees of the state university." (He voted that the faculty did not have this right.)

The Board as a whole acknowledged that loyalty was no longer a central issue. It certainly was less important than whether it had a right to assert its authority and whether faculty were obligated to obey:

A regent: Now I learn we aren't discussing communism. The issue now, as I see it, [is that] we are talking about a matter of discipline of the professors who refused to sign the oath and employment contract as submitted. There is no longer an impugning of those individuals as communists. It is now a matter of demanding obedience to the law of the Regents. . . . My position is still the same as in the past.

A second regent: Is it understood by all the regents that no accusation of communism is made against any member of the faculty on the list . . . ?

The Governor of California, Earl Warren: Regent Heller wants to know if there was any accusation that any of these people were communists or committed to its principle. He says that if that was not an issue here, he would not pursue the reading of the committee's reports.

A third regent: No regent has ever accused a member of the faculty of being a communist.[44]

Interest had even turned away from the oath itself and from the policy of implementation, and toward who had the right to establish guidelines in the selection and retention of faculty. Both faculty and the Board wanted to use their own judgment in setting the standards of employment. On this question, they became adversaries. A regent stated that the question has become, should any discipline whatever be enforced in the university, on its employees, or shall each be allowed to settle his own standard of employment. ... I don't want to lose scholars from the academic ranks, but much greater harm would result from giving in to discipline rather than individual losses.[45]

A nonsigner said:

I cannot see that for us all to sign now or to resign is in any way going to help the university or foil the Regents. In fact, it seems to me, it would be a complete victory for the Regents and it would mean complete acceptance of the principle that the Regents, not only legally, but also in actual practice, need pay no attention to the recommendations of the president, and the Committee on Privilege and Tenure. Maybe the public doesn't understand what it is all about, but the Regents do.[46]

There was no doubt that this power struggle had gained ascendance and surpassed other considerations. It had been all but forgotten that originally the debate turned on whether there should be a loyalty oath, who should sign it, and how the process should be implemented. As one regent put it:

They [the Regents] have been pussy-footing around and now are reaping the results of what they sowed. No organization can be run without course and direction. You must have that to get somewhere. This organization is drifting, and it needs to have a little more course and direction. This is one of the issues which tells whether the Regents are going to run the university or whether the staff is going to run it. I, for one, am very much opposed to pussy-footing any further to trying to work out a compromise where you stick something on the back of a contract, and it doesn't answer the question. It is a back down by the Board of Regents, and it is bad business. If you let these fellows take hold of the situation and get away with this, I am of no further use to the Board and neither will any other member.[47]

Chapters 8 and 9 will examine in more detail the possible courses and directions academic authorities could take.

Notes

1. Lewis Webster Jones, "Statement on the Heimlich-Finley Cases," 24 January 1953.
2. H. Chandler Davis, correspondence, 31 July 1954.
3. "Proceedings of the Senate Sub-committee on Intellectual Freedom and Integrity," 11 August 1954, pp. 24–26.
4. Proceedings of the meeting of the Board of Trustees of the University of Kansas City, 4 August 1953, pp. 22–27.
5. Roy J. Rinehart, correspondence to Horace B. Davis, 10 August 1953.

6. Hearing before the Executive Committee of the Board of Trustees and the President's Advisory Council, 1 December 1953.
7. Proceedings of the Board, p. 26.
8. President's Advisory Council, correspondence to Ralph E. Himstead, 29 March 1954.
9. Announcement of the dismissal of Horace B. Davis, 17 December 1953.
10. "Brief on Behalf of Dickinson College," p. 13.
11. Ibid., p. 11.
12. Ibid., p. 12.
13. Ibid.
14. Ibid., p. 14.
15. "Report of the Faculty Committee on Academic Freedom and Tenure on the Case of Dr. Laurent R. LaVallee," 28 May 1956.
16. "The Evidence and the Resolution of Censure," brief in support of protest, p. 11.
17. Report of the Executive Committee of the Board of Trustees of Dickinson College, 1 June 1956.
18. D. H. Solis-Cohen, hearings, 17 June 1953.
19. Loyalty Committee hearings, beginning 5 August 1953.
20. William H. Pearlman, correspondence to Ralph E. Himstead, 23 November 1953.
21. "Proceedings of the Special Advisory Committee to the President," 8 June 1954.
22. See ACLU, "Report on Dismissals of Two Members of Faculty of University of Michigan," 6 February 1956.
23. "Hearing before the Board of Trustees of Reed College," 13 August 1954, p. 45.
24. Stanley Moore, open letter, 3 June 1954.
25. Henry F. Cabell, correspondence to Stanley Moore, 6 August 1954.
26. Moore, open letter.
27. "Hearing," pp. 26–27.
28. Ibid., p. 37.
29. Minutes of the Board of Trustees of Reed College, 6 August 1954.
30. James A. Wechsler, *The Age of Suspicion* (New York: Random House, 1953), p. 268.
31. Hearings before the Faculty Committee of New York University, 18 February–6 March 1953.
32. Ibid.
33. Charles Hodges, Chairman of the Faculty Committee, memorandum.
34. Henry T. Heald, statement following Council's decision.
35. "The Case of Lauer vs. Gundlach: Statement of Professors Gose, Rowntree, Thompson, and Williams."
36. Ibid.
37. See "Report of the Committee on Privilege and Tenure of the Academic Senate," 13 June 1950, for a similar statement.
38. William T. Parry, affidavit submitted to the Executive Committee of the college, 12 June 1953.
39. Minutes of the meeting of the Board of Regents of the University of California, 21 April 1950.
40. Transcript of the joint meeting of the Regents' Committee to Confer with the Faculty and the Academic Senate Conference Committee, 4 January 1950.

41. Minutes of the meeting of the Board of Regents of the University of California, 13 January 1950.
42. Transcript of the joint meeting.
43. Ibid.
44. Minutes of the meeting of the Board of Regents of the University of California, 25 August 1950.
45. Ibid.
46. Edward C. Tolman, correspondence to John Hicks, 17 August 1950.
47. Minutes, 13 January 1950.

8

Publicity and Embarrassment

Generally, there were severe negative consequences for faculty whose past or present political beliefs or activities brought unwanted attention to a college or university. Largely focusing on one egregious—but in no sense unusual—case, the problems of Philip Morrison at Cornell University, this chapter examines what academic administrators did about publicity and embarrassment. Of course, the administrative officers of institutions under threat did not all react in the same manner, and incidents at Evansville College, Antioch College, and the Massachusetts Institute of Technology are also reviewed to illustrate this point.

The fate of over a third of those principals whose jobs were lost seems to have been sealed the moment they caught the attention of academic authorities. The mood in many administrative offices and board rooms was such that some individuals, no matter how inoffensive their beliefs or how harmless or innocuous their activities, were simply no longer welcome as faculty members by virtue of having brought the institution unwanted publicity. A minority of faculty survived their first episode of unfavorable publicity; it was very rare for someone to keep a job if he became a subject of controversy a second time.

For example, the University of Minnesota did not fire Joseph Weinberg, an assistant professor of physics, in 1949 after it was reported that he had been involved in espionage when employed on the Manhattan Project at the Berkeley Radiation Laboratory during World War II. However, in 1951, after he was cited for contempt of court for refusing to answer some questions in an appearance before a grand jury, the president terminated his appointment.[1] Although he was immediately found innocent, the president felt that he had failed in his resposibilities to the University of Minnesota: "Whatever his legal rights, . . . it is my belief that his judgment in this refusal to cooperate with federal authorities is incompatible with common sense and with a proper appreciation of his duty and obligation as a member of our university staff." Weinberg was also chastised by the president for failing to inform administrative authorities that he had been under investigation by the FBI in 1947 when the university hired him.

Administrators, who may have traveled from one community to another throughout a state to reassure the public that no one on campus had the remotest connection with any form of communism, were understandably embarrassed when the names of one or more faculty were mentioned in the newspaper in connection with something politically unconventional, something radical. It was particularly painful when facts surfaced that contradicted such assurances. When Frank Oppenheimer, a physicist at the University of Minnesota, denied that he had been a member of the Communist Party after he was identified as one in House Committee on Un-American Activities hearings, President James Morrill publicly defended him: "It would seem inconceivable that Dr. Oppenheimer or any other scientist so close to the heart of the atomic bomb project could even be suspected of disloyalty."[2] Less than two years later Oppenheimer admitted to the committee that he had been a member of the Communist Party in the 1930s. Not surprisingly, when a short time later Oppenheimer offered his resignation, Morrill unhesitatingly accepted it.

It was also true that some principals did hold what were seen as unorthodox ideas or had been associated with those who held such ideas. Given the mood of the country, this, of course, prompted a handful of academic administrators to take action against them.

On a number of campuses faculty were warned to give an account of any political activity "which might embarrass the university or college." Those who refused "to clarify their positions and inform the university officers and . . . [thus] embarrassed the university" strained their relationships not only with the administration but often with colleagues as well.

The notice brought by a political controversy on campus had an immediate effect on undoing reputations. Those who caught the public eye— perhaps for refusing to answer a political question or for signing a petition or for not signing a loyalty oath—were suddenly "robots," "conspirators," or "devious." Previously they might have been unobtrusive outside their departments, or regarded as "pretty average." In an instant, new and unfavorable social identities were given to many who had been known as individuals of unblemished character—some for over a long period of time.

As far as most academic administrators were concerned, a faculty member was accountable for everything he did, on or off campus. One's actions were a reflection of one's character and reflected on the institution. In contrast with the often noted lack of institutional commitment on the part of faculty in the 1980s, it was taken for granted that if anyone were to behave in a way that "brings discredit," or shows "disloyalty," or indicates a "failure in moral responsibility" so that his "usefulness . . . appears limited," his relationship with the institution "should be severed," regardless of all other considerations. This was true for faculty at both colleges and universities. In the words of President Bevis of Ohio State University:

> In his personal capacity as a citizen he was free to claim the protection of the Fifth Amendment and bear whatever personal consequences might follow. But upon beginning his relationship with the university [he] assumed obligations and responsibilities to it and his colleagues . . . .

> By refusing to say whether he had ever belonged to the Communist Party or any other related organization, whether he had ever performed services for or received funds from the Party or such organizations, [he] did grave injury to the university and its faculty. By refusing to say whether certain of his colleagues were communists he cast an unwarranted aspersion upon them individually.

> These considerations lead only to the conclusion that [he] has shown his unfitness for the position he holds. They show a lack of candor and moral integrity in matters vital to his professorial status.[3]

A corollary of this sentiment was that it was not possible for a faculty member to make a public appearance or take a stand as a "private citizen." He was first and last a faculty member of a college or university. What he did or said not only had implications for him, but for the institution where he taught. If he cast doubt on himself, he cast doubt on the college or the university, and on the administration and faculty. As President Bevis put it:

> [He] appeared not merely in this personal capacity but as an associate professor of the university. At that hearing [he] did not admit he was a communist, but he pointedly refused to deny it, claiming the protection of the Fifth Amendment. By taking this course he involved not only his own standing and prestige, but that of the university of which he was a part.

> The Fifth Amendment is indeed a guaranty that one cannot be required to make a statement which can be used as evidence against him in a criminal proceeding. But the Fifth Amendment does not refute the inferences which generally flow from the public refusal to answer pertinent questions and does not prevent our consideration of the effect of such inferences in determining [his] fitness . . . to hold professorial rank.[4]

Thus, in this instance the entanglement and harm to the institution were uppermost in the president's mind when he recommended dismissal: "My charge is that [he] failed in his duty to the university."

Members of governing boards and some faculty were no less concerned about notoriety. One trustee reported:

Now, this is not a formal hearing and the purpose of the meeting is explora-
tory. No charges have been filed against you and it is not our purpose to
conduct any inquisition. However, we cannot ignore the recent publicity
which has been given to your refusal to testify . . . in regard to possible
communistic activities.

I know that you must realize that this publicity in our local newspaper and
national magazines does great damage to the university, and I think you are
entitled to know that some thirty days after the publicity in our local newspaper the president's advisory council of the faculty informed the Board
of Trustees that it would recommend that an investigation be made of your
case. . . .

The apprehension about image was widespread—and individuals were dismissed because "continued membership [on] the . . . faculty . . . may injure
the reputation of the university as a whole."

Few administrators stood firm in the face of any potentially harmful
publicity. Some seemed to lose their composure even when the only possible damage to an institution's reputation or public relations was slight.
Most clearly saw themselves as guardians of an institution's "good name,"
rather than of its autonomy or academic integrity. In fact, it was uneasiness
about bad publicity that generally pushed administrators to take action
against a faculty member, not, as a rule, direct or indirect pressure from
public officials. The less autonomy academic administrators felt, the more
likely they were to accede to what they perceived to be the wishes of the
wider community.

It was therefore more than the spread of communism that administrators had misgivings about; any political activity to the left of New Deal
liberalism that resulted in unfavorable attention to an institution was seen
as something to be avoided. At some schools, mostly colleges, those few
faculty too visibly engaged in furthering the rights of racial minorities by
working against restrictive covenants and for equal treatment in public
places and fair employment practices put their jobs in jeopardy.

On more than a few campuses, again mostly colleges, activity in the
Progressive Party, particularly if this involved disseminating political literature or holding political discussions with students, was deemed to be
inappropriate since it was something that might be widely discussed. Administrators were therefore careful "to keep an eye on" the "communist
work" being "carried out by Young Progressives."

Those who were conspicuous in backing Henry Wallace for president
were a particular embarrassment. "His communist-controlled group," it
was believed, could do much mischief, all of it resulting in bad consequences for a college or university—and for the individuals involved. At
Oregon State College, LaVallee, who was working for the Wallace cam-

paign, according to his department head was involved in a movement to place watchers at the polls. This provoked "indignation in a community noted for the uprightness and integrity of its citizenry."[5] He was fired.

At the University of Miami, three faculty active in the Wallace for President Club were terminated for "budgetary reasons."[6] Although one pleaded, "I am backing Wallace for president, but I am violently anticommunist," it was not enough to salvage his or his colleagues' jobs, as their actions had been the subject of "a great deal of discussion" off campus.

Other Wallace campaigners, even someone whose family had been friends with the Wallace family, were accused of fronting for communists. It was not enough, as was done in this instance, to state explicitly, "I repudiate communism in theory and in practice, and always have done so." Arguing that the ideals of Wallace were "Christian" was no more successful. Campaigning for Henry Wallace in colleges located in small communities was plainly and simply unacceptable. It was reported in the newspaper, it was talked about, and, indeed, it often brought criticism.

Evansville College

Most academic administrators had a relatively low tolerance for embarrassment. As a consequence, faculty who were proving to be an embarrassment were often dismissed with what seemed from their point of view unnecessary haste. George F. Parker, an untenured assistant professor of religion and philosophy at Evansville College lost his job as the result of having accepted the chairmanship of his county's Citizens for Wallace Committee. He had been asked by the college president to resign the position, and because there was little in the local press after the request had been made, college authorities assumed that he had. He was thus routinely approved for reappointment, and received a new contract. A few weeks later Wallace made a campaign appearance in Evansville. The president reported that after it became known that Parker would preside at a rally, "an increasing flow of protests came from many sources which indicated clearly that Mr. Parker's actions were bringing a vote of no confidence in the college."

Parker attended Wallace's press conference and they were photographed together. The same evening there was a rather stormy public meeting, attended by both Wallace supporters and critics. The event and the fact that Parker played a prominent part, having given the opening invocation, were reported in some detail by the media.

The following evening the president conferred with his administrative assistant, the dean, and the college executive secretary, and a decision was made that since "Parker had failed to show good judgment and that since his actions had seriously jeopardized the college . . . his usefulness to the college was at an end."[7] As the administrative assistant to the president explained:

> My first concern about Mr. Parker and the injury he might do Evansville College occurred when Mr. Parker accepted the chairmanship of the Vanderburgh Citizens for Wallace Committee. I knew this would alienate many people in the community toward Evansville College. . . .
>
> My judgment of him was that he was being duped by the idealism expressed by Mr. Wallace and by the communists who support him, and that he was having difficulty in differentiating the acts of the communists in their dictatorial control of Russia and its satellite states with the propaganda and tactics used in this country to enlist the support of well-meaning American citizens. I looked upon him as a young intellectual who had not yet attained full maturity in judgment. . . .
>
> As the date approached for Mr. Wallace's appearance in Evansville, friends of mine, in increasing numbers, some directly and some indirectly, raised questions with me concerning the character of Mr. Parker, his beliefs, and in some instances, direct questions as to whether he was a communist.[8]

The governing board acted on the dismissal the day after the president made his decision, and this was immediately announced at a meeting of the entire faculty.:

> When Mr. George Parker, by deliberate choice, aligned himself with a political activity which could reasonably be predicted would result in an irreparable injury to Evansville College, he thereby transgressed and violated the rights of its faculty, its students and its friends, past, present and future.[9]

Parker was genuinely surprised at the speed at which events unfolded, and at how quickly his career at Evansville College ended.

In the eyes of most academic administrators, harm to an institution's public image was the very same as harm to an institution. Given this conviction, the institution was little more than the perception others held of it.

Cornell University

As the following case from Cornell University shows, some administrators took as much time as was required to force faculty to back away from any political activity that had the potential of casting the institution in an unfavorable light. Their efforts were sometimes dogged and unsparing. At Cornell, impression management became an obsession, haunting successive administrations. This example, which involved Philip Morrison, an associate professor of physics, demonstrates in detail how administrators shifted the pressures on them to a faculty member.

For a number of years, Morrison's pacifist views, appearances at left-wing political rallies, and association with alleged communist-infiltrated organizations, largely through petition signing, had been an irritant to members of the Cornell administration. A number of members of the Board of Trustees had become convinced that it would be best for Cornell if Morrison were dismissed, but were dissuaded from taking action by others who felt that there were really no viable grounds for doing so. As one trustee wrote another:

> Dear Victor:
>
> Referring to my letter to you dated January 6, 1951, I understand you have sent it on to some of the trustees with a note saying that you are now completely frustrated.
>
> I certainly want to work this thing out in the most effective way possible, but I would like to know definitely how you would proceed:
>
> 1. Would you fire Professor Morrison? If the answer to this question is yes, what is the evidence on which you would proceed?
> 2. By evidence I mean statements of witnesses which can stand up under cross-examination in a hearing which would immediately be demanded by the [American] Association of University Professors. . . .
> 4. It is my understanding that the persons who recently accused Anna Rosenberg got their information from *Counterattack*; they made their accusations before a Senate investigating committee and now the accusers of Mrs. Rosenberg may be indicted for perjury.
> 5. Do you have any way of getting from Edgar Hoover or anybody else in the FBI evidence that Professor Morrison or anyone else on the staff at Ithaca is subversive? If you have, I wish you would proceed to get it so we can act on it.
> 6. If this isn't a realistic procedure, what procedure would you suggest that would be better?
>
> I am as much concerned about this problem as you are, but I do feel that we have got to act in a manner that will not get the university in more hot water [rather] than to proceed to dismiss each person who is suspected or accused of being a communist without our having valid evidence to support the charges.[10]

At the height of the Cold War, Morrison advocated to campus audiences greater American concessions on atomic energy control, negotiations with the Soviet Union, and an immediate cease fire in Korea. At first, university authorities did not make their views publicly known. Nor did the university take any action when the right-wing press urged Cornell to dismiss

Morrison. However, when the House Committee on Un-American Activities referred to Morrison in a widely circulated report as an "important pillar of the communist 'peace' campaign," the pressure on campus authorities to do something intensified. Morrison was one of a handful of individuals given special attention in the committee's lengthy analysis of the communist influence in the "campaign to disarm and defeat the United States":

> On June 4, 5, and 6, 1948, Philip Morrison was an active participant in a Conference for Peace held in Los Angeles. Dr. Morrison was a speaker and member of the program committee at a Scientific and Cultural Conference for World Peace held on March 25–27, 1949, at the Hotel Waldorf-Astoria in New York City, under the auspices of the National Council of the Arts, Sciences, and Professions. He was a publicly announced sponsor of the World Peace Congress held in Paris on April 20 to 24, 1949.

> Professor Morrison travels up and down the country on his Red mission. According to the *Daily Worker* of February 28, 1949, he appeared before the Maryland Committee for Peace as a speaker. He was a featured speaker at the Mid-Century Conference for Peace held in Chicago, May 29, 30, 1950. The *Daily Worker* of June 16 and 20, 1950, proclaimed that Morrison had signed the World Peace Appeal. On December 14, 1949, he had signed another statement for the Committee of Peaceful Alternatives to the Atlantic Pact.

> In the issue of *National Guardian*, a leftist weekly publication, dated December 12, 1949, there is a review by Professor Morrison of a pamphlet entitled "Atomic Energy and Society." The author of the pamphlet is one James S. Allen, and it was published by International Publishers (1949), official publishing house of the Communist Party, U.S.A.

> ... James Allen's pamphlet, "Atomic Energy and Society," is unquestionably the authoritative Communist Party line on atomic energy.

> Professor Morrison, in his review, awarded high praise to Allen's pamphlet. He suggested that it "deserves sober reading." ...

> Dr. Morrison is a ready supporter of fantastic stories of accomplishment in the Soviet Union. In the November 28, 1949, issue of the *National Guardian*, Morrison was highly enthusiastic about certain "mountain-razing" experiments with atomic bombs which Soviet scientists allegedly conducted in Siberia. He cited these tall tales as "a demonstration of the peaceable use of high explosives."

> An individual so strategically situated in the scientific world was not overlooked by Soviet publicists, who singled him out for their kudos in the Moscow "Red Fleet" in mid-February 1950, and on the Moscow Soviet Home Service broadcast of July 8, 1950.

> Morrison's name is repeatedly included among the sponsors of a number of communist-front organizations, such as the American Committee for the Protection of the Foreign Born and the Joint Anti-Fascist Refugee Committee.

Professor Morrison has for some time been an open and active protagonist of the 11 communist leaders convicted for teaching the advocacy of the overthrow of the government of the United States by force and violence. His name has appeared on a number of occasions in the *Daily Worker* as a signer of statements in behalf of these men, notably on January 17, February 28, July 18, and October 28, 1949. . . .

The examples of the pro-communist sympathies and affiliations of certain scientists cited above pose a grave problem for the security of our country. It requires careful study and action.

The considerations of national security demand adequate precautionary measures in connection with all scientific personnel.[11]

Some of the most influential men of affairs took the accusations against Morrison quite seriously:

. . . I appreciate the difficulties of the situation and I hope that you will be able, by direct conference with Professor Morrison, to persuade him of the necessity for clearing a situation before participating in outside gatherings so that we may feel that while he is employed by the university of his own free will, he is not working against it.

The great responsibility which occurred to me in the last instance and which stimulated my aggressive approach to the project, is the fact that besides his own personal appearance, he brought with him a student delegation. I think we have an obligation to the students and their parents to protect Cornell from being connected or identified with subversive activities. . . . [12]

Given the mounting pressure, the university's acting president promptly called Morrison in for a conference to express his concern about the "great harm [from the publicity] to Cornell." He described in considerable "detail how Cornell" was being "injured":

I opened the discussion by saying that it was only fair to both of us to talk this matter over, as from my standpoint the situation is a very serious one because of the pressures that are being brought to bear on me from trustees, alumni and others. . . .

I then emphasized that academic freedom implies academic responsibility which involves great care of actions undertaken by professors with regard to the effect on the university. Certainly anyone drawing his salary from an institution must so conduct himself as to avoid harming that institution. . . .

I had added reports that our fund-raising activities were being harmed by his actions. . . .[13]

The acting president followed up the discussion with a letter to Morrison:

This being the case, it seems to me that in conducting any extracurricular activity you must weigh the possible injury which may be sustained by Cornell against what you may be able to accomplish toward achieving a result that you consider desirable. I explained the nature of the numerous letters I had received from trustees, alumni and others which have convinced me that these activities are bringing great harm to Cornell. . . .

I explained that one reason for asking you to confer with me was my desire to convince you that you should change the nature of some of your activities. . . .

I sincerely hope that you will consider this carefully and will decide to bring your future actions into conformity with these suggestions. . . .

"1. I urge you favorably to consider refraining from appearing on platforms in a sympathetic role with avowed or proved communists, because such action injures Cornell.
"2. I urge and request you specifically to disassociate yourself from Cornell when expressing views in a controversial area outside of your academic field.
"3. I urge you to refuse accepting sponsorship of any Cornell student group that may propose to organize for support of the Peace Crusade, an activity in a controversial area that is outside your academic field."[14]

The next day, the acting president wrote to a trustee about Morrison:

It is my opinion that we do not have sound grounds for asking for his resignation and that were we to do so we undoubtedly would become involved in an extremely bitter fight with the faculty on the campus and also with the American Association of University Professors. . . . Then it seems evident that this group would certainly not condone a dismissal based solely on guilt by association.

I am personally convinced that a dismissal or request for resignation would result in far more harm to Cornell than to continue on the course I have adopted, of trying to influence Professor Morrison to change his ways, to some extent at least, so as to remove the criticisms that are causing our alumni and others concern. Of course, I do not know that I will be successful in this attempt, but I still think it is the better course to take. Naturally new evidence, particularly proof of Communist Party membership, would alter my views.[15]

In his three-page response to the acting president, Morrison was conciliatory and indicated that he was sensitive to pressures generated by public opinion:

I am conscious indeed of the temper of the times, and I will try in every way to anticipate and to moderate any criticism so that the maximum of good both to my country and to Cornell may flow out of what I do. . . . I shall do what I can to minimize the embarrassment which such lists and statements cause to myself and to Cornell; I will not find it in my power to prevent them.[16]

He cautioned the acting president that it should not be concluded that he subscribed to all of the ideas of those with whom he appeared or in some other way was connected; he would not accept "the principle of guilt by association." It was his contention that he had been behaving responsibly and "that not all members of the public or of our Cornell community disapprove of what I have done." He therefore pleaded: "I do not believe that the Cornell tradition would have me surrender my convictions on such grave issues."

In response, the acting president again emphasized that he was primarily interested in Cornell's public image:

> I must report that . . . these [accounts of appearances with avowed or proven communists] have been powerful in inducing many persons reading them to write me of their disapproval, including proposed sanctions against the university that form the basis of my assertion that Cornell is being harmed. . . .
>
> As I have advised heretofore, your association with the American Peace Crusade and the nature of the publicity attendant to its meetings, whether rightly or wrongly, is working substantial injury to Cornell University and, I might add, to yourself. . . .
>
> All of the above adds up to my decision again to urge that you refrain from further activities connected with the American Peace Crusade. I feel that on balance the contribution to the achievement of the aim of world peace which is so important to us both, which your continuation in this organization might affect, can properly be weighed against the injury to Cornell; and that such balance will justify the suggestion I am making. . . .[17]

Cornell appointed a new president, Deane W. Malott, and, as had his predecessor, he received numerous complaints about Morrison. Malott expressed the same concerns about his "embarrassment" at having a peace activist—who moreover was a former Communist Party member—on the faculty. In the early months of his administration, Malott explained the predicament to the president of the Union Oil Company:

> Professor Philip Morrison has from time to time caused us some embarrassment, but not as much, I am sure, as would be brought forth were he to be dropped from the faculty or muzzled.
>
> The man is, we are all convinced here, not a communist. He is, however, a devoted and almost psychopathic believer in peace at any price.
>
> To understand Professor Morrison, one must know something of his background. He is a cripple, which probably means a certain inferiority complex and perhaps other psychoses which he has carried with him through life. . . .

> He has been a sore problem for a number of years here and we are doing our best to watch the situation and to prevent all possible embarrassment; but you know the troubles we would get into if we abrogate the right of freedom of speech without due cause, and supporting peace crusades does not give us adequate grounds for stopping him.[18]

When, twenty months after Morrison had received "advice" from the president's office to curtail his activities on behalf of the peace movement, it was reported in the *New York Times* that testimony to the Senate Internal Security Subcommittee revealed that he had "one of the most incriminating pro-communist records in the [entire] academic world," and President Malott formed a faculty committee to decide if there were now grounds for dismissal. The authorities at Cornell were apparently stung by the additional contention in the testimony that: "The Board of Trustees of Cornell, I can assure you from first-hand knowledge, has been fully apprised of the pro-communist activities of Professor Philip Morrison and . . . has taken no steps with respect to him."

The faculty committee took note that it was not to try Morrison; it was appointed "to consider the problems arising from the unfavorable publicity"[19] Morrison had received. The committee would give Morrison "an opportunity to describe your activities and define your position . . . in an endeavor to find the best solution to a difficult problem in which the university and you have an interest."

The committee thoroughly questioned Morrison about his political beliefs and associations. Pleased that Morrison had been "straightforward, helpful, and sincere,"[20] it affirmed that "his methods and his associations have left him open to severe censure." Yet, it was unanimous in finding that he "should not be charged with any activities which would make him guilty of such misfeasance or malfeasance as makes him unfit to participate in the relationship of teacher to student"; he was definitely "not subversive."[21] Before coming to this conclusion, however, it characterized Morrison in the following terms:

> This sense of guilt and horror [at having worked on the atomic bomb] may easily have left a blind or weakened spot in his capacity to think—one which affects his social and political concepts while having no effect upon the scientific work at which he is indisputably brilliant. At any rate he has become a rabid seeker for peace. . . .[22]

This assessment seemed to be somewhat harsh in light of the committee's failure to offer any observations about the judiciousness of the head of the organization from which the accusation emanated beyond a simple description of an interview with him:

In most profane language he accused universities and colleges of having been arrogant, shameless, and high-handed in harboring communists and fellow-travelers. His tirade continued with the further accusations that institutions of higher learning have been, for some years, faithless to their public trust by retaining and even defending subversives in the name of academic freedom, and only now "when the seat has become hot and the position entirely untenable" are they showing any concern. He called the two of us [who questioned him] "a couple of fall-guys," who within six months will be ashamed of being university staff members because of disclosures that will be made by investigations about to get under way. . . .

Beyond showing us these [index] cards Mr. Clements refused to produce any evidence as to Professor Morrison's activities. He gave two reasons: one, that he was not at all sure he wanted to cooperate with the university because information he had furnished to certain individuals in 1949 had not been acted upon; and two, (this seemed to us quite out of keeping with Mr. Clements's previous attitude), he did not like to attack individuals without conclusive evidence, because, he said, an individual might thereby be destroyed, and the individual could be a dupe.

After refusing to furnish such evidence as he may have had either to the committee members or to the university, he went on to say there is only one Ithaca person (an Ithaca businessman whom he identified) whom he knows and admires, and to whom, should this person request it, he would provide photostatic copies of all their material on Morrison at a price equal to the cost of reproduction—a cost which he quoted at $1,000.[23]

The committee concluded that although Morrison was in a sense a victim of the times, it cautioned that "only by exercising extreme discretion will he be able to avoid news comment adverse alike to himself and to Cornell. . . ."[24]

A few months later, in the spring of 1953, the Senate Internal Security Subcommittee subpoenaed Morrison to testify. In a public session, he answered all questions put to him by Senator Jenner and others about the past and the present: "I joined the Young Communist League when I was about 18, and when I was about 21, I did become a member of the Communist Party in Berkeley. I don't remember precisely which branch"; "I am not in the habit of issuing statements in general support of anyone. I think I have opposed the conviction of Mr. Dennis [General Secretary of the Communist Party] and many others under the Smith Act. I am opposed to the Smith Act as unconstitutional."[25] There was no public comment by the Cornell administration on Morrison's testimony.

The pressure and publicity—including the much-discussed report of the Senate Internal Security Subcommittee which devoted an entire section to Morrison—continued. There were threats from alumni:

Will you please do something about Professor Philip Morrison, i.e., get him off the campus. . . .

When I recently received a notice for contribution to the Cornell Alumni Fund I sent a letter to my class representative, Mr. Selden Brewer, saying I would not contribute to the Cornell Alumni Fund until Morrison is removed from the campus.[26]

There were threats of political reprisal:

The October 5, 1953, edition of *Babson's Washington Forecast* had the following squib:

"ACADEMIC FREEDOM: At a recent 'peace' rally sponsored by the *National Council of the Arts, Sciences, and Professions* . . . cited as a *communist front* by the House Un-American Activities Committee . . . the featured speaker was *Professor Philip Morrison*. Formerly with the original atom-bomb project and in possession of top secrets, the learned scholar—an admitted former Communist Party member who has never stopped aiding and abetting the red movement—*is now employed by the Cornell University Physics Department . . . which is conducting cosmic-ray research for the Navy!*"

If the above quoted item contains only a half truth, it should be investigated thoroughly. . . .

As one interested in seeing the continuance of freedom in the United States, I shall appreciate hearing from you as to whether or not there is any truth in the quoted paragraph, and, if so, whether proper steps have been taken to exclude him from learning any of the secrets of cosmic-ray research for the Navy. . . .

cc-Hon. Robert B. Anderson, Secretary of the Navy

cc-Senator Price Daniel

cc-Senator Lyndon B. Johnson

cc-Senator Joseph McCarthy[27]

Letters from around the country continued to arrive and President Malott continued to respond, to defend the university.

Mr. Robert S. Byfield
One Wall Street

. . . He is an embarrassment, to put it mildly, and I wish Cornell were completely free from embarrassments of this sort. The question, however, is always what does the least harm to the institution. I am convinced myself that to fire the man would be a breach of academic freedom at Cornell, which would reverberate across the country and in the long run do more harm than good. I am hopeful, also, that through these weeks of tension Professor Morrison may himself see the error of his ways and avoid some of the mistakes he has made in the past. . . .[28]

Mr. M. J. Davis
Hammond Bag & Paper Company
Wellsburg, W. Virginia

. . . It is true that Professor Philip Morrison has been a source of considerable embarrassment to Cornell University. His outspoken crusade for "peace at any price" regardless of his associates is, in my opinion, ill-advised and wrong; however, a thorough investigation of the man recently by a university committee could find no evidence of subversion and no just cause for recommending his removal from our faculty. . . .

He is an excellent physics teacher and has never been known to discuss politics with his students in the classroom or on the campus. He is bothered, I think, by a tremendous guilt complex because of his important part in developing the first atomic bomb.[29]

Finally, about six months after Morrison's appearance before the congressional committee, President Malott wrote Morrison, asking him "to show cause in writing to me why I should not institute proceedings for your dismissal from the university."

The continued embarrassment which you have caused Cornell University through the years has led me most regretfully to the conclusion that some action must be taken to protect the good name of the institution and those who are members of it from the continuing concern for its integrity caused by your repeated backing and support of allegedly subversive organizations far removed from your scientific work in the field of physics in which you were brought here to teach.[30]

In response, Morrison suggested that he would make even greater efforts to cooperate with university officials so as to minimize their discomfort:

I propose therefore, in an effort to demonstrate my full willingness to cooperate in "safeguarding the reputation of the university with special care," to curtail sharply my associations with organizations whose public standing has been impaired by legal actions of the Attorney General.

If I am to succeed in avoiding associations which might be embarrassing it seems to me that two clear definitions need to be made. These are the precise list of organizations with which I should refrain from association, and the nature of the associations which I will undertake to avoid. . . .

1. Let us agree upon a list of organizations, my association with which would be regarded as harmful to the university's reputation. I propose as basis for such a list either the list attached to the security forms of the United States Atomic Energy Commission, being a summary of the list issued by the Attorney General before the Supreme Court ruling; or the later list, which I do not currently possess, of the organizations he has asked to appear for a hearing. . . .

2. I will undertake to avoid, beginning some date in the near future which we

> can set (of course I cannot make the undertaking retroactive) to avoid any specified associations with such listed groups, until some happy future date when we can all feel a freer climate of public opinion. . . .

> I would suggest as a basis for discussion the following actions as constituting associations which I undertake to avoid:

> 1. Actual membership.
> 2. Personal appearance on the platform of meetings sponsored wholly or partly by such groups.
> 3. Written or other sponsorship of such groups in general, or for particular meetings or campaigns they may undertake, however proper.

He added the thought:

> I do not want to insist that I continue such an association [with an organization that has not been found to be subversive or illegal]. I still believe that a citizen has the right to do so; but I shall surrender that right in a closer interest, that of the university.[31]

The president replied that he was mostly concerned with saving the university from bad publicity and insisted on an end to such public activities:

> Because of the situation in which your previous actions and alliances have placed you, I just do not believe it can be satisfactory merely to "curtail sharply" your association with these various organizations. By reason of your past actions, your present activities must be especially discreet. . . .

> I am entirely unwilling to make an agreement with you upon any list of organizations which you should avoid. The faculty, I feel sure, would not think this a proper procedure for an administrative officer, and I myself would not think it a proper sort of control to exercise over you or any other member of the faculty. . . .

> Because so much is at stake, both from your point of view and that of the university, I cannot help but hope that you will be willing carefully to consider the advisability of withdrawing all association from organizations lying outside of your professional field.

> But I do want to point out most carefully that the decision is entirely yours. As an administrative officer I ought not to keep taboo lists, or to regulate the personal activity of any professor in Cornell University, or to make agreements of permissible conduct. . . .[32]

The president had clearly been attempting to regulate Morrison's personal activities, and as far as his rights were concerned, Morrison had been forced into a new, more limited, position.

In 1955, President Malott refused to recommend Morrison's promotion from associate to full professor. The president, however, did make a positive recommendation for promotion the following year, and in considering this, the Board of Trustees took the extraordinary step of ordering an investigation of Morrison's activities. In the opening statement at the seven-hour hearing, one of the five members emphasized the Committee of Inquiry's "concerns as to the adverse effect of certain of your associations and activities on the good name and reputation of the university and its faculty. . . ."[33] Morrison was sworn in and vigorously interrogated as if he were on trial.

In their questioning, the Board of Trustees sought information about Morrison's beliefs and actions when he was a student in the 1930s. The committee was even interested in his "political thinking when [he was] in high school."[34] More than twenty pages of testimony concerns Morrison's personal associations over the years with people mentioned in congressional hearings. He was asked to identify communists who lived in the community:

Q. Do you know anybody in Ithaca or Tompkins County at the present time who is a communist?
A. No.
Q. I have heard some intimation that there were some communists in the vicinity of Trumansburg.
A. Quite possible, but I don't know.
Q. You cannot think of any names?
A. If I could I would supply them, but I cannot.[35]

Morrison was asked to explain and justify organizations he had joined or was associated with and petitions he had signed. He was even questioned about why he had voted against a faculty resolution in 1951. A little more than 10 percent of the nearly 150-page transcript of this unusual hearing is reproduced in Appendix L. These materials leave little doubt that the Board of Trustees was very much interested in how closely Morrison had adhered to his promise not to compromise Cornell publicly and whether he was some sort of an academic anarchist who could not be depended on to abide by rules, commitments, or agreements.

The committee was apparently satisfied with Morrison's answers and in its report, which the entire Board adopted, concluded:

However, no evidence was produced to indicate that he has been a member of the Communist Party from 1942 to date. . . . None of the evidence shows that Professor Morrison ever advocated the overthrow of the government by force. . . . However, in the judgment of the committee Professor Morrison has not always exercised the degree of care called for under the circumstances in safeguarding the interests of the university in his associations. . . . Professor

Morrison ... should take special care in the future to avoid such participations as may embarrass the university.[36]

It is also evident from the excerpts of the committee's report, in Appendix M that what was uppermost in the minds of members of the Board of Trustees was the harm that some political activities of faculty could cause an institution: faculty were "put on notice"[37] that they "should take special care ... to avoid such participation as may embarrass the university."

Antioch College and the Massachusetts Institute of Technology

Few institutions experienced the protracted notoriety that Morrison brought to Cornell. From all indications, not many colleges or universities would have been as tolerant as Cornell was in the Morrison case. Most would never have allowed themselves to get into Cornell's predicament. At most colleges and universities a principal would have been promptly terminated. Of course, more often than not, little if any pressure was ever exerted on a college or university by the wider community. Moreover, even if an action resulted in compromising the academic freedom of faculty, schools generally moved quickly to stop unfavorable publicity. Only a handful of examples could be found in which administrative authorities were willing to follow procedures designed to protect faculty, even partially, in the face of off-campus pressure over an extended period of time.

Administrative authorities at Antioch College and the Massachusetts Institute of Technology (M.I.T.) were perhaps most successful in withstanding a succession of charges from politicians, civic organizations, and the media. It is obvious that it was not common sociological characteristics of the institutions that determined how they responded—Antioch is small, rural, and midwestern, while M.I.T. is large, urban, and eastern. What was common to both, however, was an uncompromising commitment on the part of administrative authorities to institutional autonomy.

Antioch College, because it is somewhat unconventional, has often had its critics, but during the Cold War years concern about communism on campus became an acute public issue. Public apprehension was fueled in 1950 after two informants for the FBI reported to the House Committee on Un-American Activities that several former Antioch students had been active in the Young Communist League before World War II. In the course of the hearings it was noted that Antioch had "the reputation of having the strongest concentration of Young Communists of any college in the country."[38]

Two years later the confessed ex-communist Harvey Matusow testified that the largest chapter in Ohio of the Young Progressives of America, described as a communist-dominated branch of the Progressive Party, was at Antioch. According to Matusow, this group controlled 40 percent of the Antioch student body of 1,200: "About 500 students ... support all the activities and the line as the YPA hands it down, and as the Communist Party on that campus hands it down through the YPA."[39]

The Antioch administration heatedly denied the charges both to sympathetic and unsympathetic audiences. In a speech to the Ohio District Rotary Conference, President Douglas McGregor pointed to the harm that fell to "The Colleges under Fire":

> But in this one respect I stand firm: The current charges concerning communism and its consequences in the colleges, and particularly the methods by which these charges are made, will, if pursued, deliver us into the hands of our enemies. ...
>
> I'm not sure Antioch—or other colleges—can continue to stand up to the mounting and ever more intense criticism of this kind. We are dependent upon public goodwill—upon *your* goodwill—for students, for money, for our very existence. ...
>
> Insist, if you will, that the colleges require their faculty and students to play the game within our traditional ground rules. This is essential, and you will have no quarrel from us about it. But I beg you to fight at every turn those who would close the free marketplace for ideas and make it a marketplace for their ideas alone.[40]

In 1954, the preoccupation with the influence of communism on the Antioch campus intensified and led in the fall to an investigation of the school by a subcommittee of the House Committee on Un-American Activities. The concerns this time were most strongly articulated by a local state senator who urged the president: "If you and Vice-President Alexander would fire about half a dozen persons connected with the school at the present time, the odium attached to Antioch would be lifted within a very short time, but instead of that you tolerate and even praise them under the guise of liberal education. ... I will carry this fight to the floor of the Ohio convention of the American Legion and the national convention. I will not rest until every vestige of communism, Marxism, pinks, leftists, socialists, radicals, etc. are eliminated from the village of Yellow Springs and the Antioch community." The president responded that he was satisfied that there were no communists on the faculty.

As promised, the attack was pressed at the district American Legion convention and then carried to other veterans groups around the state. The American Legion adopted a resolution calling for a congressional investigation to determine the extent of communist activity in Dayton, the Yellow Springs area, and on the campus of Antioch College. The legion was convinced that "certain persons associated with Antioch College and the Antioch community in and around the community of Yellow Springs have been and are now associated with various officially designated communist-front organizations."

In September, a three-man subcommittee of the House Committee on Un-American Activities held hearings in Dayton, but to everyone's surprise the only Antioch faculty member called was Robert M. Metcalf, a professor of arts and aesthetics.

In his twenty minutes on the stand, Metcalf testified that he had joined others to discuss Marxism, but that he and his friends were not in any way involved in indoctrination. In fact, he told the congressmen that he had dropped out of the group when there was talk of affiliating with students:

> In the latter part of 1945, or the early part of 1946, I became involved with a small group. As I understood, we would be a Marxist discussion group and not an organized part of the Communist Party. Some time later, and this information didn't come through to me personally, but there was an effort to make or to suggest that this group affiliate with the student group. I did not approve of this at all. I never do approve of indoctrination of any kind. I would have nothing to do with it.
>
> I said that I would then immediately withdraw from any activity in such a thing, and there was one Marxist meeting held at which the whole business was disbanded, largely because, I think, all of the people felt that we were not involved with what we had started with at all. Those people I never heard make any subversive remarks, and as far as I know personally those people got out of that organization at the same time that I did.[41]

Metcalf admitted that there were Antioch faculty members in the group of approximately ten people, but he refused to give their names on "moral" grounds. He explained his refusal through a written statement: ". . . Believing as I do . . . that the inquiry is beyond the powers of your committee, and in any event, restricted by the Bill of Rights, I shall be constrained to decline to reply to unauthorized questions, in case answering might cause other individuals unnecessary harm or embarrassment, or otherwise cause me to lose self-respect."

Metcalf was reminded by the congressmen that "our whole judicial procedure and the procedures of the investigating committees of Congress would fail if individuals would say that they do not want to give information for whatever reason it might be," and told that his refusal to answer questions would lead to a contempt citation.

The next day Antioch issued a long statement supportive of Metcalf:

> The record of Mr. Metcalf as a member of the Antioch faculty has been one of high quality. His loyalty to the American government and to Antioch College

has never been seriously questioned. There has never been any evidence of his attempting to indoctrinate or subvert in any way his students or fellow faculty members.

On the principle that an institution is the best judge of its faculty and on the basic American principles contained in the Constitution and Bill of Rights, the college sees no reason to change the status of Mr. Metcalf as a member of the Antioch College faculty because of his appearance before the House Un-American Activities Committee and the testimony given by him to that group.[42]

For its part, the American Legion was not satisfied that the examination of Antioch had been thorough enough, and attempted to keep the college on the defensive. In one of its publications it editorialized:

At the conclusion of the hearings, patriotic Americans were wondering whether the committee's investigation was not in reality a "white-wash" since approximately only one half of a day was devoted to Antioch College and the Yellow Springs area. During the proceedings, it was evident that Antioch College was not in sympathy with the congressional investigation when it promptly endorsed Professor Metcalf.

Legionnaires who have children of college age will be unwilling to send their children to colleges where evidence of subversion and un-American activities have been quite apparent, and where the high officials of the college endorse and support a faculty member who openly defied a congressional committee by refusing to name Communist Party members he had known on the same faculty.

The press also lent a hand in condemning Antioch. In March 1955, an article in the *Cincinnati Enquirer* pointed out that in one day three communists—Herbert Aptheker, "an instructor at the subversive Jefferson School of Social Science in New York," a lecturer on socialist realism in music, and Margaret Bourke-White, the photographer accused of being a member of numerous communist-front organizations—spoke on the "communist-infested campus at Antioch."

Yet, the administration's support for Metcalf did not wane. That year, President Samuel Gould made it clear that support for Metcalf had not diminished:

I have known Mr. Robert Metcalf ever since my arrival at Yellow Springs, which is now almost a year ago.

In spite of the fact that our acquaintance is of short duration, I have had occasion to look rather carefully into Mr. Metcalf's qualifications and personal character. I have found him to be a competent member of the faculty, extraordinarily skilled in his artistic specialty, and nationally recognized and respected for his work. In addition, I have discovered that he is extremely well thought of by his colleagues, is looked upon in the college and in the community as a person of high ideals, complete integrity and unswerving loyalty to his country. In my numerous contacts with him I have found no reason to doubt any of the judgments which his colleagues and others have made regarding him.

I am, therefore, pleased to state that Mr. Metcalf is one whose loyalty need not be questioned and whose personal character is attractive.[43]

Metcalf was indicted twice for contempt of Congress, first in 1955 and again in 1956 after the first charge was dismissed. The administration spearheaded an effort to raise funds to pay his legal expenses. President Gould himself wrote to individuals for financial support for Metcalf:

It is naturally impossible for the college to involve itself financially or officially in Metcalf's defense even though it recognizes the great financial need which he will have. It appears that his defense will cost thousands of dollars, and so some of us are quietly collecting contributions from members of the faculty and others who are interested either in Bob Metcalf as a person or in the merits of the case in question.

I know that you would want me to call these facts to your attention, because I have an idea that you will wish to help Bob. He is a most deserving person who has acted forthrightly according to the dictates of his conscience. He is in addition a brilliant and creative artist who should be spared as much as possible the mental anguish which will come from the financial strain this case is placing upon him.[44]

Almost five years to the day that Metcalf contended that there were limits on Congress's authority to "inquire into the beliefs, associations, and activities of individuals connected with educational institutions" and "decline[d] to reply to unauthorized questions,"[45] the case was finally dismissed on the grounds that the evidence against him was legally insufficient.

In spite of many critics and few supporters and resources, Antioch weathered the storm. With as many critics and just as few supporters, but with considerably more resources to use and at risk, M.I.T. did likewise.

All levels of the administration of M.I.T. were kept on the defensive for over a decade by the very controversial "Struik case." Dirk J. Struik, a professor of mathematics, first became a problem to the M.I.T. authorities in 1949 when, in the conspiracy trial of eleven leaders of the Communist Party, Herbert Philbrick, the FBI informant, named him as part of a top secret group of professionals in the Communist Party. Philbrick also testified that Struik had lectured on revolution to a number of communist groups. Struik insisted that he was not a member of the Communist Party, but admitted that he was a Marxist.

There was pressure on M.I.T. to investigate and to make a statement. The M.I.T. authorities responded that it would not be appropriate to take action. The school's legal counsel had studied the transcript of Philbrick's testimony and concluded that there was no "clear evidence" that Struik had advocated the violent overthrow of the government or had been involved in other illegal acts. There was also no evidence that Struik had not been satisfactorily carrying out his academic duties or that he had been disseminating communist doctrines.

Expressing both opposition to communism and a firm adherence to the principle of academic freedom, President James R. Killian, Jr. contended in a lengthy statement that these findings underlay M.I.T.'s position that Struik could not be fired. His statement was not only a defense, but an affirmation:

> ... M.I.T. seeks first a faculty and staff of thoroughly competent scholars and teachers of high integrity. Assuming this competence and integrity, it believes that its faculty, as long as its members abide by the law, and maintain the dignity and responsibilities of their position, must be free to inquire, to challenge, and to doubt in their search for what is true and good. They must be free to examine controversial matters, to reach conclusions of their own, to criticize and be criticized. Only through such unqualified freedom of thought and investigation can an educational institution, especially one dealing with science, perform its functions of seeking truth.

> The institute's attitude toward the charges which have been made against Professor Struik must be viewed against this background and in the light of these considerations. Professor Struik is an American citizen. As required in Massachusetts, he has taken the "teachers' oath" to support the constitutions of the United States and of the Commonwealth. He has only by implication been charged with illegal actions, and he staunchly denies that he has at any time committed acts that are improper for a loyal American citizen. ...

> The institute believes that Professor Struik ... should be considered innocent of any criminal action unless he is proved guilty. The institute feels that if criminal charges are to be brought against Professor Struik, they should be brought by the government and handled in orderly fashion by the courts. An educational institution has no competence to carry on a trial to determine whether a law has been broken.

> Should a member of our staff be indicted for advocating the violent overthrow of the American government or other criminal acts, or if the evidence of such actions were incontrovertible, immediate action will be taken which would protect the institute and at the same time preserve his rights. If this staff member should be convicted of this charge, he would be discharged.

> The institute also wishes to make it clear that it believes that the teacher, as a teacher, must be free of doctrinaire control originating outside of his own mind. He must be free to be critical and objective in his own way, and above all he must work in the clear daylight without hidden allegiances or obliga-

tions which require him to distort his research or teaching in accord with dictates from without. If a teacher were found to be subject to improper outside control in his teaching, the institute would regard him as incompetent.

The institute believes that one of the greatest dangers of the present Cold War and of the present fear of communism is the danger that they will cause America to relinquish or distort or weaken basic civil rights. This may be a greater danger than the occasional impact or influence of a communist.[46]

In July 1951, after Philbrick again detailed Struik's activities within the Communist Party, Struik was summoned to appear before a subcommittee of the House Committee on Un-American Activities. He took the Fifth Amendment, refusing to answer most of the committee's questions. He denied being a member of the Communist Party and denied being subject to its discipline. He also denied that he had ever committed any act of disloyalty to the United States, had ever advocated the violent overthrow of the government, or had participated in any conspiracy against it. He did state that he was an intellectual Marxist, that he was sympathetic to many Marxist doctrines.

In September, Struik was indicted by a grand jury for conspiring "to advocate, advise, counsel, and incite the overthrow by force and violence of the Commonwealth of Massachusetts" as well as the United States. The executive committee of the M.I.T. Corporation (the governing board) immediately relieved Struik of his duties, but kept him on salary pending the outcome of the trial. Once more, M.I.T. found it necessary to issue a statement:

In 1940, which was long before Professor Struik's political views and associations had been questioned, the institute, acting in accordance with the traditional academic procedure followed in nearly all large universities, granted him an appointment to its faculty with tenure. Once granted, the well-established rights of tenure can be honorably withdrawn only on evidence of a disregard of the obligations of loyalty, responsibility, and integrity which are fundamental requirements in any academic position. Until now the institute has had no basis to justify a reconsideration of Dr. Struik's status. . . .

The suspension of Professor Struik as of this date is in line with our announced policy.[47]

The faculty unanimously passed a resolution approving the administration's policies and actions.

At that point, President Killian felt the need to write a long letter to alumni, reviewing the case and reiterating M.I.T.'s position:

Throughout this episode which has caused M.I.T. deep concern, we have brought to bear the best judgment we could obtain on all aspects of the problem. We have sought to act on principle and not on expediency, and we have acted on the firm conviction that the policy ... was the honorable and proper one for an American institution dedicated wholly to American ideals and traditions and to the advancement of truth. In accordance with these ideals and traditions, our administration will not knowingly employ a member of the Communist Party.[48]

The M.I.T. administration still received inquiries and complaints, and other form letters that reiterated old arguments and set forth new ones had to be drafted. President Killian wrote:

I appreciate your candid and forthright letter about the Struik case. This case has vexed and perplexed me very much, but I feel that the course that we have been following is the wisest one for the institute. ...

The institute is seeking to deal with this matter in the best traditions and interests of basic American concepts and ideals. The institute's administration is unreservedly and unequivocally opposed to communism. The institute itself is engaged in major undertakings in behalf of the defense and security of the country at the present time, carrying a heavier burden in this regard than perhaps any other American institution.

We feel strongly that we should not attempt to set ourselves up as a judge of Professor Struik with respect to the charges which have been made against him. We do not know whether he is guilty or not guilty, and we have no way of finding out. This, it seems to me, is not a function of an educational institution. It is the proper function of the duly constituted courts. If Professor Struik is convicted, he will be discharged from the institute. During the time of the indictment, pending court action, we have taken measures through relieving him of his duties here to insure that he does not come in contact with students under the auspices of the institute. We have tried not to act in a punitive way in regard to him, but rather to make sure once he was formally indicted, and therefore came under a cloud, that he was not in a position, even if he wished to, to propagandize at the institute.

We have also been most anxious that we not create a situation in which his friends could claim that he had been unfairly treated by M.I.T. We felt that we would do this if we stopped his salary. It could then be maintained that we had denied him subsistence and the opportunity to defend himself. We felt that the institute's position would be more impregnable if we set an example of fairness and fair play. We have also tried to avoid the hazard of adversely affecting the morale of our faculty. The action taken in several institutions in connection with the communist issue has done grave damage to those institutions. Our faculty here is overwhelmingly conservative and deeply patriotic, but they look to the institute to stand on principle and not on expediency. An educational institution, it seems to me, must abide by the highest ideals, and an American institution particularly must adhere firmly to the basic American concepts of fair play and civil rights. We have tried to do this in dealing with the Struik case out of the conviction that we could do more to support our country and our American ideals by the policy that we have adopted than by following an alternative procedure that would make the institute subject to the criticism that we had acted unjustly and unfairly.

The policy that we have followed has not been lightly adopted. It has come about only after the most careful discussion and debate by the officers of the institute, members of the faculty, and members of the executive committee of the Corporation. The statements which I have issued defining our policy have been approved by our legal counsel and by the executive committee of the Corporation. . . .

I am painfully aware of the adverse reaction on the part of many people, reasonable people like yourself, and painfully aware that damage has been done to the institute by the whole episode. I am also convinced that some other course of action might do still greater damage.[49]

The fact that in 1953 three colleagues who had been members of the Communist Party testified that they had been at the same Party meetings as Struik did not give critics cause to take the pressure off M.I.T. The head of the Department of Mathematics testified to a congressional committee: "I have information that he [Struik] was at one time a member of the Communist Party." To the question, "you knew him as a member of the Communist Party?" he answered, "Yes."[50]

A 1956 United States Supreme Court decision nullified state sedition-conspiracy laws, and Massachusetts dropped its case against Struik. M.I.T. lifted his suspension, and a faculty committee (the Faculty Committee on Academic Responsibility) was appointed to review the case and make a recommendation regarding its disposition. The committee determined that conclusive evidence was lacking as to Struik's actual Party membership, advocacy of violent overthrow of the government, and improper use of the classroom. The committee deplored Struik's "present softness of attitude toward communists in Russia" and attributed it to "myopia and poor judgment. This is also true of his consistent following of the Communist Party line." The committee accused him of being less than candid in "emphasizing his Marxist and communist sympathies and minimizing his activities with Party groups." Nevertheless, it concurred that he should be reinstated: "No action [should] be taken with respect to Dr. Struik's status which, as of May 25, 1956, is that of professor of mathematics with tenure. We regret his use of the Fifth Amendment and particularly deplore its use for purposes for which it was not intended. We have concluded that Dr. Struik deserves censure for his comparative lack of candor with members of the administration."[51]

The executive committee of the M.I.T. Corporation also condemned Struik, and voted to accept and approve the faculty committee's report:

While recognizing the importance of the Fifth Amendment as an essential constitutional right, the executive committee concludes that its use by Professor Struik was conduct unbecoming an institute professor. The committee believes that a faculty member must be candid in his conversations with members of the administration and his senior colleagues relative to alleged misconduct on his part. The committee also shares with the faculty committee the conviction that Professor Struik has shown lack of concern for the welfare of the institute. It deplores his indifference to the responsibility which all members of the M.I.T. community share for protecting the good name and the welfare of the institution. . . .

In reaffirming Professor Struik's reinstatement, the executive committee in no sense endorses or condones his political views and actions. It deplores and rejects his expressed political views.[52]

In distancing itself from Struik, the Corporation also reaffirmed a belief that "no member of the Communist Party should be a member of the faculty of M.I.T."[53]

The administration of M.I.T. continued to condemn Struik, but stood by its decision not to revoke tenure or remove him. As late as December 1956, Chancellor Stratton, in testimony before the Massachusetts State Committee on Communism and Subversive Activities, commented:

Entirely apart from any question of illegal action, Professor Struik holds and has publicly advocated political opinions that are repugnant to the officers and governing bodies of this institution, to its faculty as a whole, and to the overwhelming preponderance of American citizens. Both his views and his actions have been the source of grave concern and intense embarrassment to M.I.T. He in turn has volunteered no tangible concern for the good name of the institute, nor for the respect of his colleagues.

He summed up what had become the consensus at M.I.T.

First, in the absence of a court conviction, or of more tangible evidence of criminal activities than is presently available to us, M.I.T. has no sound legal basis for the termination of Professor Struik's appointment; secondly, it is our firm belief that the principle of academic tenure is a valid one and must be respected.[54]

Tenure, Chancellor Stratton argued, is an essential element of the academic freedom vital to a university. This freedom can be maintained "only at the price of retaining in our midst an occasional member whose opinions may be unpopular and at times distasteful. We believe that the harm they [sic] may do in a healthy society—so long as they act within the law— is vastly less than the damage that results from suppression or removal." Stratton acknowledged that the position involved some risk, but was convinced that M.I.T. had to keep in mind that in estimating the magnitude of that risk "we must also consider the countervailing forces."

The commission was not convinced. In January 1957, in an effort to convince M.I.T. to finally remove him, the commission passed on its findings and reported its conclusions to the administration that Struik was indeed a communist. M.I.T. took no action.

The Portent for Faculty Autonomy

It hardly needs to be said that these incidents involving George Parker, Philip Morrison, Robert M. Metcalf, and Dirk Struik—and essentially all of the other cases in this study—were tests of the resilience of the principle of academic freedom in American colleges and universities. Since at least the founding of the American Association of University Professors in 1915, it has been a fundamental assumption of the professoriate that it cannot properly do its job and that colleges and universities cannot adequately perform their functions unless academic freedom is adhered to, without deviation. At the heart of academic freedom is not only the belief that aberrant opinion can never be grounds for dismissal, but that, off campus, faculty have the same rights to freedom of speech and action as other citizens.

Most clearly, the Morrison case shows that even when individuals were not terminated, the normative and statutory safeguards of academic freedom were a long way from being integrated into the structure of many American colleges and universities. Academic administrators principally defined what faculty could and could not do. They did not hesitate to set limits on the opinions faculty might express. During the Cold War years, some administrators felt that it was their duty to impose greater restrictions on faculty than the state imposed upon its citizens. Almost all held that faculty indeed have to answer to academic authorities for their activities outside of academic life. This, of course, was not the result of malice or of administrative encroachment. Academic authorities did not see themselves and for the most part were not perceived as being dogmatic or capricious. They were acting within a tradition that gave them this responsibility, that did not concede that faculty were autonomous professionals.

It seemed that faculty rights had advanced little since the establishment of the American Association of University Professors. In the decade after World War II, as was the case during World War I, disloyalty as defined by academic administrators was grounds for dismissal. Faculty still lacked autonomy. In fact, what determined, as much as anything, how a case developed and was resolved was the degree to which those with authority over principals exercised that authority and how much autonomy they were willing to grant to faculty. That is why the character or disposition or decision of an academic administrator was more important in the outcome of these controversies over academic freedom than what a faculty member may have done, or his institutional or professional status, or the characteristics (such as geographical location) of an institution. This conclusion is well illustrated in chapter 9.

Notes

1. "Report of Committee on Academic Freedom and Tenure," 22 May 1951; "Report of the Judicial Committee of the Senate in the Matter of the Status and Tenure Rights of Assistant Professor Joseph W. Weinberg," 9 June 1951.
2. *Minnesota Daily*, 15 and 16 July 1947.
3. "Recommendation of President Howard L. Bevis to the Board of Trustees in the Case of Dr. Byron T. Darling," released 7 April 1953, p. 6.
4. Ibid., p. 4.
5. Milton N. Nelson, correspondence to George Pope Shannon, 1 June 1949.
6. Daniel Ashkenas, Leonard Cohen, and Charles C. Davis, correspondence to Jay F. W. Pearson, 11 May 1948; Charles C. Davis, correspondence to George Pope Shannon, n.d.
7. Lincoln B. Hale, statement formulated after conferring with Messrs. McKown, Long, and Olmstead, 7 April 1948; see also similar statement by the Executive Committee of the Board of Trustees, released 11 April 1948.
8. Dean Long (Administrative Assistant to the President), statement, p. 1.
9. Ibid., p. 4.
10. Arthur H. Dean, correspondence to Victor Emanuel, 17 January 1951.
11. "Report on the Communist 'Peace' Offensive: A Campaign to Disarm and Defeat the United States," prepared and released by the Committee on Un-American Activities, U. S. House of Representatives, 1 April 1951, pp. 84–90.
12. Harold L. Bache, correspondence to T. P. Wright, 2 April 1951.
13. T. P. Wright, memorandum, 6 April 1951.
14. T. P. Wright, correspondence to Philip Morrison, 5 April 1951.
15. T. P. Wright, correspondence to Arthur H. Dean, 6 April 1951.
16. Philip Morrison, correspondence to T. P. Wright, 10 April 1951.
17. T. P. Wright, correspondence to Philip Morrison, 23 April 1951.
18. Deane W. Malott, correspondence to Reese H. Taylor, 1 February 1952.
19. S. S. Atwood, John W. MacDonald, Robert B. MacLeod, C. C. Murdock, and Herrell DeGraff, report to Deane W. Malott, 31 January 1953, p. 1.
20. Ibid., p. 7.
21. Ibid., p. 10.
22. Ibid., pp. 9–10.
23. Ibid., pp. 4–6.
24. Ibid., p. 10.
25. Testimony of Philip Morrison, transcript of hearings of the Internal Security Subcommittee of the U. S. Senate, 7 May 1953.
26. West Hooker, correspondence to Deane W. Mallot [sic], 14 April 1953.
27. O. L. James, correspondence to Deane W. Malott, 5 October 1953.
28. Deane W. Malott, correspondence to Robert S. Byfield, 18 June 1953.

29. Deane W. Malott, correspondence to M. J. Davis, 2 July 1953.
30. Deane W. Malott, correspondence to Philip Morrison, 3 December 1953.
31. Philip Morrison, correspondence to Deane W. Malott, 16 December 1953.
32. Deane W. Malott, correspondence to Philip Morrison, 23 January 1954.
33. Special Committee of the Board of Trustees of Cornell University, "Inquiry," 3 and 4 October 1956, p. 1.
34. Ibid., p. 11.
35. Ibid., pp. 140–41.
36. "Report of Committee of Inquiry concerning the Activities of Professor Philip Morrison," pp. 21–24.
37. Ibid., p. 24.
38. Harvey Matusow, quoted in *Detroit Press*, 14 August 1952.
39. Harvey Matusow, testimony before Ohio Un-American Activities Commission, 1952, and Senate Internal Security Subcommittee, 1954.
40. Douglas McGregor, "The Colleges under Fire," address to the Ohio/Rotary Conference, 17 April 1952.
41. Robert M. Metcalf, testimony, in *Investigation of Communist Activities in the Dayton, Ohio, Area*, House Committee on Un-American Activities, 1954, p. 6979.
42. "Statement on Robert M. Metcalf," 16 September 1954.
43. Samuel B. Gould, open letter, 18 March 1955.
44. Samuel B. Gould, correspondence to Paul and Helen Bernat, 20 April 1955.
45. *Antioch Record*, 11 August 1978, p. 6.
46. James R. Killian, Jr., statement, 3 May 1949.
47. Office of the president, statement, 12 September 1951.
48. James R. Killian, Jr., correspondence to M.I.T. Alumni, 27 September 1951.
49. James R. Killian, Jr., form letter to those concerned about the "Struik case," 30 November 1951.
50. "Commission Statement and Summary of the Case of Professor Dirk J. Struik," p. 2.
51. "Statement of the Executive Committee of the M.I.T. Corporation regarding the Case of Professor Dirk J. Struik," pp. 1–2.
52. Ibid., pp. 2–3.
53. Ibid., p. 2.
54. Julius A. Stratton, "Statement before the Massachusetts State Commission on Communism and Subversive Activities," 28 December 1956.

9

Diversity in Administrative Reaction and Style

There is much in these data that flies in the face of the wisdom of the day that the furor and the weight of the Cold War compelled academic administrators to take decisive action against those publicly defined as political deviants. Although most chose to, academic administrators did not have to press for sanctions against faculty. A number of cases reviewed, particularly those in chapters 6, 7, and 8, make it apparent that a wide range of options were available. In spite of the considerable clamor that "something be done" about faculty said to be subversive—that "the weight of responsibility was on the president and his staff to keep communism off . . . campus"—a small number of academic officials hardly interfered in these matters. Some administrators were very supportive of faculty; most were not. A few administrators behaved with unqualified dishonor; most did not. The differences in the degree of support for faculty are striking. Why administrators decided to move in one direction and not another is less apparent. It is clear, however, that a faculty member who was able to prove effectively that he had no connection with the communist movement did not necessarily receive any more protection from academic authorities than one who could not. Decisions tended to be arbitrary; they were determined less by what a principal may have done, or by actual pressure, or by necessity, or by institutional policy, than by administrative convenience. There is an element of capriciousness that hangs about the vast majority of cases, including many in which the outcome was favorable for individual faculty. Some faculty kept their jobs, and the fact that this minority exists is perhaps the clearest indication that a number of options were possible beyond simply moving against faculty.

Very few academic administrators went out of their way to take up the cause of a beleaguered faculty member, but some did. A single administration—and there were more than one—willing to stand by a faculty member when it would have been expedient to dismiss or punish him in some other way shows that administrators could use discretion, that choices could be made. On the one hand, presidents could (and did) conspicuously defend faculty at some risk to their own careers when the public or the press or even some members of the governing board demanded they oversee a dissident's dismissal. On the other hand, presidents could (and did) collaborate with government agents, falsify or embellish the evidence against individuals, or ignore judicious findings of a campus investigative committee that exonerated an individual.

In this chapter, we will look at the extremes in the range of administrative reactions. The cases examined, which represent administrators at their best and worst, prove that administrative authorities had considerable latitude in how to react when the politics of a faculty member became a matter of public concern. The fact that some—albeit a minority—approached the ideal of protecting the academic freedom of their faculty, one of their paramount responsibilities, more than anything else, puts the lie to the still current claim that in the frenzied early years of the Cold War academic administrators were virtually under siege, and complete capitulation was necessary to ensure institutional survival.

The fact that in a variety of institutions academic administrators went as far as to resist or to intercede with government authorities or to take up the cause on behalf of faculty under a cloud because of alleged political beliefs or activities would suggest that academic administrators around the country were aware that they could make choices. The president of Wellesley College wrote to Senator Jenner on behalf of a faculty member scheduled to appear before Jenner's subcommittee:

> Just when your letter arrived, word reached me that one of our number has been called to testify before your subcommittee in Boston on March 26. She is Louise Pettibone Smith, professor of biblical history, and a member of the faculty since 1915. I am convinced that Miss Smith is not and never has been a communist. She is deeply religious, and of a religious conviction which has no slightest relevance to Marxian socialism. In fact, Miss Smith is one of the most believing Calvinists I know. That is, she believes that man is innately sinful and cannot be saved except by the grace of God. That the "right" or "controlled" environment can create the "good" man—which I believe communist doctrine maintains—is gross error in her mind. In short, her Calvinist orthodoxy is so staunch that no Marxist would admit her to his Party, nor would she join.
>
> But she has been active in a number of groups which are listed as communist front or communist dominated ones. I would not have joined them, and I cordially disagree with her reasoning in joining them. But to the best of my knowledge she has always made clear that she is exercising her rights as a citizen, and is not acting as a professor of biblical history at Wellesley College.

And I can respect her belief in the importance of spreading the Christian gospel and in keeping open avenues of communication in order that seeds of truth may perhaps be planted.

Where she has believed in the rightness of a particular cause, she has worked with others who agree on that cause, without regard to whether she agreed fundamentally with them in philosophy or total goals. My judgment would be that it is not in her to work secretly, not to let anyone with whom she works on a particular topic fail to know the principles which motivate her.

I myself, as I said above, disagree with many of her positions, but I respect her honesty and independence. I hope that she answers forthrightly any questions which your subcommittee puts as to her own activities and opinions, and I hope that, in putting questions to her, you will bear in mind the religious orientation which motivates her, and which might well compel her to refuse to talk of anything outside her areas of sure knowledge.[1]

To be sure, there were not many of these alternate models available, but there were some, and it would have been virtually impossible not to know about them. Academic administrators could not have been unaware that it was possible for them to follow a path that would have precluded introducing political considerations into the assessment of faculty.

At both public and private institutions, in visible incidents all during the period, authorities met and even exceeded their responsiblities. These schools were no more insulated or protected from the forces of the Cold War than others. As cases at the University of Rochester and the University of Connecticut show, however, the relative calm in which administrative authorities responded to these off-campus forces led to quite different outcomes for faculty than was usual.

Resisting Pressure

The University of Rochester

The case of Bernard Peters, a physicist at the University of Rochester, is illustrative of how a university president may have been more successful in influencing the actions of government officials than were other academic administrators.

Peters was first mentioned in 1948 by the House Committee on Un-American Activities in connection with a World War II spy ring involved in stealing atomic energy secrets. There were no specific charges against Peters, but it was said that he had been relieved of his duties at the radiation laboratory of the University of California where research for the Manhattan Project was being conducted. The federal government attempted to prevent him from proceeding with a lecture trip to Europe and, for a short time on his arrival in France, took possession of his scientific papers.

The administration at the University of Rochester, believing that there was no reason to question Peters's loyalty and that the incident could have an unfavorable impact on academic and military cooperation in research, asked the government for an explanation and apology. It went as far as having the attorneys for the university write to the Secretary of the Navy to call the matter to his attention:

> If Dr. Peters has been guilty of any subversive activities, the university will discharge him at once without regard to the possible liability to him under his contract of employment. On the other hand, if the navy's suspicions are groundless, the university feels that it must continue Dr. Peters in his present work and must back him to the fullest extent in clearing himself of such suspicion. If the university does not do so, it seems to its administrative officers that there is serious danger that other university scientists engaged in navy work will hesitate to continue such work and that the university may be unable to retain them or to replace them with other scientists of like calibre. If knowledge of this situation should spread to other universities, it might also materially hamper the navy's research and scientific work throughout the country.[2]

The Navy Department had "no more specific information which may be divulged"[3] to the university beyond "that the charge was serious."

In light of the failure of the government to provide information, the attorney for the university summed up its position:

> The position of the university [was] that inasmuch as no specific charges had been made, and we knew of no facts on which to criticize him, he was in good standing with the university, its position [was] that he was presumed innocent unless and until some specific charges were made and supported satisfactorily to the university to indicate wrongful action on his part, and that until such time, the university desired to cooperate with him in his efforts at vindication.[4]

Peters was advised to ask the officials in Washington, who were responsible for his appointment as a researcher for the navy and who requested that he make the trip to Europe, for the facts of the charges against him, and if there were none, for public exoneration. This and other efforts yielded nothing. Two and a half months later, the attorneys for the university responded to the Assistant Secretary of the Navy:

> Naturally, the university is most anxious to know the present standing of Dr. Peters with the Navy Department, the nature of the charges, if any, against him, and the basis therefore. Accordingly, it would appreciate your giving

whatever information on this subject you feel can now be given. The university would also like to be authorized by you to pass on to Dr. Peters any such information which you may authorize it so to do.

From our talks with Dr. Peters, we are led to believe that the whole matter could be satisfactorily brought to a conclusion if the Navy Department would write a letter to him stating in substance that he is in good standing with the Navy Department. Because of our ignorance of the facts, we do not know whether or not such a letter would be in order, but we feel that we should pass on to you for your consideration our appraisal of the situation.[5]

The following year, Peters was questioned by the House committee in a closed session. Among other things, he was asked about past and present membership in the Communist Party and about various associates. He admitted attending communist meetings in Germany before immigrating to the United States in 1934.

It was then reported in the press that J. Robert Oppenheimer, wartime director of the atomic bomb laboratory at Los Alamos, had testified that he once characterized Peters as "a dangerous man and quite Red" to a government security officer. It was leaked by congressional investigators that Oppenheimer had told them he believed Peters had been a member of the German National Communist Party. Peters termed Oppenheimer's statements "quite untrue":

4. I have never told Dr. Oppenheimer or anybody that I had been a member of the Communist Party because I have not; but I did say that I greatly admired the spirited fight they put up against the Nazis, especially in Europe after the Nazi occupation and also that I admired the heroes who died in the concentration camp in Dachau, Germany.
5. I never advocated the overthrow of the U.S. government by force or that of any democratically-elected and operated government, but this was not my opinion in regard to the Nazi government nor is it my attitude toward Franco Spain. I think it is not only immoral, but stupid to believe that the United States government can be overthrown against the opposition of the majority of its people.
6. I have sworn to uphold the Constitution of the United States and I can take such an oath without the mental reservations which many people make who do not accept the validity of the Fourteenth and Fifteenth amendments. . . .[6]

Oppenheimer explained that although he knew Peters to have radical political views, he had never known him "to commit a dishonorable act, nor a disloyal one." He believed Peters's denial that he had ever advocated the overthrow of the government of the United States:

Dr. Peters has recently informed me that I was right in believing that in the early Nazi days he had participated in the communist movement in Germany, but that I was wrong in believing—as the article stated—that he had ever held a membership in the Communist Party. That he has today no regrets for his actions in Nazi Germany he himself has made clear in his statement that accompanied the publication of the article. . . .

The questions which were put to me by the House committee with regard to Dr. Peters arose in part because of reports of discussions between me and the intelligence officers at Los Alamos. These Los Alamos consultations took place in connection with confidential wartime assignments. I wish to make public my profound regret that anything said in that context should have been so misconstrued, and so abused, that it could damage Dr. Peters and threaten his distinguished future career as a scientist.[7]

In 1950, the State Department refused to grant Peters a passport, allegedly because his travel was "contrary to the best interests of the United States." Once again, the university came to Peters's defense and urged the government to reconsider. The president, Alan Valentine, met with several government officials, including the chief of the passport division and the first assistant in security for the Department of State, in Washington, D.C. It was the opinion of those with whom he talked that "nothing which was on the record of Peters in Washington, which they had seen, would justify their recommending to me that Peters's connection with this university should be severed, or his future connection with it in any way jeopardized or altered."[8] The president continued to support Peters:

I have told . . . Peters that nothing which I have uncovered so far in my opinion alters the relationship between Peters and this university, nor alters our high opinion of Peters as a scientist, nor alters our attitude toward him as a member of our faculty in full good standing in the university. Only new facts as yet unknown and unanticipated, unfavorable to Peters, could alter that position.[9]

Although after these initial meetings the president was not optimistic ("The whole situation is now lost in a vicious circle of various Washington departments passing the buck from one to another, and nothing further can be accomplished now."), his commitment to assist Peters did not diminish:

Lacking further evidence, it is my opinion that Peters has been very unfairly treated, in a way which should not be permitted under our system of justice. It is my further opinion that this being the case the university should do all that it can to secure justice for Peters personally, and also to protest a situation which makes such apparent injustice possible.[10]

Five weeks later, President Valentine spent an hour and a half with "one of the three top-ranking people at present in the State Department." He next issued a press release supporting Peters. He noted that he had made "the most complete personal investigation possible" of the matter.

> From that investigation nothing has emerged which in my opinion should impair our confidence in Dr. Peters as a scientist, a professor or an American citizen. He continues as a member of the university faculty in full good standing. . . .
>
> The atmosphere and procedures in these matters in Washington are at present peculiar. But we note that a man's reputation and career have been greatly threatened and perhaps even ruined without his being given an opportunity to hear the grounds for such action, to identify and face his accusers and to offer his defense. It was my impression that our government protected its citizens against such practice. In this case the citizen appears to need protection from his own government.
>
> Consequently we do not regard the case as closed, and we continue to inquire as best we can into the status of Dr. Peters and the status of American justice.[11]

The efforts and persistence of the president perhaps made a difference; in the fall, the State Department reversed itself and granted Peters a passport.

The University of Connecticut

The Zilsel case at the University of Connecticut shows that more formal participation on the part of faculty could be used by campus administrators to shape the course of an incident.

The process began in March 1953 when, at the request of the administration, a faculty committee—the Committee of Five—was appointed by the senate to investigate charges that four faculty were "communists." The committee was asked to make recommendations about each to the Board of Trustees.

At its first meeting, the Committee of Five was told that the governor had communicated to the university president his wish that the four be "immediately" dismissed.[12] It was also informed that the previous week the Board had voted that it would "not knowingly employ" or "retain" a communist.[13] The Board elaborated its position on "faculty members who may be dismissed for reasons of membership in subversive groups or failure to cooperate in instances of alleged or reported subversive associations":

> Refusal to answer questions is not related to opinions held but to possible membership in the Communist Party. Such membership is not compatible with the freedom of thought and inquiry upon which American teaching and research are based. It is no invasion of that freedom, but a necessary measure

of protection of the freedom of all of us, to seek to determine whether teachers and others in positions of trust are committed to the discipline and program of the Communist Party. . . .

The freedom to be silent is a civil right guaranteed under special circumstances by the Constitution. But academic freedom entails the obligation to render an explanation, as clearly and rationally as possible, whenever such an explanation is called for by duly constituted governmental bodies acting within the limits of their authority. . . .

Under all the circumstances of our relations to world communism, a minimum responsibility would seem to be that members of the university state frankly where they stand on matters of such deep public concern, and of such relevance to academic integrity, as membership in the Communist Party, even when by a straightforward statement they believe they might incur certain personal risks. These risks must be balanced against the risk of damage to the entire university and to the profession, incurred by refusal to testify on the grounds of possible self-incrimination. They must also be balanced against the public risks from communist conspiracy: a plea of self-incrimination may be used to shelter conspirators, and has in fact been so used by members of the Communist Party.

The legal right of any citizen to invoke the Fifth Amendment in refusing to testify is not in dispute, though the legal wisdom of its exercise is questioned. The central issue is the obligation of a member of the teaching profession, and a representative of the university, entitled by his position to freedom of teaching, research, thought, and expression, to state his position with respect to the Communist Party in the spirit of truth and courage upon the basis of which intellectual freedom is justified and valued.[14]

Unlike many of his counterparts in state universities, the president of the University of Connecticut, Albert N. Jorgensen, was evidently not overwhelmed by events. He did more than simply react; he worked to shape events so that the facts could surface before the university took a position. His actions were not designed to please the Board, the faculty, or the wider public. Over the weeks he put himself in the position of an honest broker, not a partisan. After his meeting with the governor, for example, he wrote the Governor's legal adviser that the situation presented a difficulty for the university since there was nothing in the information to indicate that any laws had been broken or even that any legal charges had been preferred. He also noted that the four should be given a right to defend themselves, and that none had been charged with present membership in the Communist Party.[15]

One of the four faculty was Paul R. Zilsel, an assistant professor of theoretical physics. Zilsel had been identified to university authorities as sometime chairman of the American Youth for Democracy while a student at the University of Wisconsin from 1943 to 1945. He was also said to have been a member of the Communist Party while at Yale University and subsequently while at Duke University up to 1949. There was a report that he was a member of the John Reed Club while at Yale, and that he had been active in the Progressive Citizens of America. All of these organizations had been cited by various government agencies as subversive. He was scheduled to appear before the House Committee on Un-American Activities the following month.

Zilsel told the Committee of Five that he had joined the Communist Party in 1946 when he was a student at the University of Wisconsin and was expelled from it in 1948 after some disagreements with Party policy. He also submitted a written statement to this effect:

> In accordance with your suggestion, I hereby reaffirm a statement made orally by me to your committee, to wit:
>
> I have not been a member of the Communist Party, formally or in any other way, at any time since the fall of 1948.[16]

He said that he had not joined any secret organization or group since 1948, and that he would not rejoin the Communist Party in the future even if its ideology or policy should undergo a change. He did not believe that the Communist Party could successfully alleviate America's social and political problems.

The chairman of the Department of Physics gave oral and written statements supportive of Zilsel. The committee also received a letter on Zilsel's behalf signed by all of Zilsel's departmental colleagues:

> During our entire association with Dr. Zilsel we have found him a man of integrity, motivated by the highest principles, and loyal in every sense to his adopted country. His words and actions on all occasions are determined entirely by idealistic standards of behavior and a self-sacrificing consideration for the rights of others. In personal conversations and dealing with him, he has always been forthright and open.
>
> He is an exceptionally effective teacher, liked and respected by his students and colleagues. He is also an able and productive scholar of great promise and international reputation in his field—having lectured by invitation at other universities and at national scientific meetings. We have found his uncompromising ideals of academic excellence a source of strength in developing high standards during this period of the expansion of the university. In general university affairs, he has exhibited an interest and a respected judgment that have resulted in his being elected to the university senate by vote of the entire faculty. The loss of Dr. Zilsel would severely lower the morale of the Physics Department.
>
> We are gratified by the efforts which the administration has made to protect the university from external pressures. We hope that it will be found possible to retain Dr. Zilsel as a valued member of our staff.[17]

This was followed by a testimonial from twenty-six past or present students.[18] On the other hand, the dean of the College of Arts and Sciences told the committee that it had been reported to him that Zilsel followed the "communist line" in a personal discussion about the Korean War, speaking, for example, about "United States imperialist aggression." Zilsel was said to have maintained that South Korea had invaded North Korea and that the war was being pursued to keep the American economy going. The faculty member who passed the information to the dean, and "shocked" him, repeated it to the committee.[19]

When Zilsel was requested to give his testimony to the congressional committee, two members of the Committee of Five went to Washington, D.C. as observers. Before his appearance, Zilsel expressed concern about compromising his personal integrity if cooperation meant that he had to "turn informer to save his own skin," if it meant answering every question under threat of losing his position, or if it meant that he would forfeit the right and responsibility to determine for himself what was proper and decent.

Zilsel described his educational background to the congressional committee, but invoked the Fifth Amendment a number of times when the questions began to focus on his relationship with the Communist Party. He did answer "I am not now a member of the Communist Party" to the question, "Mr. Zilsel, have you at any time been a member of the Communist Party?" He responded negatively to a series of questions about his being a member in 1952, 1951, 1950, 1949, 1945, 1944, 1943, 1942, 1941, 1940, and 1939. He also would not say if he ever attended Communist Party meetings. He did reply at length to one congressman's request for an explanation of what "causes American citizens to join the Communist Party."

Zilsel also relied on the Fifth Amendment in responding to questions concerning his personal associations. It is of some interest that of the two individuals he admitted knowing, one was Byron Darling, the physicist who was summarily fired from Ohio State University for invoking the Fifth Amendment. When asked, "did you know Dr. Darling, or Professor Darling, as a member of the Communist Party?" he replied: "No sir; not to my knowledge."[20]

The two representatives from the Committee of Five reported that Zilsel's attitude and behavior before the congressional committee made a favorable impression on others and added to the prestige of the University of Connecticut. However, Congressman Velde was quoted in the newspaper as saying that Zilsel had not been cooperative; Velde suggested that Zilsel might be induced to become more responsive if university authorities resolved that he could not teach. In light of his failure to cooperate fully with the congressional committee, Zilsel was "suspended . . . effective immediately and pending receipt of transcripts of your testimony yesterday in Washington and final consideration by the university Board of Trustees."[21]

Following extensive deliberations, the Committee of Five exonerated Zilsel. It concluded

> that there is no evidence to prove that Mr. Zilsel is now or has been since 1948 a member of the Communist Party, and his retention on the staff would seem, therefore, not to be in question under the March 23 action concerning communists. . . . There is no evidence that his political beliefs have influenced his teaching of physics. On the contrary, the committee has strong evidence that Mr. Zilsel is held in high esteem by his colleagues as a man of integrity, "motivated by the highest principles, and loyal in every sense to his adopted country," and is respected as an exceptionally effective teacher and as an able and productive scholar. . . .
>
> Since the congressional committee accepted Mr. Zilsel's invocation of the Fifth Amendment as a valid constitutional reason for not replying to some questions, it would seem inconsistent for the university to use this same reason for dismissal. . . .
>
> The committee believes that invoking the Fifth Amendment is not, in Mr. Zilsel's case, justifiable cause for dismissal. The committee recommends, therefore, that Mr. Zilsel's suspension be lifted, and that he be retained as a member of the faculty of the University of Connecticut.[22]

There are numerous indications that the political climate in Connecticut and the pressures on the university were no different than those around the country. President Jorgensen, however, seemed less inclined to flinch or make public relations gestures than most other academic administrators. The following letter from a funding source received the laconic and non-committal response that Jorgensen was out of the state, and that the writer could "be assured that your letter will be brought to the president's attention upon his return":

RESEARCH CORPORATION

405 Lexington Avenue
New York 17

Division of Grants

This is in further reference to my letter of March 14, 1952, which transmitted to you Research Corporation's check in the amount of $1,875 as the renewal of the grant for Dr. Paul R. Zilsel's theoretical investigations into the nature of superconductivity and superfluidity. With great regret I now ask that no expenditures beyond those irrevocably committed be made from any currently unexpended balance of these funds, and that immediate steps be taken to return to Research Corporation any such unexpended and uncommitted balance.

As a tax exempt foundation, Research Corporation is of quasi-public nature, a status which it cannot very well sustain if it knowingly and willingly supports through any grant-in-aid the work of an individual who demonstrates a lack of cooperation with our democratic governmental procedures. The stand which the public press reports Dr. Zilsel took in connection with recent testimony before a congressional committee places him in opposition to these governmental processes.

While Dr. Zilsel's reports to us have indicated accomplishment of some excellent scientific work in a very difficult area, the position which he is reported to have taken raises grave doubts in our minds concerning his objectivity of thought. As you are well aware, complete objectivity is one of the most vital ingredients of scientific research.

We will appreciate greatly an early acknowledgment of this letter.[23]

The Board of Trustees extended to Zilsel an invitation to "an informal meeting . . . to discuss with it some of the testimony which you presented to the Velde Committee. . . ."[24] Zilsel eagerly accepted, and wrote that given the nature of the discussion, "it is therefore my intention not to have counsel accompany me."[25]

In light of the pervasive attitude of campus authorities at the University of Connecticut that the facts and logic of the case should determine its outcome, it was fairly predictable that the majority of the Board of Trustees would concur with the Committee of Five that Zilsel be reinstated:

The Board of Trustees has investigated carefully the case of assistant professor Paul Rudolph Zilsel. The Board is satisfied that he is competent as a teacher and scholar. There is no evidence that Dr. Zilsel is a communist or has been at any time since coming to the University of Connecticut. As a result of its findings, the Board hereby lifts the suspension quite properly placed upon Dr. Zilsel by President Jorgensen after Zilsel's appearance before the Velde Committee and pending investigation by the Board.

The Board, however, severely censures Professor Zilsel for his refusal to cooperate fully with duly constituted federal authorities.

The Board, furthermore, expects Professor Zilsel to justify by his future performance the confidence (that the Board has) placed in him by his reinstatement.[26]

Zilsel was very much aware that the treatment he received was not at all usual:

In fact I feel that, given the political atmosphere prevalent in this country at present, the actions of the administration and the Board of Trustees, in upholding my tenure in the face of considerable pressure, have been courageous and have come as close to the maintenance of sound standards of academic freedom and political sanity as could reasonably be expected from a state university at this time. One could only wish that other universities, private as well as public, had acted as responsibly in similar cases.[27]

Bad Faith

From a faculty point of view, the way in which administrative authorities handled the Peters and Zilsel cases could hardly be faulted. Both presidents scrupulously adhered to due process; both obviously understood that their responsibilities extended to protecting junior faculty and were committed to doing this. The president of Fairmont State College—discussed in chapter 5—went even beyond these standards, insisting that the firing of a principal was unjustified. In the end, both principal and president were terminated by the governing board.

In the case of Irving Goodman, an assistant professor of chemistry at the University of Colorado, not only was there no indication that administrative authorities believed they had an obligation to individual faculty, but there was an incontrovertible lack of decency that seemed unnecessary and punitive. Juxtaposed with the atmosphere of restraint at the universities of Rochester and Connecticut—and even at the University of Colorado during the Hawkins case—the following description of the treatment of Goodman dramatically punctuates the enormous differences in the degree of support of faculty from case to case.

In 1947, Goodman was called in by the university president and asked whether he had ever been a member of the Communist Party. There were other persons present during the interview and notes were taken. Goodman admitted past membership, confirming what the president had already been told by an officer from the Office of Naval Research. Given the assurance that Goodman had quit the Party in 1945, the president approved his three-year contract.

In 1949, the university granted Goodman a leave of absence so that he could accept a Guggenheim award to study in Europe. During his second year abroad, Goodman received a letter from his department head advising him that because many in the university were concerned about charges of communist activity on campus, Goodman's contract might not be renewed. Further correspondence urged him to find another position, since his future at the university was not "rosy."

In the early spring of 1951, three senior administrators met to discuss Goodman's reappointment. The president argued that he should be terminated. Through its head, the Department of Chemistry and the dean recommended that Goodman be given a terminal year. The president refused the proposal and Goodman was officially notified that his contract would not be renewed beyond 30 June, although his leave had been extended until September:

> Dear Dr. Goodman:
>
> As you are undoubtedly aware from my letters of February 7 and March 14, 1951, there has been a serious question about the advisability of your reappointment to the staff of the Department of Chemistry after the expiration of your present three-year term which terminates June 30, 1951.
>
> The question of your reappointment has been considered seriously in connection with the preparation of the university budget for 1951–52. It has been discussed with the senior members of the staff of the Chemistry Department and, on several occasions, with the vice-president and with the dean of the college, and also in a conference with the president, vice-president, dean of the college, and myself. It has been concluded that your appointment, beyond June 30, 1951, cannot be renewed.
>
> Naturally, we regret to have to inform you of this decision, but as I told you in previous communications, you are, at the termination of your Guggenheim Fellowship, in an advantageous position to secure employment with a research organization where you should be able to carry on your work in biochemistry with satisfaction to yourself and the promise of making important contributions in the field of science and human welfare.
>
> Sincerely yours,
>
> Paul M. Dean, Head
> Department of Chemistry[28]

Goodman was told that if he quietly accepted this action, reasons for his termination would not be given. If, however, he protested, an explanation for the decision would be made public and his reputation would be adversely affected.

Goodman did object to what he called his summary dismissal and asked for an explanation. He pleaded that since his economic status would not permit a long period of unemployment, his future was in jeopardy. He asked for an extension of his leave until the fall and a letter of recommendation. The response was that in the interest of the institution the decision would stand. The Board of Regents also rejected his protest on the grounds that his case had been disposed of through routine administrative action and that his reappointment had not been recommended by his department.[29] It also made public three reasons for his dismissal:

   1. That Goodman was an active member of the American Communist Party during at least part of the time he was a member of the university faculty.

2. That he lied concerning the date of his claimed termination of such membership upon inquiry of the president.
3. That he continued his affiliation with communist activities after his claimed termination.

In stating that Goodman had not really resigned from the Communist Party in 1945 as he had told the president, the Regents did him the double disservice of branding him a liar while he was out of the country with no opportunity to defend himself. They did not make known to the public or to Goodman the source of the charges.

Actually, Goodman first learned of these reasons when he read them in a newspaper. A small, unofficial organization of faculty responded that they regarded the publication of the Regents' reasons "an action unbecoming the dignity and prestige of the institution." This same group requested that Goodman be accorded a hearing. They reminded the president that he had told the Regents that dismissal for cause would include a hearing for the accused. As it turned out, Goodman was not accorded a hearing either before or after the announcement.

It is worth repeating that for the most part these were the same university officials who treated David Hawkins so correctly; and that the University of Colorado was not the only institution where two individuals in quite similar circumstances experienced very different treatment—and, of course, outcomes—at the hands of the same administration.

Goodman was not the only principal who was unnecessarily pained. Two of the researchers terminated at Jefferson Medical College were not only refused an explanation by the dean, told that the institution had the absolute right to abrogate or alter its procedures, not given copies of the report of the committee that inquired into their loyalty, told that they would get severance pay only if they would resign and give no information to the press, but were given only three days to remove their belongings from the campus. When they resisted the plan, they were threatened with a lock-out, and the day before they were to vacate their offices the locks to their laboratories were in fact removed and replaced.

After losing its case in the courts, the administration of the University of California refused to pay lost salaries and other expenses incurred by the principals or to grant sabbatical leave credit.

In the course of hearings at Kansas City University, administrative authorities suddenly and unexpectedly brought forth a great deal of evidence relating to statements that had been made, speakers that had been sponsored, and positions that had been taken, to establish that Horace B. Davis was a communist. When the defense asked for a continuance in order to study and challenge the new charge of communism, university officials, ignoring the fact that the idea had been planted in the hearing committee's mind, simply responded that they would strike from the record the statements that they said would prove the charge of communism and denied the continuance.

At times, the behavior of administrative officers bordered on panic. Defending the firing of a young campaigner for Henry Wallace, the president of Oregon State College publicly wondered: "Why should the state pay a man who is trying to destroy the state in the interests of a foreign power whose interests are diametrically opposed to ours?" In attempting to justify the dismissal of an individual, a university president publicly and emphatically cast doubt on his character, although the man had recently been characterized by a committee investigating his political past as "candid," "open," and "honest."

The unnecessary wounding naturally took its toll. This from an active supporter of Henry Wallace whose contract was not renewed by Lycoming College:

> I do not know that it is relevant to your inquiry, but as a personal matter, it is true that my wife has been almost prostrated by this affair. She is the daughter of a Methodist minister, late of the Troy Conference; her widowed mother ninety years old lives with us. Her mother's state of health is such that any move or disturbance would be detrimental. My wife has a deep devotion to the Methodist Church arising out of her background. It has almost "broken her heart that a Board of Trustees on which are a Methodist Bishop and several Methodist preachers should deprive us of a livelihood without stating any good reason to us or to the public. For her sake, I am anxious to effect a reconciliation on the basis of reinstatement.[30]

Thus, it is clear that at any point—before, during, or after a hearing—administrators were not without choices. Some argued a case in public—invariably against a principal—through the press; others were even more thoughtful. One college president announced the suspension of a young man at a general faculty meeting without notifying him in advance.

Some administrators carefully followed due process; others dragged out old information to formulate new grievances or refused to specify charges or were vague in setting forth charges or limited an individual's right to counsel or refused to accede to the request for a hearing. Some administrators were forthright in meeting and discussing events with principals or faculty representatives; others engaged in duplicity, broke promises, and violated confidences. One college president solicited unfavorable student comments after action had already been taken against a principal. Administrators unwilling to discuss reasons for nonrenewal with a principal were less shy with the press: "He is a dull teacher"; "He is intellectually dishonest"; "We are not pleased with how he has handled his responsibilities." Two administrative officers publicly and falsely stated that they had information about a principal; neither could produce any when asked. The behavior of college presidents, more so than that of university presidents, approached the outrageous. University administrators seemed to find less difficulty than college administrators, however, in working in concert with, cultivating, following the lead of, or colluding with the public or their representatives. This was most evident in the eagerness shown by so many university officials to facilitate the investigative efforts of federal, state, and local governmental bodies.

Collusion with the Government; Tolerance for Faculty

On hearing that faculty members were to be the subject of a legislative inquiry, it was not uncommon for university presidents to contact government agencies and offer full cooperation, campus facilities, or information. Most academic administrators made their overture with speed (at the first notice in the newspaper that a hearing was planned) and very publicly. Prior to a formal inquiry, academic administrators saw it as their responsibility to convince faculty that it was necessary and proper—a "civic duty"—to testify fully, to give government representatives whatever information they wanted.

At times academic authorities went well beyond simply being helpful; they groveled before politicians and other government officials. For example, in the early years of the Cold War, the Joint Legislative Fact-Finding Committee on Un-American Activities in the State of Washington decided to investigate subversive activities on the University of Washington campus in Seattle. These hearings, inspired by the claim of one senator that probably "not less than 150" faculty members were "communists or sympathizers," were welcomed by both the administration and the Board of Regents.

Before the hearings began, the president of the Board of Regents issued a statement assuring the public and the committee that if there was evidence that showed "any faculty member to be engaged in subversive activity, it [the Board] would move immediately for such member's dismissal." President Allen added that "many friends of the university feel that this method of inquiry, bringing the situation to public view, is in the long run a healthy proceeding, however painful at the time."

Not questioning the premise that there were 150 among them who were communists or sympathizers, or concerned about a possible "abridgement" of academic freedom, President Allen urged the faculty to cooperate with the investigation:

> There is still some hope, I believe, of controlling the committee and avoiding an open conflict. As long as this hope exists, we should strive for its realization. . . . Any hostile statement directed at the committee at this time (and while this hope exists) will prejudice what chance remains of avoiding a smear and at the same time maintaining our delicate relations with conservative elements in the legislature and general public. . . . The faculty should recognize . . . the conduct of the faculty, not the tactics of the committee, are the only real determinants of whether we shall have "confusion, uncertainty and fear." If we have nothing to hide, the committee's tactics, no matter how distasteful, can scarcely be expected to have any real effect. We should save our resentment for any conduct on the part of our own people that may reflect upon us and not waste our resentment on the tactics of a committee that cannot and will not be the final judge in the matter at issue.[31]

At the hearing's conclusion, after it was found that the loyalty of at most ten faculty members would have to be examined more closely (five who admitted that they had been communists in the past, two who denied any association with the Communist Party, and three who refused to testify), the president's enthusiasm had not waned: "All things considered, I think the committee did as good a job as it could have done under the circumstances. . . . One thing has been accomplished, however; that is, to bring to view a situation that sorely needs our attention. This the hearings have done."

There is, of course, a certain logic to the joining of public colleges and universities in a common effort with the government. Administrative officers and members of the governing board of public institutions are part of the state apparatus in that they are directly or indirectly appointed by government officials, and their budgets are set by politicians. Administrators at public institutions apparently believed that it was particularly necessary for public institutions that promote themselves as performing a public service to appear vigorous in promoting the service of anticommunism. In their minds, retaining faculty whose loyalty had been questioned undercut the argument that they were providing tangible service to the state. This may be why so many campus hearings came to resemble congressional investigations and the legal proceedings that grew out of them.

It was not uncommon for a faculty member to be called to an administrator's office to be interrogated in the presence of an agent of the FBI or some other government operative. It was as common for an administrator to base the interrogation—and his assumptions and conclusions—on unsubstantiated information provided by governmental sources. Agents from a local office of the FBI were sometimes brought in—and on a few campuses former government intelligence officers or attorneys were hired—to assist administrative officials in gathering information.

To be sure, unsolicited dossiers could be received by academic administrators from anonymous sources. Even so, it was believed quite appropriate for academic administrators to initiate an investigation into the political life of faculty. This might forestall greater problems. As the president of Barnard College put it: "If the colleges take the responsibility to do their own housecleaning Congress would not feel it has to investigate." Thus, administrators did not see themselves and for the most part were not seen as being underhanded or devious, although there were stories, almost always unsubstantiated, of an administrator, generally a mid- to low-level functionary actually spying—collecting and passing information—for the government. More often than not, however, academic authorities in the midst of an on-campus investigation simply made use of information passed along by some government source. The Temple University administration, for example, after having learned the names of the political organizations with which the philosopher Barrows Dunham had been affiliated and having received his file from the FBI, had him explain this involvement at the inquiry on why he had refused to cooperate with the House Committee on Un-American Activities. Although senior administrators may not have been involved in government surveillance carried out on campus, or may have initially even been unaware of it, they did not take action against those involved when incidents were made public.

There is no way of knowing exactly how extensive the cooperation between campus authorities and government officials was. There was testimony to a congressional committee that "the college presidents of all the major California colleges cooperated with the state senate committee there, and together caused the removal of more than 100 faculty members from those universities between June 24, 1952, and . . . March 24, 1953."

Mr. Combs: That is correct. In addition to that, Mr. Morris, the committee deemed it expedient to indicate to the university administrators the necessity, particularly in the larger institutions, of employing full-time people who had had a practical experience in the field of counter-communist activities, ex-FBI agents, and ex-navy and military intelligence men. That has been followed.

On the major colleges and campuses in California such persons are working and have been since last June. They maintain a liaison with our committee. We in turn make available to them the accumulated documentation, the material that we have accumulated during the 14 years. But we soon found that it was even more necessary to prevent people from getting on faculties and obtaining positions in the educational institutions than it was to get rid of them once their positions became solidified.

So the committee developed a procedure whereby applicants for positions are referred to us, their names are, and if we do have any documentation con-

cerning their communist activity over a long period of time we make that
available to the university as a guide to indicate whether or not the individual
should be employed.[32]

There might be some hyperbole here. Yet it is less likely that the president
of Cornell University was exaggerating when he wrote to a trustee: "I have
the FBI at work to . . . try to get some dope" on Philip Morrison.[33]

Most particularly, since the appearance of faculty before a legislative
investigating committee almost always resulted in a college or university
launching its own investigation to determine if an individual was fit to hold
an academic position, this in itself created a need for information about
suspected faculty from legislative investigating committees, police agencies, and other civil authorities.

The exchange of information between campus and government offices
seemed unexceptional. The information about activities both on and off
campus was complementary. When campus officials consulted and ex-
changed information with government officials, it was usually done without the knowledge of the faculty. In those instances when it did become
public, goodwill and trust were, not surprisingly, adversely affected.

In their efforts to put themselves and their institutions in what they
believed to be the most favorable light, administrative officers displayed
cowardice more often than courage. When he was hired at one institution,
a principal made "it clear" to the dean that he had in the past been a
communist. The dean withheld the information and a letter that would
have indicated this from the president. After an investigation by the House
Committee on Un-American Activities, the dean wrote that the individual
"had denied" ever having been a communist in the original interview. The
weight of the evidence vindicated the faculty member and showed that the
dean had not told the truth in order to protect his own job. Nonetheless,
within a month after he had refused to answer some questions put to him
by the congressional committee, the principal was dismissed by the Board.

Some administrators went out of their way to punish principals econom-
ically; others were careful not to inflict additional financial strain on individuals who were already heavily burdened in other ways. Some faculty
were suspended without pay prior to a scheduled congressional appearance. Some tenured faculty dismissed on relatively short notice were
denied severance pay. Lyman Bradley, who was an associate professor of
German with more than two decades of service at New York University
and had even been department chairman, was suspended without pay for
thirty-four months before his dismissal, without severance pay, was made
final. He and sixteen other members of the Joint Anti-Fascist Refugee
Committee had been convicted for contempt of Congress after they refused

to turn over the organization's records to the House Committee on Un-American Activities. Moreover, he would not tell the congressmen how he had voted when this decision (not to turn over the records) was made. After he was sentenced to ninety days in jail in June 1947, Bradley appealed, but was forced to serve his term in the summer of 1950 when the Supreme Court made final its refusal to review the case. A few months after his suspension, Bradley attempted to persuade the chancellor that he should either return to his normal duties or be given an immediate hearing. The chancellor took the position that since Bradley was under sentence of imprisonment and a Supreme Court ruling could come at any time, he might be forced to interrupt his teaching: "I cannot agree to a recommendation to terminate your suspension under these conditions."

The president of the University of Michigan dismissed two men on 26 August and refused to pay salaries for the following academic year. In contrast, Johns Hopkins University suspended Owen Lattimore with pay for two and a half years after inconsistencies were found in his testimony before a congressional committee and he had been indicted on seven counts of perjury. All the counts were eventually dismissed and Lattimore returned to his full responsibilities. As the following example makes amply clear, a decision not to bring added trouble to a principal could be as irrevocable as one to terminate.

Patience: The Singer Case

In testimony before the House Committee on Un-American Activities in 1953, Marcus Singer, a neurobiologist from Cornell University, admitted that he had belonged to a Marxist discussion group in the early 1940s while at Harvard University. He also told the committee that he had "left the Party" in 1945. When asked if certain people were associated with his political activities, he would not fully answer:

> I am prepared to talk freely about myself, but I honestly feel in honor and conscience, I cannot . . . talk about my colleagues and associates. . . . I could never, sir, . . . trade someone's career for my own.

He assured the congressmen: "We were not subversives, sirs. We didn't follow any slavist policy. We were intellectuals. We were scholars. We were pursuing a right."[34]

Singer's position of agreeing to talk freely about his own activities while refusing to implicate others, was unpopular and consequently attracted a good deal of attention. He was denounced in some newspapers, and Cornell was urged by friends and others to fire him.

The Fifth Amendment is a protection only against self-incrimination, and so Singer was cited for contempt since he had testified fully about himself and seemed to be misusing the privilege. Near the end of 1954, Singer was indicted by a federal grand jury. The dean had written to President Malott to dissuade him from firing or suspending Singer:

> I feel strongly that nothing as derogatory as suspension is called for pending the outcome of the trial. . . . I would regard it as most unfortunate for the university to decide upon a course of action based upon specific hypothetical assumptions.[35]

Nonetheless, Singer was relieved of his teaching responsibilities and placed "on salaried leave . . . pending disposition of the indictment."

More than a year later, Singer was found guilty for refusing to testify whether he had attended meetings with certain individuals. With the conviction, some members of the Board of Trustees wanted Singer dismissed, but the president thought that unless Singer decided to appeal, he should be returned to his full duties. He wrote to Arthur H. Dean, a member of the Board: "Nothing has come out in the trial that would indicate Professor Singer is a serious moral risk as a teacher." To reinstate him, he added, "would not be 'pinning a medal on him' as you have cautioned against, but would be admitting that the courts have spoken and exacted whatever penalty was so determined."[36]

Although his punishment was not at all severe—a three-month suspended sentence and a $100 fine—Singer appealed. He was kept on salary during the appeal. The following year the conviction was upheld. No change was made in his status. A few months later his conviction was reversed and Singer was ordered acquitted. He was immediately returned to his full teaching duties.

In his letter to Dean, Malott expressed the belief that Singer "was wrong legally and morally" and that he "has been a source of considerable embarrassment to me."[37] Moreover, during the many months that the court proceedings dragged out, President Malott did not show special concern or support for Singer. Yet the president took no action and issued no statements after Singer's initial testimony or when he was cited for contempt. He also assured the faculty that "everything possible will be done to protect" Singer.[38]

Even granting the consensus at Cornell University that putting and keeping Singer on suspension for so long was unnecessary and a public relations ploy, Singer—in spite of various pressures on the administration—was not fired, and, in fact, was allowed to continue his research while he remained on salary. The Cornell administration did not waver in its course throughout the entire ordeal. Its refusal to engage in public comment "until all court procedures are completed" was adhered to fairly consistently. A letter written by President Malott in 1957 reflected an attitude that had not been changed by the events of the four years:

> We are, all of us here, quite convinced that Professor Singer is no communist and he committed no crime. . . . [He] is not interested in social causes at all and hasn't been since his student days. He answered freely every question about himself personally. Therefore, the university has no grounds to doubt his loyalty.[39]

It is of final interest that immediately after his two-and-a-half-year suspension, Singer, claiming he had six years of service, asked for and was granted a sabbatical leave.

Deception: Columbia University

Although, as previously noted, questions were occasionally raised about the integrity of principals—"What he has said can't be true. Communists are taught to lie just to lie"—the data on hand actually reveals a great deal more deception on the part of academic administrators. Moreover, it was found that both college and university presidents were just as likely to misrepresent the truth as lower-level administrative officers. Administrators did not set out to deceive; most commonly they became entangled in half-truths and misstatements in an effort to bolster a less than airtight case against a principal.

With the attitude that the end justifies the means, a small number of administrators went to great lengths not only to put principals in the most unfavorable light but to maneuver dismissals. Once it was decided that a termination was desirable, these administrators would do whatever they believed was necessary to assure this outcome. The following example from Columbia University illustrates perfectly how unlimited deviousness could have consequences not only for principals but for colleagues and institutional policy.

In an appearance before the Senate Internal Security Subcommittee, Gene Weltfish, who had taught anthropology at Columbia University for seventeen years, refused to answer questions about whether she was or had ever been a communist. Not unexpectedly, there were pressures on the university to "take immediate action" in regard to Weltfish.

University authorities had for some time been aware that Weltfish was a political activist, and, in fact, Grayson Kirk, who was first vice president then president of Columbia during the months when the publicity was most fierce, recorded in detail her affiliations with left-wing organizations. Kirk's notes reveal: "I continued to collect information concerning her activities, and I have made a substantial inquiry since her 'germ warfare' speech of June 5, 1952."[40] A tally of "organizations which have been branded as subversive" of which Weltfish was a sponsor or active member led Kirk's inventory. There were fourteen in number, beginning with:

1. *African Aid Committee, 1949–50*. This is an auxiliary of the Council on African Affairs to which reference will be made later.
2. *American Committee for the Protection of the Foreign Born, 1949–51*. In this connection, Dr. Weltfish signed a telegram to the Attorney General protesting the deportation of alien communists. (*Daily Worker*, July 28, 1949, p.2.) Similar telegrams can be found in the *Daily Worker* of August 2, 1949 and August 24, 1951.

And ending with:

13. *United Labor and Peoples Conference for May Day, 1949*.
14. *Veterans of the Abraham Lincoln Brigade*. Miss Weltfish addressed this organization in 1947. (*Daily Worker*, October 1, 1947, Page 8.)[41]

Seven more "organizations which appear on the congressional committee list but not on the list issued by the Attorney General" were enumerated:

1. *American Peace Crusade.*
2. *Ambijan.* Member of national committee.
3. *National Council of the Arts, Sciences, and Professions, 1948–51*. Dr. Weltfish is listed as a sponsor.
4. *New York State Conference of Negro Youth*. Dr. Weltfish addressed this organization on April 15, 1944.
5. *Progressive Citizens of America*. Dr. Weltfish was listed in 1947 as a sponsor.
6. *Women's International Democratic Federation*. Dr. Weltfish was a U.S. delegate to the Paris meeting of this well-known communist-front organization in 1945, where she was elected as a vice president of the Federation. (See *Daily Worker*, December 10, 1945, also *Daily Worker*, November 17, 1945, January 8, 1946, and January 20, 1946.) It is interesting to note that the executive officers of this organization include Ana Pauker, until recently foreign minister of the communist government of Rumania; Nina Popova of the U.S.S.R., one of the foremost Russian leaders of communist women's organizations; Delores Ibarrari, a Spanish communist leader; Madame Claude Viallant-Coutourrier and Dr. Weltfish.
7. *World Peace Appeal*. Dr. Weltfish is a signatory of this famous Stockholm pledge, whose communist origin has been denounced officially by the government of the United States.[42]

Among additional associations and activities of Weltfish of which the

Columbia University administration had taken note were the Congress of American Women ("This organization, as indicated by the congressional report, has followed the Communist Party line unswervingly."[43]); the Citizens Social Research Council; the End Jim Crow in Baseball Committee, 1945, the National Committee to Repeal the McCarran Act; and her signing of "a brief *amici curiae* on behalf of Dalton Trumbo and John Howard Lawson."[44]

Kirk describes his "own views ... concerning the procedures which ought to be undertaken for the solution of this problem":

POSSIBLE COURSES OF PROCEDURE

It seems to me quite clear that the connection between Dr. Weltfish and Columbia University must be severed. ...

[However] her abrupt dismissal at this time might well cause us to be charged with an arbitrary act taken for political reasons. ...

It has been suggested that this matter might appropriately be taken to the Committee of Conference, which is our highest committee in the university and which deals with matters affecting academic tenure. I am extremely reluctant to do this because at least three members of this elected committee are individuals who, in my judgment, would take the position that the university should not be concerned with the outside activities of Dr. Weltfish as long as there is no evidence that these have influenced her teaching and research. In other words, one might expect a negative result to come from the submission of this question to the Committee of Conference.

My own proposal is that we should use this opportunity for two purposes: (1) to rid ourselves of Dr. Weltfish and (2) to establish a new university policy, based on that which has been used for some years, and with success at Harvard, namely, to say that any individual on our teaching staff should not, under any circumstances, remain for more than a fixed number of years unless that individual has been put on the regular academic ladder. This "up-or-out" policy will require a little thought before its precise terms can be elaborated and their effect upon the university assessed, but I am confident that, in the long run, we would benefit from having such an arrangement. If we had had such a policy, the Weltfish problem would not be with us today. It is my proposal that we bring to the Trustees, not later than the October meeting, a policy proposal conceived along those lines. If approved, this policy could then be announced as taking effect at the end of the present academic year. Since it would include certain other persons as well as Dr. Weltfish, her elimination from the faculty could not, therefore, be the subject of as violent an internal storm as we would be compelled to weather if we were to take direct and summary action in her individual case alone.

Dean Krout concurs fully with this recommendation.[45]

In effect, Columbia University was to amend its policy governing appointments and, indirectly, its tenure rules—and terminate a number of individuals—so that it could rid itself of Weltfish.

In November 1952, the Board of Trustees adopted regulations "limiting the number of annual appointments which may be granted" to associates, instructors, and statutory lecturers.[46] The revisions prohibited them from serving more than five years unless they were given special permission by the president. As anticipated, the change made Weltfish and a number of others ineligible for reappointment. Although the faculty of the School of General Studies unanimously recommended "that she be retained"[47] and the Department of Anthropology even recommended that she be promoted, the president "decided no exception could be made." She was not renewed.

The Columbia administration adamantly denied that political considerations played any part in the drafting of the new regulations. It instead maintained that it was necessary to "tighten up" the university budget; it was all simply "a matter of academic organization." Weltfish could not be promoted because the university did not have the budget and there were no vacancies in the Department of Anthropology. In response to the inference that the decision to revise the faculty code raised other questions, that there was "an academic freedom issue [in] that there has been controversy about Dr. Weltfish's political action and statements,"[48] an assistant to the president piously stated:

> It is regrettable that the action taken last November by the university Trustees in amending the statutes for the purpose of strengthening the university's academic structure and procedures should have been interpreted by some as related only to a single member of the teaching staff. I am sure it must be obvious to those who know Columbia that the Trustees, in taking the action, had in mind the long-range academic value to the university of the amendment, rather than the case of a single individual. This view was implicit in the only statement which has been issued to the press since it became known that Dr. Weltfish was one of those affected by the amendment. Both from the point of view of the university and the various individuals concerned, it would seem unnecessary and perhaps gratuitous to introduce the political note suggested by the first paragraph of your communication.[49]

His response to a request for clarification[50] was no less moralistic:

> The amendment was adopted after long and serious consideration by the University Trustees. It will be administered by Dr. Kirk and his colleagues with thoughtfulness in the long-range interests of the university's scholarship.
>
> I have now suggested to Dr. Kirk that further comment by him or by this office bearing on the status of a single individual included in the group affected by the statute would not be a useful expenditure of time and effort.[51]

It goes without saying that such radical cynicism was the exception rather than the rule.

Notes

1. Margaret Clapp, correspondence to William E. Jenner, 19 March 1953.
2. Nixon, Hargrave, Middleton & Devans, correspondence to John L. Sullivan (Secretary of the Navy), 30 August 1948.
3. John Nicholas Brown (Assistant Secretary of the Navy), correspondence to Nixon, Hargrave, Middleton & Devans, 15 September 1948.
4. Record of conference in Dean Gilbert's Office, 28 September 1948.
5. E. Willoughby Middleton, correspondence to John Nicholas Brown.
6. "Dr. Peters Replies to Oppenheimer," *The Times-Union*, 15 June 1949.
7. J. Robert Oppenheimer, letter to the editor, *The Times-Union*, 5 July 1949 and *Democrat and Chronicle*, 6 July 1949.
8. Alan Valentine, "Memorandum of Conversations regarding the Peters Passport Case," 13 March 1950, p. 1.
9. Ibid., p. 2.
10. Ibid., p. 3.
11. University of Rochester Office of Public Information, news release, 22 March 1950.
12. Committee of Five investigating charges of communism against four members of the faculty, "Report to the Board of Trustees of the University of Connecticut," 15 June 1953, p. 1.
13. Ibid., p. 1.
14. "Minutes of the Board of Trustees of the University of Connecticut," 23 March 1953.
15. Albert N. Jorgensen, correspondence to Charles House, 6 April 1953.
16. Paul R. Zilsel, correspondence to Marcel Kessel, 12 April 1953.
17. Faculty, Department of Physics, correspondence to Marcel Kessel, 27 April 1953.
18. Students of Paul R. Zilsel, correspondence to Albert E. Waugh, 24 April 1953.
19. Committee of Five, "Report," p. 3.
20. "Hearing before Subcommittee of the Committee on Un-American Activities," House of Representatives, Eighty-third Congress, 22 April 1953.
21. Albert N. Jorgensen, correspondence to Paul R. Zilsel, 23 April 1953.
22. Committee of Five, "Report," p. 4.
23. Charles H. Schauer, correspondence to Albert N. Jorgensen, 1 May 1953.
24. Albert N. Jorgensen, correspondence to Paul R. Zilsel, 15 July 1953.
25. Paul R. Zilsel, correspondence to Albert N. Jorgensen, 16 July 1953.
26. "Minutes of the Special Meeting of the Board of Trustees of the University of Connecticut," 27 July 1953.
27. Paul R. Zilsel, correspondence to Albert E. Waugh, 23 November 1953.
28. Paul M. Dean, correspondence to Irving Goodman, 27 April 1951.
29. Announcement of the Board of Trustees of the University of Colorado, 29 June 1951.
30. Clarence R. Athearn, correspondence to George Pope Shannon, 29 August 1948.
31. Raymond B. Allen, notes of the faculty meeting, 12 May 1948.

32. "Subversive Influence in the Educational Process," report to the Committee on the Judiciary, U. S. Senate, Eighty-third Congress, 17 July 1953, p. 12.
33. Deane W. Malott, correspondence to Victor Emanuel, 28 July 1954.
34. "Hearing before Subcommittee of the Committee on Un-American Activities," House of Representatives, Eighty-third Congress, 27 May 1953, p. 1552–53.
35. Paul O'Leary, correspondence to Deane W. Malott, 3 May 1954.
36. Deane W. Malott, correspondence to Arthur H. Dean, 30 March 1956.
37. Ibid.
38. "Minutes of University Faculty Meeting," 12 May 1954.
39. Deane W. Malott, correspondence to Herbert Reynolds, 14 November 1957.
40. Grayson Kirk, "Memorandum concerning Dr. Gene Weltfish," p. 1.
41. Ibid., pp. 1–3.
42. Ibid., p. 3.
43. Ibid., p. 4.
44. Ibid., pp. 4–5.
45. Ibid., pp. 9–11.
46. Reported in a Columbia University news release, 31 March 1953.
47. Louis M. Hacker, correspondence to Grayson Kirk, 18 December 1952.
48. Students for Democratic Action, statement, 14 April 1953.
49. Robert Harron, correspondence to David Bardin, 28 April 1953.
50. Patrick Kelley, correspondence to Grayson Kirk, 28 April 1953.
51. Robert Harron, correspondence to Patrick Kelley, 1 May 1953.

10

Administrative Power, Concerns, and Pursuit of the Cold War

The Cold War in America tells us much about American politics and the American character; the Cold War on campus tells us much about the balance of power in American colleges and universities. Together, the principle of academic freedom, tenure, and the professional status of the professoriate are said to give faculty a special protection from the vicissitudes of administrative capriciousness. Yet in the early years after World War II they did not.

The Cold War on Campus and Academic Freedom

Academic freedom means that no faculty member may be dismissed for belonging to organizations or for holding opinions that are contrary to the orthodox, provided that he does not allow his associations or opinions to distort what he teaches students or how he conducts his research. These cases, however, from those at highly visible universities to those at obscure colleges, show the limits of academic freedom in a time of national insecurity. Academic administrators may give lip service to academic freedom, but they are not always committed to maintaining the ideal. In human affairs, of course, there is always a gap between an ideal and actual practice, so that even in the best of times the principle of academic freedom does not necessarily govern decision-making practices in colleges and universities.

Faculty with tenure appointments were fired with nearly the same abandon as those without tenure. The message from academic authorities was indisputable: we reserve the right, when the chips are down, to renege on tenure rules. Tenure could most appropriately be characterized as an expression of intention, not a protection of academic freedom.

The managerial prerogatives of academic administrators and governing boards are much like those of administrative authorities in other organizations. Those who work under their authority must relinquish some autonomy. Yet autonomy is one of the principal defining characteristics of the professional status and role. The consequence is that faculty are placed in a position of being less fully professional than is believed, and this position comes to be not too different from that of other employees. How these 126 cases were resolved on many American campuses clearly shows the lines of authority in colleges and universities. Institutional crises often serve to define, redefine, establish, or reestablish organizational hierarchy. In the event that changes brought about during and immediately after the war years left any doubt, the administrative response to the Cold War showed quite clearly the locus of control in American colleges and universities.

Without exception, those faculty viewed as insubordinate put themselves at special risk. Those faculty who did not cooperate with administrative authorities, and as a consequence were seen as having failed in their institutional obligations, were invariably fired. Those faculty who could not convince a president, a vice president, or a dean that they were not in or too near the Communist Party were dismissed. Some faculty who behaved in ways that pleased administrators, especially those who seemed repentant, kept their jobs. The ultimate test of breaking with the past was to appear not to be interested in protecting one's old friends. It is clear that the authorities of colleges and universities were less concerned with the political ideology of faculty than they were with institutional loyalty. There is also little doubt that a faculty member is as defenseless or vulnerable as any employee without special protection, such as that offered by a labor union.

The actions by administrators that were precipitated by Cold War tensions seem to have played some part in bringing about permanent changes in the functions of academic administrators. Academic administrators are no longer administrators—those who execute policy—but seem to have become managers—those who supervise policy and people. This formalization of social control within institutions of higher learning and the concomitant formalization of the division between faculty and administration has polarized the viewpoints of both. "We" and "they" attitudes have become more common and magnified. As a result, the academic world is less a community. Since professions are characterized by community—a sense of common experience, identity, and solidarity—the academic profession is less a profession. Moreover, the ability to defend the principles that are central to the vitality of institutions of higher learning in part depends on the consensus in the academic community about these and other matters. As this consensus is eroded, the academic community is less able to articulate its ideals to the wider society.

Throughout the Cold War years, the majority of faculty at most institutions were little more than observers. Aside from those who served on a hearing committee, most were silent witnesses. Indeed, the relationship of faculty and administration during many of the campus incidents was not unlike Levin's description of the relationship of the masses and elite during times of political hysteria:

> The role of the masses in political hysteria is fundamentally that of not opposing the elites which actually administer the repression. The masses become very frightened of imminent catastrophe. The masses . . . neither originate the conspiratorial myth nor fill in its details. They occasionally take action to eliminate and control the danger. . . . They occasionally attack alleged conspirators—but only occasionally. The hysteria is originated, promoted, sustained, and administered by elites, not masses. Like almost every political action, small groups act and large numbers react.[1]

Lazarsfeld and Thielens's observations "regarding the events of the postwar decade" that (1) because of a greater "respect for academic freedom," the governing board of a private school is "more likely to become a mediator between the community and the college" than the governing board of a public school[2] and (2) that there is a marked increase in administrative "shortcomings" with regard to "the management of academic freedom issues" in schools of low quality[3] are not fully supported by the materials examined in chapters 3 through 9. In summing up their findings, Lazarsfeld and Thielens write:

> Political pressures, to begin with, are lighter on the private schools. The trustees are then less inclined to pass them on. And the administration is often prepared to follow a policy of interposition. . . .

> The situation actually reverses in the two types of schools. In tax-supported schools, the higher the political pressures, the lower the administrative protection. But in privately endowed schools our figures indicate an impressive example of countervailing powers: the higher the political pressures, the more ready the administration to protect its faculty.[4]

There appear to be no discernible differences in the amount of pressure on public or private institutions. Moreover, the amount of pressure on an institution, private or public, did not have a great deal to do with how administrators reacted. To be sure, a disproportionate number of administrators in high-prestige, private institutions made more of an effort to protect faculty; indeed, those academic administrators inclined to protect faculty were almost always at higher quality schools, generally private. It also cannot be denied that at some of the private institutions where administrative authorities stood firm behind a principal there was considerable pressure to impose sanctions. This does not necessarily mean, however, as

Lazarsfeld and Thielens insist, that "the better schools have a more protective administration"[5] or that in tax-supported institutions faculties have less "breathing room in times of crisis" because they are "monolithic"[6] in their administrative structure. There were too many exceptions. Finally, within a school, the administration might treat one individual with a great deal of consideration and another indivividual, who objectively was no more radical, disloyal, or a threat, quite shabbily. Indeed, no universalistic criteria have emerged to protect faculty against infringements of academic freedom and other academic principles.

It would seem that most of the assertions of Lazarsfeld and Thielens "regarding the events of the post-war decade" are not supported by the facts surrounding the 126 cases from these fifty-eight institutions. Either the people they interviewed had it wrong or, more likely, Lazarsfeld and Thielens themselves have it wrong. It has become a cliché that during the Cold War years faculty at undistinguished, parochial institutions were at greater risk than those at more prestigious, visible institutions. This belief seems to be a conceit fostered largely by alumni and employees from more renowned institutions who have had access to publishers and the pages of magazines and journals.

The design of the American system of higher education is one that establishes governing boards to stand between a college or university and the community (either other elites who normally bring pressure to bear on institutions of higher learning—those above—or the public at large—those below) in order to assure that there will be no interference in academic affairs. An initial and material question, therefore, is why governing boards of colleges and universities did not defend faculty against the political repression of the Cold War. The answer is evident. There was not that much interference from government or the larger community in academic affairs. Even when there was pressure on academic authorities, there were as many reasons, for example, their responsibilities to principles and principals, not to yield as to do otherwise.

The decency of academic authorities at I.I.T. and M.I.T., at the University of Rochester and the University of Connecticut, indicates that there were choices, that faculty labeled as radicals did not have to be punished, that it was possible to stand firm. The actions of this minority of academic administrators moved the question from whether faculty who took the Fifth Amendment or who refused to sign a loyalty oath or who did not believe that they owed colleagues complete candor should never have academic appointments to whether they should sometimes not have academic appointments. This left open to all academic administrators the opportunity to evaluate competence and integrity—which are the essence of an effective tenure system, the mainstay of academic freedom—before imposing sanctions. The failure of so many academic administrators to protect their institutions was a failure in courage that created a great deal of human wreckage.

Although most faculty—those who were on institutional committees of inquiry and those who were merely powerless witnesses—behaved with decency, the actions of most academic authorities were not honorable. It did not have to be this way. The campus is supposed to be a special place—a safehold. Yet the hysteria and processes that drove out some faculty and silenced others were no different from the hysteria and processes that overwhelmed Hollywood and Washington, D.C. For the most part, there was no indication that institutions of higher learning were governed by or reflected the very highest ideals. Some might find it disconcerting that the executives of academic institutions behaved no differently than the executives of the movie industry.

It would appear that external pressures were of little significance compared to internal imperatives to remove so-called radicals from the faculties of colleges and universities. Faculty needed protection from academic administrators, who seemed driven by anticipatory subjugation, more than they needed it from congressmen or an overzealous public.

It is commonly asserted that if more judicious and democratic methods were used to appoint members of the governing boards of institutions of higher learning, this would result in more protection for faculty in that it would increase the probability that individuals who cherished academic freedom would be selected to serve. Given the latitude of academic administrators to rein in or even dismiss faculty considered politically unorthodox, a concern about the composition of governing boards seems almost incidental. More or less good will, a greater or lesser commitment to academic freedom, or the presence or absence of benevolence on the part of members of governing boards or the administrators they appoint are not what make faculty more or less vulnerable, are not what determine whether faculty who are seen as political pariahs can be fired. The power some have to separate from an institution those who they believe hold unpopular political views comes from an administrative arrangement. The relative power of faculty and administrators is a quality of the administrative structure of institutions of higher learning. To think too much about the personalities or other characteristics of administrators is to risk losing sight of the fact that behavior in institutions is largely determined by their structure and the placement and position of individuals in that structure. To increase or decrease the probability that one party can drive another from an institution, to increase or decrease faculty autonomy, would require altering structural arrangements. Since the differential distribution of authority in institutions invariably gives rise to conflict, it is naive to

believe that any substantive change can be brought about by merely changing the cast of characters without changing the authority structure. To be
sure, guarantees of due process, which would incorporate the right of
timely notice of any charge, the right to a hearing, the right to counsel, the
right to confront witnesses, the right to cross-examination, and the right to
introduce evidence on one's behalf, would protect faculty against the most
arbitrary exercise of power and could fairly and impartially regulate some
conflict.

Unwarranted Actions

In large schools and small schools, in public institutions and private
institutions, in distinguished universities and provincial colleges, administrative responses were more often anticipatory than reactive. The habit of
acquiescence appeared to be well developed among academic administrators. Of course, many responses and programs, like the introduction of
loyalty oaths, were both. When pushed by anyone other than faculty or
students, academic administrators were for the most part open to the most
implausible assertions, timid, and quite pliant. This is in keeping with
American academic tradition; American colleges and universities have always yielded to what are perceived to be public opinion and the wishes of
political and commercial forces, even in purely academic matters such as
the development of curricula.

It is now obvious that institutions of higher learning were not merely
victims of the coercive spirit of the Cold War. The Cold War was not simply
imposed on colleges and universities by diabolic forces. The Cold War on
campus was a mediated phenomenon. Academic administrators gave
character to the Cold War so that the Cold War on campus was not unlike
manifestations of other efforts of colleges and universities to control faculty labeled as deviants—ideological or social. In any organization, academic or nonacademic, negative sanctions are customarily imposed on
those who threaten social cohesion or stability. As an ideal, political, religious, or economic heretics should be more welcome on campus than
elsewhere, but this has never been the case. There are many analogies
between these Cold War years and the years during World War I when there
was a heightened concern about loyalty and a fear of the expression of
sentiments not expressly pro-American and anti-German. Faculty said to
be upsetting the status quo were censured during both periods.

The disposition of academic administrators to cultivate public relations
at the expense of other considerations was the paramount reason for the
vigorous reaction of so many of them to the Cold War. There is little
question that most administrators who moved against those faculty consid-

ered political outcasts did so in the belief that they had a special duty to correct or eliminate a condition harmful to the institution's image. To be sure, some administrators may have been convinced that they were caught up in a struggle with dangerous political ideas. Some may have shared the intolerant assumptions of those who wished to bar the ideologically impure from the American campus, and this may have kept them from adequately defending academic freedom and made it easy for them to curtail civil liberties. Surely there was a failure on the part of some to see beyond the dominant assumptions of the time. It is the responsibility of academic administrators to look beyond the question of whether faculty have public duties that involve full cooperation with civil authorities or whether communists or radicals should teach in institutions of higher learning. It is the responsibility of academic administrators to look at the relative gains and costs to institutions of higher learning and to society in dismissing faculty whose political beliefs, associations, or actions have made them a burden. Nonetheless, whether academic administrators were moved by higher ideals or less lofty reasons, they did not, as is their responsibility, protect their institutions—or faculty. Instead, many welcomed the Cold War on campus.

For the most part, faculty were victims of administrators very much concerned with maintaining their reputations and influence off campus. There was a lot less interest in appeasing constituencies on campus. Behind the Cold War on campus was more the fear of losing prestige or financial support than a conviction that forcing someone to give up his job or his politics would be ridding the campus of a dangerous element.

Indeed, if the incidents reviewed here are an indication of the extent of communist activity on American campuses in the decade after World War II, it can hardly be said that there was anything like a communist problem. Only a handful of faculty were members of the Communist Party, and there is nothing to suggest that anyone in this small minority was involved in conspiratorial activities, sabotage, or very much that would even cause civil unrest. No evidence was found that would link any of the 126 principals to subversive activities. If someone had been involved in something that was putting national security at risk, it is unlikely that some evidence of this would not have been found. This is not in any sense a study of the response to the threat of communism on campus. There was no threat. Most principals were not even conspicuously active in left-wing politics. Had there been no apprehension on the part of academic administrators, hardly anyone would have cared about their past political beliefs or activities.

If anything, the danger was not the overthrow of American institutions by force or violence but the exposure of immature minds to communist

ideology. The American way of life and national defense were not threatened, although some parents or alumni may have believed that they were.
These ideological and intellectual heretics were so unobtrusive that they
were mostly invisible until hyper-patriotic activities focused attention on
them. Perhaps the most striking finding from all of these materials is that
although political behavior and beliefs were important in getting faculty
labeled as a danger and putting their careers in jeopardy, these factors had
little to do with how events subsequently played themselves out on campus.
It was as important for faculty whose political beliefs or associations put
them under a cloud to show that they belonged and that they could fit into
the academic community as it was to prove that they were not communists
or disloyal Americans. Political confessions were not so much political tests
as a reflection that individuals understood the distribution of power in
institutions of higher learning, that they would risk embarrassing themselves and their friends rather than their administrative superiors, that they
were aware of their responsibilities of collegiality.

In essence, these were not conflicts about political ideology. They could
more aptly be described as conflicts over the definition of academic freedom. (What is academic freedom? What are the normal limits of academic
freedom? Is academic freedom an inviolable right?)

The weight of the data, in fact, suggests that academic administrators
were the creators of the Cold War on campus—that those responsible for
the integrity of academic institutions buckled under, appeased, or bowed to
what they believed was the *vox populi*. There is little doubt that academic
administrators were very much interested in extricating themselves from
what they felt were awkward situations.

This was not unforeseen. Well before the Cold War years, Thorstein
Veblen observed that what he called "captains of erudition" were "actuated
by a sharper solicitude to keep the academic establishment blameless of
anything like innovation or iconoclasm"[7]:

> Not only must a creditable publicity be provided for, as one of the running
> cares of the administration, but every feature of academic life, and of the life
> of all members of the academic staff, must unremittingly (though of course
> unavowedly) be held under surveillance at every turn, with a view to further-
> ing whatever may yield a reputable notoriety, and to correcting or eliminating
> whatever may be conceived to have a doubtful or untoward bearing in this
> respect.
>
> This surveillance of appearances, and of the means of propagating ap-
> pearances, is perhaps the most exacting detail of duty incumbent on an
> enterprising executive.[8]

Given these demands, Veblen added, the "first executive duty" is "to keep
his faculty under control."[9]

By being carriers to the campus of the public's deep concern about communism, academic administrators became part of an insidious chain reaction. Their actions did more to fan than to soothe passions occasioned by the Cold War. By being active participants in the repudiation of faculty whose ideology was somewhat to the left of dead center, they contributed to the fusing in the public mind of liberalism, radicalism, unconventional behavior, a commitment to civil rights, dissent, the American Civil Liberties Union, atheism, communism, and the *New York Times*.

It was not so much Cold War pressures as the failure of academic administrators to defend the autonomy of faculty that resulted in the sentiment that some thought and activities should be curtailed. Most administrators seemed limited by their presumptions, by the failure to ascertain what the majority of the public or alumni or benefactors would find acceptable forms of political expression. It was essentially on the basis of avoided tests that administrators concluded that there were constraints upon them and that there were limits in their repertoire of responses. Indeed, in the eyes of academic administrators the failure to defend academic freedom was justified by the implantation of constraints and limits that made such a response "impossible." Given such a view, the constraints and limits thus became prominent facts of academic life.

A disconcerting number of academic administrators abandoned common sense in their dealings with actual or alleged leftist faculty. They were not interested in how well or poorly someone taught, in intellectual qualities, in character or behavior, or if there had been dereliction of duty or moral turpitude. Few confronted suspicion with fact. Few were interested in whether someone had used the classroom or his position to indoctrinate students, whether he had surrendered his free will to a foreign power or an organization, or whether he had advocated the violent overthrow of the government. Individuals were more commonly judged by what they were presumably thinking (or what they may have at one time thought) or by their associations than by their actions. It was common to hear a university president argue that it was possible to determine the quality of a faculty member's academic work without examining it:

> Is it possible for an individual, however sincere, to embrace both the unhampered pursuit of truth and, at the same time, the doctrines and dogmas of a political party which admits of no criticism of its fundamental principles and programs? Put in another way, a teacher may be ever so sincere in his belief in communism, but can he at the same time be a sincere seeker after truth, which is the first obligation and duty of the teacher? My answer to these questions is, "he cannot." Therefore, I believe ... these men, by reason of their admitted membership in the Communist Party ... to be incompetent, intellectually dishonest, and derelict in their duty to find and teach the truth.[10]

Some administrators accused faculty of being communists "in spirit"; some condemned faculty for having a friend who was mentioned in a congressional report; others took a denial of involvement in left-wing politics as evidence of such activity since "communists always lie and can never be trusted." After deciding to fire someone who insisted that he had done nothing dishonorable or disloyal, one university president explained: "You hold the same views and beliefs now which you held while you were an active member and an officer in the Communist Party. . . . It becomes difficult to accept your disavowal of the illegal and destructive aims of the Communist Party." Such arguments were an attempt on the part of academic administrators to make their actions appear reasonable. Most academic authorities used the deductive or a priori method (rather than the inductive or pragmatic method) in their approach to these cases; they did not believe that it was necessary to rely on facts in drawing inferences or conclusions. In an ironic way this suggests that gaining power in academic institutions is probably not related to the ability to use the scientific method.

Ultimately, of course, most principals were judged by how much of an embarrassment they were thought to be. Apparently acting in the belief that the end justifies the means, some administrators abandoned principles of fair play in their efforts to terminate faculty. There are great risks, of course, when men who do not seem to have any special gift of morality become its guardians.

Academic authorities did what civic authorities could not. They became the enforcement arm of the radical right. They substituted economic punishment for the criminal punishment that the Fifth Amendment is designed to prevent. Academic authorities argued variously that invocation of the Fifth Amendment was a breach of duty to the public or to the institution, or that a principal was primarily motivated to defy congressional investigators and was therefore misusing the privilege, or that it was improper to invoke the Fifth Amendment to shield others. More often than not they seemed to be eager partners in prescriptive publicity, the practice designed to bring extralegal punishment on those who congressional committees had some reason to believe—sometimes rightly, sometimes wrongly—were communists, fellow travelers, radicals, nonconformists, or security risks. Firing people generally meant expulsion, if not from the profession of research, at least from the American college and university. It was also an infringement of basic civil liberties. The attack on those who caught the attention of academic authorities because their rhetoric, reliance on the Fifth Amendment, or work in the Wallace campaign aroused considerable indignation and negative comment did not only impinge on academic freedom, but it impinged on civil rights, including the right citizens have to act on their political views, the freedom of expression Americans in other walks of life take for granted. This restriction on basic liberties is a more fundamental loss than a denial of professional privilege.

Over the years, the discussion of the Cold War on campus has almost exclusively revolved around the question of whether those who were dismissed or punished in some other way were fairly or unfairly victimized. Is someone who may be a communist or communist sympathizer really dangerous? Should someone who may be disloyal to America or who may in some other way be untrustworthy be expeditiously dismissed? Is it fair to trample on the rights of someone who might well trample on the rights of others given the chance? Those siding with the Right have blamed the Left for the Cold War on campus. Those siding with the Left have blamed the Right. It has been taken for granted that the campus was just another arena for the larger ideological struggle taking place across America. In fact, however, the Cold War in America can be seen as incidental—as the backdrop—to the Cold War on campus in that the latter was as rooted in the politics of organizational control as in the politics of the Right or Left. The Cold War on campus was about institutional politics; ideological concerns were not as central as is commonly believed.

The Legacy

The Cold War seems to have brought a number of lasting features to American colleges and universities. All but a few academic administrators assumed and eagerly took on the function of legal arbiters of what was acceptable and unacceptable political expression, a function generally in the purview of civil authorities. Putting aside the question of whether they had the competence to carry out the duties of the police and the courts, such actions, in particular cases, redefined and broadened the responsibilities of academic administrators. More generally, they added to the confusion over what indeed are the proper and legitimate responsibilities of academic authorities and, more important, of academic institutions to the society at large. This, of course, was not the first time or the last time the question of the relationship of academic institutions to other institutions has been muddled. Since the Cold War years, however, American institutions of higher learning have stumbled about more than in the past in search of a definition and purpose—becoming entangled in the full range of human activities, from creating life to ending it.

In placing limits on what faculty could say or believe, academic administrators were also assuming the responsibility for what faculty would be permitted to say or believe. This, alongside their willingness to punish those whose political ideology was at variance with mainstream thinking, had a chilling effect on the normal exchange of ideas necessary for the development of academic work. Any decrease in political dissent would probably be matched by a decrease in dissent of any kind, by a decrease in the inclination to question. A quarter of a century later Americans still show some reluctance to engage in dialogue or debate. One striking result—a monumental irony—is that the assumptions and assertions of neo-Marxism continue to gain legitimacy as they float about the campus largely unexamined. The American academic community has slouched through the last two decades ideologically animated but very nearly intellectually moribund.

Of course, there is no way of really determining how many critics were silenced, how many took special caution in what they studied or said, or how many other factors contributed to the disinclination of American academics to examine and debate controversial ideas. Civil libertarians would have us believe that the number was significant. Whatever the case, numbers are less important than the impact all of this may have had in redefining the ideal academic: someone whose ideas are not a cause of misgivings for academic administrators, an individual whose ideas are not out of the commonplace.

Although in reality academic institutions have never been politically neutral, it was part of the lore that they were pretty nearly so and that in any case this was an ideal toward which they should strive. By making it explicit in the early Cold War years that a political test was necessary to hold an academic appointment, indeed, by bringing the Cold War on campus, academic administrators completely shattered the notion that it was possible for American colleges and universities to be politically neutral. By making political ideology and activity a concern of colleges and universities, academic administrators accelerated the politicization of colleges and universities. This politicization of the academy not only made the campus turbulence of the 1960s inevitable, but it also made it manifest that political opinion and affiliations were and would be relevant criteria for academic appointments, for retention, for dismissal.

In reviewing what he called "the silly season," Robert M. Hutchins argued that the excesses brought about by the Cold War on campus could have been avoided if administrators had relied on "the standard of competence." This

> would have protected us against teachers following a Party line or conducting propaganda. If a teacher sought to indoctrinate his pupils, which is the only circumstance under which he could be dangerous as a teacher, he would be incompetent, and should be removed as such. . . . If we had used the standard of competence we should have been free to fix our minds on the positive

responsibility of building an educational system, and with half the energy we have put into being scared to death we might have built a great one.[11]

Making merit incidental in the assessment of faculty erodes their academic freedom, as the principle of merit is the first line of defense in the protection of academic freedom. As Harold Taylor observed, with the introduction of political criteria as a "cause for retention or dismissal of university professors," academic freedom "must keep retreating to various unprepared positions, no one of which can be held for long under sustained attack."[12] The failure to use universalistic criteria in the decision-making process has long been associated with infringements of academic freedom.[13]

The political model has replaced the collegial model as the standard by which academics conduct their affairs. Few question the assumption that conflicting interests are intrinsic to all relationships between faculty and faculty, faculty and students, and faculty and administrators. Today, the administration is seldom seen as an extension of faculty. It is accepted as a fact of life that careers are as often determined by clique membership, cunning, wirepulling, bureaucratic agility, or holding the correct opinions (depending on one's circumstances, Right, middle, or Left) as by ability or intellectual contribution. Pressure groups compete for resources and attention. Successful administrators are those who best understand how to wield power. It is taken for granted that relations between departments and between colleagues will be marked by suspicion and tension. The preoccupation with conspiracy abounds. Conspiratorial theories have become central to more and more historical, social scientific, and literary interpretations. In fact, a general sense of paranoia has permeated academic life. In short, traditional structures and notions of authority of institutions of higher learning—and in the wake of this, traditional ideals of objective scholarship—have been weakened.

Since the early Cold War years, it has become an indisputable tenet of the conventional wisdom that the interests of the government and the interests of higher learning are the same. Prior to that time, of course, public service was a central function of academic institutions, particularly land-grant colleges and universities. However, since the onset of the Cold War years, the meaning of public service has evolved considerably—from working for the greater good as defined by elites to working for the greater good as defined by politicians. In many academic departments it is now considered necessary and proper for the curriculum and research programs to be an extension of the domestic and foreign policies of the goverment. Government service has become the first duty of higher education. To more and more academics, the national interest means what those in the government or the foundations who have money to throw at colleges and universities say is the national interest. Physical scientists work on dooms-day weapons, while social scientists busy themselves with the dispossessed. The humanist who can celebrate the American dream can win a free air-plane trip and three nights at a Holiday Inn.

Thus, through the servility or arrogance of a few hundred academic administrators, these legacies of the Cold War are now an integral part of academic life on a few thousand campuses. An academic career has come to be defined as just that—a career, something one does to earn a living. Less and less often is academic life seen as a calling, an arena for personal fulfillment and service. The Cold War on campus did more than pre-cipitously end a number of academic careers. It warped and weakened the institutional structure of colleges and universities that sustained the ideal that the life of the mind was worth pursuing, that learning could be an end in itself.

Notes

1. Murray B. Levin, *Political Hysteria in America* (New York: Basic Books, 1971), p. 146.
2. Paul F. Lazarsfeld and Wagner Thielens, Jr., *The Academic Mind* (Glencoe, Ill.: Free Press, 1958), pp. 185–86.
3. Ibid., p. 187.
4. Ibid., p. 183.
5. Ibid., p. 191.
6. Ibid., p. 183.
7. Thorstein Veblen, *The Higher Learning in America* (New York: Hill and Wang, 1959), p. 167.
8. Ibid., pp. 168–69.
9. Ibid., p. 185.
10. Raymond B. Allen, "The President's Analysis," *Communism and Academic Freedom: The Record of the Tenure Cases at the University of Washington* (Seattle: University of Washington, 1949), p. 90.
11. Robert M. Hutchins, "The Meaning and Significance of Academic Freedom," *The Annals* 300 (1955): 73.
12. Harold Taylor, "The Dismissal of Fifth Amendment Professors," *The Annals* 300 (1955): 81.
13. Lionel S. Lewis, *Scaling the Ivory Tower: Merit and Its Limits in Academic Careers* (Baltimore: Johns Hopkins University Press, 1975).

Appendix A
Preparing the List of Institutions

An exhaustive search was made in order to generate as complete a list as possible of colleges and universities in which political issues surfaced as germane to holding an academic appointment. Initially, the records of the American Association of University Professors, the organization to which faculty would most likely turn if they felt that their academic freedom had been violated, were twice checked over. From an examination of various listings, it was estimated that for a little more than the decade under consideration, the American Association of University Professors had received close to 550 complaints, of which slightly less than one-third, around 175, revolved around questions of academic freedom. In about one-third of these academic freedom cases, the complainant charged that political beliefs or activities were relevant to the judgment and action of institutional authorities. Thus, the indications were that there were roughly fifty-five dossiers in the American Association of University Professors' archives that could provide information pertinent to this study. Close to that number of cases were actually found in the archives. However, an examination of these records revealed that some of the files were quite thin, containing little more than a letter of inquiry. The American Association of University Professors does not launch a complete investigation every time a charge is brought against an institution. Indeed, there is no follow-up to almost half the initial contacts. A case may involve nonreappointment, for example, a circumstance that does not usually generate enough particulars to make a full inquiry practicable. At the other extreme, however, cases that involved the revocation of tenure would be a challenge of tenets to which the American Association of University Professors is committed, and the evidence indicates that such incidents were indeed given full consideration.

Names of other potential institutions were derived from ascertaining the institutional affiliations of witnesses called before legislative committees to testify about communism and other political activities on campus in the years before and after World War II. Inquiring into communism in education was the special province of Representative Velde's House Committee on Un-American Activities and Senator Jenner's Senate Internal Security Subcommittee. The latter published information on over ninety "teachers and other staff members of educational institutions who invoked the Fifth Amendment regarding their Communist Party membership or admitted such membership." Other listings, such as one of witnesses who in 1953 appeared before one of the congressional committees that had set out to expose communists in education and "refused on the grounds of the Fifth Amendment of the Constitution to answer at least some of the questions," provided additional names that might otherwise have been overlooked. Among educators who were called to recount their past or present political affiliations, about two-thirds had academic appointments, so that this publicizing of their identities provided additional leads to a few of the less notorious academic freedom controversies. The newly gained prominence also, unfortunately, was responsible for the fact that some of the cases ever existed, in that charges in some instances were lodged against individuals only after the publication of these lists brought names to the attention of academic authorities.

There is considerable published material about some *causes célèbres*, most notably the case that ended in the dismissal of three faculty from the University of Washington in Seattle and the protracted loyalty oath controversy at the University of California that, after tensions eased and the dust settled, resulted in the dismissal of eighteen individuals.

Cases of less distinction were also covered by newspapers and magazines, and it was possible to add a handful of names of institutions to our roster by utilizing published indexes. Other secondary sources, such as privately published accounts, dissertations, and institutional histories, supplemented the data base. Available archival materials were consulted when practicable and necessary. These materials were sometimes extensive. At the University of Washington, for example, there were over thirty volumes of typed transcript covering a month and a half of testimony. Although some institutions had complete files on incidents, others had next to nothing; at a few institutions, there was not only no record of the incident, but none of the individual who was supposedly involved. Universities generally had fuller records than did colleges. At many institutions, large portions of materials that were said to exist could not be located or were confidential, thus inaccessible.

Preliminary procedures generated a list of over 100 institutions that seemed to merit study. This number was quickly reduced by a quarter, mostly due to the elimination of institutions where no trace could be found that state or national loyalty concerns had intruded on campus life with any force. Of the remainder, incidents with names attached were brought to light at sixty-seven institutions; enough particulars were gathered for fifty-eight to warrant inclusion in the study. Many incidents involved only one individual, but close to half involved the appointments of two or more faculty.

Presumably this fifty-eight is a significant proportion of the national total, although there is no way of knowing this for a fact. This is not the population of institutions that might merit inclusion in this study, for surely there were some that did not come to my attention. There are no records, for example, of situations where individuals whose politics were suspect were unable to find jobs or were obliged to accept an appointment below their qualifications. Nor is it a sample of the campus disquietude with political overtones in the decade after World War II, as basically benign incidents that did not have negative repercussions were not likely to have become part of academic folklore or written history.

Needless to say, there were other manifestations on campus of the political tensions wrought by the Cold War. These 126 cases at fifty-eight institutions, however, were clearly its most visible and perhaps most far-reaching result. It is apparent that their chilling effect on the expression of all ideas by both faculty and students was significant, although in fact there is no way to measure adequately their full impact.

Although a large number of documents were found in the Washington, D.C., office of the American Association of University Professors, the libraries and archives of the following were also a rich source of information: Antioch College; the University Archives of the State University of New York at Buffalo; the University of Colorado; Office of the Secretary, Columbia University; Historical Manuscripts and Archives, the University of Connecticut; Department of Manuscripts and University Archives, John M. Olin Library, Cornell University; Professor Lee Lorch for materials regarding Fisk University; Susan Furry for material regarding Harvard University; Office of the Dean, School of Advanced Studies, Illinois Institute of Technology; University Archives, Indiana University; Institute Archives and Special Collections, Massachusetts Institute of Technology; Michigan Historical Collections, Bentley Historical Library, the University of Michigan; the University of Minnesota; University Archives, the Ohio State University; Reed College Archives; Houston Collection, Rensselaer Polytechnic Institute Archives; Department of Rare Books and Special Collections, University of Rochester Library; Esther Raushenbush Library, Sarah Lawrence College; the College Archives, Smith College; Department of Rare Books and Manuscripts, Vassar College; Archives of the Margaret Clapp Library, Wellesley College; Yale University Archives. Some letters, memoranda and reports were made available with the understanding that individuals and institutions named therein not be identified; thus, the above list is not quite complete.

Appendix B
Statistical Profile of
the American Campus, 1946-1956

A. Institutions:

Year	Total	4-Year Colleges	Junior Colleges
1946	1,768	1,304	464
1948	1,788	1,316	472
1950	1,863	1,345	518
1952	1,891	1,380	511
1954	1,862	1,344	518
1956	1,850	1,383	467

B. Income and Expenditures for Higher Education:

Year	Income	Expenditures
1946	$1,169,394,000	$1,088,422,000
1948	2,027,052,000	1,883,269,000
1950	2,374,645,000	2,245,661,000
1952	2,562,451,000	2,471,008,000
1954	2,945,550,000	2,882,864,000
1956	3,603,370,000	3,499,463,000
1939-40		674,688,000
1949-50		2,245,661,000

C. Enrollments:

Year	Total	Public Institutions	Private Institutions
1947	2,338,226	1,152,377	1,185,849
1949	2,444,900	1,207,151	1,237,749
1951	2,101,962	1,037,938	1,064,024
1953	2,231,054	1,185,876	1,045,178
1955	2,653,034	1,476,282	1,176,752
1956	2,918,212	1,656,402	1,261,810

D. Degrees Conferred:

Year	Total	Bachelor's Male	Bachelor's Female	Master's	Doctorate or Equivalent
1946	157,349	58,664	77,510	19,209	1,966
1948	317,607	175,615	95,571	42,432	3,989
1950	496,874	328,841	103,217	58,183	6,633
1952	401,203	225,981	104,005	63,534	7,683
1954	357,327	186,884	104,624	56,823	8,996
1956	377,698	198,615	110,899	59,281	8,903

E. Number of Faculty:

Year	Total	Male	Female
1946	165,324	116,134	49,190
1948	223,660	164,616	59,044
1950	246,722	186,189	60,533
1952	244,488	187,136	57,352
1954	265,911	204,871	61,040
1956	298,910	230,342	68,568

F. Faculty Salaries:

Average Annual Salaries at Large State Universities:

	1947	and	1953
Professors	$5,300		$7,000
Associate Professors	4,300		5,600
Assistant Professors	3,500		4,600
Instructors	2,800		3,700

Some Non-professorial Salaries:	**1947**	**and**	**1953**
Physicians	$10,726		$15,000
Executive Officials, Large Railroads	9,070		11,592
High School Principals (cities over 500,000)	6,396		9,156
Dentists	6,610		8,500
Railroad Conductors	4,862		6,676
High School Principals (cities between 30,000-100,000)	4,700		6,523
High School Teachers (cities over 500,000)	4,047		5,526
Automobile Workers	3,143		4,947
Elementary School Teachers (cities over 500,000)	3,200		4,817
High School Teachers (cities between 30,000-100,000)	2,774		4,292
Bituminous Coal Miners	3,212		4,198
Elementary School Teacher (cities between 30,000-100,000)	2,288		3,682
Telephone Operators	2,428		3,224

Sources: Department of Health, Education, and Welfare, Office of Education, *Biennial Survey of Education in the United States*; U.S. Department of Education, National Center for Education Statistics; Beardsley Ruml and Sidney G. Tickton, *Teaching Salaries Then and Now: A 50-Year Comparison with Other Occupations and Industries*, New York: The Fund for the Advancement of Education, 1955.

Appendix C
Example of Congressional Testimony*

Mr. Velde: Now, you are willing to give us the street address, residence, at the present time. As I understand it, you refuse to give your residence and the street address of your residence when you were in Boston; is that right?

Professor: Yes, sir.

Mr. Tavenner: Now, Professor, during the course of the investigation that has been conducted by this committee as to the purpose of the Communist Party in attempting to organize persons within the teaching profession at Harvard University and at Massachusetts Institute of Technology, and also for the purpose of determining just what the Communist Party objectives were in doing that, and also for the purpose of determining the extent of success or failure of the Communist Party in that enterprise, the committee has learned that you were affiliated with that same group. It appears in the testimony of Dr. Robert Gorham Davis, who testified before this committee on February 25, 1953. He told the committee that two persons took part in his recruitment into the Communist Party, and that you were one of those. At the time he did not know you were a member of the Party, but after he, himself, became a member he ascertained that you were a member of the Party.

Now, if that be true, you are in a position to give this committee information within your knowledge of the things it is inquiring into.

So, I want to begin by asking you whether or not the testimony of Mr. Davis was true or whether it was false that you were a member of the Communist Party at Harvard University.

Professor: Is that your question?

Mr. Tavenner: Yes.

Professor: Well, that question, with regard to the truth of the testimony of—of the—reluctant informer, Mr. Davis, I decline to answer on two grounds: The first and principal—principal ground is that I assert the privilege against self-incrimination and, secondly, it appears to me, although I haven't consulted counsel on this specific point—it appears to me—

Mr. Tavenner: Let me suggest you do—

Mr. Velde: You may at any time—

Mr. Tavenner: —consult counsel.

Mr. Velde: —consult counsel.

Professor: Sir, I'll continue my answer, having consulted counsel.

*"Hearing before Subcommittee of the Committee on Un-American Activities," House of Representatives, Eighty-third Congress, 19 May 1953.'

As I say, the first and principal reason is that of the Fifth article in the Bill of Rights. The second reason is that I—I believe, since I have not had the opportunity to cross-examine Mr. Davis, that I have a right under the Sixth—Sixth article of the Bill of Rights to refuse to answer.

Mr. Velde: What questions would you ask Mr. Davis if you had the privilege to cross-examination here?

I want to state for your own benefit and for the benefit of counsel this is not a court of law. This is an investigating committee. It is a legislative committee, authorized by the House of Representatives, and we are out, duty-bound, to ascertain facts and information relative to subversive activities in the United States, report to Congress, report to the American people, for remedial legislation.

I ask you again to reconsider your answer to that question, and to, if you can see it within your own conscience, with your own rights under the Constitution, answer the question and give us the information that you have.

Obviously, you were a member of the Communist Party at Harvard. There is no reason why you shouldn't tell us about it.

Professor: Well, sir, I think the answer—the question whether I knew the informer, Davis, would tend to degrade and incriminate me, and I also do think that— that a congressional hearing should at least—at least morally, if not legally—I am not prepared to judge the law—should grant the right of cross-examination. Whether it is a legal right or not, I suppose, is for the Supreme Court to ultimately decide; but, to me, it seems the justice—the Fifth Article of the Bill of Rights speaks specifically about criminal cases, but has been extended to cover congressional hearings. So, in my non—non-legal opinion the Sixth Article could be interpreted in the same spirit.

Mr. Clardy: You misinterpret, but at any rate the question the chairman asked you hasn't been answered. He asked you that if you were permitted to do something our rules do not authorize—and that is to cross-examine Mr. Davis— what subject or what questions did you want to ask him?

Professor: Well, that seems to me to be a very ify question, as the late President Roosevelt would say, and I would have to prepare—I would prepare for that particular contingency when it arose—would prepare my questions then— but I am not prepared to ask them in a vacuum.

Mr. Clardy: Well, you knew when you came here today that the rules of this committee did not permit the procedure you are talking about, and you made no effort to explore the subject of what you would ask at all, then?

Professor: Well, sir, you may—you know I made an effort by means of a letter I wrote to you to explore the possibility of testifying without informing on people, and your committee has denied me that right. It's quite true I didn't explore every possible contingency that might arise. . . .

Mr. Tavenner: Not understanding fully just what importance you put upon these various assignments of grounds for your refusal to answer, I want to ask you the question in this form: Were you a member of the Communist Party at any time while you attended Harvard University?

Professor: Well, I attended as a student—
You mean as a student?

Mr. Tavenner: Yes; let us put it that way first—while you attended as a student.

Professor: Well, speaking of the period before I obtained my Ph. D. degree—the period before I obtained my Ph. D. degree from Harvard—I can answer that I was not a member of the Communist Party.

Mr. Clardy: I didn't hear the concluding part of that.

Professor: I was not a member of the Communist Party—

Mr. Tavenner: And it would be—

Professor: —at that time.

Mr. Tavenner: You entered Harvard in 1930; you received your Doctor's degree in 1932—

Professor: Yes, sir. . . .

Mr. Tavenner: Well, were you a member of the Communist Party during that period of time, between 1933 and 1937?

Professor: That—on that question, I decline to answer; I claim the privilege against self-incrimination.

Mr. Tavenner: Was there any period during that time, between 1933 and 1937, when you were not a member of the Communist Party?

Professor: I claim the privilege, sir.

Mr. Tavenner: Well, during the year 1933, to be more specific—

Mr. Velde: Just a minute, Mr. Tavenner.

You claim the privilege?

Professor: I claim the privilege.

Mr. Velde: And refuse to answer?

Professor: Yes, sir.

Mr. Tavenner: To be a little more specific, were you a member of the Communist Party in 1933?

Professor: I decline to answer on the same grounds—that is, on the grounds of the—of the Fifth Article of the Bill of Rights.

Mr. Tavenner: Now, while you were a student at Harvard—that is between 1930 and 1932—were you a member of the Young Communist League?

Professor: No, sir. . . .

Mr. Tavenner: Now, during the period you were such an assistant, were you a member of the Young Communist League at any time during that period?

Professor: I would like to consult my attorney before answering that.

Sir, that question I must also decline to answer on the same grounds.

Mr. Tavenner: Now, Professor, a witness testified under oath before this committee that he was a member of the Young Communist League as early as 1934 and a man by the name of Harry Marks—M-a-r-k-s—was the head of the group and that the meetings were held at [your] home . . . in a rooming house.

Were any meetings of the Young Communist League held at your home in 1934—

Professor: I decline—

Mr. Tavenner: —or thereafter?

Professor: I decline to answer on the same grounds.

Mr. Tavenner: Isn't it a fact that you refused to testify a few moments ago as to where you resided between 1933 and 1937 due to the fact that Communist Party meetings were held in your home?

Professor: No, sir; that is not a fact.

Mr. Tavenner: How is that?

Professor: That is not my understanding of it. I refused to testify as to my address—address in Boston.

Mr. Scherer: Was it because Communist Party meetings were being held at that address?

Professor: I don't have to explain the reason.

Mr. Scherer: Well, if you—

Professor: The reason was explained at that time.

Mr. Scherer: If you decline to answer, you have the right to decline; but I am asking the question, sir,—

Professor: Yes, sir.

Mr. Scherer: —is that the reason you declined to give the Boston address, because Communist Party meetings were held at that address?

Professor: I don't think, sir, it would be wise for me to explain the reason—the reason why—

Mr. Clardy: Witness—

Mr. Velde: Just a minute.

Professor: —the reason why I decline.

Mr. Velde: Mr. Scherer has the floor.

Mr. Scherer: You decline?

Professor: I decline to answer on the grounds that it might tend—my answer might tend to incriminate me.

Mr. Tavenner: Were you acquainted with Herbert Ellis Robbins—R-o-b-b-i-n-s?

Professor: I decline to answer on the grounds that it might tend to incriminate me.

Mr. Tavenner: Were you acquainted with Harry Marks?

Professor: I decline to answer on the same grounds.

Mr. Tavenner: Are you acquainted with an investigator of this committee, Mr. George E. Cooper, who is sitting to my left?

Professor: Yes, sir.

Mr. Tavenner: Did Mr. Cooper serve the subpoena on you for your appearance at this hearing?

Professor: Yes, sir.

Mr. Tavenner: Do you recall the date?

Professor: Well, I think the date was May 9th, sir, this year.

Mr. Tavenner: On examination of the subpoena I find that it was served, according to the return thereon, on May 8, 1953. Is that in accordance with your recollection?

Professor: Well, sir, I can identify the date in this way: I can identify the day. It was the same day the university issued a statement of policy to its faculty. I am sure of that, and I can say this also on the date: It was a Friday. Now, if Friday was the 8th, I will agree it was the 8th; but if Friday was the 9th, I would say the subpoena was served on the 9th.

Mr. Tavenner: Do you recall talking to Mr. Cooper on that occasion and, in the course of your conversation, that you admitted to him that you belonged to the Communist Party at Harvard?

Professor: Well, that seems to be another way of getting me to answer the question I declined to answer.

I decline to answer that question on the same grounds.

Mr. Clardy: Mr. Chairman.

Mr. Velde: Mr. Clardy.

Mr. Clardy: I ask that the witness be directed to answer the question. I think there is no basis whatsoever for raising the Fifth Amendment in that circumstance.

Mr. Velde: The chair concurs with the gentleman from Michigan. The witness is directed to answer the question.

Professor: May I have the question please?

Mr. Tavenner: Will you repeat the question, please, sir?

Professor: I would like to consult my attorney before answering that question.
Sir, I deline to answer the question on the grounds of self-incrimination.

Mr. Tavenner: Were you asked the question by Mr. Cooper of whether you knew Isadore Amdur, a Norman Levinson, Robert G. Davis and Dirk J. Struik—S-t-r-u-i-k—to which you replied that you did and you admitted attending meetings with them?

Professor: My understanding is Mr. Cooper asserts that I said I attended meetings with all of those names—

Mr. Tavenner: With Isadore Amdur, Norman Levinson—

Mr. Velde: Just a minute, Mr. Counsel. Let the witness finish his answer.

Professor: I think I finished—with all the individuals you named?

Mr. Tavenner: Yes.

Mr. Velde: I'm sorry. Proceed.

Mr. Tavenner: Yes, sir.

Mr. Velde: At this point it is going to be necessary for the members of the committee to answer a roll call, and the committee will be in recess for 20 minutes. . . .

Mr. Velde: And let the record show that the witness has admitted that he wrote the letter.

Mr. Clardy: And that this is his signature on the letter, and it is dated . . . May 15, 1953, and addressed to you, Mr. Chairman:

"I have been subpoenaed to appear before your committee on May 19. Before testifying, I would like to make a request.

"Conscious of no wrong-doing, I am well aware that some past associations or activities might be used against me under present circumstances, in which there is widespread disrespect in high places for the Bill of Rights. However, in view of my desire to protect the good name of my university, I am prepared to set aside personal apprehensions, to waive my privilege of not testifying against myself, and to answer freely and frankly any relevant questions about my own activities, provided"—and that word is underlined—"that your committee agrees not to ask me to name or identify any other person. I will not play the conscious role of informer. I will not get innocent people into trouble. If I did, I would lose all self-respect and forfeit the confidence of my colleagues and students. I request you, therefore, to respect my conscientious scruple, making it possible for me to waive my constitutional protection and testify more fully than I otherwise can. Respectfully."

and signed by your name. . . .

Mr. Clardy: All right, then, having made that statement, isn't it a fact that at the time you wrote the letter, and indeed right down to the the very time prior to your appearing on the stand, that you were perfectly willing to tell this committee all about your past associations and connections, provided that we did not interrogate you about the identity of other persons?

Professor: Well, what I stated in that letter is true.

Mr. Clardy: That is the fact, isn't it?

Professor: I meant what I said when I wrote the letter, if that is what you are asking.

Mr. Clardy: I can't hear you. I wish—

Professor: I meant what I said when I wrote the letter.

Mr. Clardy: Well, just answer my question, then: My statement of it is an accurate statement, then, isn't it?

Professor: Well, we have so many statements of it now—

Mr. Clardy: Well, we will put it this way: Do you still adhere to and mean what you said in your letter?

Professor: I better consult my attorney on that.

Mr. Clardy: You may.

Professor: Sir, my answer is that the letter was written in good faith and I meant what I said in the letter. The letter contained a provision, and that having— that provision and the request not having been granted, the entire letter is now null and void. It is like an offer which is not accepted. The entire thing is of no effect at the present time, as far as I can see.

Mr. Clardy: Oh, I see. You thought you could bargain with the committee and not having obtained your price that what you said then would be of no importance; is that what you are trying to tell us?

Professor: No, sir. If the offer had been accepted, the condition—the situation would now be different from what it is. . . .

Mr. Clardy: One final question: If the committee should at this time inform you that it will not ask you any questions about the identity of any of the persons associated with you in the testimony that we have called to your attention, but would confine our questions to asking you merely about your own actions and past associations, would you answer the questions?

Professor: May I consult my attorney?

Mr. Clardy: You may.

Professor: Sir, my answer is that if you at this time grant the request I made in the letter, I would stand by the letter, although at the moment I feel my personal apprehensions are stronger that they were when I wrote it. . . .

Appendix D
Excerpts from Minutes of Meetings of the Regents of the University of Colorado

The Denver members of the Regents of the University of Colorado met in Regent Bromley's office in Denver on January 31, 1951 at 11:00 A.M. . . . .

President Stearns announced that the purpose of the meeting was to consider a course of action in connection with a current news release and press comments concerning Professor David Hawkins of the University of Colorado who was called to testify in December, 1950, before the House Un-American Activities Committee in Washington, D.C. The President reviewed briefly Professor Hawkins's appointment to the faculty in 1947, prior to which time he was on the faculty of George Washington University and, during the years 1943–45, a scientist and historian in the Los Alamos, New Mexico Atomic Research Laboratory.

President Stearns said that Professor Hawkins, upon receiving his summons to Washington in December, volunteered the information that he had become a member of the Communist Party in 1938 but, in disagreement with the tenets of that organization, had discontinued his membership and affiliation in 1943. Subsequently, according to information received from the director of the Los Alamos Laboratory, Hawkins had been cleared for work in the Laboratory.

President Stearns posed two questions,

1. Should there be an investigation of alleged communist affiliates among the members of the faculty and, if so, who should conduct it?
2. What should be the policy in connection with the loyalty oath which the laws of Colorado require of teachers?

It was agreed that if the Governor and the legislature feel that an investigation is desirable, it will be welcomed; meanwhile, the Regents will pursue the matter through established procedures not only in regard to Professor Hawkins but any other members of the university faculty against whom specific charges of communist affiliation may be brought.

The deliberations of the [Executive] Committee will be reported to the Board in a special session on Friday, February 2. The agenda for that meeting will include the consideration of whether faculty members should be required to take the loyalty oath; what action, if any, should be taken against Professor Hawkins; and the course to be followed in conducting an investigation of faculty members.

Pursuant to the Notice of Call made a part of these minutes, the Regents of the University of Colorado met in Special Session [February 2, 1951] at 12:30 P.M. at the Denver Club, Denver, Colorado. . . .

President Stearns briefed the Regents on the deliberation of the Executive Committee which met January 31, 1951.

It was moved that the Regents require the Oath of Allegiance. The motion was seconded and unanimously carried.

Referring to the action to be taken on charges against Professor David Hawkins, the President suggested that the machinery for investigating specific charges against any faculty member is provided in the Faculty Committee on Privilege and Tenure. Dean Dyde suggested that it was not within the purview of the Committee to originate the charges, but that they could be asked to report to the Regents on specific charges.

It was moved that the case of Professor Hawkins be referred to the Faculty Committee on Privilege and Tenure on charges to be specified by President Stearns, to be heard and report thereof to be made to the Regents for their final action. The motion was seconded and unanimously carried.

In the matter of the proposed investigation of subversive persons reported to be in the employ of the university, four methods of conducting such an investigation were considered: (1) by the Regents, (2) by agency or by counsel selected by the Regents, (3) by referral to the Committee on Privilege and Tenure, (4) by a committee of the state legislature. After full discussion, the following resolution was moved, seconded and unanimously carried.

> WHEREAS it has come to the attention of the Board of Regents that there are reports of subversive persons in the employ of the University,
>
> NOW THEREFORE BE IT RESOLVED that the Regents employ experienced and qualified investigative counsel to investigate and make findings and report thereof to the Board of Regents with all convenient speed, and that such plan be referred to the Attorney General for concurrence.

A regular meeting of the Regents of the University of Colorado was held in the President's office, Boulder, Colorado, February 16, 1951 at 10:00 o'clock. . . .

Oath of Allegiance

President Stearns reported that following the Regents' meeting of February 2, a meeting of the faculty was called at which he read from Chapter 146, Colorado Statutes Annotated, Sections 235, 236, 237, regarding the oath of allegiance to be required of all teaching members of the staff. A similar meeting was held in the Department of Medicine. Since that time, practically all of the full-time members of the teaching staff have signed the oath and also a large number of the non-teaching staff who did so voluntarily. Hereafter, the oath will be required of all faculty members at the time of their employment.

The Hawkins Case

President Stearns read a letter which he had written on February 9, 1951 to the Senate Committee on Privilege and Tenure referring to it the case of Professor David Hawkins for its determination of the truth or falsity of specified allegations, and requesting the committee to make recommendations as to whether or not Professor Hawkins is a fit person to teach at the University of Colorado. The letter is attached as *EXHIBIT A.* . . .

[Portions of *Exhibit A*, Letter to Senate Committee on Privilege and Tenure]

6. Pursuant to this procedure, in accordance with the statement of duties laid upon the Committee on Privilege and Tenure and in accordance with the established practices of the university, whenever questions arise concerning the revocation of the appointment of a faculty member for the good of the university, the matter of his qualifications for the continuation of tenure is referred to the Senate Committee on Privilege and Tenure for a full and fair investigation and hearing and the making of findings of fact and recommendations to the president.
7. Questions have arisen concerning the qualifications of Professor David Hawkins of the university faculty to continue in his present appointment. He now holds the position of professor of philosophy in the College of Arts and Sciences, serving until the time of his normal retirement unless such tenure is terminated earlier for cause.
8. Accordingly, by action taken by resolution of the Board of Regents at a special meeting duly called and held for that purpose on February 2, 1951, I am instructed to refer to your committee the case of David Hawkins, to determine the truth or falsity of the following allegations, and on the basis of your findings to reach conclusions and make recommendations as to whether or not he is a fit person to teach at the

University of Colorado:
(a) It is alleged that on his own testimony before the Committee on Un-American Activities of the House of Representatives Professor Hawkins was a member of the American Communist Party from 1938 to 1943;
(b) It is alleged that Professor Hawkins did not disclose his alleged former membership in the American Communist Party to the university when he was being considered for appointment thereto;
(c) It is alleged that he did not disclose his alleged former membership in the American Communist Party to his superior when he was appointed to the staff of the laboratory at Los Alamos in 1943;
(d) It is alleged that he has refused to answer certain questions propounded to him by the Committee on Un-American Activities of the House of Representatives of the United States Congress after having taken an oath to tell the truth, the whole truth and nothing but the truth;
(e) It is alleged that his answers to certain of the questions propounded to him by the Committee on Un-American Activities of the House of Representatives of the United States Congress were evasive;
(f) It is alleged that Professor Hawkins while acting as sponsor for the Marxist study group, an organization on the campus of the University of Colorado, permitted said group to become a political action committee rather than to restrict its activities to its function as a study group as authorized by its charter;
(g) It is alleged that his separation from the American Communist Party was never clearly defined by formal resignation and was nominal rather than real.

WHEREFORE, the committee is requested to investigate the foregoing, to determine its conclusions concerning the qualifications of Professor Hawkins to continue to serve as a member of the faculty of the University of Colorado and to make its recommendation to the president with all convenient speed.

General Investigation

The President reported that in compliance with Regents' instructions at the meeting of February 2, he had employed attorneys Dudley Hutchinson, Jr. of Boulder, and Harold E. Hafer of Fort Collins to conduct an investigation into alleged subversive persons reported to be in the employ of the university. The investigative counsel is to report its findings to the Regents with all convenient speed. . . .

Appendix E
Testimony by a State Legislator before the Regents of the University of Colorado*

President Stearns: Are there any persons here who care to present any pertinent testimony in this matter?

Mr. A. W. Hewett: President Stearns, and members of the Board of Regents: I am interested, not particularly as an individual, but as a representative of the people of the State of Colorado. I don't want to give you any of my opinions, nor draw any conclusions. I want to merely state a few rather pertinent facts that seem to be more or less the common knowledge of most of the people of the State.

The people of the State are particularly interested in this institution, in its well being, and in its progress, and in its continuance as a developer of American ideals and individuals.

I would like to call to the attention of the Regents, if they have not seen this before, the copyrighted article of Fulton Lewis, Jr. under date line, I believe, of February the 5th, which has received circulation throughout the nation, and which is substantiated in its statements. If someone will read it, I would like to have it read.

President Stearns: It will be received and put into the record.

Mr. Hewett: That is all right, but it is a statement of fact, and has been substantiated by the facts taken from the reports of the Un-American Activities Committee of the United States [House of] Representatives.

Mr. Bromley: If you want it in, Mr. Hewett, why don't you read it into the record?

Mr. Hewett: I am not too good as a reader. I think perhaps a lot of you that have not read this might be interested in what is being circulated throughout the State, and what many people in the State of Colorado have had the opportunity to read, and perhaps in some cases, or in many cases they might have some reason to believe.

Mr. Bundy: I wonder about this reading. I have no particular objection to this excepting that the introduction of the opinions of columnists can be carried on forever.

Mr. Hewett: That is true.

President Stearns: Wouldn't it be sufficient if we accepted it into the record?

Mr. Hewett: That is all right with me. I might say it was sent to me by one of the

*"Transcript of Final Hearing before Board of Regents," 11 May 1951.

293

illustrious sons of the university here, and with his comments regarding the article.

Mrs. Boyd: Mr. Chairman, should not this material, if it is introduced as new evidence, be made available to Mr. Hawkins?

Mr. Hawkins:. Mr. Chairman, I would just like to say that I have read the statement, and I have considered it to be a libelous statement.

Mr. Hewett: I am not introducing it on my own. That is merely what is being circulated, what the people of the State of Colorado have had the opportunity to read, and in many cases perhaps believe. It is pretty much substantiated by these reviews and reports of the Un-American Activities Committee of the United State House of Representatives. I think it was pretty well proven here. That is, this conference referred to in the review of the Scientific and Cultural Conference for World Peace, sponsored by the National Council of Arts, Sciences, and Professions held in New York City, March 25, 26, and 27, 1949. It does list approximately five hundred names here of individuals who either belong to the Communist Party, are members of various communist front organizations who have supported individual communists in their campaigns for elections, or have represented them as counsel. These names, perhaps a good many of them, might be familiar to a lot of you. They are here, almost five hundred of them, which shows the association of this group that sponsored this particular conference, and this is the report of "The Communist Peace Offensive, A Campaign to Disarm and Defeat the United States," prepared and released by the Committee on Un-American Activities, U.S. House of Representatives, Washington, D.C., dated April 1, 1951, and on page 105 Professor David Hawkins is listed as a sponsor of that conference.

In the testimony as given before this Committee on Un-American Activities in Washington, pages 3442, 3443, 3444, is the substantiation of the testimony of the fact that a sponsor of this communist peace offensive, associated with the approximately five hundred individuals who were either communists, or belonged to the communist front organizations, or represented as counsel communists, or in some other way connected with those. [sic]

Those are the only facts I have to put before the Regents, and for the public. They are not my conclusions; they are just simple facts that are available to everyone.

Mr. Bundy: Is that the official name of the organization, "The Communist Peace Offensive?"

Mr. Hewett: That is right. "Report on the Communist Peace Offensive." That is the title given this review by the Un-American Activities Committee.

Mr. Bundy: That is the title of the book, but is that the title of the organization?

Mr. Bromley: The title of the organization was Scientific and Cultural Conference for World Peace arranged by the National Council of the Arts, Sciences, and Professions.

Mr. Bundy: National Council of the Arts, Sciences, and Professions. I see.

Mr. Hewett: I submit those for what they are worth.

Mr. Charlton: Who got this out?

Mr. Hewett: That is the Un-American Activities Committee.

President Stearns: Are there any further questions by the Board?

Mr. Bundy: Does the Committee on Un-American Activities say that the sponsors of this organization are communists?

Mr. Hewett: No, it doesn't. They are all listed there in the categories in which they are known to be, either communists or merely members of the communist front organizations.

Mr. Bromley: How was Doctor Hawkins listed, do you recall?

Mr. Hewett: Merely listed as a sponsor of this world peace movement. The two conferences according to the date line, took place at the same time in New York City at the Waldorf-Astoria Hotel.

President Stearns: No objection?

Mr. Hawkins: Except the one already stated to the Fulton Lewis article.

Presiden Stearns: Mr. Hawkins has no objection to the introduction of these in evidence with the exception of the statement which he has already made, that is, including the statement he has already made. Is there any interrogation of Mr. Hewett? . . .

Appendix F
Example of Formal Charges*

Before the Faculty Committee on Tenure and Academic Freedom
EDWARD H. LAUER, Complainant
vs.   } Complaint
JOSEPH BUTTERWORTH, Respondent

Comes now the complainant and complaining of the respondent alleges:

PREMISE NO. 1

The complainant is Dean of the College of Arts and Sciences at the University of Washington.

PREMISE NO. 2

The respondent is a member of the faculty of said University of Washington and teaches in the Department of English, of which said complainant is the Dean.

PREMISE NO. 3

The Communist Party of the United States is not a political party in the sense that it freely and openly advocates that the form of government and social order advocated by Karl Marx should be substituted for the form of government and social order existing in the United States of America, and that such substitution should be openly accomplished by peaceful constitutional means.

During all of the times mentioned herein said Communist Party has insisted on the interpretation of Marxism as laid down by Lenin, and in more recent years by Stalin. It has, moreover, required that its members conceal their identity, take on assumed names, deny membership and use any means, even though considered false and fraudulent under the American conception of that term, to attain its ends, and has required undeviating compliance with the mandates of Stalin and the Soviet government in connection with the attitude to be taken and the deceptions to be made by Party members respecting public issues as they have arisen in this country from time to time.

*Edward H. Lauer, complaint before the Faculty Committee on Tenure and Academic Freedom.

297

It has, moreover, required the performance of various tasks and programs assigned to the Party members, and such members have risen in Party esteem and their importance has increased in Party councils in proportion to the time given by them to the carrying out of Party policies as directed by higher Party officials, either through the Party itself or through organizations created or sponsored by them, which are large in number and are popularly known as communist fronts.

PREMISE NO. 4

During its 1947 session, the legislature of the State of Washington took cognizance of the dangers inherent in members of the various state institutions belonging to said Communist Party, and by legislative enactment appointed a committee, legally designated as the Legislative Committee on Un-American Activities (popularly known and hereinafter designated as the Canwell Committee), which committee was charged with the duty of investigating communist infiltration into the various state institutions and/ or other agencies operating in the State of Washington. In this connection said committee was also given the power to subpoena witnesses and take their testimony under oath. The legality of said committee was thereafter approved by the Supreme Court of the State of Washington, in the case of State ex rel. Robinson vs. Fluent, reported in 130 Wash., Dec., page 179.

PREMISE NO. 5

In the Administrative Code of the University of Washington, the chapter on Tenure and Terms of Appointment of Faculty Members has the following provision:

Section IV. Removal for Cause

Persons having tenure under the provisions of this act may be removed from the faculty of the university for one or more of the following reasons:

(a) Incompetency
(b) Neglect of duty
(c) Physical or mental incapacity
(d) Dishonesty or immorality
(e) Conviction of a felony involving moral turpitude

Proceedings for the removal of such persons shall be conducted in accordance with the rules of procedure hereinafter described (see Chapter IV, Part II).

PREMISE NO. 6

Respondent is a member of the faculty of the University of Washington, entitled to "tenure . . . during good behavior and efficient and competent service," according to the provisions of Chapter IV, Section I, of said administrative code.

CHARGE NO. I

Respondent is and for many years past has been a member of the Communist Party.

CHARGE NO. II

At a general faculty meeting on May 12, 1948, the president of the university, Dr. Raymond B. Allen, explained to faculty members that the Canwell Committee would, no doubt, undertake a full-scale investigation of communist activities on the university campus. He then and there emphasized in this connection that no member of the faculty could expect the administration to defend any faculty member who had been carrying on in secrecy activities the nature of which was unknown. The clear meaning of his statement was that any member of the faculty so engaged and desiring the protection of the university was in duty bound not to withhold pertinent facts concerning affiliations which might embarrass the university.

Notwithstanding the membership of respondent in the Communist Party, either then or theretofore, no effort was made by him to explain his connection with said Party to Dr. Allen, or to any other responsible superior faculty member, nor did he in any wise endeavor to assist them in preparing for any hearings that might be held or charges that might be made against the university because of membership in and association with the Communist Party at any time, but to the contrary remained silent, and thereby knowingly concealed facts which it was his duty to disclose, and he particularly concealed the fact that he was or had been a member of the Communist Party.

CHARGE NO. III

Thereafter and before the Canwell hearings herein referred to, the Honorable Albert F. Canwell, Chairman of the Canwell Committee, gave to President Allen the names of six (6) members of the faculty whom, he said, he was prepared to prove were either past or present members of the Communist Party. The respondent, above named, was one of the six (6) and the president of the university scheduled an individual conference with him. At that conference respondent equivocated and/or failed and refused to disclose to the president whether he then was or ever had been a member of the Communist Party.

CHARGE NO. IV

As a member of the Communist Party respondent consistently followed the so-called "party line," that is to say, the instructions emanating from Moscow, and by such membership placed himself in a position where he could not be an honest man nor a free agent in teaching the truth wherever it led. During a portion of that period the communist line required that a member of the Party should decry the European war between Hitler and the democratic nations of western Europe as an imperialistic war, and

Party members assigned to such duty picketed the White House and in their propaganda described President Roosevelt as a "war monger." After the German attack upon Russia said party line, without explanation, was immediately changed and the war against Russia [*sic*] became a war to save democracy, with the Communist Party, through its leaders in this country, advocating immediate help to the Western powers through the medium of war, if necessary.

Thereafter, when the U.S. became involved in the war the Communist Party, through its members and devotees, insisted upon the so-called Western front or invasion of Europe as early as the spring of 1942, and continuously thereafter clamored for such invasion, notwithstanding the fact that the Western powers, and especially the United States, were unprepared to undertake such an invasion until the summer of 1944, and notwithstanding the fact that the United States delayed any such invasion until advised by its military leaders that the invasion had a reasonable chance of success.

Throughout these various inconsistent policies of the Communist Party, respondent adhered to the so-called party line, thereby demonstrating his dishonesty and incompetency to remain on the faculty of the University of Washington.

CHARGE NO. V

In compliance with the requirements of the Communist Party and in neglect of duty to the University of Washington, respondent has at all times during his membership spent a large part of his time attending Party meetings and meetings of various organizations sponsored by said Party and known as communist fronts, and in assisting in the preparation of various kinds of propaganda to further the communist cause and to assist in the establishment of Marxism, in the United States as that philosophy has been explained and determined by Lenin and Stalin, and in said Party exploited the fact that he was a member of the faculty of the University of Washington.

CHARGE NO. VI

At the conference with the president, referred to in Charge No. III above, respondent was advised that he doubtless would be called as a witness at the Canwell hearings, and that for the good of the university he should make a full disclosure of any present or former connection with the Communist Party.

Thereafter, respondent, by legal subpoena, was called as a witnesss to testify at a hearing of the Canwell Committee on the 22nd day of July, 1948, and then and there took and subscribed to the following oath, legally given to him:

> I hereby swear that I will tell the truth, the *whole* truth, and nothing but the truth, so help me God.

Notwithstanding the taking of such oath, respondent refused to testify to pertinent matters, and especially refused to say whether he then was or ever had been a member of the Communist Party. Such refusal on respondent's part was a dishonest and an immoral act and was in defiance of the president's admonition, and again demonstrating his unfitness for membership on the university faculty.

CONCLUSION AND PRAYER

For the reasons above given respondent has brought contumely and disrespect upon the University of Washington; his behavior has been bad; he has neglected his duty; he has been dishonest and incompetent; he cannot render efficient and competent service, and he has demonstrated his professional unfitness to remain as a member of the university faculty.

WHEREFORE, complainant prays that this committee recommend to the president of the university that said respondent be discharged of his duties and removed as a member of said faculty.

Edward H. Lauer
Dean of the College of Arts and Sciences

Appendix G
The Consequences of Taking
the Fifth Amendment

Part I

Report of the Findings of the Trustee-Faculty Committee
in re Dr. Alex Novikoff
June 12, 1953

To the President and Board of Trustees of the University
of Vermont and State Agricultural College
Burlington, Vermont

Gentlemen:

Your committee composed of the following faculty members, Professors
T. M. Adams, A. G. Mackay, and P. A. Moody, and the following trustees,
C. H. Brown, R. F. Joyce, and F. W. Shepardson, herewith submit to you
their findings and recommendations concerning the Dr. Alex Novikoff
matter.

The committee in its entirety met on five different occasions. At two of
these meetings Dr. Novikoff and the following persons gave statements, and
submitted to extensive questioning: Dr. B. Pearson, Professor of Pathology
and Chairman of the Department, Dr. F. W. Dunihue, Professor of Histo-
logy and Embryology, Dr. W. Van B. Robertson, Professor of Biochemistry
and Associate Professor of Experimental Medicine, and Dr. A. B. Soule,
Professor of Radiology, all of the University of Vermont Medical College
faculty; Stanley Burns Jr. and George Higgins, second year students in the
University of Vermont Medical College; Rabbi Max P. Wall of Burlington;
and Father T. D. Sullivan, Chairman of the Department of Biology at St.
Michael's College. From the persons above listed, the following facts were
shown:

Dr. Novikoff was born in Russia, arriving in the United States at the age
of six months, and is now a citizen of the United States by virtue of the
naturalization of his father. He is a graduate of Franklin K. Lane High
School in Brooklyn, and received the degrees of B.S., M.A., and Ph.D.
from Columbia University. His teaching and research experience have been
at Brooklyn College, at the Jefferson School of Social Science at New York

303

City, at the University of Wisconsin, and at the University of Vermont since 1948, where he is now Professor of Experimental Pathology and Associate Professor of Biochemistry in the College of Medicine, and a career research specialist.

The background of Dr. Novikoff shows him to have been brought up in Brooklyn in a family of below moderate means; that he was assisted by the family in going through Columbia, but likewise worked and contributed to his own education; that he went to Brooklyn College as a teacher, directly after his undergraduate work.

All the information that we have been able to obtain shows:

1. That since being connected with the University of Vermont, he has not been a member of the Communist Party, nor has he directly, indirectly, or by implication taught communist philosophy to any students therein; and further that there is no evidence of connection with the Communist Party subsequent to the year 1945.
2. That he is a sincere and tireless worker in the field of science, allowing himself to become completely absorbed in his work, and spending long hours within the laboratory.
3. That he has won the respect of his associates as a person as well as a scientist.
4. That he has not advocated, and does not now advocate, subversive activities and the overthrowing of the government of the United States, but to the contrary thereof, specifically states that he has never been connected with any such activity and would not be, under any consideration.
5. That his candid attitude, his willingness to testify in all honesty, and to cooperate with the committee, were of the highest level.
6. That if he were ever a member of the Communist Party, and we believe he might have been while at Brooklyn College, there is nothing about his statements or actions which would indicate that he has intended or expected to return to such line of thinking, but to the contrary thereof, he now completely renounces communism and its philosophy.
7. That he has taken the Freeman's Oath of the State of Vermont, and the loyalty oath of the University of Vermont; that he has registered for the draft and has expressed a willingness to serve in the armed forces of the United States; that he did serve the armed forces in an advisory capacity; and that he never did a treasonable act against the United States.
8. That he was called before the Jenner Committee on at least two occasions: first when he was given the privilege of testifying privately and naming names covering possible communists whom he knew, and secondly, when he was brought before the committee in public hearing, under oath, and invoked the Fifth Amendment, which was his right under Article 5 of the Amendments to the United States Constitution, which is as follows:

No person shall be held to answer for a capital, or otherwise infamous crime, unless on a presentment or indictment of a grand jury, except in cases arising in the land or naval forces, or in the militia, when in actual service in time of war or public danger; nor shall any person be subject for the same offense to be twice put in jeopardy of life or limb; *nor shall be compelled in any criminal case to be a witness against himself*, nor be deprived of life, liberty, or property, without due process of law; nor shall private property be taken for public use, without just compensation.

9. That he recognizes the authority of any congressional committee to call him before it for questioning, and he agrees with the announced intention of eliminating the influence of the power of those seeking to overthrow the government of the United States as just and proper; but even with that thought in mind, he still invoked the Fifth Amendment for what appear to be the following reasons:

    (a) Self-incrimination: an unalterable fear of dire results against himself through an unconscious and unintended error of fact by some statement of his while under oath, together with the same fear of error by a third person, made either by design or as above indicated.

    (b) Moral reasons: first, arising from a sense of scientific honesty, and second, childhood discipline against informing as being a wrong within itself.

    (c) A feeling that the method used by the committee might be commonly referred to as a "witch hunt" or "smear campaign."

Using the facts as above stated, this committee feels that Dr. Novikoff is not now a communist; that he has done no communistic teaching at the University of Vermont; that he is a sincere man of science and a person of veracity; that among other reasons, his failure to answer to the congressional committee was his method of protection against what seemed to him inquisitorial methods of investigation and infringement upon his personal liberty and intellectual freedom; and that while he might have been in error because of confusion about the rights which the Amendment confers upon a person, and while legally, as well as technically, his position may not be wholly defensible, nevertheless he was convinced in his own mind of his moral rights in the matter.

This committee would not hesitate to recommend retaining Dr. Novikoff on the faculty of the Medical College of the University of Vermont, if he had not invoked the Fifth Amendment, because we feel that he is, as of now a good citizen of the United States, together with being an excellent teacher and scientist, and of great value to the Medical College. We also feel that he might have had a good reason for invoking the Fifth Amendment, so that the Trustees may in absolute honesty feel, that even though he did invoke the Fifth Amendment, he should be retained.

This committee feels that the use of the Fifth Amendment is a regrettable practice and a most undesirable one which cannot reflect credit on a faculty member or on the university. The committee therefore recommends that should further cases of the type arise, the faculty member so concerned be informed of the Trustees' deep feeling in the matter and that the faculty member be instructed by the attorney of the university of the limited reasons for use of this Amendment.

Signed:

R. F. Joyce, Chairman

C. H. Brown

P. A. Moody

T. M. Adams

F. W. Shepardson

A. G. Mackay, M.D.

Since each case is judged on its individual merits, we the undersigned members of this committee recommend, in view of all the circumstances in the case of Professor Alex Novikoff, that he be retained on the faculty, unless further evidence with regard either to his past or future activities should at any time give reason to alter this decision.

Signed:

R. F. Joyce, Chairman

P. A. Moody

T. M. Adams

F. W. Shepardson

A. G. Mackay, M.D.

To the President and Board of Trustees of the University
of Vermont and State Agricultural College
Gentlemen:

I regret very much that I cannot agree with the final recommendation of the fellow members of this committee whose opinion I respect and admire a great deal. You will note that I signed with the other members of the committee down to the last recommendation which of itself should indicate to you that I am in accord with them to that point.

Because of my unwillingness to agree with them in the final recommendation, I feel it is my duty to explain to the Trustees my reasons therefor.

I have not been able to escape the conclusion that anyone who invokes the protection of the Fifth Amendment must accept that fact that by so doing, he, of his own choosing, calls into question the quality of his citizenship. I believe it is not the privilege of a citizen when invoking his rights under the Fifth Amendment to be doing so for the purpose of protesting and taking issue with the legality of the questions, or for the purpose of contesting the propriety of a particular procedure, because it is my belief that it is the basic duty of every citizen to answer to the truth to all proper questions before an authorized tribunal, regardless of the consequences even to others of his answers. And I further believe that a man who exercises this privilege either genuinely believes his words may incriminate him or he is using the privilege improperly. I feel had he not invoked the Fifth Amendment, and even though he had been a communist, that he should be retained. I have no doubt but what he has no interest in or leanings toward the Communist Party as of this time.

Respectfully yours,
(Signed) C. H. Brown

Part II

Summary before the Board of Review by the Attorney for the University of Vermont

Mr. Lisman: Mr. Chairman, it has been charged in the first instance, and I'm going to address myself directly to the charges. We have had a lot of eloquence this afternoon. We've had a great deal of "beating about the bush." If I am guilty of eloquence from now on it is wholly unintentional. If I do any "beating about the bush" that, too, is unintentional.

I am going to address myself to the first charge, that Dr. Novikoff is guilty of conduct which justifies his discharge in that when summoned to testify before a sub-committee of the United States Senate Judiciary Committee investigating the subversive influence in the educational process,—I would like to underline that—investigating the subversive influence in the educational process—I am going to skip a little bit—when questioned concerning his connections with the Communist Party, if any, prior to 1948, he claimed privilege under the Fifth Amendment.

This morning and this afternoon we have heard testimony, though it hasn't come from Dr. Novikoff, he declined to testify as to anything that happened prior to 1948 or even as to anything that happened after that, if it would open up something that happened before 1948, we heard from others, witnesses whom he produced, that he was a communist at one time. And it didn't stop there. There was positive evidence that he was the leader of a communist-dominated union.

This board, certainly the Board of Trustees, feels that the mere fact that a man claims privilege under the Fifth Amendment should not in and of itself warrant his discharge from the university. But Dr. Novikoff is charged with something more than claiming privilege in and of itself. Dr. Novikoff, under the evidence that stands before this board, was a leader of one of the communist fronts, a communist-dominated teachers' union. Does not such a man have a greater obligation to his country than any other? Does not such a man, in view of what we all know of the communist conspiracy in this country, does not such a man have a duty to disclose the information which he gained as a leader? Such a man if discharged from the university faculty is not being discharged for the claim of privilege in and of itself. He is being discharged because, having knowledge, particular knowledge, knowledge not available to the ordinary communist even, of activities inimical to the security of this country nevertheless refuses in an investigation of the subversive influence in the educational process to give to a congressional committee the benefit of his knowledge.

In my opinion such conduct constitutes moral turpitude. In my opinion you are not only justified in discharging Dr. Novikoff under the first charge, but further you are justified in discharging him on the ground of moral turpitude under the first charge.

As to the second charge that he improperly invoked the Fifth Amendment for the protection of others and not for his own protection, you heard Dr. Novikoff testify. He testified that he invoked the Fifth Amendment for three reasons, one of which his feeling that the Jenner Committee was an unconstitutional committee, or, at least, that its procedures were unconstitutional, he regarded as a minor objection to the committee. The other two grounds were that he would have incriminated himself had he testified and that he did not want to subject others, others, to the investigative process. He said that the last two were intertwined, in effect, that he couldn't distinguish one from the other, that he couldn't tell which was the dominant feeling.

Now, when he was examined with reference to this claim he became evasive. He was asked numbers of questions, all of which boiled down to the one with which Mr. Mower started, as to what he would incriminate himself if he stood on his privilege, and he took refuge behind what had happened prior to 1948. Now, there were other events concerning which he did not take such refuge. You will remember Mr. Mower went quite a ways afield, and you will remember that there were certain things that could have referred to events prior to 1948 as to which he did not take refuge, but as to this matter he did.

I submit that that shows that Dr. Novikoff did not claim his privilege in good faith; that he was not fearful of incriminating himself; or else that he was not fearful of involving others; and whatever his reason for having claimed the benefit of the Fifth Amendment he has not yet given it to us. On the contrary his evasiveness, his loss of memory tend to show that he had a reason which was not a good reason, whatever it may have been.

And now I come to the last charge which, in my opinion, is the one that Dr. Novikoff has himself most clearly proved. Now, I realize that I am in the position of advocate here. I realize that I am representing a board which has preferred charges and that it is my duty to press those charges and to show you, if possible, that they have been proven. I want to assure you, however, that the statements that I am making I am making in all sincerity. I want to say that when I consider Dr. Novikoff has proved himself guilty of these charges, that I am not doing so merely in the office of a devil's advocate. I am doing it because I believe that that is the net result of the hearing today.

Had Dr. Novikoff taken the stand and testified freely and fully before the Jenner Committee we wouldn't be here. But we haven't required that he do that entirely. Up until today we said that the mere fact that he didn't claim his privilege wouldn't matter. I've asked you to consider, however, what has happened today; I asked you to consider that we know now something that we never knew before, that he was a leader in this movement; that he was a leader of the communist conspiracy; he was a leader of a communist-dominated union. Now, I ask you to consider something further—I ask you to consider his attitude today. Regardless of all else he certainly owes [to] the Board of Trustees and to its agencies a duty of frankness, forthrightness and candor. I think the Bishop, who testified, used the terms "candor" and "forthrightness," and I wish we could have found those same qualities in Dr. Novikoff that he referred to.

Certainly regardless of whether or not he owes that duty to anyone else, the Jenner Committee or anyone else, he owes it to the Board of Trustees. He owes it to this committee because how else can you pass upon his competence. And yet, he refused to be considered a witness. He was only willing to testify if his evidence was not on the record. When he finally agreed to be a witness it was only on such a condition that it was impossible to examine him on anything that referred to a date earlier than 1948.

I consider, and I believe you will, that his refusal to cooperate with the Board of Trustees and with this Board of Review is evidence in support of the third charge. It is evidence that shows that Dr. Novikoff right along has refused to disclose fully his connections with the Communist Party prior to 1948. That's what the third charge is. I feel, ladies and gentlemen, that when you have given this matter due consideration you will decide that Dr. Novikoff is guilty of conduct which justifies his discharge. And I am inclined to think you will go further and find that that conduct constitutes moral turpitude.

Part III

Resolution Adopted by Trustees
University of Vermont
Re: Dismissal of Dr. Alex B. Novikoff from Faculty of
University of Vermont, September 5, 1953

Whereas, when Dr. Alex B. Novikoff claimed privilege under the Fifth Amendment on April 23, 1953, before a sub-committee of the United States Senate Judiciary Committee, his fitness to remain on the faculty of the University of Vermont and State Agricultural College became the subject of inquiry under Paragraph 2 of the policy of the university regarding individuals called before congressional investigating committees, which reads in full as follows:

"1. No known communist will be permitted on the staff of the university.
"2. Any faculty member claiming privilege under the Fifth Amendment will be immediately relieved of his teaching duties. A faculty-trustee committee will be set up at once to investigate the circumstances of the case, and upon its recommendation appropriate action will be taken.
"3. A faculty member who admits previous membership in the Communist Party, but who now claims he is no longer a member shall be investigated by a faculty-trustee committee who will make recommendations on his fitness to continue on the staff of the university.

"4. A person who is charged with being a communist and denies under oath any such connection will be investigated by a faculty-trustee committee should evidence be presented to indicate the possibility of perjury."

And whereas a faculty-trustee committee, appointed April 28, 1953, under the provisions of the above policy, conducted an initial investigation into the circumstances of the case and provided full opportunity to Dr. Novikoff to express himself in private both on and off the record;

And whereas the Board of Trustees on June 20, 1953, after considering the findings and recommendations of the faculty-trustee committee and all other information at hand, voted:

"That Dr. Novikoff be indefinitely suspended without pay, from any further duties at this institution as of July 15, 1953, unless on or before that date he advises the president in writing of his willingness to go down and appear before the Jenner Committee and answer fully and freely any questions that committee may see fit to put to him, and that on or before that date he offers to the Jenner Committee to do so."

And whereas the Board of Trustees on August 14, 1953, following the suspension that became effective July 15, 1953, informed Dr. Novikoff in writing that a Board of Review had been constituted under the provisions of Article X, Section 14, of the Organization of the University of Vermont and State Agricultural College, to consider the following charges against him;

"1. That Dr. Alex B. Novikoff is guilty of conduct which justifies his discharge, in that when summoned to testify before a sub-committee of the United States Senate Judiciary Committee, investigating the subversive influence in the educational process, he testified freely concerning his activities since coming to the university in 1948, but when questioned concerning his connections with the Communist Party, if any, prior to 1948, he claimed privilege under the Fifth Amendment.

"2. That Dr. Novikoff is guilty of conduct which justifies his discharge, in that when summoned to testify before a sub-committee of the United States Senate Judiciary Committee, investigating the subversive influence in the educational process, he improperly invoked the Fifth Amendment for the protection of others and not for his own protection.

"3. That Dr. Novikoff was guilty of conduct which justifies his discharge, in that he has refused to disclose fully his connection with the Communist Party prior to 1948, if any."

And whereas a hearing was held by the Board of Review on August 29,

1953, under the provisions of Article X, Section 14 of the Organization of the University of Vermont and State Agricultural College, which reads in full as follows:

"14. The final decision concerning a termination for cause of a continuous appointment, or the dismissal for cause of a teacher previous to the expiration of a term of appointment, is vested in the Board of Trustees.

"However, in the consideration of such termination or dismissal, the counsel of members of the teaching staff is vital; and therefore, a board of review, consisting of the trustees, the policy committee of the senate, and four teachers of the college directly concerned shall be constituted to consider all such matters.

"In all cases where the facts are in dispute, the accused teacher shall be informed in writing before the hearing of the charges against him and shall have the opportunity to be heard in his own defense by all bodies concerned in his case. He shall be permitted to have an advisor of his own choosing who may act as counsel.

"There shall be a full stenographic record of the hearing available to the parties concerned. In the hearing of charges of incompetence, the testimony shall include that of teachers and other scholars either from the University of Vermont and State Agricultural College, or from other institutions, or both.

"Teachers on continuous tenure who are dismissed for reasons not involving moral turpitude or financial exigency, and who are relieved of their duties at this institution shall receive from the University of Vermont and State Agricultural College, for not less than one year from the date of notification of dismissal, that portion of their salaries which is normally paid for their teaching duties at the University of Vermont and State Agricultural College."

And whereas the Board of Review at the conclusion of its deliberations following the hearing on August 2, 1953 [*sic*], recommended to the Board of Trustees that Dr. Alex B. Novikoff is guilty of conduct which justifies his dismissal from the faculty;

THEREFORE, the Board of Trustees has dismissed Dr. Alex B. Novikoff from the faculty of the University of Vermont and State Agricultural College as of September 5, 1953, with the provision that he be immediately notified of his dismissal and that he receive terminal salary of $7,500 through September 5, 1954, under the final provision contained in Article X, Section 14 of the Organization of the University of Vermont and State Agricultural College under which these dismissal proceedings have been conducted:

And the Board of Trustees states in connection with this action:

1. that the dismissal of Dr. Novikoff is based on the circumstances of his own particular case and does not, therefore, indicate any change in policy of the Board of Trustees that the invoking of privilege under the Fifth Amendment is not, in and of itself, cause for dismissal;
2. that the subject matter of charge No. 2, involving possible improper invocation of the Fifth Amendment was not a factor considered by the Board of Trustees in its final action; and
3. that the dismissal of Dr. Novikoff represents the considered opinion of the Board of Trustees that he has failed to display to a sufficient degree in his actions and statements during the past five months, both before the committee of Congress and before the university bodies, the qualities of responsibility, integrity, and frankness that are fundamental requirements of a faculty member. The actions referred to include, but are not limited to, his invoking of the Fifth Amendment.

Appendix H
An Example of Administrative Dominance
of a Committee*

President Bevis: Professor Darling and gentlemen, the principal object of our coming together here this morning is to hear what you have to say about your appearance before the House Un-American Activities Committee which was, I believe, on March the thirteenth. I don't think I need rehearse the facts. They are known to you and I think known to all of us. You did appear before the committee in Washington. Following your testimony there, I issued an order of suspension until the record of your appearance might be studied.

On the twenty-fourth of March I sent you a letter in which I set forth the questions that were raised in my mind growing out of the study of the record of your appearance and now pursuant to the University rule, we want to have this administrative hearing; we want to give you an opportunity to set forth whatever you want to say in explanation or defense of anything you want to say. I have asked the three vice presidents, Mr. Taylor, Mr. Heimberger, and Mr. Stradley, and the assistant to the president, Mr. Luxon, to sit with me, and I have also asked three members of the Faculty to sit in on this hearing, Professors Hoagland, Alpheus Smith, and Lawrence Kauffman. The focal point of the conference, I may as well say, is consideration of your fitness to continue to hold the rank of associate professor in The Ohio State University.

Dr. Darling: I would like to explain a note on necessity for postponing the hearing. The first thing is that the time is too short in which to retain counsel and prepare proper presentation. For days after I returned from Washington, I had continual harassment from the press, photographers, and a few cranks, and I have had a tremendous number of calls from the faculty members concerned, and from colleagues and students. There were a number of meetings of faculty groups which I felt I was obliged to attend, such as the Conference Committee of the Teaching Staff and the American Association of University Professors. All these things have taken up considerable time. During all this time I tried to obtain an attorney to represent me both locally and throughout the state, and I regret that in spite of repeated attempts to obtain counsel, up to this minute I have been unable to get anyone who would be able to represent me on such a short notice of only eight days for the following reasons.

*"Hearing of the Case of Byron Thorwell Darling," 2 April 1953, pp. 7–16.

313

First, most of them were already tied up so that they could not possibly take me
even if they wished.
Second, others were able to determine after a number of calls that they would not be
able to represent me. With several I spent many hours discussing my case,
only to be told the last day that they might not be able to present my case as I
would want them to. I now have several lawyers interested but they insist that
they would need about a week, since this is Easter Sunday weekend, in which
to prepare and get acquainted with the facts of the case. One lawyer, Mr.
James Paradise of Cincinnati, who appeared to be interested in my case, said
that he could take it on Thursday or Friday of next week. I feel that in view of
these difficulties that I am encountering in obtaining proper representation
that it is only fair that I be given at least a week to ten days in which to retain
counsel and prepare for a useful and fair trial, hearing, that is; and furthermore, an extension of time does not involve any departmental difficulties
inasmuch as I have been relieved of my teaching duties.
President Bevis: I received from you a letter yesterday, Mr. Darling, about noon, in
which you said this is a request for postponement of the hearing and in which
you said further that "I had not previously intended to ask anyone to represent me, but I now feel it desirable to follow the recommendation of certain
faculty groups." I had a telegram last evening about 9 o'clock, I think, from
Mr. Paradise in Cincinnati, who, I understand, is an attorney although I don't
know him, saying that you had discussed this matter with him. I'll read his
telegram:

> Byron Darling discussed the case tonight via long distance and asked
> whether I would accept retainer. Am greatly interested in case but would
> like opportunity full personal discussion before deciding whether to repre-
> sent him. Understand he has had great difficulty obtaining representation
> on comparatively short notice. Prior commitments make it impossible
> my coming to Columbus before end of next week. Deeply appreciate
> favorable consideration of postponement about ten days. Issues involved
> vital to Darling and of great public importance. No prejudice can result in
> postponement since Darling is relieved of duty.
>
> Signed James C. Paradise

To that I sent this reply which may come to your attention:

> Dr. Darling has known since March thirteen that he would have to present
> defense. Was advised on March twenty-fourth of date of hearing and
> urged by me to have representatives. Now states he has decided only last
> evening to seek counsel. Hearing is administrative, not judicial. Cannot
> agree to postponement.

Dr. Darling: The letter that was written there was written in some haste after the
meeting of the AAUP. In fact, I had help from Professor (Robert E.) Math-
ews, and I wish to state that it is a fact that I have tried to obtain counsel
during the time, but when I didn't seem to see that anyone was interested
much, I began to get discouraged and feel like what I would do was just
prepare it myself. But after the AAUP meeting, in which they prepared a

resolution strongly urging me to get counsel, I decided to try to get a postponement and continue my efforts. Now, I think it's only fair that one have legal representation in a situation if we are to have a fair hearing. The rules of procedure for this type of hearing are not generally known or set, and I think that the importance of the case, not only to myself but from the standpoint of academic tenure rules, and so forth, is so important that one must, in order to have a fair hearing, have counsel.

President Bevis: Am I correct, Mr. Darling, in my information that you did prepare and present to the meeting of the AAUP day before yesterday a written statement of some 20 minutes in length in which you set forth your situation.

Dr. Darling: Yes.

President Bevis: It is difficult to understand why, Mr. Darling, you come in at this last moment, yesterday noon, first; last night at nine o'clock again, asking for postponement for the reasons you assigned. You have known certainly since the thirteenth of March that you would need to make an explanation because that was the date on which the suspension was given you. Prior to that time I think you had been urged to provide yourself with counsel. In your conference with Dr. Heimberger before you went to Washington Dr. Heimberger urged you to get counsel.

Dr. Darling: That was with respect to the hearing in Washington. I didn't know what the rules, tenure rules and rules of procedure, were here. It wasn't until I got back and met with Professor (Paul A.) Varg of the Conference Committee of the Teaching Staff that I learned that there were rules like this.

President Bevis: In my letter to you on March twenty-fourth I urged you to get representatives; to come provided with them. Our difficulty is understanding why at this date you need to postpone this hearing for the reasons assigned. You evidently have your own thinking in mind. You wrote it out, presented it to the AAUP. This is an informal proceeding. It won't be conducted according to the rules of court procedure. You can say anything you want. Anybody here can say anything he wants. After all, the thing we want to find out is what is your explanation, of your refusal to answer a long series of questions in your hearing in Washington before the House Un-American Activities Committee. That isn't a technical matter. You can make any explanation you want.

Dr. Darling: Well, you see I don't know what the procedure here will be.

President Bevis: Let me tell you what the procedure will be. May I tell you what the procedure will be? I am simply going to ask you to explain your answers and your refusals to answer which are set forth in the record of your hearing in Washington. That is the procedure. I am not going to ask the questions all over again. I stated to you in my communication that your appearance in Washington raised certain serious questions in my mind about your fitness to continue to be a professor, in The Ohio State University. Those questions are in my mind. Now, the only procedure here is that we would like to know what you have to say by way of explanation—anything you want to say. The procedure is just as simple as that.

Dr. Darling: But there are questions of a legal nature involved in the explanation which—I am not a lawyer. I am just a physicist. If you want me to talk physics right now, I can do it. I am capable of it and I know I can do that. But, with regard to the testimony, these legal questions, I just am not a lawyer, and I explained to you that I have been trying continuously to get representation and piled on top of that all this other business. I would like to make it a fair hearing, but I feel that in order to do that I can only do it with legal representation.

President Bevis: I have difficulty, Mr. Darling, squaring your statement with your letter of April first, which was yesterday, which, after referring to proceedings of the preceding day, says that "I had not previously intended to ask anyone to represent me, but I now feel it desirable to follow the recommendation of these faculty groups." The point in my mind is that there seems to me to have been a good deal of time allowed purposely, as I wrote you in my letter yesterday answering your letter. I deliberately and purposely set the hearing a considerable time in advance in order that you might have full opportunity to obtain counsel or any other representative that you wanted to have come speak for you. It really isn't a complicated question.

Dr. Darling: I have explained about that letter. Well, it was rather hastily drawn in order to get something over here early and that all the facts that should have been put in it didn't get into it. I explained how the difficulties I've had in trying to get representation led me to a discouragement and so I thought, well, what am I going to do? Then I thought, well, there wasn't much use of having a hearing, so I had come to the opinion that I wouldn't need representation. Then, the meeting of the AAUP was held and they strongly urged me to get representation, and so I just have been continually trying. I think I understand that you are a lawyer.

President Bevis: I used to be.

Dr. Darling: All right, you used to be. I think you will agree that there are legal questions involved here; that I am not a lawyer, and that even a lawyer in a similar situation would understand that it was wise to have legal representation.

President Bevis: I appreciate your including lawyers among those who might understand. It is my feeling, Mr. Darling, that fair and ample opportunity has been accorded you to find counsel. You have no assurance yet that if a continuance were granted that you would have counsel. Mr. Paradise wired me to the effect that he didn't know whether he wanted to take the case. He wanted to make up his mind about it after he talked to you.

Dr. Darling: President Bevis, what is the rush? I have explained that I have tried and have been trying and I have had all these other things. Now in the coming—if you would give me an extension I will continue to try; and I can't, of course, just guarantee, but what I would plan to do is try not to—see, so many other things have interrupted me and that I would just try to concentrate on that, and what I would like to do is make this a fair hearing and do the best I can toward the university.

President Bevis: Mr. Darling, the questions here aren't essentially legal questions but questions of truth. What are the facts? You know what they are. You are not under oath here.

Dr. Darling: Well, I didn't even know that, but what I am—you see, not only the truth but it is a matter of why I used essentially my rights and privileges at various places in the testimony; and this requires legal knowledge, and it is for that reason that I believe that it would be better for all of us if I could have representation.

President Bevis: If you wouldn't mind leaving the room for a minute, I'll consult with those present.

(President Bevis discussed Dr. Darling's request with the seven observers at some length. Upon decision to grant a 48-hour continuance, Dr. Darling was asked to return to the room.)

President Bevis: Professor Darling, in your earnest plea for another opportunity to secure counsel, we are willing to continue this case until Saturday morning at ten o'clock. Beg your pardon?

Dr. Darling: Which Saturday?

President Bevis: Saturday morning of this week at ten o'clock. I think it will give counsel an opportunity to familiarize himself with the issues which in my judgment are not intricate. Due to the fact that you have already had considerable length of time in which to seek counsel, it is my feeling that we would not be doing you an injustice if we proceeded now, but we want to be sure that you have an opportunity to be represented if you want to be. The hearing will be continued until Saturday morning at ten o'clock.

Dr. Darling: I don't know whether Mr. Paradise can make it Saturday morning.

President Bevis: If you desire to have the case continued until Saturday morning at ten o'clock, we will continue it.

Dr. Darling: Well, I would like to say that it is my intention to answer all the questions, and it is your estimation of the thing that the legal danger is not difficult. I have no way of knowing that; but this—really, I think, if Mr. Paradise, for example, is tied up and can't be here, assuming that your statement about the intricacies of the thing are not great, why it places me in a difficult position of trying to find somebody. I tried and I think perhaps Mr. Paradise would probably take it if he is not tied up.

President Bevis: Saturday morning isn't usually a very busy time; he could probably come up here on Saturday morning.

Dr. Darling: Well, would it be all right to call and see if he could make that at that time?

President Bevis: If you want. I am continuing the case to Saturday morning at ten o'clock. There won't be any further continuance.

Dr. Darling: You won't give me a week?

President Bevis: I think you have had ample time, Professor Darling, to have done what you are asking to do now. You put off until yesterday asking for continuance; apparently you put off until last night getting in touch with Mr. Paradise. Mr. Paradise wired me to the effect that you had just talked to him.

Dr. Darling: That's right, but Mr. Paradise is not the only lawyer I—

President Bevis: That's my point. I judge Mr. Paradise has not been your regular counsel.

Dr. Darling: No, I had—

President Bevis: Have you ever met him?

Dr. Darling: No.

President Bevis: You've never met him. Professor Darling, we can continue Saturday morning or we can go ahead now—whichever you prefer.

Dr. Darling: Well, would Mr. Paradise—he is very busy, and I think he would take an interest—would like to take an interest in the case because he is an attorney for the American Civil Liberties Union, and I think that he wouldn't represent me as an attorney for them, that is just as an attorney. That is why I feel that he may have a definite interest in it and would, if he is not too busy. He would probably be able to appear if there was a little more time granted.

President Bevis: In view of the length of time you have had to do this, Professor Darling, it seems to me that it would not be unfair to go ahead with the hearing this morning, but we want to afford you the opportunity to have counsel if you desire it. I don't think we ought to continue the case indefinitely, but I will continue it if you desire until Saturday morning at ten o'clock, or we can proceed now.

Dr. Darling: All right, I will accept the continuance.

President Bevis: The case will be continued until Saturday morning at ten o'clock.

(The hearing was adjourned at this point to meet at 10 a.m. Saturday, April 4).

Appendix I
Committee Action in the Case of Two
Junior Faculty

Report of the Faculty Committee on Reviews and Appeals
on the Case of Mr. L. R. LaVallee and Dr. Ralph Spitzer

The Faculty Committee on Reviews and Appeals convened February 17, 1949 to give consideration to the letters of appeal that had been filed with the Chairman on February 14, 1949 by L. R. LaVallee, Assistant Professor of Economics and Dr. Ralph Spitzer, Associate Professor of Chemistry. These letters, following prescribed procedure, were cleared through the President's office on February 18 by letter of reference from the Dean of Administration.

The contentions raised in the letters by each man were:

1. That he had been denied academic freedom in that he had been dismissed for reasons other than academic performance.
2. That the Administration had violated AAUP-recommended procedure by taking action without conference with the departments concerned.

In view of these serious charges made against the administration, hearings were held with Mr. LaVallee and Dr. Spitzer, and, upon invitation of the committee during the period February 22 to March 5, with all staff members responsible for the appointment or reappointment of Mr. LaVallee and Dr. Spitzer. Complete stenographic notes were taken for the use of the committee. During these hearings Dr. Spitzer and Mr. LaVallee further alleged that their dismissals were based on their political activities.

Due to the similarity of allegations, and similarity of findings of fact, this report combines the opinion of the committee with respect to both cases.

Based on the evidence secured it is clear to your committee:

1. That both Mr. LaVallee and Dr. Spitzer are on temporary or short-term appointments. It is well established both locally and nationally that such appointments do not carry privileges of tenure and are subject to

319

termination at the expiration of the term by the mere act of giving timely notice of the desire to terminate. The committee deems it significant, however, that in each case valid reasons for non-renewal, other than those alleged, were presented to the committee through oral testimony, by correspondence drawn from administrative files, and by statements filed with the committee.

2. That the desirability of re-employing Mr. LaVallee for the present academic year, 1948-49, had been seriously questioned in the spring of 1948. His further employment beyond 1948-49 was the subject of recurrent conferences on departmental, school and institutional levels during the present academic year with subsequent notification on January 14, 1949 that he would not be reappointed.
3. That the desirability of reappointing Dr. Spitzer or of granting him a leave of absence during 1949-50 had been questioned last October. The decision not to tender him a reappointment was made at the culmination of various consultations on departmental, school, and institutional levels extending over the preceding several months, the last of which was on the 8th of February 1949, following which such notification was given Dr. Spitzer.

The Committee concludes:

1. That at no time during their employment at this institution has either man been denied academic freedom.
2. That the decision to terminate their employment at the end of their current appointments was taken for reasons deemed sufficient by those responsible for administrative action. In no way were the decisions not to reemploy influenced by reputed membership in the Progressive or any other political party.
3. That, according to the evidence presented, the provisions of AAUP-recommended procedure have been fully complied with.
4. That the decision not to reemploy neither violated existing contract rights nor denied due process.
5. That none of the evidence presented supports any of the allegations made by Mr. LaVallee and Dr. Spitzer.

It is the opinion of the committee, based upon careful investigation and consideration, that President Strand acted entirely within his administrative rights and in the discharge of his official duties in the decision not to renew the appointments of Mr. LaVallee and Dr. Spitzer.

Aside from any bearing that it might have upon this investigation, the committee is of the opinion that it is, and should be, the prerogative of the President to make the final decision as to who should be appointed, or reappointed, to the staff of the institution for which he is responsible to the State.

March 15, 1949

The Faculty Committee on Reviews and Appeals
Signed:
[Professor of Business Administration]
[Associate Professor of Engineering]
[Professor of Physics]

Appendix J
Edited Transcript of Hearing
at a Private University

June 1953

Chancellor: Will you start the record if you please. Professor P., there are some additional questions the committee would like to ask you under the same understanding with which we have proceeded in other sessions. Would anyone like to ask Professor P. a question?

Dean P.: I have two or three I would like to ask. Professor P., you spoke with considerable appreciation of the minority opinions of Justices Douglas and Black in the Dennis case. I wonder what your comment would be on this quotation from Justice Douglas's recent book *North from Malaya* as quoted in a review in the *New York Times*. He writes, "the loyalty of a communist whether he be a Huk in the Phillipines, or a guerilla in Malaya, or a comrade in North Korea is to the Russian fatherland first. Russia today is empire building, using fifth columns within the various countries to destroy existing governments." Now would you go along with Justice Douglas on that statement?

Professor P.: Well, I don't have first-hand knowledge of the Asiatic communist movement he speaks of. From my second-hand knowledge, I wouldn't interpret it the way he does. It doesn't seem to me, for example, that the Chinese communists are primarily Russian nationalists, by any means. I would say my impression is they definitely have an independence. They think of Soviet Russia as an ally, but I feel that, for example, the Chinese communists make their own decisions. I would say in that case that definitely that from what I know of the history, for instance, of their leader Mao Tse-tung, he has often differed from the policy that the Russians advise and follows his own judgment in those things. My own feeling is that the Asiatic communists think of Russia as a sort of big brother. They think of it as being opposed to the imperialist powers, the European imperialist powers, whom they regard as their main enemies. But I don't feel at all that there is anything of Russian nationalism in their viewpoint. That seems to me to be a very poorly chosen characterization, I would say, judging from a second-hand account.

Dean P.: I assume that, while he is writing here of Asiatic communists, that he means to make a general statement about communists wherever found.

Professor P.: Very likely he does. If he applies it to them I should think he would apply it to any of them because they have more obviously shown their independence.

Dean P.: What would you say about this statement as applied to American communists?

Professor P.: As applied to American communists? Well, except perhaps for the minority of them, who happen to be of Russian extraction, I wouldn't say that there is a Russian nationalism in them.

Dean P.: Would you say that their first loyalty, however, is to the Soviet government in Moscow?

Professor P.: Not in an unconditional sense. Only as long as they think that the communist government in Russia, in the Soviet Union, is representing the interests of the workers of the world better than any other government, they will go along with it.

Dean P.: Is that their opinion would you say?

Professor P.: It is generally their opinion, but you notice occasionally it happens they lose that opinion and then they fall away. I mean, you get groups, say, like followers of Trotsky or, for that matter, Tito, other communists like that. When they once come to believe that the Soviet government is not representing the interests of the workers of the world, or their own particular country, then they go away from it, which, to me, seems to show that the basic thing is not Russian nationalism nor that the Soviet government, come what may, above everything they are loyal to that. But it shows, rather, that their loyalty to the Soviet Union is conditioned by their belief that the Soviet government better represents the interests of the workers of the world generally. As soon as they have any reason to depart from that belief then they depart from their loyalty, such loyalty as they have.

Dean P.: They depart also from the Communist Party, don't they?

Professor P.: Ordinarily they depart from the Communist Party, except in cases like Tito where the whole Party went with him.

Dean P.: Now, this is not a question. You said, I think, the last time that you were here that you have not, by any means, agreed with everything that the Soviet government has done in the postwar years, and that you would be willing I believe you said, to specify. Now, I wonder if you would mention a few actions of the Soviet government with which you have found fault, or which you have been disposed to criticize.

Professor P.: I could mention one or two off hand. I thought they made a mistake in their attitude toward the Marshall Plan proposal in forbidding countries like Czechoslovakia and others to go along with that. Most of the European countries, I mean countries like France and England, did not want to break up European unity at this time and they and, as I understand it, it was really at their insistence that the United States government proposed to include countries like Finland and Czechoslovakia, and so on. So, the Soviet government by refusing to allow them, appeared as the villain who was breaking up European unity. I think this was a big mistake on their part.

Dean P.: Would you agree or disagree with the Russian view that the Marshall Plan was one form of American imperialism?

Professor P.: Well, actually I think, it did serve purposes of American imperialism, and so I can understand the Soviet objection. I think it was not the kind of more or less disinterested policy that UNNRA, for instance, was.

Dean P.: How do you define American imperialism in the present period?

Professor P.: How do I define American imperialism?

Dean P.: Yes, what do you mean by American imperialism when you say that the Marshall Plan was a form of American imperialism?

Professor P.: Well, American imperialism is predominantly an economic type, rather than colonial, although I notice that we did pick up some land in the Pacific in the last war. But mainly it is economic in character and is a drive to get economic domination of the world.

Dean P.: Was that the purpose of the Marshall Plan, to get economic domination of Europe?

Professor P.: Well, I don't know. When you speak of purpose, different people have different purposes. Undoubtedly, different people supported it, and I wouldn't want to say what General Marshall's purpose was, for instance. I don't really know. But I do think that the fact that it was supported by dominant economic groups in this country suggests to me that they did think of it as serving their purposes of increasing American influence and control in Europe.

Dean P.: Without pursuing that any further, are there any other instances you would mention where you think the Soviet government has been wrong?

Professor P.: Well, I think they must have made some serious mistakes in their relations with Yugoslavia, Tito. Now I don't profess to understand that situation altogether, and I don't know who's telling the truth about it, and so on. But I do have a feeling that there must have been insufficient recognition on the part of the Soviet Union of the necessity of these other countries to have an independent policy.

Dean P.: In matters that have affected the United States more directly than that did, is there anything else that you would criticize?

Professor P.: In direct relation to the United States? Well, let me think about that. I don't know what you would mean would be more directly related to the United States. I mean we have our finger in every pie in the world, so almost anything they do would touch the United States. But I don't think of anything more directly affecting it, unless perhaps I would say that I think they perhaps should have exercised more of a restraining hand on the North Koreans, just as we should sometimes have exercised maybe more of a restraining hand on the South Koreans if we are going to be in there at all. So they have some share in the responsibility, perhaps, for the Korean mess. I don't think they have the major responsibility, but I would admit they have some share in the responsibility.

Dean P.: You mentioned three instances: the Marshall Plan, the relations with Tito, and the relations with North Korea in which you think they may have been wrong?

Professor P.: Yes.

Dean P.: That about completes the list as far as you think of it now?

Professor P.: Well, I think if I went into every event in which they participated probably I could find many criticisms. Those stand out in my mind as the ones that have struck me forcibly. Well, I can mention, of course, in Germany, too, there have probably been cases where their policy could be criticized, as well as that of the Allies.

Dean P.: All right, that is enough on that. Now I have one more question. I think nobody has asked this. We have your word that you have not been a member of the Communist Party since 1946. Do you or do you not consider yourself a communist aside from Party membership?

Professor P.: Do I consider myself a communist, that is, a non-Party communist? Well, that's hard to answer frankly. I hadn't thought of labeling myself exactly.

I think the label would be a fair one provided I could make my own interpretation of it. It is possible that I could fairly be described as a non-Party Communist with qualifications, it would have to be interpreted in my own way, and not anybody else's way.

Professor S.: We were talking the other day, Mr. P., about the First Amendment, freedom of speech, freedom of press, and so on, and you said that you could support a minority revolution if that minority had its own freedoms suppressed. Is that fair?

Professor P.: No, I don't believe I said that I would support a minority revolution if the minority had its freedoms suppressed. I thought what I said was that if the majority wasn't given the right to take power peaceably, democratically, then I might support their revolution against the minority government.

Professor S.: You, however qualified, suggested you would want to make your own interpretation of the majority, such as the majority of the working class, or the majority of the proletariat.

Professor P.: Well, I said that I thought the communist leaders would make their own interpretation. In some cases they might be satisfied with a strong majority of the working class and some support from other sections of the population. But as for my own view, I think, my recollection is that as I tried to clarify that, that I would say that there should be majority support in the United States. At any rate, there should be a clear indication of majority support before there would be any justification for a revolutionary movement.

Professor S.: Well, considering, that is, the hypothetical case the Communist Party took power in this country, would you then subscribe to Vishinsky's remark written in 1948 in the Law of the Soviet State where he says, and this is a quotation, "in our State naturally there can be no place for freedom of speech, press, and so on, for the foes of socialism"? That is quoted incidentally, in Mr. Justice Douglas's dissenting opinion in the Dennis case, where he goes on to comment: "Our concern should be that we accept no such standard for the United States." How would you view that, if by chance the Communist Party achieved power in this country?

Professor P.: Well, personally, on that point I agree more with Justice Douglas than with Mr. Vishinsky. I think that in the United States opposition to socialism should be permitted. Only if, let us say, pro-capitalists were still attempting a counter-revolution, were attempting to overthrow the government supported by the majority, only then would I condone suppressing their opposition. I would think that would be my own opinion.

Professor S.: Well, on that basis would you consider it appropriate for the majority today to suppress the freedom of speech of a conspiratorial Communist Party in this country?

Professor P.: Well, I would think that they should act on the kind of principles that Holmes and Brandeis tried to outline. If there were a clear and present danger of overthrow of the government by a conspiratorial group, I would consider them justified in acting against that group. But if it's a question, even if it's a question, regardless of what group may advocate it, but if some group does advocate that in some hypothetical future situation there should be violent overthrow of the government, that, in my opinion, wouldn't justify suppressing them.

Professor S.: This brings me back, Mr. P., to the problem of advocacy and propaganda, a distinction that I found difficult to follow, and I recall a statement made by Father R. Knox in a publication some years ago in which he said about the Roman Catholic Church, "we demand freedom in the name of your principles; we shall deny it in the name of ours." Can you accept that as an ethical proposition?

Professor P.: Well, I think it is a consistent view. Of course, I don't share Father Knox's views, but I think it is a consistent view. I think, too, it seems to me that it is consistent for a communist, even if he happens to be one like myself who would have no objections at all to curtailing pro-capitalist opinion in a socialist country. I think it is consistent for him, too, to say that he prefers capitalism with democracy with the Bill of Rights to capitalism without it, even though he would still more prefer a socialist form of government, which might temporarily not have any freedom for certain minorities, but perhaps that doesn't directly answer your question. You are really asking, I suppose, do I approve of the spirit of Knox's view that you can ask someone to grant you a freedom that you wouldn't grant them.

Professor S.: That is an ethical question, as I see it.

Professor P.: Yes.

Professor S.: Putting that one aside, have you read an article by Hannah Arendt in the *Commonweal* for March 20, 1953, called "The Ex-Communists"?

Professor P.: No, I haven't.

Professor S.: In which she discriminates according to her own use of the terms "ex-communists" and "former communists," and as I read her article, she would put Chambers and Budenz as ex-communists and you as a former communist. Do you make that clear distinction, or a distinction similar to that, perhaps using more precise terms than she does?

Professor P.: Why, yes, if it is a question of being anti-communist, I am not an anti-communist. I wouldn't say I am an anti-communist; I would say that I'm a former communist and not an anti-communist. I consider, my conception, that truly to be a communist you have to be an active member of the Communist Party, in my view. Although I allowed that if someone wanted to call me a non-Party Communist, I would accept that, but only so long as you keep in the non-Party because a true communist should be an active member of some Communist Party and so I would say that I'm a former communist and hence a non-communist but not an anti-communist.

Dean A.: I'd like to have you clarify your remarks in response to Dr. S.'s earlier question. Did I infer correctly that you would prefer socialism without a Bill of Rights to capitalism with a Bill of Rights?

Professor P.: Well, I didn't express a judgment on that. I said that some communists undoubtedly would. I don't know whether I want to make a choice on that alternative without having the particular circumstances more concretely before my mind. In a particular situation I might make a concrete choice, see which of the two was the lesser evil. In any case, I think that socialism with a Bill of Rights is the goal, is the ideal I would be interested in. It would only be a question of which of these two inferior forms was closer to it in a particular situation, capitalism with a Bill of Rights and some chances of progressing, or socialism which temporarily had denied a Bill of Rights. I would have to decide in the particular situation there. I mentioned this question because some communists would definitely, most of them perhaps, would definitely take socialism without a Bill of Rights and I am just saying that I think they are consistent, however, in preferring capitalism with a Bill of Rights to capitalism without a Bill of Rights. That's perfectly reasonable and consistent that they should have that preference even if they would prefer socialism without a Bill of Rights.

Dean A.: Does, in your opinion, the Communist Party in Russia today stand for and work for socialism?

Professor P.: Yes, I believe the Communist Party in Russia is working for socialism, I would say that. I think they are not always, perhaps, working for international socialism as much as people think, but they certainly stand for socialism in the Soviet Union, I would say that.

Dean A.: Is Russia a democracy as you understand it?

Professor P.: Well, the word democracy needs to be qualified, I think, in any case. You would have to say something like that it's something like a proletarian democracy, it is certainly not a democracy in the American sense. Of course, as the Russians would say, it's a proletarian democracy, not a bourgeois democracy. It certainly doesn't actually have many forms of democratic freedom which would seem to be desirable which I hope they will have some day when they no longer fear defeat in world war, and things of that sort.

Dean A.: Following up this, in your reply to Dean P.'s questions, you would have no objections then to the use of secret police by the Russians, or perhaps you would feel that they do not use secret police?

Professor P.: Well, I have no doubt they have secret police. They certainly have needed them at some time. Whether they might not be better off without them now I don't know. Maybe they would be better off without them now. They feel, of course, and probably correctly, that capitalist countries are constantly trying to get agents in there. They need some means of combating that, of course, but I really don't know enough about how their secret police operate at the present time. I don't want to pass a judgment as to whether they should have them or not. I would say offhand that is for the Russian communists to decide whether they need secret police. I would want to have a good deal of evidence before feeling justified in having an opinion on that.

Chancellor: Could the chair interpolate a question, Dean A.? Awhile ago you said you were not anti-communist and a little later you said that there were probably a good many communists who would be willing to take socialism without a Bill of Rights in preference to capitalism with a Bill of Rights. Are you anti that kind of communist, or not?

Professor P.: Well, I would have some disagreements with them but I don't believe that he is such a danger that he needs to be suppressed if you mean in that sense. I don't think that kind of communist has to be suppressed in this country. I don't think that he is any particular danger to the country at the present time.

Chancellor: But I'm still not clear whether you personally repudiate that position or whether you do not wish categorically to repudiate it.

Professor P.: Well, all I can say there is that I am not prepared to make a blanket judgment and say that in any case capitalism with or without a Bill of Rights is necessarily better than socialism without a Bill of Rights. I'm not prepared to make a blanket judgment on that.

Chancellor: Will you proceed, Dean A., if you have more questions?

Dean A.: In your discussion with us you indicated that you resigned from the directorship of the workers' school in Boston in approximately 1938?

Professor P.: Yes sir.

Dean A.: And you remained a member of the Party until 1942?

Professor P.: Yes.

Dean A.: I believe you gave us some of your employment history from 1938 to 1942, but I wasn't at all clear as to the nature of your activity with and for the Communist Party. Could you elaborate on that a bit?

Professor P.: Yes, sir. I gave you my full employment history, I believe. Well, I think I told you most of the things, principal, at any rate, that I did in the Party. That is I was active in Party branches. For instance, I would be active in a street branch, that would mean such things as this—on Sunday morning we would go out selling the *Daily Worker* house-to-house. I would take part in that kind of work. Or we would, of course, have regular meetings of the branch.

Dean A.: You were not an employee of the Communist Party?

Professor P.: No, I was not an employee. I was never paid by the Party for any activity.

Dean A.: To your knowledge, was there any subversive activity going on under the sponsorship of the Communist Party at that time, or espionage?

Professor P.: Well, I never heard anything about espionage. I mean, of course, every country engages in espionage. Naturally, the Soviet Union was engaged in espionage, but I never heard it discussed or proposed in the Party.

Dean A.: To your knowledge?

Professor P.: No, I never heard anyone propose that Party members undertake it, or anything of that sort. The question never came up, actually, in my mind. If it had, I would have considered it highly desirable that active Party members should have absolutely nothing to do with espionage. I think the Soviet Union should recruit its agents outside of the Communist Party. That would have been my view.

Dean A.: To your knowledge, then, during that period the Communist Party, the Russian government was not using the Communist Party for espionage, as far as you know?

Professor P.: Not to my knowledge, no. If it was, I had no knowledge.

Dean A.: Have you heard anything since that would make you feel that it was or was not?

Professor P.: Well, I haven't read all these confessions of all these various people. I gather that some communists have engaged in espionage for the government. The details of this I don't know. As far as I know it has never been in any way something that was part of Party procedure, practices or policy. I would say it was a question of it being on an individual basis of the Soviet government and its agents recruiting people. And I gather apparently they may have at some times recruited Communist Party members into this activity. As I say, to me it seems unfortunate that that should happen, but I suppose it has happened. As I say, as far as I know, it was on an individual basis of some individual being recruited because a Soviet agent thought he was a possibility for it. I don't know of any evidence that it was something recommended by the Party or considered by it, but, of course, I haven't been in for, the period since 1942, of course, I can't speak from inside knowledge.

Dean A.: You are not convinced, then, that the Russian government used the Communist Party as an organization in the United States as an agent for its espionage work?

Professor P.: No, I haven't seen conclusive evidence of that, that they used the Party as such. I don't know that I have seen, I can't recall that I have seen, any good evidence.

Dean A.: Have you read Whittaker Chambers's book?

Professor P.: No, I've only read a few excerpts; I haven't read his book.

Professor H.: Were you aware at that time when you were a member of the Party of the existence of the Third International?

Professor P.: Oh, yes.

Professor H.: What was your conception of the role of the Third International in the communist movement?

Professor P.: Well, I considered it was, while it existed, that is, a gathering together of the different Parties of the different countries into an international organization to give advice and support to each other, and to consult on policies of concern to all of them. I never conceived of it as something which should mean one Party dictated to another Party; that wasn't the principle of it, at any rate. Maybe sometimes it acted that way, but that was not the way I thought of it, as dictation by one Party to another, but rather an international gathering together of the Parties of the different countries for their mutual interests.

Professor H.: Where was the head of this Third International?

Professor P.: Well, the head of it was usually in Moscow.

Dean A.: I believe in your earlier discussion you listed a number of things that you were willing to repudiate and some that you were not. One was a belief in Marxism, I believe?

Professor P.: Yes.

Dean A.: Right. I would like to know, I am intensely ignorant of Marxism as such, whether in your opinion it is a set of economic or social laws, or whether it is a set of principles that should govern social change, or whether it is a program of social reform.

Professor P.: You want to know what I conceive Marxism to be?

Dean A.: As a category. Perhaps it is like a physical law or perhaps it is a set of principles that should govern social change.

Professor P.: I know really very little of most of the things you mentioned. That is, however, primarily I think of it as a set of principles, not in the sense, however, of certain laws set down once and for all, but in the sense of a growing body of principles, analogous, let us say, to some term like Christianity or Protestantism or some other term of that sort. That is, a set of principles which are not to be defined once and for all but which has a certain growth. They start, of course, with the writings of Marx and Engels. They have their basis there, but I think of them as something to be modified and grow with time. And so when I say I would be willing to call myself a Marxist, I mean that in some form of this set of principles and developments from it I would be willing to adhere to it.

Dean A.: One final question—do you believe a pro-Fascist should enjoy academic freedom?

Professor P.: Well I think I discussed that, but I will discuss it again. I am inclined to think that probably as long as his pro-Fascism doesn't involve the kind of violent racial prejudice which would affect his fairness to his students, I think I would tolerate him. I might not like him, but I would tolerate him. I would consider that to hold consistently to a set of principles of academic freedom, one could expect to be accepted, you would have to say a pro-Fascist should be tolerated. But, on the other hand, if his pro-Fascism included, for instance, hostile utterances against certain racial groups and if it seemed that this sort of thing carried over into his relations with his students, then it seems to me that goes beyond the limits of academic freedom because it affects his impartiality as a teacher. So long, so to speak, as it is on an intellectual plane, and it doesn't come from the level of affecting adversely his relations with students, I would tolerate him.

Professor S.: Professor P., on the, I think, second day you made reference to Socrates, and then to Hermes. The next day you rather apologized for the rhetoric, but I didn't feel it was rhetoric referring to them. I have to ask a question, which is rather deeply ingrained in my mind, involving the notion of philosophy or rather of wisdom. And I think my question probably could not be phrased to a person who was not a teacher of philosophy in similar circumstances. My question is phrased in this fashion, perhaps one might say it is a double question: As a teacher of philosophy, would you be happy in an institution where your philosophical and political, economic, and social views might be integrated? Or if you prefer, this question: Do your views, philosophical, political, economic, social seem to you to be inconsistent with your being a teacher of philosophy? And I do not limit teacher of philosophy to your specialty, symbolic logic, but to a teacher of philosophy in a comparatively small liberal arts college where it is necessary for you to do such courses as "Highlights of Philosophy" and to teach freshmen and sophomores a philosophical view.

Professor P: Well, it seems to me that my views, political, philosophical, and economic, are perfectly consistent with my teaching philosophy in a liberal arts college like this. I don't think that they have ever hampered me. Of course, they might if I had other pedagogical views. That is, if I considered it necessary to propagandize constantly for my views, then, no doubt, it would have been inconsistent, at least with a happy stay at this university. But I have always considered that the best way to teach philosophy is to present to the students as well as I can different views, and I always endeavor to present as sympathetically as I can all the different views within the particular area of thought that we are considering. And I may say I think you will find many of my students are often puzzled as to what view I do accept. I think I do a pretty good job of presenting quite sympathetically a large variety of philosophical views. Any view, for instance, I have at any time found sympathetic I can do a pretty good job of giving a good, fair, sympathetic presentation.

And so if I can do this, if I can make the students understand the different viewpoints, and at the same time try to teach them to think critically about the viewpoints and make criticisms of the different viewpoints, then I think I have laid the basis for them to make their own judgments. Now, I have a long range hope that, in the long run, people will consider all the different views, consider them carefully and critically, and will tend to come toward a view like my own. Now, maybe they won't, maybe they won't come toward a view like mine, and I am sure that many of my students come to quite different views, of course, even if they are influenced by me. I don't know to what extent they are influenced by me, but even if they are, they may very well find, well, let's say I gave such a sympathetic account of, well, let's say of someone like Nietzsche that a student might be inclined in that direction, for all I know, rather than any other. But I have the view that in the long run if people think carefully, if they try to see the different viewpoints, try to think themselves into the different points of view, and then stand back and try to evaluate them, well, I feel that in the long run they will tend toward a view like my own. Whether they tend toward a view like my own or not, I feel that it is the way they will tend to arrive toward the truth in the matter. So I see nothing at all, I have never felt that there was any inconsistency in teaching philosophy in a liberal college with my views, and I have never found that it offered any difficulty. I have never had any complaints in that regard. If I have had complaints, it might be, well, I was too strict or something like that, but I never had any complaints about propagandizing for my view, or things of that sort. So it never seemed to me that there was any difficulty at all in this regard. I don't know whether that answers all of your questions or not.

Chancellor: Could I follow with a question? Have you ever regularly assigned to your students vigorous critiques of Marxism or Leninism as a part of their regular assignment?

Professor P.: Well, most of the courses never discuss Marxism or Leninism. Now, there are some that have. In the, well, in the ethics course, there is a book there, *Ethics and Society*, which does discuss Marxism and Leninism to some extent.

Chancellor: Sympathetically?

Professor P.: Well, the writer in the end doesn't agree essentially with Marxism or Leninism, but he presents a rather sympathetic account, on the whole. It is sympathetic, but it is critical at the same time, and in the end, the criticism prevails, but he does give a good deal of merit, you might say, to the Marxist view. Now actually in teaching a class, sometimes I haven't even got that far in the book, but when I have got that far, I would say in the class I usually emphasized a sympathetic presentation of the Marxist position in a general way, and I can't say that I require them to read a more severe critique of it than that book. I felt the chances are that they are much more likely to be exposed to attacks on Marxism than to an understanding presentation of it, so I would think that even from a more liberal point of view, let us say, it seemed they are more in need of having a sympathetic understanding of Marxism than a vigorous critique of it, which is quite easy to get nowadays. They can get that from many sources, and Rader's book does at least give them some critique even if it isn't quite as hostile as some people might want, but it does contain a critique of it. It by no means accepts Marxism, or still less, Leninism.

Chancellor: I've just one or two more questions at this point. As I looked over the transcript, you indicated that you distinguish between advocacy of doctrines and indoctrination.

Professor P.: Yes, sir.

Chancellor: You indicated that at least while you were in the Labor School students were free to accept or reject your position. Do you look upon this as, that is, leaving students free to accept or reject your position, do you look upon this as the essential meaning of freedom of students to learn?

Professor P.: Well, it's an essential element of it. I don't know whether that is sufficient by itself, but, of course, that's one essential element.

Chancellor: Well, is it sufficient, and if not, how is it insufficient?

Professor P.: Well, to have a genuine freedom to learn, lots of things are necessary. They have to have a teacher who knows what he is talking about. They have to, at least, be encouraged to study and think for themselves. They can't be compelled to, but they have to be encouraged to do their own thinking. From the standpoint of, let us say, a liberal arts college, I would say for freedom to learn they have to have some opportunity to be exposed to diverse opinions, which, naturally, was not so much the case in the Progressive Labor School. The Progressive Labor School, of course, was not an academic institution. It was frankly one-sided, like a church school would be, but certainly in a liberal arts college it is reasonable to say that students should be exposed to different points of view, if possible, through teachers with different points of view, but where that doesn't exist, the teachers have to make some effort themselves to present different points of view than their own to the students.

Chancellor: One more question on this type of topic. You indicated that off campus you would regard students in the character of any younger citizens. Do you consider that this permits you to indoctrinate students with communist principles so long as it does not take place on the campus?

Professor P: Well, I don't know whether it permits me but I wouldn't indoctrinate them with communist doctrines.

Chancellor: Well, I would like to know if you think it permits you?

Professor P: I'm afraid I have lost the question.

Chancellor: I'll be glad to restate it. You indicated that off campus you would regard students in the character of any younger citizens. Do you consider that this should permit you to indoctrinate students with communist principles so long as it does not take place on the campus?

Professor P: Well, now, when I say off campus that's not to be taken too strictly. If it's a case of a student in my class, let us say, who comes to my house, then that is not essentially different from his coming to my office. When I say off campus I mean without any relation to campus activities. I should make that point of clarification. A question as to which side of Main Street it is on would not be the decisive thing. It's a question of relationship. Now, suppose there is a student not in any class of mine with whom I have no official teacher-pupil relation, the question is, should I be permitted to indoctrinate him off the campus? Is that it?

Chancellor: That's essentially the question. I'm perfectly willing to have the question stated that way.

Professor P: Permission is a question of someone or something permitting. Do you mean should the university permit me to do it?

Chancellor: No. Should you yourself think it was perfectly permissable to do so?

Professor P: Well, I don't think it is permissable for me to do so, no. I would not consider it proper, if that is your question. I would not do it; I would not consider it proper to do it.

Chancellor: Why, then, did you state originally that you thought that off campus you would regard students in the character of younger citizens?

Professor P: Well, I wouldn't indoctrinate the younger citizens either off the campus, so that's consistent with that.

Chancellor: Have you had any meetings of students in your home to discuss Marxism, Leninism, or communism?

Professor P: I haven't had any meetings of . . . students.

Chancellor: Well, have you had meetings of other students in your home for these purposes?

Professor P: Well, I had a group of people. I wouldn't call them students except that they were studying dialectical materialism at that time. In that sense they were students. I did have such a group at one time that met informally once in a while at my house. Maybe one or two of them were students in the sense that they were taking extension courses, or things of that sort. I can't say that none of them were students, but it wasn't a group of students as such. I did once have a group that met at my house, and I led discussions on dialectics, or dialectical materialism. I did do that once.

Chancellor: Did you use any communist literature in these discussions?

Professor P.: Well, yes, some of the literature was by communist writers.

Chancellor: Are there any additional questions?

Professor M.: I have one additional question. Have you, in connection with that work, talking with students, have you taken part in any student activities at the university? Have you been advisor to any groups or helped them with programs, or anything of that nature?

Professor P.: Well, as a matter of fact I brought two documents here; I was going to present which would bear on this. The only group I have ever been advisor to, as it happens, was the Inter-Fraternity Council, and I have two letters which acknowledge my work there. I thought I might put them in the record. This is the only campus group that I have ever been advisor to, and if you think it is relevant, I will read you—well perhaps one of them is enough—the letter that the president of the Inter-Fraternity Council wrote. It is on the stationary of the Inter-Fraternity Council, dated December 7, 1950: "Dear Dr. P.: On behalf of the member fraternities of this organization I would like to thank you sincerely for your work as faculty advisor to this group. The interest that you displayed proved decisively that we made a wise choice when we offered you the advisorship. I only hope that your successors will prove as worthy. Again let me express our appreciation and thank you. Inter-fraternally, Michael B., President." There is a shorter letter from the next president William C. S. of the IFC, that is dated June 18, 1951: "Dear Dr. P.: Enclosed please find your Inter-Fraternity Council key. The Council is awarding you this key in recognition of your services as faculty advisor." That is signed "Inter-fraternally, William C. S., President, IFC." Now I was faculty advisor for a little over a year with that group. I succeeded Professor B. in that office. That is the only group I have been faculty advisor of on the campus.

Professor M.: How were you chosen faculty advisor for that group?

. . . .

Appendix K
Noncooperation: Three Views

I. A College President[1]

This memorandum is submitted to the Board of Trustees for its consideration only. In accordance with the resolution of the Board of July 9, 1954, any statements herein are made in confidence.

To the Trustees of Reed College:

On June 2, 1954, Stanley Moore was called to testify before a subcommittee of the House Committee on Un-American Activities. Claiming the protection of the First and Fifth amendments to the Constitution, he refused to answer questions regarding membership in the Communist Party or activities connected therewith, including the question whether he was then a member of the Communist Party. Both before and after his appearance Professor Moore has been named before the Committee as having been a member of the Communist Party.

In accordance with the request of the Trustees, I have conducted an informal inquiry touching upon: (1) the professional conduct of Professor Moore according to generally accepted standards, including possible misuse of his position in informal relations with students, and (2) his alleged relationship with the Communist Party and all pertinent facts bearing thereon.

Owing to Professor Moore's absence in New York, communication with him has been difficult. My informal inquiry has been impeded by this fact and by Professor Moore's apparent unwillingness to discuss informally any of the questions raised in the committee hearings or subsequently in my own inquiry. His position with respect to this inquiry has been stated in two open letters and in a series of communications, all of which are on file and available for examination by the Board.

Professor Moore stated in an open letter of 3 June 1954 that "it is an abuse of power for an employer to question an employee about his politics" and has subsequently explained that his use of the term "politics" was

335

meant to include "revolutionary politics." I cannot accept this point of view.

I believe that membership in the Communist Party today is not consistent with membership in a college faculty. It is beyond the scope of political beliefs and associations and also beyond the scope of academic freedom. It makes impossible the confidence which must be extended to a faculty member if he is to perform his duties with academic freedom.

I recognize that in a criminal trial the use of the Fifth Amendment carries no implication of guilt. I recognize also the serious disadvantages which congressional investigation procedure places upon an individual. I do not believe that the use of the Fifth Amendment in a congressional investigation is in itself sufficient grounds for dismissal, but at the same time deplore its use as a matter of policy.

Moreover, I believe that refusal by a faculty member to answer questions regarding present membership or activity in the Communist Party makes it necessary for the college to inquire into the full facts. In such an inquiry the college has a right to expect, and the faculty member has a duty to respond with, full candor.

Professor Moore has consistently refused to discuss the questions raised in this inquiry and has also indicated that if these questions are to be pursued, he desires that a formal hearing be held.

I can only recommend, therefore, that a formal hearing be afforded him.

Respectfully,

II. A Faculty Committee[2]

The initial question of fact, whether there was such refusal to give information to the Special Committee of the Trustees as would constitute the basis of the charge, is a matter for the judgment of the Board, and the council does not wish to comment on it.

Whether such refusal, if established, is evidence of a lack of the cooperation that should be expected of a faculty member, depends on whether the information asked for can properly be required. Academic tenure, and academic and civic freedom put the burden of proof on those who base a charge on political belief and affiliation. To require a teacher to answer questions on such matters is contrary to this principle. The absence of limitations on lawful political associations has been a long-standing policy of the college, and no such limitation has been made a condition of appointment or of the grant of indefinite tenure. It should, therefore, not now be applied to a faculty member on tenure. If membership in the Communist Party were made illegal, the College would take the change into account. But, whatever the effect of the change, until then refusal to answer on grounds of principle should not be construed to be lack of cooperation.

A third question is whether failure to cooperate with the Board of Trustees, if it were established, is adequate cause for termination of tenure or any disciplinary action. The answer to this question is dependent on how we answer the question, "to whom and for what is the duty of cooperation owed?" A college or university teacher is a member of a professional community of teachers and scholars, and it is to a college or university as such a community that he is immediately responsible. Through this community he shares in its responsibility to society for education and scholarship. A board of trustees has a part in this responsibility as sponsor and protector of the body of teachers and scholars. The relationship is not simply nor essentially that of employer and employees, but that of collaborators in a common academic enterprise. Cooperation is, as an official of the AAUP says, not definable in terms of obedience. Neglect of duty should be seen rather in a larger context, that of the purposes and standards of the particular educational institution and of the general principles of academic freedom and tenure. We emphasize that the obligation is a loyalty to a set of fairly well understood professional principles and to a college community and that this is, in our mind, clearly distinguished from obedience to the formal authority of any particular group or person in the community. This distinction should be recognized in reaching any judgment about failure to cooperate.

Decision concerning the termination of the tenure of a faculty member is a grave matter. It should be based not just on some specific failure (if this is proved) but on the total record of his services as teacher and as citizen and an overall evaluation of these services to the college and to education according to the established standards of the profession.

- - - - -

The recommendation of the council in this case was: that there has been no significant failure of cooperation which justifies disciplinary action, and that, even if the Board holds that there has been a failure of cooperation and takes a more serious view of this than the council does, we most strongly urge the Board not to consider such failure as a decisive reason for termination of tenure.

III. A Governing Board[3]

On June 2, 1954, Stanley Moore was called to testify before a subcommittee of the House Committee on Un-American Activities in Washington, D.C. Claiming the protection of the First and Fifth amendments to the Constitution, he refused to answer questions regarding membership in the Communist Party or activities connected therewith, including the question whether he was then a member of the Communist Party.

On June 19, 1954, Professor Moore was named before the Committee, meeting in Portland, as having been a member of the Communist Party during the period from August 8, 1948, to December, 1948.

We recognize that in a criminal trial the use of the Fifth Amendment carries no implication of guilt. We do not believe that the use of the Fifth Amendment in a congressional investigation is in itself grounds for dismissal, but we do deplore as a matter of policy its use by a faculty member.

Moreover, since we are not engaged in a criminal trial, we cannot ignore the serious questions which its use may leave unanswered. Refusal by a faculty member to answer questions regarding present membership or activity in the Communist Party makes it necessary for the college to inquire into the full facts.

In such an inquiry the college has a full right to expect, and the faculty member has a duty to respond with, full candor. Failure to do so would be justifiable grounds for dismissal.

We believe it was our duty, in view of these circumstances, to inquire fully into the question of Professor Moore's relationship to the Communist Party and into his conduct as a member of the Reed College faculty as it might have been influenced by such a relationship.

In doing so we acted in accordance with an earlier resolution of the Trustees, which read as follows:

> It has not been and is not the policy of the college to examine the conduct of any member of the faculty unless there is substantial evidence of misconduct or unless the good name of the college or the individual requires it.
>
> The Trustees will determine any case brought before them on its own merits, in the light of all relevant facts, and only after careful examination of the full facts and in doing so will solicit the assistance and advice of the president and the faculty.

In accordance with this resolution, the Faculty Council, the president of the college and a committee of trustees have conducted separate, but cooperative inquiries and have reported their findings and recommendations to the Board of Trustees at its meeting of August 6, 1954.

Professor Moore's position with respect to our inquiry has been set forth in an open letter of June 3, 1954, in which he stated, "it is an abuse of power for an employer to question an employee about his politics."

More particularly, at a meeting of August 3, 1954, with the committee of our members, Professor Moore refused to disclose to them any information concerning his past or present membership in the Communist Party.

We believe that membership in the Communist Party today is not consistent with membership in a college faculty. It is beyond the scope of political beliefs and associations and also beyond the scope of academic freedom. It makes impossible the confidence which must be extended to a faculty member if he is to perform his duties with academic freedom. Academic freedom can never be used for the aid of those who would destroy academic and all freedoms.

We therefore consider that an inquiry into these matters has been both necessary and proper and that Professor Moore's refusal to cooperate has been misconduct.

At its meeting of August 6, 1954, the Board of Trustees voted to bring charges against Professor Moore and to afford him a formal hearing before the Board on August 13, 1954.

Charges respecting his failure to cooperate have been delivered to Professor Moore prior to this hearing. A stenographic record of the hearing has been made and a copy will be provided him. He has been afforded the opportunity to have counsel of his choosing and to be heard in his own defense. The members of the Faculty Council and the president of the college have been present at the hearing and have had opportunity to confer with the Board of Trustees prior to their reaching a decision.

After careful consideration of the facts set before us in the hearing we have concluded that the evidence presented has established conclusively the charges presented.

In view of Professor Moore's public assertion that when he was first employed the College expressed indifference to his politics, we have found that at no time did he state or did any of the college authorities have knowledge that he was a member of the Communist Party.

It has never been the policy of this Board of Trustees to knowingly employ or retain as a member of the faculty a member of the Communist Party.

We recognize the function of the faculty as advisers to the president and the function of the President as the adviser to the Board of Trustees on matters of educational policy, but in matters such as have been presented at this hearing, the ultimate responsibility is that of the Board of Trustees.

Notes

1. Duncan S. Ballantine, correspondence to the Board of Trustees of the Reed College, 5 August 1954.
2. "Summary of the Views of the Faculty Council," presented orally after the hearing of the charge against Stanley Moore, 13 August 1954.
3. "Statement by the Board of Trustees of the Reed Institute," 13 August 1954.

Appendix L
From the Meeting Held 3 and 4 October, 1956 between Professor Philip Morrison and Five Members of the Board of Trustees of Cornell University

Q. If you were to join an organization . . . [Paul] Robeson was in today, would you feel you could do that within the spirit of this agreement?

A. I think this is a good question, but it is actually directed to Robeson. He has become a symbol.

Q. It is only an illustration of what can happen. Having in mind an agreement with the University, whatever the ultimate content, would you feel that you could obey the spirit of the agreement and join an organization in which Robeson was a member?

A. So far as the spirit of the agreement is concerned, Yes; but so far as the expediency of the association is concerned, no doubt I would say "No" to it.

Q. I think you said these agreements represented rather an expedient result than complete agreement in principle?

A. We ought to go even farther back. I think Mr. Robeson is neither treasonous nor subversive, but excitable. I do not think it brings him in the purview of this agreement.

Q. But looking at it in terms of the harm to Cornell University and opposing yourself to a choice between those two things, would you feel it calls for avoidance?

A. I would say I do not think the agreement calls for that. I think the implications of the agreement suggest it but the agreement does not put it in words. He is neither treasonous nor subversive. I cannot say I would absolutely refuse to join.

Q. Is it not correct that when this agreement was made you were trying to reach some basis for avoiding harm through such an association?

A. I think I would not associate with him in any way politically, but if a group wanted to bring him here to sing I would feel moved by conscience to support that group.

Q. If you were asked to join another organization with political objectives in which he was a member, would you?

A. I hate to condemn him for all time. I would say that if he did what he did in 1951, I would not, but otherwise maybe.

Q. But would you do it, having regard for your responsibilities to the university vis-a-vis any feeling against Robeson?

A. I would have to weigh it in view of what interpretation might be put on it. It is a difficult matter. I would not say I would not have an association with a man I really admire. I cannot say. I would say that I would sift the expediency of it to determine whether it was a big risk and what would happen to me and the University. But if it seemed to be a slight risk I might be willing to face it.

Q. But you have had a rather disturbing experience of some considerable impact in his case?

A. Yes.

Q. Now, having had it, as of today if you were asked to join an organization in which he is a leading figure, would you feel you should consider it at all?

A. I feel it would depend very much on the circumstances. I would not say that I would associate with him under any circumstances for any cause not in the interest of the University.

Q. As of today, in view of your recent experience and as you value yourself, would you think you should avoid it in the interest of the university?

A. It would be very easy for me to say that I would, but it would not be so. I do not want to trouble the University or myself, but I cannot brand a man in this way. I have not seen him for three years but between 1951 and 1954 he modified considerably. In 1951 I might have avoided it, but I might conceivably be led to associate with him again if circumstances were different.

Q. You are not on trial but my questions might make it seem so. I was simply trying to find by illustration this area of agreement and where it begins and ends in your mind.

A. These are questions about a difficult and complicated situation which we are now trying to settle in every way we can. If we had a definite agreement which would say what I can and cannot do, I would live up to it if possible. Actually I have not associated with Robeson for three or four years. The situation has not come up, and that should be taken as part of the evidence. You asked what I would do; if it did happen I would be inclined to do nothing at all.

Q. Still using him just as a symbol, having in mind his frequent trips to Russia and his frequent statements of how wonderful Russia is compared to this country, and his influence on a great many people; having further in mind that in the average person's mind he is definitely a communist; and having in mind the probable effect on Cornell if he should come to Cornell to make a speech on some political subject, you would probably back him or sponsor him?

A. I would not mind if he wanted to speak on a political subject. The university has had communists.

Q. Would not that in your opinion violate your agreement with Dr. Wright or President Malott because of the adverse publicity it would bring to Cornell, by thoughts which are in the minds of the people and by statements in the newspapers, whether or not you agree with them?

A. I would not interpret it as a breach of good faith. I would think a long time before doing it. I would doubt that I would do it.

Q. Would you think that it would bring discredit to Cornell and thereby violate your understandings? You have to make a judgment whether actions might carry discredit in a certain set of circumstances.

A. I think the situation is so complicated that we cannot take it hypothetically.

Q. But you are also saying, recognizing all the problems that have come up at

Cornell with the result of misinterpretation by the press, and which may or may not be so, that today, knowing what you know and what might be done with this, in all probability you would not sponsor it, but you just don't want to be put in the position of saying you would not?

A. That is right.

Q. If it came up as of today you probably would not sponsor it because of expediency?

A. I would say to him: "If you want to come, come and sing," and I would debate the question with him.

Mr. Scheetz:

Q. I think what we are facing is probably the last choice. I think what we are talking about is the practicality of the situation. I think we are trying to deal with a highly loaded problem, one which anyone as sensitive as you are is constantly going to face, but we are now in a position here at Cornell that what you say or do in any way may be misinterpreted. We cannot allow you the freedom of expediency. We must say are we willing to be expeditious any more than three or four or five years ago before the question came up. Our concern, and my personal concern, is that you face the practicalities more than ever before and are you willing to face them as never before?

A. I think the record shows that. I do not think I have received any unfavorable publicity for several years. I have been attacked by organizations that make a living out of it and who will always make something of it. I have tried very hard to keep out of the general newspaper columns.

Recessed at 6:00 P.M. October 3, 1956.

Q. Since your agreements with Dr. Wright, have you joined any so-called communist-front organization which you had good reason to believe was in fact a communist front or was maneuvered or set up by the Communist Party or somebody on behalf of the communist movement?

A. Since my agreement with Dr. Wright I certainly have joined very few organizations.

Q. Answer, please, what specific organizations?

A. If you tell me the one you mean I will tell you the occasion. My criteria is not whether I have joined but why.

Mr. Scheetz:

Q. Professor, we understand your desire to have a particular organization named to explain why you did join, but this was a general question, whether you know of any organization which you joined which was really under the discipline of or set up by the Communist Party or someone in its behalf. I think that is a general question which you should be able to answer directly, simply because we ask whether you associated with or joined any organization of that type.

We do not know what organizations you may have joined. That is why it is a general question, and I hope you think it is fair.

Mr. Treman:

Q. In fairness to you, the question is: Did you know when you joined it, or sponsored it, or lent your name to it, that it was in fact a communist front or maneuvered by the Communist Party for its purposes, since your arrangements with Dr. Wright? That is to distinguish from those you may have learned later were in fact maneuvered by the communist movement. I am asking specifically whether when you joined, or lent your name, or sponsored any of these so-called fronts, did you in fact know?

A. It is very easy to say "No" to the questions, but I am trying to be candid and explain. I deny the incidence of such organizations. I am prepared to raise that question because your question is full of implications and I am trying to deny the implications.

Q. Do you deny in substance that there are any organizations which are so-called communist fronts, leaving out any of your own connections?

A. I think this is true of the majority of the organizations.

Q. But there are some you are willing to state are maneuvered?

A. Not to my knowledge, but there may be some.

Q. My point is specifically your personal connection with any which to your knowledge were communist dominated when you joined or sponsored or lent your name to them. We are not trying to to go back to Dr. Wright's arrangements in 1951.

A. I cannot be put in this position. There are organizations set up ad hoc; for example, the committee to defend Mr. Trachtenberg. Mr. Trachtenberg was one of the defendants in the second Smith Act trials, a publisher, with a publishing house, and the principal charges alleged against him were the facts that in the books his house published there was material which tended to support the overthrow of the government by force and violence. I think the United States government cannot constitutionally indict or convict the publisher of such books. I have certainly contributed money and lent a little support, wrote letters, directed to his defense. The Trachtenberg committee was no doubt exclusively a communistic organization but the purpose was not communistic. Trachtenberg was openly a communist. He was tried and convicted, and asked for assistance as a publisher with the right to publish books. The question does not arise whether it was communist dominated.

Mr. Littlewood:

Q. You do not question the motives of others who might have sponsored it, but your purpose in sponsoring it had nothing to do with communism?

A. That is right.

Q. Can you make that explanation categorically as to every organization that you joined since your conference with Dr. Wright?

A. That is a very hard thing to do.

Mr. Scheetz:

Q. Yesterday the professor said that in this type of instance he considered it a safe type of association. Whether the person was subversive or not, he felt the fellow was entitled to a trial with due process and he excluded them in his mind. I think we ought to ask concerning other types of association.

A. I have never been under the domination of the Communist Party or any of its members directly or indirectly since I came to Cornell, let alone since I discussed these matters with Dr. Wright, and have never gone into any organization which I found under this domination. But that does not mean I do not intend to enter into organizations organized by the Communist Party for the benefit of certain people to defend their rights on some particular position. No categorical answer is possible. I have very little in common with the American Communist Party during the last decade. That is quite clear from my whole actions and policy. . . .

Mr. Treman:

Q. You did sponsor this conference?

A. Yes.

Q. What were the purposes of the conference that led you to be willing to sponsor it?

A. As I understand it, it was to be an effort to try in an election year to make some kind of political mark of the kind the Progressive Party made in 1948.

Q. Do you recall receiving any other literature except that one letter?

A. I received some sort of description of the program of the meeting.

Q. I show you this paper marked "Call to Conference for Legislation in the National Interest" which on the second page includes a program, and ask if this is what you refer to?

Q. This document looks familiar to me. Yes.

A. Is your name on that as one of the sponsors at that time?

A. No, I was late in answering this.

Q. In other words, your name does not appear on the printed original call to conference?

A. That is right. Because I wanted to see what was involved before I took any step.

Q. Will you refer to the second page of this and say which of the talks, or whether all of them, led you to be interested enough to let them use your name?

A. The most interesting was "Survival or Extinction, Congress on the Brink of War."

Q. Because of your great interest in peace and peace activities?

A. Because I am a citizen. This is an election year and we hear a lot of politics this year. I debated in my mind whether this would start trouble, especially since it was a political activity in a presidential year, involving Congress, whether it would make trouble, and I thought it would be safe enough to join as a matter of expediency. I was wrong.

Q. When you wrote that you wanted to become a sponsor you did not consider you were violating your good faith toward Cornell, President Malott, and Dr. Wright?

A. That is right.

Mr. Littlewood:

Q. Did you discuss this with any of your associates or seek counsel?

A. No.

Q. But you had originally in your letter to Dr. Wright of April 18, 1951 suggested, at the end of your letter, that you would seek counsel in particular cases. This was not such?

A. Not a particular case. Between 1951 and 1955 there were many in which I was interested. I made an appeal to President Malott to set up hard criteria to govern me and he refused. After that I thought I would be bound by my own judgment.

Q. Did you think the agreement with President Malott superseded your agreement with Dr. Wright?

A. Yes. That was my view.

Q. Did not Mr. Malott both orally and in his correspondence urge you to refrain from anything which would in any way bring criticism to Cornell?

A. Yes. But he said he was unwilling to do anything. I did not see how he could have it both ways. Either I would use my own judgment as a citizen as to my minimum activity—very difficult for a person with strong views—or I can do what I did, ask the university to give me a definite course. The university refused the responsibility and I accepted the responsibility.

Mr. Scheetz:

Q. Am I not correct in saying that President Malott's position was that he should not be telling people what organizations they should be joining in politics or any other field? We all share the view that that would be an intolerable situation. That was the real reason why he said you would have to take the responsibility of doing whatever sifting you saw fit to do. Don't you think that was a proper posture for the president to take in this situation?

A. I do. But I do not think it is then fair to say that I am violating an implied or implicit agreement. It cannot be both ways, make an agreement and still leave the path open to me to use my own judgment. You can tell me to make an agreement and not to exercise my own judgment.

Q. Reverting to yesterday's discussion, you recall we were talking about the phrase in the agreement, that you would not knowingly associate with an organization that was subversive or treasonous. Then we discussed the question of expediency, and, if I understood you correctly, you said you would evaluate these situations in terms of expediency?

A. Yes.

Q. And I think that you acquiesced in the idea that the agreements do contemplate an expedient judgment in these matters as to what would harm Cornell. Let me suggest to you that we then got into the discussion of, for example, supporting defenses in court, and I want to be sure I have it correctly, when we were talking about expediency, in addressing your attention to these agreements, it did pose the problem of what would be the harm to Cornell and something for you to evaluate.

A. Yes. I don't mind being called to account for bad judgment on political questions. If I have failed I desire, deserve, to make amends. But I object to having my good faith questioned on the ground of expediency. You cannot make an agreement on the ground of expediency. Perhaps I have failed. I don't know. I resent the implication. In my mind this specific agreement, which was rather general in the first place, was superseded by the position that nothing can be done, by telling me to use my judgment in each case.

Q. As the record shows, Yes. One can understand why you would resent any suggestion about your good faith. That is not what we are suggesting here. It is a question of how you relate this particular sponsorship to the agreement, and as you have just said it might have been an error of judgment but not a question of good faith, and I am not impugning your good faith. We are trying to see how this thing is operating and what problems it presents because there is a substantial risk that this organization would land, as did the others, on the Attorney General's list.

A. Yes, I agree I am in the wrong in being connected with it. I was a one-shot sponsor for the conference. I do not think it has the material to grow into a more suitable organization.

Mr. Treman:

Q. In that literature there were two types of units that were being set up. I think one was called "Committee on Continuation" which was assigned to each of the four panels, and then there were "Committees of Correspondence" [that were] supposed to spread the gospel for the particular legislation throughout the country. Did you become identified with either of those committees?

A. No.

Q. You say it was a one-shot proposition on the sponsorship. The organization is still in existence is it not?

A. I have had some correspondence but I don't regard myself as being associated with it or a sponsor of its further activities. I seem to recall I received a draft copy of the by-laws to vote on by mail. I wrote that I did not like the scheme, did not think it was viable; I did not think of myself as part of the organization as it was reconstrued [sic].

Q. Did you put that in a letter?

A. Yes.

Q. Do you have a copy of the letter?

A. No. I wrote it in June.

Q. Do you have a copy of the by-laws?

A. I think I returned it with the vote against them.

Q. You did not formally resign in any other way, except by that letter?

A. No. I am not trying to get off the hook. The pressure of the Board of Trustees on this made me more careful. I did not want to disassociate too formally.

Mr. Scheetz:

Q. About this faculty statement of policy, I think the way the record now stands it may not be entirely fair. As I recall the testimony yesterday, when you were asked about the statement as it refers to the question of advocacy of the overthrow of the government, you said you did not recall whether you voted against it but today you would vote against it. I hope you think this is a fair question, but this is a matter of some extent between you and your faculty colleagues. Say if you think it unfair. The university faculty on May 1, 1918 drew up a statement of policy as to behavior at that time. Then this question came up again in May 1951 and the action taken at that time involved two things; one was a definition of misconduct in relation to this topic, and the other was a reaffirmation of the policy that was adopted in 1918. I would like to take first the 1918 statement and I will read it. Perhaps you should also have a look at it. The first paragraph reads: "The faculty maintains that each of its members in writing or speaking has the same rights and duties as any other citizen." Second paragraph: "The faculty believes that each of its members in exercising his rights of free speech should realize that in the minds of many citizens he occupies a representative position and that in consequence the reputation of the university lies partly in his hands." Third paragraph: "The faculty recognizes that each of its members is bound in the present crisis to safeguard the reputation of the university with special care." Thinking of these three paragraphs in the context of May 1951 and the present context, do you disagree in any particular with them?

A. No, and especially the first paragraph.

Q. You think it is valid today?

A. Yes.

Q. Therefore you do not mean when you say you would vote against it that you would vote against that if it came up?

A. No. But I think the legislation has two parts.

Q. And the other thing is: "It is the sense of the faculty that any member of the faculty who, publicly, or in his contacts with students, advocates the overthrow of the government of the United States, or of a State or Territory of the United States, by force or violence, or the accomplishment of political change by a means not permitted by the Constitution of the United States or of the State of New York is guilty of misconduct." I understand you said yesterday you would vote against that.

A. Yes.

Q. Would you mind explaining why you feel that that is not a proper precept for the guidance of a professor?

A. It was by no means unanimously passed.

Q. Was most of the faculty for it?

A. Oh, yes.

Q. Would you consider yourself bound by that?

A. Yes.

Q. Even though you disagree?

A. Yes.

Q. What do you take exception to in that?

A. It is beneath the dignity of the university. It says if a man commits a crime he should be considered to be guilty of misconduct. This is a subterfuge. The acts stated are all criminal under the law. If a man commits a crime he should not be punished for misconduct. If a man commits murder, which is a crime, he would not be accused of misconduct. This appears to me to be a device to make it easier to dismiss a non-conforming faculty member on grounds that would not have the hard certainty of placing it on a more substantive ground. It is not misconduct to advocate overthrow of the government by violence, it is a crime. This was adopted in a spirit not proper. This does not mean that I think a man who advocates overthrow should go unpunished, but that if he advocates it he should not be called guilty of misconduct. There should be a redefinition of misconduct. All other acts are then listed as such. The writers of the legislation did not have hard proof in mind but they wished to color it to allow them to censure a man without it. It does not mean it was misuse but lends itself to misuse. It is not proper legislation. I should like to request that the record show whether there was a substantial number of faculty members who voted against this proposal. I would have voted against it. It is not at all unlikely, but I don't remember whether I did then.

Mr. Scheetz: I think you should see why the thing is important and valuable to me as well as to the rest of us, as to why you would have voted against it.

Professor Corson: May I say something? This matter was the subject of bitter debate before the ballot.

Mr. Scheetz:

Q. I think it was right to clear up Dr. Morrison's answer to the question.

A. I am in full agreement. I understand the motives of Mr. Scheetz and I am grateful for it, but I cannot think this constant defensive attitude on certain rights and privileges should be entered into in my particular case as a supposed cause of misinterpretation of the record. I think that those who voted for such legislation should be asked to give their reason for voting for it.

Q. It so happens that in this world of affairs a particular action in this whole setting might be taken by some people to have implications just of the kind you fear and therefore to find out what the basis of your voting against it was helps to supply an answer and we were interested in knowing it. It does mean that you are constantly being asked questions, explaining why you do things, but we are still only in search of an explanation to get the record straight.

A. But is it really proper to call me to account for all allegations which I feel I may make by right, privilege and law? I cannot explain them all.

Q. We are only trying to get some understanding on the periphery of what we are talking about.

A. I would like to ask what other point of view someone might have. Is there any right point of view where the right of a faculty member to vote against something is in question?

Q. But I think this has risk of carrying doubt in the minds of other people. I do not think you should be questioned generally on the subject nor should any other professor, but only in this particular context there is such a risk. I say that to you from my observation and I think it is useful to have your explanation on the record and in your interest, but it is not our business why you vote "Yes" or No. We would want the full faculty to understand that we would not sponsor any taking to task of a professor as to why he voted pro or con.

A. But I still feel it would be more proper to inquire as to my substantive views and ask what I think of persons who have done this and that and not take off from the standpoint of why I voted this or that way.

Mr. Littlewood:

Q. I think this specific line of questioning was intended to find out why you would have voted against it again.

A. I was first asked was I at the meeting; did I recall how I voted, and I volunteered the information that I would have voted against it. I don't think the question was even raised. It partakes of an impropriety which I think is behind the whole proceeding and I am most disturbed.

Professor Morrison left the Meeting at 11:00 A.M. to hold class.

Appendix M
Excerpts from Report of Committee of Inquiry Concerning the Activities of Professor Philip Morrison, Cornell University

VII

There is much in Professor Morrison's history that shows association with many known communists and membership in or connection with many known communist fronts. Also, it is clear that from his school days in 1933 through 1941 he was an active member of the Young Communist League or of the Communist Party. However, no evidence was produced to indicate that he has been a member of the Communist Party from 1942 to date. Professor Morrison appears to have simply drifted out of the Party instead of formally resigning. None of the evidence shows that Professor Morrison ever advocated the overthrow of the government by force.

Professor Morrison's attitudes toward the Communist Party are quite different from those generally prevalent in the United States. He does not appear to believe that the various communist fronts with which he has been associated have primarily promoted the interests of the Communist Party rather than the humanitarian and egalitarian ends stated to be their objectives. He has applied different criteria of circumspection than most non-communists would use in evaluating the organizations he has supported.

Due to his own past, his position with the university, and his other relationships, he states that decisions as to whether or not he should join an organization as a sponsor or member must be for him a matter of expediency. In other words, he must at times in his own mind submerge his belief in certain principles in the interests of expediency. This suggests a conflict of motivations.

Professor Morrison has had abundant opportunity to become acquainted with the operations of the Communist Party and patterns of activity within the communist movement. The committee concludes, therefore, that he should be in a position to exercise a high degree of circumspection in determining when an association with organizations which include in their membership or sponsorship Party members or communists would be harmful to the university. He appears to have sorted through the organizations looking for his support and become associated with those which, in his opinion, existed primarily not to advance communism but to advance other specific humanitarian objectives. But there is reason to believe that his peculiar evaluation of the Communist Party and the indicated psychological conflict may interdict his circumspection in such matters. This may account for the fact that sponsoring participation in an organization by known communists or members of the Communist Party does not appear to be a deterrent or to inspire more careful investigation on the part of Professor Morrison as a prelude to association. It has not in the past and may not in the future. This is illustrated by the case of the Conference for Legislation in the National Interest, which in the opinion of the committee was sponsored by Professor Morrison without adequate investigation and consideration.

In the opinion of this committee, no evidence has been produced to substantiate charges that Professor Morrison is unfit to be a teacher in accordance with the Faculty Statement of Policy. However, in the judgment of the committee, Professor Morrison has not always exercised the degree of care called for under the circumstances in safeguarding the interests of the university in his associations.

VIII

The Committee recommends that the Board state its feeling that the relationship of a teacher to his institution and his associates involves responsibility in all areas of behavior, and that consequently Cornell University, its Trustees and Administration are appropriately concerned with any teacher's non-academic behavior however great his professional competence may be. Particularly in the case of the teaching profession, fragmentation is not feasible or desirable; behavior within and without the classroom is an integrated matter.

The Board may desire further study and investigation than this committee has undertaken. Such study and investigation would require special investigators and would be a long and costly proceeding. This committee does not believe that the evidence merits such action and recommends against it.

Professor Morrison should be put on notice that under all these circumstances he should take special care in the future to avoid such participations as may embarrass the university.

Therefore the committee recommends that the Board of Trustees requests the president to give Professor Morrison formal notification that he must take particular care in the future to avoid any actions or participations that may embarrass the university.

The committee further recommends that this inquiry be terminated and the committee discharged. . . .

Index